BUDDHIST PARABLES

Head of Future Buddha

Graeco-Indian School of Gandhara First or Second Century A.D.

From the original in the Pennsylvania Museum, Philadelphia

BUDDHIST PARABLES

TRANSLATED FROM THE ORIGINAL PALI

By

EUGENE WATSON BURLINGAME

GYAN

Published by

Gyan Publishing House
5, Ansari Road
Daryaganj, New Delhi-110002
Phone: 011-47034999, 9811692060
E-mail: books@gyanbooks.com

Distribution Network
gyanbooks.com
India, USA, Canada, UK, Australia, France

ISBN : 978-81-212-6637-6 (PB)
First Published, 1922

2nd Impression 2022

Printed at: Gyan Press, Delhi.

BUDDHIST PARABLES
Author: EUGENE WATSON BURLINGAME

BUDDHIST PARABLES

TRANSLATED

FROM THE ORIGINAL PĀLI

BY

EUGENE WATSON BURLINGAME

FELLOW OF THE AMERICAN ACADEMY OF ARTS AND SCIENCES

LECTURER IN PĀLI (1917-1918) AT YALE UNIVERSITY

A parable, O monks, I here give unto you,
that ye may understand the meaning of the matter.
Majjhima Nikāya, i. 117, 155.

NEW HAVEN

YALE UNIVERSITY PRESS

LONDON · HUMPHREY MILFORD · OXFORD UNIVERSITY PRESS

MDCCCCXXII

TO MY GRANDMOTHER

WHO WHEN I WAS A BOY TAUGHT ME LETTERS

AND TOLD ME STORIES MANY AND VARIOUS

CONTENTS

PREFACE

THIS volume contains upwards of two hundred similes, allegories, parables, fables, and other illustrative stories and anecdotes, found in the Pāli Buddhist texts, and said to have been employed, either by the Buddha himself or by his followers, for the purpose of conveying religious and ethical lessons and the lessons of common sense. Much of the material has never before been translated into English.

CHAPTERS I-III contain parables drawn, with a single exception, from the Book of the Buddha's Previous Existences, or *Jātaka Book*. This remarkable work relates in mixed prose and verse the experiences of the Future Buddha, either as an animal or as a human being, in each of 550 states of existence previous to his rebirth as Gotama. The *textus receptus* of this work represents a recension made in Ceylon early in the fifth century A. D., but much of the material is demonstrably many centuries older. For example, the stanzas rank as Canonical Scripture, and many of the stories (including Parables 4 and 14 and 27) are illustrated by Bharahat sculptures of the middle of the third century B. C. Parable 6 is taken from the Book of Discipline or *Vinaya*, and was very possibly related by the Buddha himself.

With Parable 1, *The grateful elephant*, compare the story of Androclus and the lion, and Gesta Romanorum 104. With Parable 2, *Grateful animals and ungrateful man*, compare E. Chavannes, Cinq Cents Contes 25; A. Schiefner, Tibetan Tales 26; Gesta Romanorum 119; and the following stories in Grimm, Kinder- und Hausmärchen: 17 Die weisse Schlange, 60 Die zwei Brüder, 62 Die Bienenkönigin, 85 Die Goldkinder, 107 Die beiden Wanderer, 126 Ferenand getrü un Ferenand ungetrü, 191 Das Meerhäschen. For additional parallels, see J. Bolte und G. Polivka, Anmerkungen zu den Kinder- und Hausmärchen der Brüder Grimm, Märchen 17, 62, 191.

Parable 9, *Vedabbha and the thieves*, is the original of Chaucer's Pardoner's Tale. With Parable 10, *A Buddhist Tar-baby*, compare E. Chavannes, Cinq Cents Contes 89 and 410; also the well-known story in Joel Chandler Harris, Uncle Remus, His Songs and His Sayings. With Parable 13, Part 1, *Gem, hatchet, drum, and bowl*, compare Grimm, Kinder- und Hausmärchen: 36 Tischchen deck dich, Goldesel, und Knüppel aus dem Sack; 54 Der Ranzen, das Hütlein, und das Hörnlein. For additional parallels, see Bolte-Polivka. A more primitive form of Parable 15, *A Buddhist Henny-Penny*, will be found in A. Schiefner, Tibetan Tales 22. Compare the well-known children's story of the same name. Parables 5 and 14 are the oldest known prototypes of Panchatantra, Book 2, Frame-story.

Chapter IV contains four specimens of *Jātaka* parables in early and late forms. Compare also Chapter II, Parables 6 and 7; and Chapter VIII, Parables 45 and 47, with Chapter III, Parables 8 and 11, respectively. The reader will observe that in the earlier (Canonical) versions, the Future Buddha has not yet become identified with any of the *dramatis personae*. This material is offered as a contribution to the history of the evolution of the Buddhist Parable.

Chapter V contains four remarkably fine old parables which may well have been related by the Buddha himself.

Chapter VI contains several typical specimens of a variety of parable which will undoubtedly be new to many students of religious literature—the Humorous Parable.

Chapter VII contains several specimens of Parables on Death. With Parable 30, *Kisā Gotamī*, compare E. Chavannes, Cinq Cents Contes 224; Budge, Ethiopic Pseudo-Callisthenes, pp. 306-308, 374-376; Sir Edwin Arnold, Light of Asia, Book 5; John Hay, Poems, The Law of Death. A modern Burmese version of Parables 30 and 31 combined will be found in H. Fielding Hall, Soul of a People, pp. 272-278. For a Tibetan version of Parable 31, *Paṭācārā*, see Tibetan Tales, pp. 222-226. Parable 31 is one of the three principal sources of the legend of St. Eustace, the other two being Jātakas 12 and 547. For a recent treatment of the history of this legend, see H. Delehaye, La légende de saint Eustache, Bull. de l'Acad. roy. de Belgique (Classe des lettres), 1919, pp. 175-210. Compare the history of Faustus, Faustinus, and Faustianus, in the Clementine Recognitiones, 200 A. D. (outline in Dict. Chr. Biog., i. 569-570); Gesta Romanorum 110; Golden

Legend, St. Eustace; Early English metrical romance of Sir Ysumbras; and the story of Abu Sabir in the Arabian Nights (Burton, Supplemental Nights, i. 81-88).

Chapter VIII contains, in the form of an imaginary dialogue between an unbeliever and the Buddhist sage Kumāra Kassapa, a lengthy discussion of the subject: "Is there a life after death?" In order to refute objections advanced by the unbeliever, the sage relates thirteen remarkably fine parables, finally vanquishing his antagonist. The arguments *pro* and *con* are the same that have been used ever since men began to discuss this important subject. The dialogue forms one of the chapters of the Long Discourses, one of the oldest of the Buddhist books, but is quite modern in its freshness.

Chapter IX contains several parables from a commentary on the *Añguttara Nikāya* composed by Buddhaghosa in the early part of the fifth century A. D. The first two parables in Chapter VII are from the same source. Parallels from a commentary on the *Dhammapada* composed by a contemporary of Buddhaghosa will be found in the author's *Buddhist Legends.*

Parable 49, *Ghosaka,* has traveled all over the world. For the principal Oriental versions, see J. Schick, Corpus Hamleticum, Berlin, 1912. For an interesting Chinese Buddhist version, see E. Chavannes, Cinq Cents Contes 45. This story appears to be the source of the ninth century apocryphal legend of the seven marvels attending the birth of Zoroaster; see the author's paper in Studies in Honor of Maurice Bloomfield, pp. 105-116. For some interesting European derivatives, see Gesta Romanorum 20 and 283; Golden Legend, Pope St. Pelagius; William Morris, Old French Romances, King Coustans the Emperor (thirteenth century); Schiller's ballad Fridolin; Grimm, Kinder- und Hausmärchen, 29 Der Teufel mit den drei goldenen Haaren. For additional derivatives, see Bolte-Polivka, i. 286-288. The story of Amleth in the Danish History of Saxo Grammaticus contains two derivatives, of which one is utilized by Shakespeare in Hamlet.

Chapter X is a miscellaneous collection of parables from early sources. These parables are all much older than the beginning of the Christian era, and it is altogether probable that some of them, more particularly Parables 57, 58, 59, 60, 63, and 65, enshrine the very words of the Buddha himself.

Chapter XI contains numerous selections from a collection of imaginary dialogues between Menander, Greek king of Bactria, 125-95 B. C., and the Buddhist sage Nāgasena. §§ 1-7 are probably as old as the beginning of the Christian era; §§ 8-13 are probably not older than the beginning of the fifth century A. D. The illustrative material is wonderfully vivid and beautiful, and the expositions of Buddhist teaching on the non-existence of the soul and on Nibbāna (Nirvāṇa) are of prime importance to all students of the History of Religions.

Chapters XII-XV contain selections from the Long and Medium-length Discourses of the Buddha, two of the oldest of the Buddhist books. References to the Buddhist Scriptures in the Bhābrā edict of Asoka, and other considerations, amply justify the statement that the Pāli originals of these four chapters, and of Chapters V, VIII, and X as well, are, in their present form, at least three centuries anterior to the Christian era. Chapters XII and XIII elucidate fully the Practice of Meditation enjoined by the Buddha on his followers as the Way of Salvation. Chapters XIV and XV deal with the problem of conduct and its future rewards and punishments. These chapters should be of particular interest to students of the History of Religions.

Chapter XVI is a miscellaneous collection of parables turning on the Sacrifice of the Body and Blood and on the closely related Sacrifice of the Eyes,—favorite motifs in Buddhist fiction. These parables illustrate in a very striking manner the beginnings and early development of Mahāyāna doctrines. Parables 204-206 are adaptations of translations by the author from the *Dhammapada Commentary*, published in *Buddhist Legends*. Parables 207, 210, and 212 are English translations of French translations of Chinese translations of Sanskrit originals dating from about the beginning of the Christian era. Parables 208 and 209 are adaptations of C. H. Tawney's translations from the *Kathāsaritsāgara*, corrected with reference to the original text. As a collection, the *Kathāsaritsāgara* is a late work, but most of the material is very old. Parable 215 is a literal translation from this work. Parables 211 and 216 are translations from the Buddhist Sanskrit work *Divyāvadāna*, a collection of legends compiled in the second or third century A. D.

Parables 213 and 214, the finest of the Buddhist parables turning on the Sacrifice of the Eyes, are from the Pāli, and are very old. Parable 214, *Subhā of Jīvaka's Mango Grove,*—a veritable Indian *Comus,*—is taken from the Stanzas of the Nuns, a canonical work, and is at least as old as the third century B. C. From Parable 214 are derived the four Buddhist-Christian parables with which the chapter closes. The oldest of these, Parable 219, was composed in Greek at Rome by John Moschus in 615 A. D. The author expressly says that he heard the story in Alexandria. Parable 220 occurs in the *Exempla* of Jacques de Vitry, a manual of illustrative stories for the use of preachers compiled early in the thirteenth century. It is the original of innumerable Medieval versions. Parables 217 and 218 date from the fourteenth or fifteenth century.

The book is thus a collection of specimens of an unusually interesting type of literary composition; a text-book of the teachings of the Buddha, presented just as the Buddha and his followers presented them, by discourse and example; and a collection of good stories,—all in one. It contains much that will interest children; it also contains much that will puzzle the profoundest philosopher.

ACKNOWLEDGMENTS

Just as the thought of preparing a translation of the legends embodied in the *Dhammapada Commentary* was first suggested to my mind by a query of Professor T. W. Rhys Davids in his American Lectures on Buddhism (page 69), so also the thought of publishing a volume of selections of Buddhist parables and illustrative stories was first suggested to my mind by Mrs. C. A. F. Rhys Davids's articles on *Buddhist Parables and Similes* in the *Open Court* for 1908, and on *Similes in the Nikāyas* in the *Journal of the Pāli Text Society* for 1906-1908. I need hardly say that in common with other students of the Pāli texts I am deeply indebted to the enthusiastic and persevering labors of these two distinguished scholars.

But it is chiefly to three distinguished American scholars that I owe the inspiration of the series of volumes of which this book is one,—Professor Charles Rockwell Lanman of Harvard University, Professor Maurice Bloomfield of the Johns Hopkins University, and the late Professor Morris Jastrow of the University of Pennsylvania. Through his exercises in the Fables of Bidpai, the late Professor Jastrow first opened my eyes to the immense possibilities of this body of literature. In innumerable ways, such as will readily suggest themselves to those who knew him well, he assisted me in my work, and through his untimely death I have suffered a profound personal loss. Under Professor Bloomfield I studied for many years, and through his exercises in the Vedas, in the fiction-collections of India, and in Comparative Grammar, laid the foundations of a sound philological method. Professor Lanman first opened the Pāli texts to me, and did more than any other to assist me to interpret them. It is not only a duty but a pleasure to record my indebtedness to these three distinguished scholars.

I wish also to thank Professor E. Washburn Hopkins of Yale University for a careful review of the manuscript of the present work, and for many helpful suggestions.

I am greatly indebted to Mr. Andrew Keogh, Librarian of Yale University, and to Mr. James I. Wyer, Director of the New York State Library, for generous facilities accorded me in the loan of books. I am also under obligations to Professor Lanman for the loan of a rare copy of Buddhaghosa's *Añguttara Commentary*, Colombo, 1904. It is from this text that the translations of Buddhaghosa's Legends of the Saints have been made.

I have to thank Mr. Langdon Warner, Director of the Pennsylvania Museum, Philadelphia, for permission to reproduce the beautiful Graeco-Buddhist head which forms the frontispiece to the present volume.

Last, but by no means least, my most hearty thanks are due to Mr. George Parmly Day, President of the Yale University Press, for invaluable assistance rendered in connection with the execution and publication of this book.

E. W. B.

Yale University,
New Haven, Connecticut,
June 1, 1918. [*Revised to September 1, 1922.*]

INTRODUCTORY NOTE

GOTAMA BUDDHA was born nearly twenty-five centuries ago in the city of Kapila, in North-East India. Kapila was the principal city of the Sakya tribe, and his father was king of the tribe. *Gotama* was his family name. *Buddha* means *Awakened* or *Enlightened*, that is to say, awakened or enlightened to the cause and the cure of human suffering.

The Buddhist Scriptures tell us that when Gotama was born, the angels rejoiced and sang. An aged wise man inquired: "Why doth the company of angels rejoice?" They replied: "He that shall become Buddha is born in the village of the Sakyas for the welfare and happiness of mankind; therefore are we joyful and exceeding glad."

The wise man hastened to the king's house, and said: "Where is the child? I, too, wish to see him." They showed him the child. When he saw the child, he rejoiced and was exceeding glad. And he took him in his arms, and said: "Without an equal is he! foremost among men!" Then, because he was an old man, and knew that he was soon to die, he became sorrowful and wept tears.

Said the Sakyas: "Will any harm come to the child?" "No," replied the wise man, "this child shall one day become Buddha; out of love and pity for mankind he shall set in motion the Wheel of Religion; far and wide shall his religion be spread. But as for me, I have not long to live; before these things shall come to pass, death will be upon me. Therefore am I stricken with woe, overwhelmed with sorrow, afflicted with grief."

Seven days after Gotama was born, his mother died, and he was brought up by his aunt and stepmother. When he was nineteen years old, he married his own cousin. For ten years he lived a life of ease, in the enjoyment of all the comforts and luxuries which riches and high position could give him. When he was twenty-nine years old, a change came over him.

For many centuries, it has been a common belief in India that when a human being dies, he is at once born again. If he has lived a good life, he will be born again on earth as the child of a king or of a rich man, or in one of the heavens as a god. If he has lived an evil life, he will be born again as a ghost, or as an animal, or in some place of torment.

According to this belief, every person has been born and has lived and died so many times that it would be impossible to count the number. Indeed, so far back into the past does this series of lives extend that it is impossible even to imagine a beginning of the series. What is more to the point, in each of these lives every person has endured much suffering and misery.

Said the Buddha: "In weeping over the death of sons and daughters and other dear ones, every person, in the course of his past lives, has shed tears more abundant than all the water contained in the four great oceans."

And again: "The bones left by a single person in the course of his past lives would form a pile so huge that were all the mountains to be gathered up and piled in a heap, that heap of mountains would appear as nothing beside it."

And again: "The head of every person has been cut off so many times in the course of his past lives, either as a human being or as an animal, as to cause him to shed blood more abundant than all the water contained in the four great oceans."

Nothing more terrible than this can be imagined. Yet for many centuries it has been a common belief in India. Wise men taught that there was a way of escape, a way of salvation. If a person wished to avoid repeated lives of suffering and misery, he must leave home and family and friends, become a monk, and devote himself to fasting, bodily torture, and meditation.

The Buddhist Scriptures tell us that when Gotama was twenty-nine years old, he saw for the first time an Old Man, a Sick Man, a Dead Man, and a Monk. The thought that in the course of his past lives he had endured old age, sickness, and death, times without number, terrified him, and he resolved to become a monk.

Leaving home and wife and son, he devoted himself for six years to fasting, bodily torture, and meditation. Finally he became convinced that fasting and bodily torture were not the way of salvation, and abandoned the struggle. One night he had a wonderful experience. First he saw the entire course of his past lives. Next he saw the fate after death of all living beings. Finally he came to understand the cause of human suffering and the cure for it.

Thus it was that he became Buddha, the Awakened, the Enlightened. He saw that the cause of rebirth and suffering was craving for worldly pleasures and life and riches. He saw that if this craving were uprooted, rebirth and suffering would come to an end. He saw that this craving could be uprooted by right belief, right living, and meditation.

For forty-five years the Buddha journeyed from place to place, preaching and teaching. He founded an order of monks and nuns, and won many converts. He lived to be eighty years old. Missionaries carried his teachings from India to Ceylon and Burma and China and Tibet and Japan. In a few hundred years the religion of the Buddha had spread over the whole of Asia. Hundreds of millions of human beings have accepted his teachings.

In at least two respects, the teachings of the Buddha were quite remarkable. In the first place, he insisted on the virtue of moderation. He urged upon his hearers to avoid the two extremes of a life devoted to fasting and self-torture and a life of self-indulgence. In the second place, he taught that a man must love his neighbor as himself, returning good for evil and love for hatred. But this was not all. He taught men to love all living creatures without respect of kind or person. He taught men not to injure or kill any living creature, whether a human being or an animal, even in self-defense. All war, according to the teaching of the Buddha, is unholy.

In the course of time it came to be believed that Gotama had become Buddha as the fruit of good deeds performed in countless previous states of existence, especially deeds of generosity. At any time, had he so desired, he might have uprooted craving for worldly pleasures and life and riches by meditation, and thus have escaped the sufferings of repeated states of existence. But this he deemed an unworthy course. Out of pity and compassion and friendliness for living creatures, he preferred to be reborn again and again, to suffer and to die again and again, in order that, by the accumulated merit of good works, he might himself become enlightened and thus be able to enlighten others.

In comparison with the career of the Future Buddha, devoted to the performance of good works, unselfish, generous to the point of sacrificing his own body and blood, the career of the monk, isolated from the world, selfish, seeking by meditation to uproot craving for worldly pleasures and life and riches, seemed low and mean. The disciple began to imitate his Master. Thus began the Higher Career or Vehicle of Mahāyāna or Catholic Buddhism, as distinguished from the Lower Career or Vehicle of the more primitive Hīnayāna Buddhism of the Pāli texts. Thus did the quest of Buddhahood supplant the quest of Nibbāna. This development took place long before the beginning of the Christian era.

NOTE ON PRONUNCIATION OF PĀLI NAMES

With certain exceptions, both vowels and consonants are pronounced as in Latin and Greek,—the vowels in the so-called Continental manner. Exceptions: short *a* is pronounced like *u* in *but; e* and *o* are short in closed syllables, otherwise long; *c* is pronounced like *ch* in *church, j* as in *judge; kh, gh, ch, jh, ṭh, ḍh, th, dh, ph,* and *bh* are true aspirates, *th,* for example, being pronounced like *th* in *hothouse, dh* like *dh* in *madhouse; ṭ, ṭh, ḍ, ḍh, ṇ,* and *ḷ* are modified dentals, being pronounced with the tip of the tongue turned up and drawn back; *ṁ* indicates nasalization of the preceding vowel. Accent as in Latin.

BIBLIOGRAPHICAL NOTE

For an account of the Buddha's life and teachings, see T. W. Rhys Davids's articles *Buddha* and *Buddhism* in *Encyclopaedia Britannica,* 11th edition. See also Hermann Beckh, *Buddhismus* (*Buddha und seine Lehre*), Sammlung Göschen, Berlin und Leipzig, 1919-1920. On Buddhism as a world-religion, see H. Hackmann, *Buddhism as a Religion,* London, 1910. On the history of Buddhist doctrine, see Louis de la Vallée Poussin's article *Mahāyāna* in Hastings's *Encyclopaedia of Religion and*

Ethics; also the same author's *Bouddhisme: Opinions sur l'Histoire de la Dogmatique,* Paris, 1909. For admirable brief treatments of the subject of New Testament parables, with full bibliographies, see E. E. Nourse's article *Parable* (*Introductory and Biblical*) in Hastings's *Encyclopaedia of Religion and Ethics,* and A. Jülicher's article *Parables* in *Encyclopaedia Biblica.* For a scholarly treatment of the problem presented by *Mark* iv. 11, 12, see A. Loisy, *L'évangile selon Marc,* pp. 128-133.

CHAPTER I

PARABLES FROM THE BOOK OF THE BUDDHA'S PREVIOUS EXISTENCES ON THE GRATEFULNESS OF ANIMALS AND THE UNGRATEFULNESS OF MAN

1. THE GRATEFUL ELEPHANT

Where there's a will, there's a way.

Jātaka 156 : ii. 17-23.

Relying on Noble-heart. This parable was related by the Teacher while he was in residence at Jetavana with reference to a certain monk who relaxed effort. Said the Teacher to him: "Of a truth, monk, did you not, in a previous state of existence, by exerting yourself, get and give to a young prince no bigger than a piece of meat, dominion over the city of Benāres, a city twelve leagues in measure?" So saying, he related the following Story of the Past:

In times past, when Brahmadatta ruled at Benāres, there was a carpenters' settlement not far from Benāres. In this settlement lived five hundred carpenters. They would go up-stream in a boat, cut timber for building materials for houses in the forest, and prepare houses of one or more stories on the spot. Then, marking all of the timbers, beginning with the pillars, they would carry them down to the river-bank, load them on a boat, return to the city with the current, and for a price build for any particular person any particular kind of house he desired to have built. Then they would go back to the forest and get building materials once more. Thus they made their living.

One day, not far from the camp where they were fashioning timbers, a certain elephant trod on an acacia splinter, and the splinter pierced his foot. He suffered intense pain, and his foot became swollen and festered. Maddened with pain, hearing the sound of those carpenters fashioning timbers, thinking to himself,

"With the help of these carpenters I can get relief," he went to them on three feet and lay down not far off. The carpenters saw that his foot was swollen, and on drawing closer, saw the splinter in his foot. So making incisions all round the splinter with a sharp knife, they tied a cord to the splinter, removed the splinter with a pull, let out the pus, washed the wound with hot water, and by applying proper remedies, in no very long time made the wound comfortable.

When the elephant was well, he thought: "I owe my life to these carpenters; now I ought to do something for them." From that time on he helped the carpenters remove trees, rolled them over and held them for the carpenters while they were fashioning them, brought them their tools, and held the measuring-cord, taking it by the end and wrapping his trunk about it. As for the carpenters, when it was time to eat, each one of them gave the elephant a morsel of food; thus in all they gave him five hundred morsels of food.

Now that elephant had a son, and he was pure white, a noble son of a noble sire. So the following thought occurred to the elephant: "I am now old. I ought therefore to give my son to these carpenters to help them in their work, and myself go away." Without saying a word to the carpenters, he entered the forest, and leading his son to the carpenters, said: "This young elephant is my son. You gave me my life; I give you this elephant by way of paying the fee which I owe to my physicians. Henceforth he will work for you."

Then he admonished his son: "Henceforth you are to do whatever it was my duty to do." Having so said, he gave his son to the carpenters and himself entered the forest. From that time on the young elephant obeyed the commands of the carpenters, was patient of admonition, performed all of the duties. They fed him also with five hundred morsels of food. After doing his work, he would descend into the river and play, and then come back. And the carpenters' children used to take hold of him by the trunk and play with him, both in the water and on dry land.

Now noble animals, whether elephants or horses or human beings, never dung or stale in the water. Therefore he also did not dung or stale in the water, but attended to nature's needs out of the water, right there on the river-bank. Now one day the god rained up the river. A half-dry cake of elephant-dung, washed away by the rain-water, came down the river and drifted along until it stuck and lodged in a clump of bushes near the landing-place of the city of Benāres.

Now the king's elephant-keepers, with the thought in their minds, "We'll let the elephants bathe," led five hundred elephants to the river-bank. Smelling the odor of the dung of a noble elephant, not a single elephant would descend into the river, but all whisked up their tails and started to run away. The elephant-keepers told the elephant-trainers. Thought the latter: "There must be some offensive object in the water." So they had the water purified, and seeing the dung of a noble elephant in that clump of bushes, and knowing, "That's what's the trouble there," they had a chatty brought, filled with water, the dung dissolved in it, and therewith the bodies of the elephants sprinkled. Their bodies became sweet-scented. Then they descended into the river and bathed.

The elephant-trainers reported that incident to the king, remarking: "That noble elephant should be sought out and brought to you, your majesty." The king made haste up the river with boats and rafts; with rafts bound up-stream he reached the place of abode of the carpenters. The young elephant, playing in the river, on hearing the sound of the drum, went and stood by the carpenters. The carpenters went forth to meet the king, and said: "Your majesty, if you have need of timber, why did you yourself come? why shouldn't you have sent men to get it?" "I didn't come for timber, I assure you, but I came for this elephant." "Take him and go, your majesty."

The young elephant would not go. "What, pray, will you have done, elephant?" "Have the carpenters paid for my keeping, your majesty." "Very well, I will," said the king. He had a hundred thousand pieces of money laid near each of the elephant's four feet, near his trunk, and near his tail. But for all that the elephant would not go. When, however, pairs of cloths had been given to all of the carpenters, when under-garments had been given to the carpenters' wives, and when the proper attentions had been paid to the children he had played with, then the elephant turned around, and eyeing the carpenters and their wives and their children as he went, accompanied the king.

The king took the elephant, went to the city, and caused both city and elephant-stable to be adorned. He caused the elephant to make rightwise circuit of the city and to be taken into the elephant-stable. He adorned the elephant with all the adornments, sprinkled him, made him his riding-animal, elevated him to the dignity of a friend, gave him half his kingdom, and had him treated as himself. From the day when the elephant arrived, the king obtained complete mastery over all the Land of the Rose-apple.

As time thus went on, the Future Buddha received a new conception in the womb of the chief consort of that king. When her unborn child was ripe for birth, the king died. Now if the elephant had known that the king was dead, it would have broken his heart then and there. So they said not a word to the elephant about the king's death, but waited on him just as if nothing had happened.

But when the king of Kosala, who ruled over the country immediately adjoining, heard that the king was dead, he reflected: "The kingdom, they say, is empty;" and came with a large army and surrounded the city. The citizens closed the gates of the city and sent the following message to the king of Kosala: "The chief consort of our king is about to give birth to a child. The soothsayers have told us: 'Seven days hence she will give birth to a son.' If, on the seventh day, she gives birth to a son, we will give battle,—not the kingdom. Wait that long." "Very well," said the king in assent. On the seventh day the queen gave birth to a son. On the day when he received his name, because, as they said, "He is born extending a noble heart to the multitude," they gave him the name Noble-heart, Alīnacitta.

Now from the day he was born, the citizens fought with the king of Kosala. But because they had no man to lead them in battle, the force, large as it was, gave way little by little in the conflict. Ministers reported this fact to the queen, saying: "We fear that if the force continues thus to give way, we shall lose the battle. But the state elephant, the king's friend, does not know that the king is dead, that his son is born, and that the king of Kosala has come to fight." And they asked her: "Shall we let him know?" "Yes," said the queen, assenting. She adorned the boy, laid him in a head-coil of fine cloth, came down from the terrace, and accompanied by a retinue of ministers, went to the elephant-stable, and laid the Future Buddha at the feet of the elephant. Said she: "Master, your friend is dead. We didn't tell you because we were afraid it would break your heart. Here is the son of your friend. The king of Kosala has come and has surrounded the city and is fighting with your son. The force is giving way. Do you either kill your son or get and give him the kingdom."

Then the elephant with his trunk caressed the Future Buddha and lifted him up and put him on his shoulders and cried and wept. Then he lowered the Future Buddha and laid him in the arms of the queen, and with the words, "I will capture the king of Kosala!" went out of the elephant-stable. Then the ministers clad him with armor and adorned him, and unlocking the city-gate, went out in his train.

As the elephant went out of the city, he trumpeted the Heron's Call, making the multitude tremble and quake, and frightening them away. He broke down the stockade, seized the king of Kosala by the top-knot, and carried him and laid him at the Future Buddha's feet. And when men rose to kill him, he would not let them, but set the king free with the admonition: "Henceforth be careful; do not presume on the youth of the prince."

Thenceforth the Future Buddha had complete mastery over all the Land of the Rose-apple. No other adversary dared to stand up against him. When the Future Buddha was seven years old, he received the ceremonial sprinkling and became known as King Noble-heart. He ruled with righteousness, and when his life was come to an end, departed, fulfilling the Path to Heaven.

When the Teacher had related this parable, he uttered, as Supreme Buddha, the following pair of stanzas:

Relying on Noble-heart, a mighty host, delighted,
Captured Kosala alive, dissatisfied with his army.

So also the monk who has found a Reliance,
Who exerts strenuous effort,
Who cultivates the Exalted States
To the attainment of Nibbāna,
Shall, in due course, reach
The Destruction of all Bonds.

2. GRATEFUL ANIMALS AND UNGRATEFUL MAN

Driftwood is worth more than some men.

Jātaka 73: i. 322-327.

True is this saying of some men of the world. This parable was related by the Teacher while he was in residence at Veḷuvana with reference to Devadatta's going about for the purpose of killing him. For while the Congregation of Monks, sitting in the Hall of Truth, were discussing Devadatta's wickedness, saying, "Brethren, Devadatta knows not the Teacher's virtues, but is going about for the sole purpose of killing him," the Teacher drew near and asked: "Monks, what is the subject that engages your attention now as you sit here all gathered together?" "Such-and-such," was the reply. "Monks," said the Teacher, "not only in his present state of existence has Devadatta gone about for the purpose of killing me; in a previous state of existence also he went about for the purpose of killing me in the same old way." Then, in response to a request of the monks, he related the following Story of the Past:

Prince Wicked.

In times past Brahmadatta ruled at Benāres. He had a son named Prince Wicked, and Prince Wicked was as tough and hard as a beaten snake. He never spoke to anybody without either reviling him or striking him. The result was that both by indoor-folk and by outdoor-folk he was disliked and detested as much as dust lodged in the eye or as a demon come to eat.

One day, desiring to sport in the water, he went to the river-bank with a large retinue. At that moment a great cloud arose. The directions became dark. He said to his slaves and servants: "Come, fellows! take me and conduct me to mid-stream and bathe me and bring me back." They led him there and took counsel together, saying: "What can the king do to us! Let's kill this wicked fellow right here!" So they said to him: "Here you go, bird of evil omen!" So saying, they plunged him into the water, made their way out of the water again, and stood on the bank.

As the courtiers returned to the king, they reflected: "In case we are asked, 'Where is the prince?' we will say, 'We have not seen the prince; it must be that upon seeing a cloud arise he plunged into the water and went on ahead of us.' " The king asked: "Where is my son?" "We do not know, your majesty. A cloud arose. We returned, supposing: 'He must have gone on ahead of us.' " The king caused the gates to be flung open, went to the river-bank, and caused them to search here and there. "Search!" said he. Nobody saw the prince.

As a matter of fact, in the darkness caused by the cloud, while the god was raining, the prince, swept along by the river, seeing a certain tree-trunk, clambered on it, and sitting astride of it, traveled along, terrified with the fear of death, lamenting.

Snake, rat, parrot, and man.

Now at that time a resident of Benāres, a certain treasurer, who had buried forty crores of wealth by the river-bank, by reason of his craving for that wealth, had been reborn on top of that wealth as a snake. Yet another had buried thirty crores of wealth in that very spot, and by reason of his craving for that wealth, had been reborn on the spot as a rat. The water entered their place of abode. They went out by the very path by which the water came in, cleft the stream, and went until they reached the tree-trunk bestridden by the royal prince. Thereupon one climbed up on one end, the other on the other, and both lay down right there on top of the tree-trunk.

Moreover, on the bank of that very river there was a certain silk-cotton tree, and in it lived a certain young parrot. That tree also, its roots washed by the water, fell on top of the river. The young parrot, unable to make headway by flying while the god was raining, went and perched on one side of that very tree-trunk. Thus did those four persons travel together, swept along by the river.

The Future Buddha befriends animals and man.

Now at that time the Future Buddha was reborn in the kingdom of Kāsi in the household of a Brahman of high station. When he reached manhood, he retired from the world and adopted the life of an ascetic, and building a leaf-hut at a certain bend in the river, took up his abode there. At midnight, as he was walking up and down, he heard the sound of the profound lamentation of that royal prince. Thought he: "It is not fitting that that man should die in sight of an ascetic like me, endowed with friendliness and compassion. I will pull him out of the water and grant him the boon of life." He calmed the man's fears with the words, "Fear not! fear not!" Then, cleaving the stream of water, he went and laid hold of that tree-trunk by one end, and pulled it. Powerful as an elephant, endowed with mighty strength, with a single pull he reached the bank, and lifting the prince in his arms, set him ashore.

Seeing the snake, the rat, and the parrot, he picked them up also, carried them to his hermitage, and lighted a fire. "The animals are weaker," thought he. So first he warmed the bodies of the animals; then afterwards he warmed the body of the royal prince and made him well too. When he brought food also, he first gave it to those same animals, and afterwards offered fruits and other edibles to the prince. Thought the royal prince: "This false ascetic does not take it into his reckoning that I am a royal prince, but does honor to animals." And he conceived a grudge against the Future Buddha.

A few days after that, when all four had recovered their strength and vigor and the river-freshet had ceased, the snake bowed to the ascetic and said: "Reverend Sir, it is a great service you have done me. Now I am no pauper. In such-and-such a place I have buried forty crores of gold. If you have need of money, I can give you all that money. Come to that place and call me out, saying: 'Longfellow!'" So saying, he departed. Likewise also the rat addressed the ascetic: "Stand in such-and-such a place and call me out, saying: 'Rat!'" So saying, he departed.

But when the parrot bowed to the ascetic, he said: "Reverend Sir, I have no money; but if you have need of ruddy rice,—such-and-such is my place of abode,—go there and call me out, saying: 'Parrot!' I'll tell my kinsfolk, have them fetch ruddy rice by the cart-load, and give it to you. That's what I can do!" So saying, he departed.

But that other, the man, because it was his custom to betray his friends, said not so much as a word according to custom. Thought he: "If you come to me, I'll kill you!" But he said: "Reverend Sir, when I am established in my kingdom, be good enough to come and see me; I'll furnish you with the Four Requisites." So saying, he departed. And in no very long time after he had gone, he was established in his kingdom.

Gratefulness of animals.

Thought the Future Buddha: "I'll just put them to the test!" First he went to the snake, and standing not far off, called him out, saying: "Longfellow!" At the mere word the snake came out, bowed to the Future Buddha, and said: "Reverend Sir, in this place are forty crores of gold; carry them all out and take them with you!" Said the Future Buddha: "Let be as it is; if occasion arises, I'll think about it." So saying, he let the snake go back.

Then he went to the rat and made a noise. The rat also behaved just as had the snake. The Future Buddha let him also go back. Then he went to the parrot and called him out, saying: "Parrot!" The parrot also, at the mere word, came down from the top of the tree, and bowing to the Future Buddha, asked: "Tell me, Reverend Sir, shall I speak to my kinsfolk and have them fetch you self-sown rice from the region of Himavat?" Said the Future Buddha: "If I have need, I'll think about it." So saying, he let the parrot also go back.

Ungratefulness of man.

"Now," thought the Future Buddha, "I'll test the king!" He went and passed the night in the king's garden, and on the following day, having put on beautiful garments, entered the city on his round for alms. At that moment that king, that betrayer of friends, seated on the back of his gloriously adorned state elephant, accompanied by a large retinue, was making a rightwise circuit of the city. Seeing the Future Buddha even from afar, he thought: "Here's that false ascetic, come to live with me and eat his fill! That he may not make known in the midst of this company the service he has rendered me, I'll straightway have his head cut off!"

He looked at his men. Said they: "What shall we do, your majesty?" Said the king: "Here's a false ascetic, come to ask me for something or other, I suppose. Without so much as giving that false ascetic, that bird of evil omen, a chance to look at me, take that fellow, bind his arms behind his back, conduct him out of the city, beating him at every cross-roads, cut off his head in the place of execution, and impale his body on a stake!" "Very well," said the king's men in assent. They bound the Great Being, guiltless as he was, and started to conduct him to the place of execution, beating him at every cross-roads. The Future Buddha, wherever they beat him, uttered no lament, "Women! men!" but unperturbed, uttered the following stanza:

> True is this saying of some men of the world:
> "Driftwood is worth more than some men!"

[*Native gloss:* A stick of wood washed up on dry land is of some use: it will cook food; it will warm those who are shivering with the cold; it will remove dangerous objects. But an ingrate is worse than useless.]

Thus, wherever they beat him, did he utter this stanza. Hearing this, wise men who stood by said: "But, monk, what is the trouble between you and our king? have you done him some good turn?" Then the Future Buddha told them the whole story, saying: "I alone, by pulling this man out of a mighty flood, have brought suffering upon myself. I speak as I do because I keep thinking: 'Alas! I have not heeded the words of wise men of old!' "

Hearing this, Warriors and Brahmans and others, residents of the city, became enraged. Said they: "This king here, this betrayer of friends, has not the slightest conception of the virtues of this embodiment of the virtues, this man who has granted him the boon of his own life! What have we to gain through him! Capture him!" And rising in all quarters, they slew him, even as he sat on the back of the elephant, by hitting him with arrows and spears and rocks and clubs. And laying hold of his feet, they dragged him and threw him back of the moat. And conferring the ceremonial sprinkling on the Future Buddha, they established him in the kingdom. The Future Buddha ruled righteously.

Again one day, desiring to test the snake, the rat, and the parrot, he went with a large retinue to the place of abode of the snake and called him out, saying: "Longfellow!" The snake came, bowed to him, and said: "Here's your money, master; take it." The king entrusted to his ministers wealth amounting to forty crores of gold. Then he went to the rat and called him out, saying: "Rat!" The rat also came, and with a bow handed over to him wealth amounting to thirty crores. The king entrusted that also to his ministers. Then he went to the place of abode of the parrot and called him out, saying: "Parrot!" The parrot also came, and reverencing his feet, said: "Master, shall I fetch rice?" Said the king: "When there is need of rice, you may fetch it; come, let's go."

With the seventy crores of gold, causing those three animals also to be carried along, he went to the city. And ascending to the grand floor of his magnificent palace, he caused that wealth to be stored and guarded. For the snake to live in, he caused a golden tube to be made; for the rat, a crystal cave; for the parrot, a golden cage. For the snake and the parrot to eat, he caused every day sweet parched grain to be given in a vessel of gold purified with fire; for the rat, grains of perfumed rice; he gave alms and performed the other works of merit. Thus those four persons, one and all, dwelt together in unity and concord all their days, and when their days were come to an end, passed away according to their deeds.

Said the Teacher: "Monks, not only in his present state of existence has Devadatta gone about for the purpose of killing me; in a previous state of existence also he went about for the purpose of killing me in the same old way." Having related this parable, he joined the connection and identified the personages in the Birth-story as follows: "At that time King Wicked was Devadatta, the snake was Sāriputta, the rat was Moggallāna, the parrot was Ānanda, but he that gained a kingdom and became a King of Righteousness was I myself."

3. ELEPHANT AND UNGRATEFUL FORESTER

The whole earth will not satisfy an ungrateful man.

Jātaka 72: i. 319-322.

To an ungrateful man. This parable was related by the Teacher while he was in residence at Veḷuvana with reference to Devadatta. The monks, seated in the Hall of Truth, were saying: "Brethren, Devadatta the ungrateful knows not the virtues of the Tathāgata." The Teacher drew near and asked: "Monks, what is the subject that engages your attention now, as you sit here all gathered together?" "Such-and-such," was the reply. "Monks," said the Teacher, "not only in his present state of existence has Devadatta proved ungrateful; in a previous state of existence also he was ungrateful just the same. At no time soever has he known my virtues." Then, in response to a request of the monks, he related the following Story of the Past:

In times past, when Brahmadatta ruled at Benāres, the Future Buddha received a new conception in the region of Himavat in the womb of an elephant. When he came forth from his mother's womb, he was pure white, like a mass of silver; moreover his eyes were like globules of jewels, and from them shone forth the Five Brightnesses; his mouth was like a crimson blanket; his trunk was like a rope of silver, ornamented with spots of ruddy gold; his four feet were as if rubbed with lac. Thus his person, adorned with the Ten Perfections, attained the pinnacle of beauty.

Now when he reached the age of reason, elephants from all over Himavat assembled and formed his retinue. Thus did he make his home in the region of Himavat, with a retinue of eighty thousand elephants. After a time, perceiving that there was contamination in the herd, he isolated himself from the herd and made his home quite alone in the forest. Moreover, by reason of his goodness, he became known as Good King Elephant.

Now a certain resident of Benāres, a forester, entered the forest, seeking wares whereby to make his living. Unable to distinguish the directions, he lost his way, and terrified with the fear of death, went about with outstretched arms lamenting. The Future Buddha, hearing those profound lamentations of his, thought: "I will free this man from his suffering." And impelled by compassion, he went to him.

The instant that man saw the Future Buddha, he fled in fright. The Future Buddha, seeing him in flight, halted right where he was. The man, seeing that the Future Buddha had halted, himself halted. The Future Buddha came back. The man fled a second time, but halting when the Future Buddha halted, thought: "This elephant halts when I flee, and approaches when I halt. He has no desire to do me harm, but without a doubt desires only to free me from this suffering." And summoning up his courage, he halted.

The Future Buddha approached him and asked: "Why, Master man, do you go about lamenting?" "Master, because I couldn't distinguish the directions, lost my way, and was afraid of death." Then the Future Buddha conducted him to his own place of abode, and for a few days gladdened him with fruits and other edibles. Then said the Future Buddha: "Master man, don't be afraid; I'll conduct you to the path of man." And seating him on his back, he proceeded to the path of men.

But that man, that betrayer of friends, even as he sat on the back of the Future Buddha, thought: "If anybody asks me, I must be able to tell him where this elephant lives." So as he went along, he noted carefully the landmarks of tree and mountain. Now the Future Buddha, having conducted that man out of the forest, set him down on the highway leading to Benāres, and said to him: "Master man, go by this road; but as for my place of abode, whether you are asked or not, say nothing to anybody about it." So saying, he took leave of him and went back to his own place of abode.

Now that man went to Benāres, and in the course of his walks came to the street of the ivory-carvers. And seeing the ivory-carvers making various kinds of ivory products, he asked: "But, sirs, how much would you make if you could get the tusk of a real live elephant?" "What are you saying, sir! The tusk of a live elephant is far more valuable than the tusk of a dead elephant." "Very well! I'll fetch you the tusk of a live elephant." Accordingly, obtaining provisions for the journey and taking a sharp saw, he went to the place of abode of the Future Buddha.

When the Future Buddha saw him, he asked: "For what purpose have you come?" "I, sir, am a poor man, a pauper, unable to make a living. I came with this thought in my mind: 'I will ask you for a fragment of one of your tusks; if you will give it to me, I will take it and go and sell it and with the money it brings make a living.'" "Let be, sir! I'll give you tusks, if you have a sharp saw to cut them off with." "I brought a saw with me, sir." "Very well, sever the tusks with your saw and take them and go your way." So saying, the Future Buddha bowed his knees together and sat down like a cow. The man actually cut off his two principal tusks!

The Future Buddha, taking those tusks in his trunk, said: "Master man, not with the thought, 'These tusks are not dear to me, not pleasing to me,' do I give you these tusks. But dearer to me than these a thousand times,—a hundred thousand times,—are the Tusks of Omniscience, which avail to the comprehension of all things. May this gift of tusks which I here bestow enable me to attain Omniscience!" So saying, as it were sowing the Seed of Omniscience, he gave him the pair of tusks.

The man took them and went and sold them. When the money

they brought was gone, he went to the Future Buddha again and said: "Master, the money I got by selling your tusks turned out to be no more than enough to pay off my debts. Give me the rest of your tusks!" "Very well," said the Future Buddha, consenting. And ordering all things precisely as before, he gave him the rest of his tusks.

Those also did that man sell, and then came back again. "Master," said he, "I cannot make a living. Give me the stumps of your tusks!" "Very well," said the Future Buddha, and sat down precisely as before. That wicked man trod on the Great Being's trunk,—that trunk which was like unto a rope of silver; climbed up on the Great Being's temples,—those temples which were like unto the snow-clad peaks of Kelāsa, with his heel kicking the tips of the tusks and loosening the flesh; and having mounted the temples, with a sharp saw severed the stumps of the tusks, and went his way.

But even as that wicked man receded from the vision of the Future Buddha, the solid earth, which extends for a distance of two hundred thousand leagues and four Inconceivables more, which is able to endure such mighty burdens as Sineru and Yugandhara, such foul-smelling and repulsive objects as dung and urine,—even the solid earth, as if unable to endure the wickedness he had piled upon it, burst asunder and yawned. Instantly from the Great Waveless Hell flames of fire shot forth, enveloped that man, that betrayer of friends, wrapping him, as it were, in a blanket proper for death and laid hold of him.

When that wicked man thus entered the earth, the tree-spirit resident in that forest-grove thought: "An ungrateful man, a man who will betray his friends, cannot be satisfied, even if he be given the kingdom of a Universal Monarch." And making the forest ring, proclaiming the Truth, the tree-spirit uttered the following stanza:

> To an ungrateful man
> Ever looking for an opening
> You may give the whole earth
> And yet not satisfy him.

Thus did that tree-spirit, making the forest ring, proclaim the Truth. The Future Buddha, having remained on earth during the term of life allotted to him, passed away according to his deeds.

Said the Teacher: "Monks, not only in his present state of existence has Devadatta proved ungrateful; in a previous state of existence also he was ungrateful just the same." Having completed the parable, he identified the personages in the Birth-story as follows: "At that time the man who betrayed his friend was Devadatta, the tree-spirit was Sāriputta, but Good King Elephant was I myself."

CHAPTER II

PARABLES FROM THE BOOK OF THE BUDDHA'S PREVIOUS EXISTENCES AND FROM THE BOOK OF DISCIPLINE, ON UNITY AND DISCORD

4. QUAIL, CROW, FLY, FROG, AND ELEPHANTS

The biter bit.

Jātaka 357: iii. 174-177.

Hearing that the monks of Kosambi were quarreling, the Exalted One went to them and said: "Enough, monks! No quarreling! No brawling! No contending! No wrangling!" Then he said: "Monks, quarrels, brawls, contentions, wrangles,—all these are unprofitable. For because of a quarrel even a tiny quail brought about the destruction of a noble elephant."

In times past, when Brahmadatta ruled at Benāres, the Future Buddha was reborn as an elephant. He grew up to be a fine big animal, acquired a retinue of eighty thousand elephants, and becoming the leader of a herd, made his home in the Himālaya region. At that time a tiny female quail laid her eggs in the elephants' stamping-ground. When the eggs were hatched, the fledglings broke the shells and came out. Before their wings had grown and while they were yet unable to fly, the Great Being came to that spot with his retinue of eighty thousand elephants in search of food.

When the tiny quail saw him, she thought: "This elephant-king will crush my fledglings and kill them. Well, I will ask of him righteous protection for the defense of my little ones." So folding her wings and standing before him, she uttered the first stanza:

I salute you, elephant of sixty years,
Forest-ranger, glorious leader of a herd;
With my wings I do you homage.
I am weak: do not kill my little ones.

Said the Great Being: "Do not worry, tiny quail; I will protect your little ones." And he stood over the fledglings, and the eighty thousand elephants passed by. Then he addressed the tiny quail: "Behind us comes a single solitary elephant; he will not obey our command. If you ask him also when he comes, you may obtain safety for your little ones." So saying, he went his way.

The tiny quail went forth to meet the solitary elephant, did homage to him with her wings, and uttered the second stanza:

> I salute you, solitary elephant,
> Forest-ranger, pasturing on mountain and on hill;
> With my wings I do you homage.
> I am weak: do not kill my little ones.

The solitary elephant, hearing her words, uttered the third stanza:

> I will kill your little ones, tiny quail.
> What can you do to me? You are a weakling.
> Even a hundred thousand like you
> Could I crush with my left foot.

And so saying, he pulverized her little ones with his foot, washed them away with a torrent of urine, and went his way trumpeting. The tiny quail perched on the branch of a tree and thought: "Just now you go your way trumpeting. In only a few days you will see what I can do! You do not understand that the mind is stronger than the body. Ah, but I will make you understand!" And threatening him, she uttered the fourth stanza:

> For not alway does strength avail;
> For strength is the destruction of a fool.
> Elephant-king, I will do you harm,
> You who killed my little ones since I was weak.

Thus spoke the tiny quail. For a few days she ministered to a crow. The crow was pleased and said: "What can I do for you?" Said the tiny quail: "Master, there is only one thing I want done. I expect you to peck out the eyes of that solitary elephant." "Very well," assented the crow. The tiny quail then ministered to a green fly. The fly also said: "What can I do for you?" Said the tiny quail: "When this crow has put out the eyes of the solitary elephant, I wish you would drop a nit on them." "Very well," assented the fly also. The tiny quail then ministered to a frog. Said the frog: "What can I do?" Said the tiny quail: "When this solitary elephant has gone blind and seeks water to drink, then please squat on the mountain-top and croak; and when he has climbed to the top of the mountain, then please hop down and croak at the bottom. This is all I expect of you." The frog also, hearing her words, assented, saying, "Very well."

Now one day the crow pecked out both of the elephant's eyes, and the fly let a nit drop on them. The elephant, eaten up by maggots, maddened with pain, overcome with thirst, wandered about seeking water to drink. At that moment the frog, squatting on the mountain-top, let out a croak. The elephant thought: "There must be water there;" and climbed the mountain. Then the frog hopped down, and squatting at the bottom, let out a croak. The elephant thought: "There must be water there." And going to the brink of the precipice, he tumbled and fell to the foot of the mountain, and met destruction.

When the tiny quail realized that he was dead, she cried out: "I have seen the back of my enemy!" And pleased and delighted, she strutted over his shoulders, and passed away according to her deeds.

> Behold the quail, the crow, the fly, the frog!
> They slew the elephant! Behold the hatred of the haters!

5. QUAILS AND FOWLER

In union there is strength.

Jātaka 33: i. 208-210.

Then said the Exalted One to those monks: "Monks, be united; do not wrangle. For because of a wrangle many thousand quails lost their lives."

IN times past, when Brahmadatta ruled at Benāres, the Future Buddha was reborn as a quail, and lived in the forest with a retinue of many thousand quails. At that time a certain quail-hunter used to go to the haunt of the quails and attract them by imitating a quail's whistle. When he perceived that they had assembled, he would throw a net over them and huddle them all together by trampling the edges. Then he would fill his basket, go home, and sell them. Thus he made his living.

Now one day the Future Buddha said to those quails: "This

fowler is bringing our kinsfolk to destruction. I know a way by which he shall not be able to catch us. From this time on, the moment he throws the net over you, let each quail stick his head through a single mesh, lift the net, and carrying it wherever you will, let it down on some thorn-brake. This done, we can escape each through his own mesh." They all assented, saying, "Very well!"

When the net was thrown over them on the following day, they raised the net precisely as the Future Buddha had told them to, dropped it on a certain thorn-brake, and themselves escaped from under. Twilight came on with the fowler still busy disentangling the net from the brake, and he went away absolutely empty-handed. On the next day, and thereafter also, the quails did the very same thing. The fowler also, busy every moment until sunset disentangling the net, got nothing, and went home absolutely empty-handed.

Now his wife got angry and said: "Day after day you return empty-handed; I suppose there is some other household outside you have to provide for too." Said the fowler: "My dear, there is no other household I have to provide for. The fact is, these quails are acting in unison. The moment I throw the net, they depart with it and drop it on a thorn-brake. But they will not live in unity forever. Do not worry. When they fall to wrangling, I will return with them all and bring a smile to your lips." And he recited the following stanza to his wife:

> United, the birds go away with the net;
> But when they fall out, they'll come into my power.

Now after only a few days had passed, one quail, lighting on the feeding-ground, accidentally trod on the head of another. The other was offended and said: "Who trod on my head?" "I did, but accidentally; do not be offended." But the other was offended just the same. They bandied words and wrangled with each other, saying, "You alone, I suppose, lift the net!"

While they wrangled, the Future Buddha thought: "There is no safety for a wrangler. From this moment they will not lift the net. Then they will come to a sorry end. The fowler will get his chance. It is impossible for me to live in this place." And he went elsewhere with his own retinue.

As for the fowler, he came back after a few days, imitated a quail's whistle, and when the quails had assembled, threw the net over them. Then said one quail: "They say that in the very act of lifting the net, you lost the down on your head. Now lift!" Said another: "They say that in the very act of lifting the net, you lost your wing-feathers. Now lift!"

Even as they said: "You lift!" "You lift!" the fowler tossed the net. And huddling them all together, he filled his basket, and went home and brought a smile to the lips of his wife.

And for the second time the Exalted One said this to those monks: "Enough, monks! No quarreling! No brawling! No contending! No wrangling!"

But in spite of this, they paid no attention to his words. Thereupon the Exalted One related the following Story of the Past:

6. BRAHMADATTA, DĪGHĪTI, AND DĪGHĀVU

Love your enemies.

Vinaya i. 342-349.

In olden times at Benāres, Brahmadatta king of Kāsi was rich, possessed of great wealth, ample means of enjoyment, a mighty army, many vehicles, an extensive kingdom, and well filled treasuries and storehouses. Dīghiti king of Kosala was poor, possessed of meagre wealth, scanty means of enjoyment, a small army, few vehicles, a little kingdom, and unfilled treasuries and storehouses.

Now Brahmadatta king of Kāsi drew up his fourfold army and went up against Dīghīti king of Kosala. And Dīghīti king of Kosala heard: "Brahmadatta king of Kāsi, they say, has drawn up his fourfold army, and is come up against me." Then to Dīghīti king of Kosala occurred the following thought: "Brahmadatta king of Kāsi is rich, possessed of great wealth, ample means of enjoyment, a mighty army, many vehicles, an extensive kingdom, and well filled treasuries and storehouses. But I am poor, possessed of meagre wealth, scanty means of enjoyment, a small army, few vehicles, a little kingdom, and unfilled treasuries and storehouses. I am not strong enough to withstand even a single clash with Brahmadatta king of Kāsi. Suppose I were merely to countermarch and slip out of the city!"

Accordingly Dīghīti king of Kosala took his consort, merely countermarched, and slipped out of the city. Thereupon Brahmadatta king of Kāsi conquered the army and vehicles and territory and treasuries and storehouses of Dīghīti king of Kosala, and took possession. And Dīghīti king of Kosala with his consort set out for Benāres, and in due course arrived at Benāres. And there, in a certain place on the outskirts of Benāres, Dīghīti king of Kosala resided with his consort, in a potter's dwelling, in disguise, in the guise of a wandering ascetic.

Now in no very long time the consort of Dīghīti king of Kosala became pregnant. And this was her craving: She desired at sunrise to see a fourfold army drawn up, clad in armor, standing in a pleasant place, and to drink the rinsings of swords. Accordingly the consort of Dīghīti king of Kosala said this to Dīghīti king of Kosala: "I am pregnant, O king. And this craving has arisen within me: I desire at sunrise to see a fourfold army drawn up, clad in armor, standing in a pleasant place, and to drink the rinsings of swords." "Whence are we, wretched folk, to obtain a fourfold army drawn up, clad in armor, standing in a pleasant place, and the rinsings of swords?" "If, O king, I do not obtain my desire, I shall die."

Now at that time the Brahman who was the house-priest of Brahmadatta king of Kāsi was a friend of Dīghīti king of Kosala. Accordingly Dīghīti king of Kosala approached the Brahman who was the house-priest of Brahmadatta king of Kāsi. And having approached, he said this to the Brahman who was the house-priest of Brahmadatta king of Kāsi: "Sir, your female friend is pregnant. And this craving has arisen within her: She desires at sunrise to see a fourfold army drawn up, clad in armor, standing in a pleasant place, and to drink the rinsings of swords." "Very well, O king, we also will see the queen."

Now the consort of Dīghīti king of Kosala approached the Brahman who was the house-priest of Brahmadatta king of Kāsi. The Brahman who was the house-priest of Brahmadatta king of Kāsi saw the consort of Dīghīti king of Kosala approaching even from afar. And seeing her, he rose from his seat, adjusted his upper robe so as to cover one shoulder only, and bending his joined hands in reverent salutation before the consort of Dīghīti king of Kosala, thrice breathed forth the utterance: "All hail!

A king of Kosala dwells in thy womb! All hail! A king of Kosala dwells in thy womb!" Then he said: "Be not distressed, O queen. You shall obtain your desire to see at sunrise a fourfold army drawn up, clad in armor, standing in a pleasant place, and to drink the rinsings of swords."

Thereupon the Brahman who was the house-priest of Brahmadatta king of Kāsi approached Brahmadatta king of Kāsi. And having approached, he said this to Brahmadatta king of Kāsi: "Thus, O king, the signs appear: To-morrow at sunrise let the fourfold army be drawn up, clad in armor, standing in a pleasant place, and let the swords be washed." Accordingly Brahmadatta king of Kāsi ordered his men: "Do as the Brahman who is my house-priest has said." Thus the consort of Dīghīti king of Kosala obtained her desire to see at sunrise a fourfold army drawn up, clad in armor, standing in a pleasant place, and to drink the rinsings of swords. And when that unborn child had reached maturity, the consort of Dīghīti king of Kosala brought forth a son, and they called his name Dīghāvu. And in no very long time Prince Dīghāvu reached the age of reason.

Now to Dīghīti king of Kosala occurred the following thought: "This Brahmadatta king of Kāsi has done us much injury. He has robbed us of army and vehicles and territory and treasuries and storehouses. If he recognizes us, he will cause all three of us to be put to death. Suppose I were to cause Prince Dīghāvu to dwell outside of the city!" Accordingly Dīghīti king of Kosala caused Prince Dīghāvu to dwell outside of the city. And Prince Dīghāvu, residing outside of the city, in no very long time acquired all the arts and crafts.

Now at that time the barber of Dīghīti king of Kosala resided at the court of Brahmadatta king of Kāsi. The barber of Dīghīti king of Kosala saw Dīghīti king of Kosala residing with his consort in a certain place on the outskirts of Benāres, in a potter's dwelling, in disguise, in the guise of a wandering ascetic. When he saw him, he approached Brahmadatta king of Kāsi. And having approached, he said this to Brahmadatta king of Kāsi: "O king, Dīghīti king of Kosala is residing with his consort in a certain place on the outskirts of Benāres, in a potter's dwelling, in disguise, in the guise of a wandering ascetic."

Thereupon Brahmadatta king of Kāsi ordered his men: "Now

then, bring Dīghīti king of Kosala with his consort before me." "Yes, your majesty," said those men to Brahmadatta king of Kāsi; and in obedience to his command brought Dīghīti king of Kosala with his consort before him. Then Brahmadatta king of Kāsi ordered his men: "Now then, take Dīghīti king of Kosala with his consort, bind their arms tight behind their backs with a stout rope, shave their heads, and to the loud beating of a drum lead them about from street to street, from crossing to crossing, conduct them out of the South gate, hack their bodies into four pieces south of the city, and throw the pieces in the four directions."

"Yes, your majesty," said those men to Brahmadatta king of Kāsi; and in obedience to his command took Dīghīti king of Kosala with his consort, bound their arms tight behind their backs with a stout rope, shaved their heads, and to the loud beating of a drum led them about from street to street, from crossing to crossing.

Now to Prince Dīghāvu occurred the following thought: "It is a long time since I have seen my mother and father. Suppose I were to see my mother and father!" Accordingly Prince Dīghāvu entered Benāres, and saw his mother and father, their arms bound tight behind their backs, their heads shaven, being led about, to the loud beating of a drum, from street to street, from crossing to crossing. When he saw this, he approached his mother and father.

Dīghīti king of Kosala saw Prince Dīghāvu approaching even from afar. When he saw him, he said this to Prince Dīghāvu: "Dear Dīghāvu, do not look long! Do not look short! For, dear Dīghāvu, hatreds are not quenched by hatred. Nay rather, dear Dīghāvu, hatreds are quenched by love."

At these words those men said this to Dīghīti king of Kosala: "This Dīghīti king of Kosala is stark mad, and talks gibberish. Who is Dīghāvu to him? To whom did he speak thus: 'Dear Dīghāvu, do not look long! Do not look short! For, dear Dīghāvu, hatreds are not quenched by hatred. Nay rather, dear Dīghāvu, hatreds are quenched by love'?" "I am not stark mad, I assure you, nor do I talk gibberish. However, he that is intelligent will understand clearly." For the second and the third time Dīghīti king of Kosala spoke thus to Prince Dīghāvu, and those men spoke thus to Dīghīti king of Kosala.

Then those men led Dīghīti king of Kosala with his consort about from street to street, from crossing to crossing, conducted them out of the South gate, hacked their bodies into four pieces south of the city, threw the pieces in the four directions, posted a guard of soldiers, and departed.

Thereupon Prince Dīghāvu entered Benāres, procured liquor, and gave it to the soldiers to drink. When they were drunk and had fallen, he gathered sticks of wood, built a pyre, placed the bodies of his mother and father on the pyre, lighted it, and with joined hands upraised in reverent salutation thrice made sunwise circuit of the pyre.

Now at that time Brahmadatta king of Kāsi was on an upper floor of his splendid palace. And Brahmadatta king of Kāsi saw Prince Dīghāvu, with joined hands upraised in reverent salutation, thrice making sunwise circuit of the pyre. When he saw this, the following thought occurred to him: "Without doubt that man is a kinsman or blood-relative of Dīghīti king of Kosala. Alas, my wretched misfortune, for no one will tell me the facts!"

Now Prince Dīghāvu went to the forest, wailed and wept his fill, and wiped his tears away. Then he entered Benāres, went to the elephant-stable adjoining the royal palace, and said this to the elephant-trainer: "Trainer, I wish to learn your art." "Very well, young man, learn it." Accordingly Prince Dīghāvu rose at night, at time of dawn, and sang and played the lute with charming voice in the elephant-stable.

Brahmadatta king of Kāsi heard him as he rose at night, at time of dawn, and sang and played the lute with charming voice in the elephant-stable. Hearing him, he asked his men: "Who was it, pray, that rose at night, at time of dawn, and sang and played the lute with charming voice in the elephant-stable?" "Your majesty, it was a young man, the pupil of such-and-such an elephant-trainer, who rose at night, at time of dawn, and sang and played the lute with charming voice in the elephant-stable." "Very well, bring that young man to me." "Yes, your majesty," said those men to Brahmadatta king of Kāsi; and in obedience to his command brought Prince Dīghāvu to him.

"Was it you, young man, who rose at night, at time of dawn,

and sang and played the lute with charming voice in the elephant-stable?" "Yes, your majesty." "Very well, young man, sing and play the lute for me." "Yes, your majesty," said Prince Dīghāvu to Brahmadatta king of Kāsi; and in obedience to his command, desiring to win his favor, sang and played the lute with charming voice.

Thereupon Brahmadatta king of Kāsi said this to Prince Dīghāvu: "You, young man, may wait upon me." "Yes, your majesty," said Prince Dīghāvu to Brahmadatta king of Kāsi, and obeyed his command. And Prince Dīghāvu rose in advance of Brahmadatta king of Kāsi, retired after him, obeyed his every command, conducted himself in a pleasing manner, spoke in a friendly manner. And in no very long time Brahmadatta king of Kāsi appointed Prince Dīghāvu to a highly confidential position.

Now Brahmadatta king of Kāsi said this to Prince Dīghāvu: "Now then, young man, harness the chariot; I wish to go a-hunting." "Yes, your majesty," said Prince Dīghāvu to Brahmadatta king of Kāsi. And having, in obedience to the king's command, harnessed the chariot, he said this to Brahmadatta king of Kāsi: "Your majesty, the chariot is harnessed for you; do as you think fit." Thereupon Brahmadatta king of Kāsi mounted the chariot; Prince Dīghāvu drove the chariot. In such wise did he drive the chariot that the army went one way, the chariot the other.

Now when he had gone a long way, Brahmadatta king of Kāsi said this to Prince Dīghāvu: "Now then, young man, unharness the chariot. I am tired: I wish to lie down." "Yes, your majesty," said Prince Dīghāvu to Brahmadatta king of Kāsi; and in obedience to his command unharnessed the chariot and sat down on the ground cross-legged. And Brahmadatta king of Kāsi lay down, placing his head in Prince Dīghāvu's lap. So tired was he that in the mere fraction of a moment he fell asleep.

Thereupon to Prince Dīghāvu occurred the following thought: "This Brahmadatta king of Kāsi has done us much injury. He has robbed us of army and vehicles and territory and treasuries and storehouses. And he has killed my mother and father. This would be the very time for me to satisfy my hatred!" And he drew sword from sheath. Then to Prince Dīghāvu occurred the following thought: "My father said to me in the hour of death: 'Dear

Dīghāvu, do not look long! Do not look short! For, dear Dīghāvu, hatreds are not quenched by hatred. Nay rather, dear Dīghāvu, hatreds are quenched by love.' It is not fitting that I should transgress the command of my father." And he returned sword to sheath. And this happened a second time, and a third time.

Suddenly Brahmadatta king of Kāsi rose, frightened, agitated, alarmed, terrified. Thereupon Prince Dīghāvu said this to Brahmadatta king of Kāsi: "Why, your majesty, did you rise so suddenly, frightened, agitated, alarmed, terrified?" "Right here, young man, Prince Dīghāvu, son of Dīghīti king of Kosala, fell upon me with his sword in a dream. Therefore I rose suddenly, frightened, agitated, alarmed, terrified."

Then Prince Dīghāvu, stroking the head of Brahmadatta king of Kāsi with his left hand, and drawing his sword with his right hand, said this to Brahmadatta king of Kāsi: "I, your majesty, am Prince Dīghāvu, son of Dīghīti king of Kosala. You have done us much injury. You have robbed us of army and vehicles and territory and treasuries and storehouses. And you have killed my mother and father. This would be the very time for me to satisfy my hatred!"

Thereupon Brahmadatta king of Kāsi prostrated himself on his face at the feet of Prince Dīghāvu, and said this to Prince Dīghāvu: "Grant me my life, dear Dīghāvu! Grant me my life, dear Dīghāvu!" "How have I the power to grant your majesty your life? Your majesty, however, might grant me my life." Very well, dear Dīghāvu. You grant me my life, and I will grant you your life." Then Brahmadatta king of Kāsi and Prince Dīghāvu granted each other their lives and shook hands and swore an oath not to injure each other.

Then Brahmadatta king of Kāsi said this to Prince Dīghāvu: "Now then, dear Dīghāvu, harness the chariot; let us be going." "Yes, your majesty," said Prince Dīghāvu to Brahmadatta king of Kāsi. And having, in obedience to the king's command, harnessed the chariot, he said this to Brahmadatta king of Kāsi: "Your majesty, the chariot is harnessed for you; do as you think fit." Thereupon Brahmadatta king of Kāsi mounted the chariot; Prince Dīghāvu drove the chariot. In such wise did he drive the chariot that in no very long time he came up with the army.

Then Brahmadatta king of Kāsi entered Benāres, caused the

ministers of his council to be assembled, and said this: "If, sirs, you were to see Prince Dīghāvu, son of Dīghīti king of Kosala, what would you do to him?" Some spoke thus: "We, your majesty, would cut off his hands." Others spoke thus: "We, your majesty, would cut off his feet." "We would cut off his hands and feet." "We would cut off his ears." "We would cut off his nose." "We would cut off his ears and nose." "We, your majesty, would cut off his head." "Sirs, this is Prince Dīghāvu, son of Dīghīti king of Kosala; it is not permissible to do anything to him. He has granted me my life, and I have granted him his life."

Then Brahmadatta king of Kāsi said this to Prince Dīghāvu: "When, dear Dīghāvu, your father said to you in the hour of death: 'Dear Dīghāvu, do not look long! Do not look short! For, dear Dīghāvu, hatreds are not quenched by hatred. Nay rather, dear Dīghāvu, hatreds are quenched by love,' what did your father mean by that?" "When, your majesty, my father said to me in the hour of death: 'Not long,' what he meant was: 'Do not cherish hatred long.' This, your majesty, is what my father meant when he said to me in the hour of death: 'Not long.' When, your majesty, my father said to me in the hour of death: 'Not short,' what he meant was: 'Do not break with your friends quickly.' This, your majesty, is what my father meant when he said to me in the hour of death: 'Not short.'

"When, your majesty, my father said to me in the hour of death: 'For, dear Dīghāvu, hatreds are not quenched by hatred. Nay rather, dear Dīghāvu, hatreds are quenched by love,' what he meant to have me understand was this: Your majesty has killed my mother and father. Were I to deprive your majesty of life, your majesty's well-wishers would deprive me of life, and my well-wishers would deprive yours of life. Thus that hatred would not be quenched by hatred. But as matters stand, your majesty has granted me my life, and I have granted your majesty his life. Thus hatred has been quenched by love. This, your majesty, is what my father meant when he said to me in the hour of death: 'For, dear Dīghāvu, hatreds are not quenched by hatred. Nay rather, dear Dīghāvu, hatreds are quenched by love.' "

Thereupon Brahmadatta king of Kāsi exclaimed: "O how wonderful, O how marvelous, that this Prince Dīghāvu should understand in its fulness a matter which his father expressed so briefly!"

And he restored to him the army and vehicles and territory and treasuries and storehouses of his fathers, and gave him his daughter in marriage.

"For, monks, of these kings who took the rod, who took the sword, such is said to have been the patience and gentleness. How much more, monks, should you, who have retired from the world under a Doctrine and Discipline so well taught, let your light so shine in this world as to be known of men as patient and gentle." And for the third time the Exalted One said this to those monks: "Enough, monks! No quarreling! No brawling! No contending! No wrangling!"

7. DĪGHÀVU AND THE KING OF BENĀRES

Love your enemies.

Jātaka 371: iii. 211-213.

Such as you are, O king. This parable was related by the Teacher while he was in residence at Jetavana with reference to the quarrelsome monks of Kosambi. For when they came to Jetavana and begged his pardon, the Teacher addressed them: "Monks, you are my own legitimate sons, born of the words of my mouth. Now it is not proper for sons to trample under foot admonitions given them by their father. But you have not obeyed my admonitions. Wise men of old, even when bandits who had slain their mother and father and had taken their kingdom at last came into their hands in the forest, reflected, 'We will not trample under foot the admonitions given us by our mother and father,' and refrained from killing them." So saying, he related the following Story of the Past:

Now that Prince Dīghāvu, as the king of Benāres lay in the forest with his head in his own lap, seizing him by the top-knot, drawing his sword, with the thought in his mind, "Now I will cut off the head of this slayer of my mother and father, this bandit, and hack it into fourteen pieces," at that moment remembering the admonition given him by his mother and father, thinking, "Though I renounce life, I will not trample under foot their admonition; I will only frighten him," uttered the first stanza:

> Such as you are, O king, you have come into my power!
> Is there any means by which you can escape disaster?

Then the king uttered the second stanza:

> Such as I am, O prince, I have come into your power!
> There is no means by which I can escape disaster.

Then the Future Buddha uttered the rest of the stanzas:

> Good deeds, O king, and nothing else,
> Good words, O king, and nothing else,
> Protect a man in the hour of death;
> Worthless is any other kind of wealth.

> *He abused me, he struck me, he defeated me, he robbed me:*
> If any cherish this thought, their hatred never ceases.

> *He abused me, he struck me, he defeated me, he robbed me:*
> If any cherish not this thought, their hatred ceases.

> *For never in this world do hatreds cease through hatred;*
> *Through love alone do hatreds cease:* this is an eternal law.

Now when he had thus spoken, the Future Buddha said, "I, great king, have no desire to harm you; but do you kill me!" and placed his sword in the king's hand. As for the king, he said, "Neither have I any desire to harm you," and swore an oath. Returning to the city with the prince, he showed him to his ministers and said: "This, gentlemen, is Prince Dīghāvu, son of the king of Kosala. He has granted me my life. It is not permissible to do anything to him." So saying, he gave him his own daughter in marriage and established him in the kingdom which belonged to his father. Thenceforth the two ruled as kings in unity and concord.

When the Teacher had related this parable, he identified the personages in the Birth-story as follows: "At that time the mother and father were the royalties of to-day; Prince Dīghāvu was I myself."

CHAPTER III

PARABLES FROM THE BOOK OF THE BUDDHA'S PREVIOUS EXISTENCES ON DIVERS SUBJECTS

8. TWO CARAVAN-LEADERS

Adhere to the Truth.

Jātaka 1: i. 95-106.

One day Anāthapiṇḍika the treasurer, accompanied by five hundred disciples of heretical teachers, went to Jetavana monastery, saluted the Exalted One, presented offerings, and sat down. Likewise did those disciples of heretical teachers salute the Tathāgata and sit down, close beside Anāthapiṇḍika. And they gazed at the countenance of the Teacher, resplendent with the glory of the full moon; at his form, a form like that of Great Brahmā, adorned with the greater and lesser marks of beauty, encircled with a radiance a fathom deep; at the solid rays of a Buddha which issued from his body, forming, as it were, garland after garland and pair after pair.

And to them the Teacher, as it were a young lion roaring the lion's roar on a table-land in the Himālaya mountains, as it were a cloud thundering in the rainy season, as it were bringing down the Heavenly Ganges, as it were weaving a rope of jewels, with a voice like that of Great Brahmā, endowed with the Eight Excellences, captivating the ear, delighting the heart, preached a pleasing discourse on the Doctrine, diversified in divers ways.

The heretics, after listening to the discourse of the Teacher, believed in their hearts, and rising from their seats, burst asunder the refuge of the heretical teachers and sought refuge in the Buddha. From that time on they regularly accompanied Anāthapiṇḍika to the monastery with offerings, listened to the Doctrine, gave alms, kept the Precepts, observed Fast-day. Now the Exalted One departed from Sāvatthi and went back again to Rājagaha. When the Tathāgata departed, the heretics burst that refuge asunder, sought refuge once more in the heretical teachers, lapsed once more into their former position.

When the Exalted One returned to Sāvatthi and learned what had happened, he said to those backsliders: "Laymen, in former times also men mistook for a refuge what was no refuge at all, grasped with the grasp of reason, with the grasp of contradiction, and in a wilderness haunted by demons came to a sorry end, becoming the food of ogres. But men who laid hold of Truth absolute, certain, consistent, obtained safety in that very wilderness." Having so said, he became silent.

Thereupon Anāthapiṇḍika the householder, rising from his seat, saluted and applauded the Exalted One. And joining his hands and pressing them to his head in token of reverent salutation, he spoke as follows: "Reverend Sir, it is clear to us that these laymen just now burst asunder the Supreme Refuge and chose instead speculation. But the fact that in former times, in a wilderness haunted by demons, men who chose speculation were destroyed, while men who chose Absolute Truth were saved,—that fact is hidden from us and clear to you alone. It were indeed well were the Exalted One, as it were making the full moon rise in the heavens, to make this fact clear to us."

Then the Exalted One aroused the attention of the treasurer by saying: "I, O householder, fulfilled the Ten Perfections during a period of time which cannot be measured, and penetrated Omniscience, for the sole purpose of rending asunder the doubt of the world. Lend ear and listen as attentively as though you were filling a golden tube with lion-marrow." Thereupon, as it were cleaving the Vault of the Snow and releasing the full moon, he revealed circumstances hidden by rebirth:

In times past, in the kingdom of Kāsi, in the city of Benāres, there was a king named Brahmadatta. At that time the Future Buddha was reborn in the household of a caravan-leader. In the course of time he grew to manhood, and went about trading with five hundred carts. Sometimes he went from east to west, sometimes from west to east. In the same city of Benāres there was another caravan-leader besides, a foolish, short-sighted, resourceless fellow.

At that time the Future Buddha took a valuable lot of goods from Benāres, filled five hundred carts, made preparations for the journey, and was all ready to start. Likewise that foolish caravan-leader also filled five hundred carts, made preparations for the journey, and was all ready to start.

The Future Buddha thought: "If this foolish caravan-leader goes at the same time I go, and a thousand carts travel along the road together, even the road will not be big enough. It will be difficult for the men to find firewood and water, and difficult for the oxen to find grass. Either he or I should go first." So he had the man summoned, told him the situation, and said: "It is out of the question for both of us to go at the same time. Will you go first, or follow after?"

Thought the foolish caravan-leader: "There are many advantages in my going first. There will not be a single rut in the road over which I travel; my oxen will eat grass which has not been touched; my men will have leaves for curry which have not been touched; the water will be clear; I can sell my goods at whatever price I choose to set." So he said: "I, sir, will go first."

As for the Future Buddha, he saw many advantages in going second, for the following considerations presented themselves to his mind: "Those who go first will make smooth the rough spots on the road; I shall go by the same road they have gone; the oxen that go first will eat the old tough grass, and my oxen will eat the fresh grass which will have sprung up in the meantime; wherever they pluck leaves, fresh leaves for curry will have sprung up and will be at the disposal of my men; in places where there is no water, they will dig wells and obtain a supply, and we shall drink water from wells dug by others. Moreover, price-fixing is like depriving men of life! If I go second, I can sell my goods for whatever price they have fixed." Accordingly, seeing all these advantages in going second, he said: "You, sir, go first." "Very well, sir," said the foolish caravan-leader. So harnessing his carts, he set out, and in due course passing beyond the habitations of men, he reached the mouth of the wilderness.

(Wildernesses are of five kinds: robber-wildernesses, beast-wildernesses, waterless wildernesses, demon-wildernesses, famine-wildernesses. Where the road is infested with robbers, it is called a robber-wilderness. Where the road is infested with lions and other beasts of prey, it is called a beast-wilderness. Where there is no water for bathing or drinking, it is called a waterless wilderness. If it is infested with demons, it is called a demon-wilderness. If it lacks roots and hard food and soft food, it is called a famine-wilderness. Of these five kinds of wildernesses, this wilderness was both a waterless wilderness and a demon-wilderness.)

Therefore that caravan-leader set many huge chatties in the carts and had them filled with water before he struck into the sixty-league wilderness. Now when he reached the middle of the wilderness, the ogre who lived in the wilderness, thinking, "I will make these men throw away the water they took," created a car to delight the heart, drawn by pure white young oxen; and surrounded by ten or twelve demons bearing in their hands bow, quiver, shield, and weapon, decked with water-lilies both blue and white, head wet, garments wet, seated in that car like a very lord, the wheels of the car smeared with mud, came down that road from the opposite direction.

Both before him and behind him marched the demons who formed his retinue, heads wet, garments wet, decked with garlands of water-lilies both blue and white, carrying in their hands clusters of lotus-flowers both red and white, chewing the fibrous stalks of water-lilies, streaming with drops of water and mud.

Now caravan-leaders, when the wind is ahead, to avoid the dust, ride in front, sitting in their cars, surrounded by their attendants. When it blows from behind, they ride behind in precisely the same way. But at this time the wind was ahead; therefore that caravan-leader rode in front.

When the ogre saw him approaching, he caused his own car to turn out of the road and greeted him in a friendly manner, saying: "Where are you going?" The caravan-leader also caused his own car to turn out of the road, allowing room for the carts to pass, and standing aside, said to that ogre: "We, sir, are just approaching from Benāres. But you are approaching decked with water-lilies both blue and white, with lotus-flowers both red and white in your hands, chewing the fibrous stalks of water-lilies, smeared with mud, with drops of water streaming from you. Is it raining along the road by which you came? Are the lakes completely covered with water-lilies both blue and white, and lotus-flowers both red and white?"

When the ogre heard his words, he said: "Friend, what's this you're saying? Do you see that dark green streak of woods? Beyond that point the entire forest is one mass of water; it rains all the time; the hollows are full of water; in this place and in that are lakes completely covered with lotus-flowers both red and white." As the carts passed, one after another, he inquired: "Where are you going with these carts?" "To such-and-such a country." "What are the goods you have in this cart,—and in that?" "Such-and-such."

"The cart that approaches last moves as though it were excessively heavy; what goods have you in that?" "There is water in that." "In bringing water thus far, of course, you have acted wisely. But beyond this point you have no occasion to carry water. Ahead of you water is abundant. Break the chatties to pieces, throw away the water, travel at ease." And having so said, he added: "You continue your journey; we have some business that detains us." The ogre went a little way, and when he was out of their sight, went back again to his own city of ogres.

Now that foolish caravan-leader, out of his own foolishness, took the advice of the ogre, broke the chatties to pieces, threw away all of the water, leaving not so much as a dribble, and caused the carts to move forward. Ahead there was not the slightest particle of water. For lack of water to drink the men grew weary. They traveled until sundown, and then unharnessed the carts, drew them up in a contracted circle, and tied the oxen to the wheels. There was neither water for the oxen nor gruel and boiled rice for the men. The weakened men lay down here and there and went to sleep. At midnight the ogres approached from the city of ogres, slew both oxen and men, every one, devoured their flesh, leaving only the bare bones, and having so done, departed. Thus, by reason of a single foolish caravan-leader, they all met destruction. The bones of their hands and all their other bones lay scattered about in the four directions and the four intermediate directions; five hundred carts stood as full as ever.

As for the Future Buddha, he waited for a month and a half from the day when the foolish caravan-leader set out, and then set out from the city with five hundred carts. In due course he reached the mouth of the wilderness. There he had the water-chatties filled, putting in an abundant supply of water. Then, sending a drum around the camp, he assembled his men and spoke as follows: "Without first obtaining my permission, you must not use so much as a dribble of water. In the wilderness there are poison-trees: any leaf or flower or fruit which you have not previously eaten, you must not eat without first obtaining my permission." Having thus admonished his men, he struck into the wilderness with his five hundred carts.

When he reached the middle of the wilderness, that ogre showed himself in the path of the Future Buddha in precisely the same way as before. When the Future Buddha saw him, he knew: "In this wilderness is no water; that is what is called a waterless wilderness. Moreover this fellow is fearless, red-eyed, casts no shadow. Without a doubt this fellow caused the foolish caravan-leader who went first to throw away all his water, and having thus brought weariness upon him and his company, devoured them. But, unless I am mistaken, he does not know how wise and resourceful I am."

Accordingly the Future Buddha said to the ogre: "You go your way. We are traders. Unless we see water farther on, we shall not throw away the water we have brought. But wherever we do see water, there we shall throw away the water we have brought, and having thus lightened our carts, shall continue our journey." The ogre went a little way, and when he was out of sight, went back again to his own city of ogres.

Now when the ogre had gone, the men asked the Future Buddha: "Noble sir, these men said: 'Do you see that dark green streak of woods? Beyond that point it rains all the time.' And the men who said it approached garlanded with garlands of water-lilies both blue and white, carrying clusters of lotus-flowers both red and white, chewing the fibrous stalks of water-lilies, heads wet, garments wet, with drops of water streaming from them. Let us throw away the water and go quickly with lightened carts."

The Future Buddha, hearing their words, caused the carts to halt, assembled all of his men, and asked: "Has any one of you heard that there is either a lake or a pool in this wilderness?" "Noble sir, we have not so heard. This is what is called a waterless wilderness." "Just now some men said: 'Beyond that dark green streak of woods it is raining.' Now how far does a rain-wind blow?" "A matter of a league, noble sir." "But has a rain-wind touched the body of even a single one of you?" "It has not, noble sir." "How far off is a cloud-head visible?" "A matter of a league, noble sir." "But has any one of you seen even a single cloud-head?" "We have not, noble sir." "How far off is lightning visible?" "Four or five leagues, noble sir." "But has any one of you seen a flash of lightning?" "We have not, noble sir." "How far off can the sound of a cloud be heard?" "A matter of one or two leagues, noble sir." "But has any one of you heard the sound of a cloud?" "We have not, noble sir."

"Those are not human beings; those are ogres. They must have come with the thought in their minds: 'We will make these men throw away their water, weaken them, and devour them.' The foolish caravan-leader who went first was not resourceful. Undoubtedly he must have thrown away the water at their behest, grown weary, and been devoured; the five hundred carts must stand as full as ever. To-day we shall see them. Do not throw away even so much as a dribble of water, but drive ahead as fast as ever you can." With these words he bade them drive forward.

Proceeding, he saw the five hundred carts as full as ever, and the bones of the men's hands and all their other bones scattered in all directions. He had the carts unharnessed and a stockade built by drawing them into a contracted circle. He had both men and oxen given their supper betimes, and the oxen lie down in the centre of the circle formed by the men. He himself, assisted by the leaders of the force, kept watch during the three watches of the night, sword in hand, and allowed the dawn to rise upon him standing there.

On the following day, very early in the morning, he had his men do all their chores, feed the oxen, discard the weak carts, substitute strong ones, throw away goods of little value, substitute those of great value. And going to the place where he would be, he sold his goods for twice or thrice the price, and together with his entire company went back again to his own city.

When the Teacher had related this parable, he said: "Thus, householder, in times past those who grasped with the grasp of speculation came to a sorry end, but those who grasped Absolute Truth escaped from the hands of demons, went in safety to the place where they would be, and went back again to their own place." And having thus joined the two parts of this Parable of Absolute Truth, he, the Supremely Enlightened, uttered the following stanza:

> Some adhered to Absolute Truth, sophists to less than this.
> Knowing this, a wise man should lay hold on Absolute Truth.

Said the Teacher in conclusion: "At that time the wise caravan-leader was I myself."

9. VEDABBHA AND THE THIEVES

Cupidity is the root of ruin.

Jātaka 48: i. 252-256.

Whoever seeks advantage by wrong means. This was said by the Teacher while he was in residence at Jetavana with reference to a disobedient monk. For to this monk the Teacher said: "Monk, not only in your present state of existence are you disobedient, but in a previous state of existence also you were just as disobedient. And through this same habit of disobedience, because you disregarded the words of wise men, you were cleft in twain with a sharp sword and left lying on the road. And through your own fault, and yours alone, a thousand men met destruction." So saying, he related the following Story of the Past:

In times past, when Brahmadatta ruled at Benāres, there lived in a certain little village a certain Brahman who knew a charm called the Vedabbha charm. This charm, we are told, was beyond price, of great worth. When the moon was in conjunction with a certain constellation, the Brahman would look up at the sky and recite that charm, and straightway the Rain of the Seven Jewels would rain from the sky.

At that time the Future Buddha was learning the arts and crafts in the house of that Brahman. Now one day the Brahman, accompanied by the Future Buddha, departed from his own village and set out for the kingdom of Cetiya on some business or other. Along the road, at a certain place in the forest, five hundred Despatcher-thieves were in the habit of committing outrages on travelers. They captured both the Future Buddha and the Brahman Vedabbha.

(But why were these thieves called *Despatcher-thieves?* We are told that whenever they captured two persons, they would *despatch* one of them to fetch ransom-money; therefore they were appropriately called *Despatcher-thieves.* For example, if they captured father and son, they would say to the father: "Fetch us ransom-money first; then you may take your son and go." Similarly, if they captured mother and daughter, they would despatch the mother; if they captured an older and a younger brother, they would despatch the older; if they captured teacher and pupil, they would despatch the pupil.)

So it was on this occasion. Having captured the Brahman Vedabbha, they despatched the Future Buddha. The Future Buddha bowed to his teacher and said: "I will return in the course of a day or two. Have no fear. However, do as I tell you. To-day will occur the conjunction of the moon which causes the Rain of Riches. Under no circumstances, because you cannot endure your misfortune, must you recite the charm and cause the Rain of Riches. If you do so, you will yourself come to ruin, and these five hundred thieves likewise." Having thus admonished his teacher, he went for the ransom-money.

When the sun had set, the thieves bound the Brahman and laid him down. At that very moment, from the eastern quarter rose the disk of the full moon. The Brahman surveyed the constellations and reflected: "The conjunction of the moon which causes the Rain of Riches is at hand. Why should I endure misfortune? I will recite the charm, cause the Rain of Riches, give the riches to the thieves, and go where I please."

Accordingly he addressed the thieves: "Well, thieves, for what purpose did you capture me?" "For ransom-money, noble sir." "If you want ransom-money, quickly free me from my bonds, bathe my head, clothe me with new garments, perfume me with scents, deck me with flowers, and set me on my feet." The thieves, hearing his words, did so. The Brahman, knowing the conjunction of the moon, recited the charm and looked up at the sky. Straightway jewels fell from the sky.

The thieves gathered up that wealth, wrapped it in folds of their upper garments, and went their way. The Brahman followed close behind them. Now a second pack of five hundred thieves captured the first pack of thieves. "For what purpose did you capture us?" inquired the first. "For ransom-money," replied the second. "If you want money, capture this Brahman. It was he who, by looking up at the sky, caused a Rain of Riches; he is the man who gave us this wealth."

The second pack released the first, captured the Brahman, and said to him: "Give us wealth too." Said the Brahman: "I would gladly give you wealth. But the conjunction of the moon which causes the Rain of Riches will not occur for a year yet. If you want money, have patience, and I will cause the Rain of Riches then." At this the thieves became enraged and said: "Oh, you rascally Brahman! You caused a Rain of Riches for others but a moment ago, but you tell us to hold our patience for another year!" So saying, they cleft the Brahman in twain with a sharp sword and left him lying on the road.

Then the second pack pursued the first pack hotly, fought with them, killed every man of them, and took the spoils. Again dividing into two packs, they fought with each other until one pack of two hundred and fifty had killed the other. Continuing in this wise, they killed each other off until there were only two men left. Thus those thousand men came to ruin. Now those two men, having gotten away with the spoils by a ruse, hid the spoils in a thicket near a certain village. One sat guarding the spoils with sword in hand; the other, having procured rice, entered the village to have some porridge cooked.

"Cupidity is the root of ruin!" The man sitting by the spoils reflected: "When this fellow returns, this wealth will have to be divided into two portions. Suppose I were to strike him with the sword and kill him the very moment he returns!" So girding on his sword, he sat watching for his companion to return.

His companion reflected: "That wealth will have to be divided into two portions. Suppose I were to put poison in the porridge, let that fellow eat it, cause his death, and get the spoils for myself alone!" So when the porridge was done, he ate some himself, put poison in the rest, and then took it and went to the thicket.

The moment the second thief took that porridge out and set it down, the first thief cleft him in twain with his sword and flung his remains away in a secluded spot. Then he ate that porridge and himself died on the spot. Thus, by reason of that wealth, every one of those men came to ruin.

As for the Future Buddha, he returned in the course of a day or two with the ransom-money. Not seeing his teacher where he had left him, but seeing the spoils scattered all about, he reflected: "It must be that my teacher disregarded my words and caused the Rain of Riches; it must be that all of those men have come to ruin." And he continued his walk along the highway.

As he proceeded, he saw his teacher lying on the highway, cleft in twain. Thought he: "My teacher disregarded my words and is dead." Then he gathered firewood, built a pyre, cremated his teacher, and honored him with forest-flowers.

As he proceeded, he saw farther on five hundred thieves who had met destruction; farther on yet, two hundred and fifty; and so on until finally he came upon two. Thought he: "These thousand thieves have come to ruin save only two. There must be two thieves besides. They also could never have restrained themselves. Where can they be?"

As he proceeded, he saw the footprints of the two thieves who had entered the thicket with the spoils. Proceeding farther, he saw first a heap of riches wrapped up in a bundle, and then one of the two thieves dead with a porridge-bowl overturned beside him. Then he knew all. "Such-and-such they must have done," thought he. Then he reflected: "Where can that fellow be?" Making a search, he found his body also flung away in a secluded spot. Then he reflected:

"Our teacher, because he disregarded my words, through his own habit of disobedience, through his own fault, has come to ruin. Moreover through him a thousand men besides have perished. Alas! By employing wrong means, for no reason at all, seeking gain for themselves, these thieves, like our teacher, must all have come to a fearful end indeed!". And he recited the following stanza:

> Whoever seeks advantage by wrong means, comes to grief.
> Thieves slew Vedabbha, and all met destruction.

Thus, by the recitation of this stanza, did the Future Buddha preach the Doctrine. And the spirits of the forest made the forest ring with their applause. Then said the Future Buddha: "Just as our teacher, putting forth effort by wrong means, at the wrong time, caused the Rain of Riches, and thus himself met destruction and became the cause of others' ruin, precisely so whoever else besides shall exert himself, seeking advantage for himself by wrong means, shall himself come to ruin and shall become the cause of others' ruin."

Employing right means, the Future Buddha removed that wealth to his own home, and during the remainder of the term of life allotted to him gave alms and performed the other works of merit. And when his life came to an end, he passed away, fulfilling the Path to Heaven.

Said the Teacher: "Monk, not only in your present state of existence are you disobedient, but in a previous state of existence also you were disobedient. And because of your habit of disobedience you came to a fearful end." And having completed this parable, he identified the personages in the Birth-story as follows: "At that time the Brahman Vedabbha was the disobedient monk, but the pupil was I myself."

10. A BUDDHIST TAR-BABY

Keep the Precepts.

Jātaka 55: i. 272-275.

The man whose heart clings not. This parable was related by the Teacher while he was in residence at Jetavana with reference to a monk who relaxed effort. For, addressing that monk, the Teacher asked: "Monk, is it true, as they allege, that you have relaxed effort?" "True, Exalted One!" "Monk," said the Teacher, "in former times wise men exerted themselves on an occasion when it was necessary for them to exert themselves, and by so doing attained the glory of dominion." So saying, he related the following Story of the Past:

In times past, when Brahmadatta ruled at Benāres, the Future Buddha received a new conception in the womb of the chief consort of that king. On the day when he received his name, his parents, after delighting eight hundred Brahmans with all of the Pleasures of Sense, inquired regarding the signs. The Brahmans, skilled in the discernment of signs as they were, seeing that he possessed the signs of a Great Man, made the following prediction: "Great king, the prince possesses merit; upon your decease he will attain the sovereignty; he will become the foremost man in the Land of the Rose-apple, and will be celebrated, will be renowned, for his deeds with the five weapons." His parents, hearing these words of the Brahmans, in selecting a name for the prince, gave him the name Prince Five-weapons.

Now when he reached the age of discretion, when he was about sixteen years of age, the king addressed him. "Son," said the king, "acquire the arts and crafts." "Under what teacher shall I acquire them, your majesty?" "Son, go acquire them under a world-renowned teacher who resides in the city of Takkasilā in the kingdom of Gandhāra; here is the fee for you to give to this teacher." So saying, he gave him a thousand pieces of money and sent him on his way.

The prince went there and acquired the arts and crafts. Having so done, he took the five weapons which his teacher gave him, bowed to his teacher, departed from the city of Takkasilā, and girded with the five weapons, struck into the road leading to Benāres. On the way he came to a certain forest infested by an ogre named Sticky-hair. Now at the mouth of the forest men who saw him tried to dissuade him from entering, saying: "Sir prince, do not enter this forest; an ogre named Sticky-hair lives here; he kills every man he sees."

The Future Buddha, confident of himself, fearless as a maned lion, entered the forest just the same. When he reached the heart of that forest, that ogre showed himself to the Future Buddha. He had increased his stature to the height of a palm-tree; he had created for himself a head as big as a summer-house with bell-shaped pinnacle, eyes as big as alms-bowls, two tusks as big as giant bulbs or buds; he had the beak of a hawk; his belly was covered with blotches; his hands and feet were dark green.

Having shown himself to the Future Buddha, he said: "Where are you going? halt! you are my prey!" But the Future Buddha said to him: "Ogre, I knew what I was about when I entered this forest. You would do well to be careful about attacking me, for with an arrow steeped in poison will I pierce your flesh and fell you on the spot!" Having thus threatened him, the Future Buddha fitted to his bow an arrow steeped in deadly poison and let fly.

It stuck right to the ogre's hair. Then he let fly, one after another, fifty arrows. All stuck right to the ogre's hair. The ogre shook off every one of those arrows, letting them fall right at his feet, and approached the Future Buddha. The Future Buddha threatened him once more, and drawing his sword, smote him with it. The sword, thirty-three inches long, stuck right to the ogre's hair. Then he hit him with a spear. That also stuck right to his hair. Perceiving that the spear had stuck, he smote him with a club. That also stuck right to his hair.

Perceiving that the club had stuck, he said: "Master ogre, you have never heard of me before. I am Prince Five-weapons. When I entered this forest infested by you, I took no account of bows and such-like weapons; when I entered this forest, I took account only of myself. Now I am going to beat you and pound you into powder and dust!" Having thus made known his determination, with a yell he struck the ogre with his right hand. His hand stuck right to the ogre's hair. He struck him with his left hand. That also stuck. He struck him with his right foot. That also stuck. He struck him with his left foot. That also stuck. Thought he: "I will beat you with my head and pound you into powder and dust!" He struck him with his head. That also stuck right to the ogre's hair.

The Future Buddha, snared five times, stuck fast in five places, dangled from the ogre's body. But for all that, he was unafraid, undaunted. As for the ogre, he thought: "This is some lion of a man, some man of noble birth,—no mere man! For although he has been caught by an ogre like me, he appears neither to tremble nor to quake! In all the time I have harried this road, I have never seen a single man to match him! Why, pray, is he not afraid?" Not daring to eat him, he asked: "Youth, why are you not afraid? why are you not terrified with the fear of death?"

"Ogre, why should I be afraid? for in one state of existence one death is absolutely certain. What's more, I have in my belly a thunderbolt for weapon. If you eat me, you will not be able to digest that weapon. It will tear your insides into tatters and fragments and will kill you. In that case we'll both perish. That's why I'm not afraid!" (In these terms, we are told, the Future Buddha referred to the Weapon of Knowledge within himself.)

Hearing this, the ogre thought: "What this youth says is true, every word of it. From the body of this lion of a man, my stomach would not be able to digest a fragment of flesh even so small as a kidney bean. I'll let him go!" Terrified with the fear of death, he let the Future Buddha go, saying: "Youth, you're a lion of a man! I'll not eat your flesh. Do you, this moment released from my hand, even as the moon is released from the Jaws of Rāhu, go gladden the circle of your kinsfolk and well-wishers!"

Then said the Future Buddha to the ogre: "Ogre, I'll go presently. But you, because in a former state of existence also you wrought evil, have been reborn as an ogre, cruel, red-handed, feeding on the flesh and blood of others. If in this state of existence also, so long as you live, you do evil deeds, you will go from darkness to darkness. But from the moment you saw me, it has been impossible for you to do evil deeds. Such a crime as taking the life of living beings means rebirth in hell, in the animal kingdom, in the region of the fathers, in the world of the fallen deities; should you be reborn in the world of men, you will live but a short time and soon pass away."

In such wise did the Future Buddha recite the disadvantages of doing deeds contrary to the Precepts, and the advantages of keeping the Five Precepts. With one reason after another he terrified the ogre, preached the Doctrine to him, subdued him, made him self-denying. Having established him in the Five Precepts, he bade him practice them. Then he transformed him into a spirit entitled to receive offerings in the forest, and having admonished him to be heedful, departed from the forest. At the mouth of the forest he told his story to human beings. Then, girded with the five weapons, he went to Benāres and visited his mother and father. After a time becoming established in the kingdom, he ruled righteously, gave alms and performed the other works of merit, and passed away according to his deeds.

The Teacher, having related this parable, uttered, as Supreme Buddha, the following stanza:

> The man whose heart clings not,
> Whose mind clings not,
> Who cultivates the Exalted States
> To the attainment of Nibbāna,
> Shall, in due course, reach
> The Destruction of all Bonds.

11. TWO DICERS

Take care!

Jātaka 91: i. 379-380.

On a certain occasion the Exalted One reproved the monks for handling their property carelessly. Said he: "Monks, careless handling of property is like careless handling of deadly poison. For men of old, through carelessness, not knowing what was the matter, ate poison, and as a result experienced great suffering." So saying, he related the following Story of the Past:

In times past, when Brahmadatta ruled at Benāres, the Future Buddha was reborn in a household of great wealth. When he reached manhood, he became a dicer. Now a second dicer used to play with the Future Buddha, and he was a cheat. So long as he was winning, he would not break the play-ring; but when he lost, he would put a die in his mouth, say, "A die is lost!" break the play-ring, and make off.

The Future Buddha, knowing the reason for this, said: "Let be!

I shall find some way of dealing with him." So taking the dice to his own home, he painted them with deadly poison and let them dry thoroughly. Then, taking them with him, he went to the second dicer's and said: "Come, sir, let us play at dice." "Yes, sir," said the second dicer, and marked out the play-ring.

As the second dicer played with the Future Buddha, he lost, and put a die in his mouth. Now the Future Buddha, seeing him do this, said: "Just swallow! Later you will know what that is." And to rebuke him he recited the following stanza:

> Smeared with the strongest poison
> Was the die the man swallowed, but knew it not.
> Swallow, O swallow, wicked dicer!
> Later it will taste bitter to you.

Even as the Future Buddha spoke, he swooned from the effect of the poison, rolled his eyes, dropped his shoulders, and fell. Said the Future Buddha: "Now I must grant him his life." So giving him an emetic containing herbs, he made him vomit. Then, giving him ghee, honey, and sugar to eat, he made him well. Finally he admonished him: "Never do such a thing again." And having performed almsgiving and the other works of merit, the Future Buddha passed away according to his deeds.

When the Teacher had completed this parable, he said: "Monks, careless handling of property is like careless handling of deadly poison." Then he identified the personages in the Birth-story as follows: "At that time the wise dicer was I myself."

12. BRAHMADATTA AND MALLIKA

Overcome evil with good.

Jātaka 151: ii. 1-5.

On a certain occasion King Pasenadi Kosala, after deciding litigations in the Hall of Justice, came hastily to pay his respects to the Teacher. Said the Teacher: "Great king, to decide litigations righteously and justly is a good thing. It is the Path to Heaven. But this is no remarkable thing, that you, receiving admonition from an Omniscient Buddha like me, should decide litigations righteously and justly. This alone is remarkable, that kings of old, listening to the words of men who were wise but not omniscient, decided litigations righteously and justly, avoided the Four Evil Courses, kept inviolate the Ten Royal Virtues, ruled justly, and departed fulfilling the Path to Heaven." Then, in response to a request of the king, he related the following Story of the Past:

In times past, when Brahmadatta ruled at Benāres, the Future Buddha received a new conception in the womb of his chief consort. The queen received the treatment customary for the protection of an unborn child, and the Future Buddha passed out of the womb of his mother in safety. On his name-day he received the name Prince Brahmadatta. In due time he grew up. When he was sixteen years old, he went to Takkasilā, acquired proficiency in all the arts and crafts, and on the death of his father, became established in the kingdom.

He ruled righteously and justly. He avoided the Four Evil Courses in rendering judgments. Since he himself ruled so righteously, the ministers of justice also transacted their affairs with an eye to righteousness alone. Since the ministers of justice transacted their affairs righteously, there were no men who brought dishonest litigations. For lack of them, hubbub over litigations in the king's courtyard ceased. Every day ministers of justice took their seats in the place of litigation, but seeing no one come for litigation, departed. The place of litigation became abandoned.

The Future Buddha thought: "Since I have been ruling righteously, no men at all have come for litigation, the hubbub has ceased, the place of litigation has become abandoned. The time has come for me to find out whether I have any fault. If I know, 'This, for example, is a fault in me,' I will get rid of it and have to do with good qualities only." From that time on he mingled with indoor-folk and tested them with the question, "Is there anybody who says I have a fault?" He met with no one who said he had a fault, but heard mentioned only his own good qualities. "It may be because these people are afraid of me that they refrain from mentioning faults in me and speak only of my good qualities."

He tested the outdoor-folk, but among them also met no one. He tested those who dwelt within the city. He took his stand in the settlements at the four gates and tested those who dwelt without the city. Among them also he met with no one who said he had a fault, but heard mentioned only his good qualities. "I will test the countryside," thought he. So turning over the kingdom to his ministers, he mounted his chariot, departed from the city in disguise, accompanied only by his charioteer, and went as far as the frontier testing the countryside. Meeting with no one who said he had a fault, but hearing mentioned only his good qualities, he turned back from the frontier and started back for the city on the highway.

Now at this time a king of Kosala named Mallika, a righteous ruler, was also trying to find out whether he had any faults. Meeting with no one among either indoor-folk or others who said he had a fault, but hearing mentioned only his own good qualities, he went to that region testing the countryside. Both kings met face to face in a single wagon-track leading through a swamp. There was no room for either chariot to turn out.

Now King Mallika's charioteer said to the charioteer of the king of Benāres: "Get your chariot out of the way!" Said the charioteer of the king of Benāres: "Master charioteer, get your chariot out of the way! In this chariot sits the lord of the realm of Benāres, the mighty king Brahmadatta!" Retorted King Mallika's charioteer: "Master charioteer, in this chariot sits the lord of the realm of Kosala, the mighty king Mallika! Get your chariot out of the way! Make room for the chariot of our king!" Thought the charioteer of the king of Benāres: "He also is every inch a king, to be sure. What's to be done?" He came to the conclusion: "This is the way: I will find out the ages of the two kings and cause the chariot of the younger to turn out and make room for the chariot of the older."

Accordingly the charioteer of the king of Benāres asked the other charioteer the age of the king of Kosala. Comparing the ages of the two kings, he discovered that both kings were of exactly the same age. He then made inquiry regarding the extent of his kingdom, his army, his wealth, his reputation, and his position in respect of caste, race, and family. He discovered: "Both are lords of kingdoms three hundred leagues in extent; they are equals as regards army, wealth, and reputation; they are in the same position in respect of caste, race, and family." Then he thought: "I will make room for that king who is more advanced in the practice of morality." Accordingly the charioteer of the king of Benāres asked the charioteer of the king of Kosala: "What is your king's practice of morality like?" The charioteer of the king of Kosala replied: "Such-and-such is our king's practice of morality." And proclaiming, as though they were good qualities, only the faults of his own king, he uttered the first stanza:

> Firmness he flings in the face of the firm;
> Mallika overcomes kindly with kindness,
> Good with good, evil with evil.
> Such is this king. Charioteer, turn out of the road.

But the charioteer of the king of Benāres said to him: "What! Are these the good qualities of your own king which you have just recited?" "Yes." "Well! If these are his good qualities, what must his faults be like? Now then, listen." So saying, the charioteer of the king of Benāres uttered the second stanza:

> He overcomes anger with kindness,
> He overcomes evil with good,
> The niggard with gifts, the liar with truth.
> Such is this king. Charioteer, turn out of the road.

Hearing these words, King Mallika and his charioteer both got down from the chariot, unharnessed the horses, removed the chariot, and gave the road to the king of Benāres.

The king of Benāres admonished King Mallika, saying: "Thus and so must one do." Having so said, he went to Benāres, gave alms and performed the other works of merit, and when his term of life was come to an end, fulfilled the Path to Heaven.

As for King Mallika, he accepted the admonition of the king of Benāres, tested the countryside, met with no one who said he had a fault, and went to his own city. Having given alms and having performed the other works of merit, when his term of life was come to an end, he also fulfilled the Path to Heaven.

When the Teacher, for the purpose of admonishing the king of Kosala, had related this parable, he identified the personages in the Birth-story as follows: "At that time King Mallika's charioteer was Moggallāna, the king was Ānanda, the charioteer of the king of Benāres was Sāriputta, but the king was I myself."

13. KING DADHIVĀHANA

Evil communications corrupt good manners.

Jātaka 186: ii. 101-106.

On a certain occasion the Teacher addressed the monks as follows: "Monks, contact with the corrupt is a bad thing, an injurious thing. Indeed, why should it be necessary to discuss the injurious effect on human beings of contact with the corrupt, when in times past even a senseless mango tree, with flavor as sweet as the flavor of celestial fruit, through contact with sour, unpalatable nimbs, turned sour and bitter?

Part 1. Gem, hatchet, drum, and bowl.

In times past, when Brahmadatta ruled at Benāres, four Brahman brothers in the kingdom of Kāsi adopted the life of ascetics, and building a row of leaf-huts in the Himālaya region, took up their abode there. The eldest of the four brothers died and was reborn as Sakka. Knowing who he had been, he went from time to time, every seven or eight days, and ministered to his former brothers.

One day he saluted the eldest ascetic, sat down on one side, and asked: "Reverend Sir, is there anything you need?" The ascetic, who was suffering from jaundice, said: "I need fire." Sakka gave him a little hatchet. Said the ascetic: "Who will take this and fetch me wood?" Then Sakka said to him: "When, Reverend Sir, you need wood, just rub this hatchet with your hand and say: 'Please fetch me wood and make me a fire.' And the hatchet will fetch wood, make a fire, and turn it over to you."

Having given him the little hatchet, Sakka went to the second ascetic and asked: "Reverend Sir, what do you need?" Past his leaf-hut ran an elephant-track. Since the elephants bothered him, he said: "The elephants annoy me; drive them away." Sakka presented a drum to him, saying, "Reverend Sir, if you beat this side, your enemies will flee; if you beat that, they will become kindly disposed and will surround you with a fourfold army."

Having given him the drum, Sakka went to the youngest ascetic and asked: "Reverend Sir, what do you want?" He also was afflicted with jaundice; therefore he said: "I want curds." Sakka gave him a bowl of curds, saying: "If you invert this and make a wish, the curds will turn into a mighty river, will set flowing a mighty flood, and will even be able to get and give you a kingdom." So saying, he went his way.

From that time on the little hatchet made fire for the eldest brother; when the second brother beat the drum, the elephants fled; the youngest brother enjoyed his curds.

At that time a boar, rooting among the ruins of a village, caught sight of a gem endowed with magical power. He bit the gem, and by its magical power rose into the air. Seeing a little island in mid-ocean, he thought: "There now is the place for me to live." So he descended and made his home in a pleasant place under a fig tree.

One day the boar lay down at the foot of that tree, placed the gem in front of him, and fell asleep.

Now a certain man who lived in the kingdom of Kāsi, driven from home by his mother and father with the remark, "He's no good to us," went to a certain seaport, hired himself out to mariners, and embarked on a ship. In mid-ocean the ship sprang a leak, and he floated to that island on a plank. While seeking wild fruits he saw that boar. Creeping up, he seized the gem. By its magical power he rose into the air. Seating himself on the fig tree, he thought: "This boar, become an air-voyager by the magical power of this gem, lives here, I suppose. But I must not go back without first of all killing him and eating his flesh." He broke off a twig and let it fall on the boar's head. The boar woke up, but not seeing the gem, ran this way and that, all of a tremble. The man sitting in the tree laughed. The boar looked, and seeing him, ran his head against the tree, and died then and there. The man came down, made a fire, and cooked the boar's flesh and ate it. Then he rose into the air and passed over the tops of the Himālayas.

Seeing a region of hermitages, he descended at the hermitage of the eldest ascetic. He lived there for two or three days, performed the major and minor duties for the ascetic, and saw the magical power of the little hatchet. "This I must get," thought he. Accordingly, after demonstrating to the ascetic the magical power of the gem, he said: "Reverend Sir, take this gem and give me the little hatchet." The ascetic, having a desire to travel through the air, took the gem and gave him the little hatchet.

The man took the little hatchet and went a short distance.

Then he rubbed the little hatchet and said: "Little hatchet, chop off the ascetic's head and bring me the gem." The little hatchet went and chopped off the ascetic's head and brought him the gem. The man put the little hatchet in a secret place, and then went to the second ascetic and lived with him for a few days. Seeing the magical power of the drum, he gave the second ascetic the gem, took the drum, and in the same way as before caused his head also to be cut off. Then he approached the youngest ascetic. Seeing the magical power of the bowl of curds, he gave the youngest ascetic the gem, took the bowl of curds, and in the same way as before caused his head to be cut off.

Then he took the gem and the little hatchet and the drum and the bowl of curds, and rose into the air. Halting not far from Benāres, he sent, by the hand of a certain man, the following message to the king of Benāres: "Give me battle or the kingdom!" As soon as the king heard the message, he said: "Let's catch the bandit;" and sallied forth. The man beat the proper side of the drum, and a fourfold army surrounded him. Perceiving that the king had deployed his forces, he turned the bowl of curds loose. A mighty river began to flow, and the multitude sank down in the curds and were unable to extricate themselves. Then he rubbed the little hatchet and said: "Bring me the king's head." The little hatchet went and brought the king's head and laid it at his feet. Not a single soldier had the power to lift a weapon. Accompanied by a mighty force, the man entered the city and caused himself to be sprinkled king. Having become king under the name Dadhivāhana, he ruled with righteousness.

Part 2. Corrupt fruit from a good tree.

One day, while he was amusing himself in the mighty river, in an enclosure formed by a net, there floated up and lodged in the net a single mango fruit fit for the gods. When they lifted the net they saw it and gave it to the king. It was of large size, as big as a water-pot, perfectly round, and of a golden color. The king asked his foresters: "What is that the fruit of?" "The fruit of a mango tree." Having eaten it, he caused the stone to be planted in his own garden, and to be sprinkled with milk and water. The tree sprouted, and in the third year bore fruit.

Great was the honor rendered to the mango. They sprinkled it with milk and water, they made marks of the spread hand with scented ointment on it, they festooned it with wreaths and ropes of flowers, they burned lamps with perfumed oil before it, and round about it they hung a curtain of fine cloth.

The fruit was sweet and of a golden color. When King Dadhivāhana sent the fruit of the mango to other kings, he pierced with a maṇḍu thorn the spot where the sprout starts, for fear a tree might sprout from the stone. When, after eating the mango fruit, they planted the stone, nothing happened. "What, pray, can be the cause of this?" they inquired, and discovered the cause.

Now a certain king summoned his gardener and asked: "Can you spoil the flavor of King Dadhivāhana's mango fruit and make it bitter?" "Yes, your majesty." "Very well, go." So saying, he gave him a thousand pieces of money and sent him off. The gardener went to Benāres, caused the king to be informed that a gardener had arrived, managed to have himself summoned by the king, and entering the palace, made obeisance to the king. "Are you the gardener?" asked the king. "Yes, your majesty," said the gardener, and described his own marvelous powers. Said the king: "Go, assist our gardener."

From that time on the two men cared for the garden. The newly arrived gardener caused flowers to blossom out of season and fruits to grow out of season, and made the garden a charming place. The king, pleased with the new gardener, dismissed the old gardener, and gave the new gardener exclusive charge of the garden. The new gardener, realizing that the garden was in his own hands, planted nimbs and pot-herbs and creepers all around the mango tree.

In the course of time the nimbs grew up. Roots with roots, branches with branches, were in contact, entangled, intertwined. Merely through this contact with the sour, unpalatable nimbs, the sweet fruit of the mango turned bitter, and its flavor became like the flavor of the leaves of the nimbs. The gardener, knowing that the fruit of the mango had turned bitter, fled.

Dadhivāhana went to the garden and ate a mango fruit. As soon as he put the mango into his mouth, perceiving that the juice tasted like the vile juice of the nimb, he was unable to swallow it, and coughing it up, spat it out. Now at that time the Future Buddha was his counsellor in temporal and spiritual matters.

The king addressed the Future Buddha: "Wise man, this tree is just as well cared for now as it was of old. But in spite of this, its fruit has turned bitter. What, pray, is the reason?" And by way of inquiry he uttered the first stanza:

> Color, fragrance, flavor, had this mango before.
> Receiving the same honor, why has the mango bitter fruit?

Then the Future Buddha told him the reason by uttering the second stanza:

> Your mango, Dadhivāhana, is surrounded with nimbs,
> Root in contact with root, branches entwine about branches.
> Through contact with the bad, therefore your mango has bitter fruit.

The king, hearing his words, had every one of the nimbs and pot-herbs chopped down, the roots pulled up, the sour earth round about removed, sweet earth put in its place, and the mango fed with milk and water, sweetened water, and perfumed water. Through contact with sweet juices the mango became perfectly sweet again. The king gave the regular gardener sole charge of the garden, and after living out his allotted term of life, passed away according to his deeds.

14. ANTELOPE, WOODPECKER, TORTOISE, AND HUNTER

In union there is strength.

Jātaka 206: ii. 152-155.

On a certain occasion the Buddha related the following story:

In times past, when Brahmadatta ruled at Benāres, the Future Buddha was an antelope and made his home in a certain thicket in a forest, not far from a certain lake. Not far from that same lake, on the tip of a certain tree, perched a woodpecker. Moreover in the lake a tortoise made his home. Thus did those three live together as friends, kindly affectionate one towards another.

Now a certain hunter, on his way through the forest, seeing the tracks of the Future Buddha at the place where the animals went to drink, set a trap, resembling an iron foot-chain, only made of leathern strips, and went his way. In the very first watch of the night the Future Buddha, coming to drink of the water, became entangled in the trap and cried the cry of a captured animal.

When he made that sound, from the tip of the tree came the woodpecker and out of the water came the tortoise. And they took counsel together, saying: "What's to be done now?" Then said the woodpecker, addressing the tortoise: "Master, you have teeth; you saw this trap in two. I'll go and manage things in such a way that that hunter sha'n't come near. Thus, if the two of us do our very best, our friend will save his life." And explaining this matter, he uttered the first stanza:

> Come, tortoise! use your teeth, and cut the leathern trap!
> I'll manage things in such a way the hunter shall not come!

The tortoise began to chew the strips of leather. The woodpecker went to the village where the hunter lived. At the first signs of dawn, the hunter took his knife and started to leave the house. The bird, observing that he was leaving the house, shrieked, flapped his wings, and struck him in the face just as he was coming out of the front door. Thought the hunter: "I have been struck by a bird of evil omen." So he went back, lay down for a little while, and then got up again and took his knife.

The bird knew: "This fellow first came out of the front door. This time he will come out of the back door." So he went and perched back of the house. As for the hunter, he thought: "When I went out of the front door, I saw a bird of evil omen. This time I will go out of the back door." So he went out of the back door. Again the bird shrieked, flew at him, and struck him in the face. The hunter, struck once again by that bird of evil omen, made up his mind: "That bird will not permit me to go out." So he went back, lay down until the dawn came up, and when it was dawn, took his knife and went out. The bird went quickly and told the Future Buddha: "The hunter is coming!"

At that moment the tortoise had chewed all of the strips except just one strap. But his teeth had got to the point where they were ready to drop, and his jaws were smeared with blood. The Future Buddha saw the hunter, knife in hand, coming on with lightning-speed. Cutting that strap, he entered the wood. The bird perched on the tip of the tree. But the tortoise was so weak that he continued to lie right there. The hunter threw the tortoise into a sack and hung the sack on some stump or other.

The Future Buddha came back, looked about, and perceived

that the tortoise had been taken captive. "I will grant my friend the boon of life!" he resolved. So feigning weakness, he showed himself to the hunter. "That antelope must be very weak," thought the hunter: "I will kill him." And knife in hand, he started after him. The Future Buddha, keeping not too far away and not too near, led him on and entered the forest. When he thought he had gone far enough, he disguised his tracks, went by another path with the speed of the wind, lifted the sack on his horn, flung it on the ground, broke it open, and let out the tortoise. As for the woodpecker, he came down from the tree.

The Future Buddha, admonishing his two friends, said: "I, through you, have obtained my life. You have done for me what a friend should do for a friend. At any moment the hunter may come and catch you. Therefore, Master woodpecker, do you take your fledglings and go elsewhere; and do you, Master tortoise, enter the water." They did so.

The Teacher, as Supreme Buddha, uttered the second stanza:

The tortoise entered the water,
The antelope entered the wood,
The woodpecker from that dangerous path
Took his fledglings far away.

When the hunter returned to that spot and saw nothing at all, he took the tattered sack and went to his own house in deep dejection. As for those three friends, they lived all their lives long with never a break in their friendly relations, and then passed away according to their deeds.

When the Teacher had related this parable, he identified the personages in the Birth-story as follows: "At that time the hunter was Devadatta, the woodpecker was Sāriputta, the tortoise was Moggallāna, but the antelope was I myself."

15. A BUDDHIST HENNY-PENNY

Much ado about nothing.

Jātaka 322: iii. 74-78.

On a certain occasion the Teacher, referring to the self-mortification of the Hindu ascetics, said to the monks: "Monks, there is no value, no merit, in their self-mortification. It is like the 'rat-a-tat' the little hare heard." Said the monks: "We do not understand what you mean by saying that it is like the 'rat-a-tat' the little hare heard. Tell us about it, Reverend Sir." So in response to their request the Teacher related the following Story of the Past:

In times past, when Brahmadatta ruled at Benāres, the Future Buddha was reborn as a lion, and when he grew up, lived in a forest. At that time, near the Western Ocean, grew a grove of cocoanut trees intermingled with Vilva trees. There, at the foot of a Vilva tree, under a cocoanut sapling, lived a little hare. One day, returning with food, he lay down under a cocoanut leaf and thought: "If this earth should collapse, what would ever become of me?"

At that very instant a Vilva fruit fell on top of the cocoanut leaf. At the sound of it the little hare thought: "This earth is certainly collapsing!" And springing to his feet, back he ran, without so much as taking a look. As he was running away as fast as he could in fear of death, another little hare saw him and asked: "Why, pray, are you running away in such a fright?" "Oh, don't ask me!" And he kept right on running, in spite of the fact that the other little hare kept asking: "Oh! what is it? Oh! what is it?" The other little hare turned around, and without so much as taking a look, said: "The earth is collapsing here!" He also ran away, following the first.

In the same way a third little hare saw the second, and a fourth the third, until finally there were a hundred thousand little hares running away together. A deer saw them,—also a boar, an elk, a buffalo, an ox, a rhinoceros, a tiger, a lion, and an elephant. Seeing, each asked: "What's this?" "The earth is collapsing here!" Each ran away. Thus, in the course of time, there was an army of animals a league in size.

At that time the Future Buddha, seeing that army running away, asked: "What's this?" "The earth is collapsing here!" When the Future Buddha heard this, he thought: "No such thing! The earth is collapsing nowhere! It must certainly be that they failed to understand something they heard. But if I do not put forth effort, they will all perish. I will grant them their lives."

With the speed of a lion he preceded them to the foot of a mountain and thrice roared the roar of a lion. Terrified with fear of the lion, they turned around and stood all huddled together.

The lion made his way in among them and asked: "Why are you running away?" "The earth is collapsing!" "Who saw it collapsing?" "The elephants know." He asked the elephants. Said the elephants: "We don't know; the lions know." Said the lions: "We don't know; the tigers know." The tigers: "The rhinoceroses know." The rhinoceroses: "The oxen know." The oxen: "The buffaloes." The buffaloes: "The elks." The elks: "The boars." The boars: "The deer." The deer: "We don't know; the little hares know."

When the little hares were asked, they pointed out that little hare and said: "He's the one that told us." So the lion asked the little hare: "Friend, is it true, as you say, that the earth is collapsing?" "Yes, master, I saw it." "Where were you living when you saw it?" asked the lion. "Near the Western Ocean, in a grove of cocoanut trees mingled with Vilva trees. For there, at the foot of a Vilva tree, under a cocoanut sapling, beneath a cocoanut leaf, I lay and thought: 'If the earth collapses, where shall I go?' That very instant I heard the sound of the earth collapsing. So I ran away."

The lion thought: "Evidently a Vilva fruit fell on top of that cocoanut leaf and made a 'rat-a-tat,' and this hare here, hearing that sound, came to the conclusion: 'The earth is collapsing!' I will find out for a fact." So the lion, taking the little hare with him, reassured the throng, saying: "I am going to find out for a fact whether or not the earth collapsed at the spot where the little hare saw what he saw; having so done, I will return. Until I return, all of you remain right here."

So taking the little hare on his back, he sprang forward with the speed of a lion. And setting the little hare down in the cocoanut grove, he said: "Come, show me the spot where you saw what you saw." "I don't dare, master." "Come, don't be afraid." The little hare, not daring to approach the Vilva tree, stood no great distance off and said: "That, master, is the spot where it went 'rat-a-tat.' " So saying, he uttered the first stanza:

> "Rat-a-tat" it went,—I wish you luck,—
> In the region where I dwell.
> But as for me, I do not know
> What made that "rat-a-tat."

When the little hare said this, the lion went to the foot of the Vilva tree, looked at the spot beneath the cocoanut leaf where the little hare had lain, and observed that a Vilva fruit had fallen on top of the cocoanut leaf. And knowing for a fact that the earth had not collapsed, he took the little hare on his back, went quickly, with the speed of a lion, to the assemblage of animals, informed them of all the facts, reassured the throng of animals by saying, "Fear not," and released the little hare.

For if, at that time, the Future Buddha had not come to the rescue, they would all have run down into the sea and perished. It was through the Future Buddha that they obtained their lives.

Hearing a Vilva fruit fall,—"rat-a-tat,"—the hare ran.
Hearing the hare's words, a host of animals were frightened.

Those who have not attained consciousness of their portion,
Those who follow the voice of others,
Those who are given to heedlessness,—the foolish,—
They attain what others attain.

But those who are endowed with morality,
Those who delight in the tranquillity of wisdom,
Those who abstain and refrain from worldly delights,—the wise,—
They attain not what others attain.

(These three stanzas were uttered by the Supremely Enlightened One.)

When the Teacher had related this parable, he identified the personages in the Birth-story as follows: "At that time the lion was I myself."

CHAPTER IV

PARABLES FROM THE BOOK OF THE BUDDHA'S PREVIOUS EXISTENCES IN EARLY AND LATE FORMS

16. PARTRIDGE, MONKEY, AND ELEPHANT

Reverence your elders.

A. Canonical version.

Vinaya ii. 161-162.

On a certain occasion the Exalted One admonished a company of monks to show proper respect for their elders. Said he:

In former times, monks, on a slope of Himavat, grew a huge banyan tree. Near it lived three friends: a partridge and a monkey and an elephant. They lived without respect or deference for each other, having no common life. Now, monks, to these friends occurred the following thought: "If only we knew which one of us was the oldest, we would respect, reverence, venerate, and honor him, and we would abide steadfast in his admonitions."

Accordingly, monks, the partridge and the monkey asked the elephant: "How far back sir, can you remember?" "Sirs, when I was a youngster, I used to walk over this banyan tree, keeping it between my thighs; the little tips of the shoots would just touch my belly. As far back as that, sirs, can I remember."

Next, monks, the partridge and the elephant asked the monkey: "How far back, sir, can you remember?" "Sirs, when I was a youngster, I used to sit on the ground and eat the little tips of the shoots of this banyan tree. As far back as that, sirs, can I remember."

Finally, monks, the monkey and the elephant asked the partridge: "How far back, sir, can you remember?" "In yonder open space, sirs, grew a huge banyan tree. I ate one of its fruits and voided the seed in this place. From that sprang this banyan tree. At that time also, sirs, I was the oldest."

Thereupon, monks, the monkey and the elephant said this to the partridge: "You, sir, are our elder. You will we respect, reverence, venerate, and honor, and in your admonitions will we abide steadfast."

Accordingly, monks, the partridge prevailed upon the monkey and the elephant to take upon themselves the Five Precepts, and himself also took upon himself the Five Precepts and walked therein. They lived in respect and deference for each other, and had a common life. After death, upon dissolution of the body, they were reborn in a place of bliss, in a heavenly world. This, monks, was called the Holy Life of the Partridge.

> Men versed in the Law who honor the aged
> Have praise even in this life
> And in the next life are in bliss.

B. Uncanonical version.

Jātaka 37: i. 217-220.

On a certain occasion the Teacher admonished a company of monks to show proper respect for their elders. Said he: "In former times, monks, even animals reflected: 'But it is not becoming in us that we should live without respect or deference for each other, having no common life. Let us find out which one of us is the oldest, and to him let us offer respectful greetings and the other marks of courtesy.' And when, after diligent inquiry, they knew, 'He is our elder,' to him did they offer respectful greetings and the other marks of courtesy. And having so done, they departed, fulfilling the Path to Heaven." So saying, he related the following Story of the Past:

In times past, on a slope of Himavat, near a certain huge banyan tree, lived three friends: a partridge, a monkey, an elephant. They were without respect or deference for each other, having no common life. And to them occurred the following thought: "It is not proper for us to live thus. Suppose we were to live hereafter offering respectful greetings and the other marks of courtesy to that one of us who is the oldest!" "But which one of us is the oldest?" they considered. "This is the way!" said the three animals one day as they sat at the foot of the banyan tree.

So the partridge and the monkey asked the elephant: "Master

elephant, since how long have you known this banyan tree?" He said: "Friends, when I was a young elephant, I used to go with this banyan sapling between my thighs. Moreover, when I stood with the tree between my thighs, the tips of its branches used to rub against my navel. Thus I have known this tree from the time it was a sapling."

Next the other two animals, in the same way as before, asked the monkey. He said: "Friends, when I was a young monkey, I used to sit on the earth, extend my neck, and eat the tips of the shoots of this banyan tree. Thus I have known it since it was very small."

Finally the other two animals, in the same way as before, asked the partridge. He said: "Friends, in former times, in such-and-such a place, grew a huge banyan tree. I ate its fruits and voided its seed in this place. From that sprang this tree. Thus I know this tree from the time when it had not yet sprouted. Therefore I am older than you." Thus spoke the partridge.

Thereupon the monkey and the elephant said to the wise partridge: "Master, you are older than we. Henceforth to you will we offer respect, reverence, veneration, salutation, and honor; to you will we offer respectful greeting, rising on meeting, homage with joined hands, and proper courtesy; in your admonitions will we abide steadfast. From this time forth, therefore, be good enough to give us admonition and needed instruction."

From that time forth the partridge gave them admonition, established them in the Precepts, and himself also took upon himself the Precepts. And those three animals, established in the Precepts, showed respect and deference for each other, and had a common life. When their life was come to an end, they attained the goal of a heavenly world. The taking upon themselves by these three animals of the Precepts was called the Holy Life of the Partridge.

"For, monks, those animals lived in respect and deference for each other. Why is it that you, who have retired from the world under a Doctrine and Discipline so well taught, do not live in respect and deference for each other?"

When the Teacher had thus related this parable, he assumed the prerogative of One Supremely Enlightened and uttered the following stanza:

Men versed in the Law who honor the aged
Have praise even in this life
And in the next life are in bliss.

When the Teacher had thus extolled the practice of honoring the oldest, he joined the connection and identified the personages in the Birth-story as follows: "At that time the elephant was Moggallāna, the monkey was Sāriputta, but the wise partridge was I myself."

17. THE HAWK

Walk not in forbidden ground.

A. Canonical version.

Saṁyutta v. 146-148.

Thus have I heard: Once upon a time the Exalted One was in residence at Sāvatthi, at Jetavana, in Anāthapiṇḍika's Grove. At that time the Exalted One addressed the monks: "Monks!" "Reverend Sir!" replied those monks to the Exalted One. The Exalted One said this:

In olden times, monks, a hawk attacked a quail with violence and caught it. Now, monks, as the hawk was carrying off the quail, the quail thus lamented: "I am indeed unfortunate, I possess little merit,—I who walked in forbidden ground, in a foreign region. If to-day I had walked in my own ground, in the region of my fathers, this hawk would not have been equal to a combat with me."

"But, quail, what is your feeding-ground? What is the region of your fathers?"

"A field of clods, turned up by the plow."

Then, monks, the hawk, not exerting his strength, not asserting his strength, released the quail. "Go, quail! Even there you will not escape from me." Then, monks, the quail went to the field of clods, turned up by the plow, and mounting a big clod, stood and called the hawk: "Come now, hawk, I dare you! Come now, hawk, I dare you!"

Then, monks, the hawk, not exerting his strength, not asserting his strength, flapped both his wings and attacked the quail with violence. When, monks, the quail knew: "This hawk is coming for me with a vengeance!" he entered a crack in that very clod. And, monks, the hawk struck his breast against that very clod.

"For, monks, so it goes with whoever walks in forbidden ground, in a foreign region. Therefore, monks, walk not in forbidden ground, in a foreign region. If, monks, you walk in forbidden ground, in a foreign region, the Evil One will obtain entrance, the Evil One will obtain lodgment. And what, monks, is forbidden ground, a foreign region? The Five Pleasures of Sense. What are the Five? Pleasurable Sights, Sounds, Odors, Tastes, Contacts. And what, monks, is lawful ground, the region of the fathers? The Four Earnest Meditations. What are the Four? Meditation on the Body, on the Sensations, on the Thoughts, on the Conditions of Existence. Walk, monks, in lawful ground, in the region of the fathers. If, monks, you walk in lawful ground, in the region of the fathers, the Evil One will not obtain entrance, the Evil One will not obtain lodgment."

B. *Uncanonical version.*

Jātaka 168: ii. 58-60.

A hawk flying strong. This stanza was recited by the Teacher while in residence at Jetavana to explain his own meaning in the Parable of the Bird. For one day the Teacher addressed the monks: "Walk, monks, in lawful ground, in the region of the fathers." So saying, he recited the Saṁyutta Suttanta found in the Mahāvagga. Then he said: "You just stay where you belong. In former times even animals, because they left their own ancestral region and walked in forbidden ground, fell into the bands of their enemies, but through their own intelligence and resourcefulness escaped from the hands of their enemies." So saying, he related the following Story of the Past:

In times past, when Brahmadatta ruled at Benāres, the Future Buddha was reborn as a quail, and made his home in a field of clods, turned up by the plow. One day he said to himself: "I will seek food in a foreign region." So he left off seeking food in his own region and went to the edge of a wood. Now while he was picking up food there, a hawk saw him and attacked him with violence and caught him. As the hawk was carrying off the quail, the quail thus lamented: "I am indeed mighty unfortunate, I possess very little merit,—I who walked in forbidden ground, in a foreign region. If to-day I had walked in my own ground, in the region of my fathers, this quail would certainly not have been equal to coming to a combat with me."

"But, quail, what is your feeding-ground? What is the region of your fathers?"

"A field of clods, turned up by the plow."

Then the hawk, not exerting his strength, released him. "Go, quail! Even there you will not escape." The quail went there, and mounting a big clod, stood and cried to the hawk: "Come now, hawk!"

The hawk, exerting his strength, flapped both his wings and attacked the quail with violence. But when the quail knew: "This hawk is coming for me with a vengeance!" he turned and entered a crack in that very clod. The hawk, unable to check his speed, struck his breast against that very clod. Thus the hawk, with heart broken and eyes bulging out, met destruction.

When the Teacher had related this Story of the Past, he said: "Thus, monks, even animals, when they walk in forbidden ground, fall into the hands of their adversaries; but when they walk in their own ground, in the region of their fathers, they humble their adversaries. Therefore you also must not walk in forbidden ground, in a foreign region. If, monks, you walk in forbidden ground, in a foreign region, the Evil One will obtain entrance, the Evil One will obtain lodgment. If, monks, you walk in lawful ground, in the region of the fathers, the Evil One will not obtain entrance, the Evil One will not obtain lodgment." Then, revealing his omniscience, he uttered the first stanza:

> A hawk flying strong, attacked with violence
> A quail standing in his feeding-ground, and thus met death.

Now when the hawk had thus met his death, the quail came out and exclaimed: "I have seen the back of my enemy!" And standing on his heart and breathing forth a solemn utterance, the quail uttered the second stanza:

> Endowed with sense, delighting in my own feeding-ground,
> My enemy gone, I rejoice, intent on my own good.

The Teacher, having proclaimed the Truths by the narration of this fable, identified the personages in the Birth-story as follows: "At that time the hawk was Devadatta, but the quail was I myself."

18. SNAKE-CHARM

A blessing upon all living beings!

A. Canonical version.

Vinaya ii. 109-110.

Now at that time a certain monk was bitten by a snake and died. They reported that fact to the Exalted One.

ASSUREDLY, monks, that monk had not suffused the four royal families of snakes with friendly thoughts. For, monks, if that monk had suffused the four royal families of snakes with friendly thoughts, in that case, monks, that monk would not have been bitten by a snake and died.

What are the four royal families of snakes?

The Virūpakkhas are a royal family of snakes.

The Erāpathas are a royal family of snakes.

The Chabyāputtas are a royal family of snakes.

The Kaṇhāgotamakas are a royal family of snakes.

Assuredly, monks, that monk had not suffused the four royal families of snakes with friendly thoughts. For, monks, if that monk had suffused the four royal families of snakes with friendly thoughts, in that case, monks, that monk would not have been bitten by a snake and died.

I permit you, monks, to suffuse these four royal families of snakes with friendly thoughts; for self-preservation, for self-defense, to effect Protection of Self. And this, monks, may be effected in the following way:

There is friendship 'twixt me and Virūpakkha snakes,
There is friendship 'twixt me and Erāpatha snakes,
There is friendship 'twixt me and Chabyāputta snakes,
There is friendship 'twixt me and Kaṇhāgotamaka snakes.

There is friendship 'twixt me and living beings without feet,
There is friendship 'twixt me and living beings with two feet,
There is friendship 'twixt me and living beings with four feet,
There is friendship 'twixt me and living beings with many feet.

Let no living being without feet injure me!
Let no living being with two feet injure me!
Let no living being with four feet injure me!
Let no living being with many feet injure me!

Let all creatures that live,—let all creatures that breathe,—
Let all creatures that exist,—one and all,—
Let all meet with prosperity!
Let none come unto any adversity!

Infinite is the Buddha! Infinite is the Doctrine! Infinite is the Order!

Finite are creeping things,—snakes and scorpions, centipedes, spiders and lizards, rats and mice!

I have wrought defense for myself! I have wrought protection for myself!

Begone, living beings!
I here do homage to the Exalted One and to the Seven Supreme Buddhas!

B. Uncanonical version.

Jātaka 203: ii. 144-148.

There is friendship 'twixt me and Virūpakkha snakes. This parable was related by the Teacher while he was in residence at Jetavana with reference to a certain monk.

The story goes that while he was splitting wood at the door of the room where the monks took hot baths, a snake came out of a hole in a rotten log and bit him on the big toe. He died on the spot. The news of his death and of how he came to die spread throughout the monastery. In the Hall of Truth the monks began to discuss the incident: "Brethren, such-and-such a monk, they say, while splitting wood at the door of the room where the monks take hot baths, was bitten by a snake and died on the spot."

The Teacher drew near and inquired: "Monks, what is the subject that engages your attention as you sit here all gathered together?" "Such-and-such," said they. "Monks," said the Teacher, "if that monk had cultivated friendship for the four royal families of snakes, the snake would not have bitten him. For even ascetics of old, before a Buddha had arisen, cultivated friendship for the four royal families of snakes, and thus obtained deliverance from the perils that arose through those royal families of snakes." So saying, he related the following Story of the Past:

In times past, when Brahmadatta ruled at Benāres, the Future Buddha was reborn in the kingdom of Kāsi in the household of a Brahman. When he reached manhood, he renounced the pleasures of sense, retired from the world and adopted the life of an ascetic, and developed the Supernatural Powers and the Attainments. By supernatural power, in the region of Himavat, at a bend in the Ganges, he created a hermitage, and there he resided, surrounded by a company of ascetics, diverting himself with the diversions of the Trances.

At that time, on the bank of the Ganges, reptiles of various kinds wrought such havoc among the ascetics that many of them lost their lives. Ascetics reported that fact to the Future Buddha. The Future Buddha caused all of the ascetics to be assembled, and said to them: "If you would cultivate friendship for the four royal families of snakes, the snakes would not bite you. Therefore from this time forth, cultivate friendship for the four royal families of snakes in the following way." So saying, he recited this stanza:

> There is friendship 'twixt me and Virūpakkha snakes,
> There is friendship 'twixt me and Erāpatha snakes,
> There is friendship 'twixt me and Chabyāputta snakes,
> There is friendship 'twixt me and Kaṇhāgotamaka snakes.

Having thus pointed out to them the four royal families of serpents, he said: "In case you are successful in cultivating friendship for these, reptiles will not bite you or annoy you." So saying, he recited the second stanza:

> There is friendship 'twixt me and living beings without feet,
> There is friendship 'twixt me and living beings with two feet,
> There is friendship 'twixt me and living beings with four feet,
> There is friendship 'twixt me and living beings with many feet.

Having thus set forth Cultivation of Friendship in the usual form, he next set it forth by way of prayer, reciting this stanza:

> Let no living being without feet injure me!
> Let no living being with two feet injure me!
> Let no living being with four feet injure me!
> Let no living being with many feet injure me!

Next, setting forth Cultivation of Friendship without respect of persons, he recited this stanza:

> Let all creatures that live,—let all creatures that breathe,—
> Let all creatures that exist,—one and all,—
> Let all meet with prosperity!
> Let none come unto any adversity!

"Thus," said he, "cultivate friendship for all living beings without respect of persons." Having so said, he spoke once more, to bid them meditate on the virtues of the Three Jewels. Said he: "Infinite is the Buddha! Infinite is the Doctrine! Infinite is the Order!"

When the Future Buddha had thus pointed out that the virtues of the Three Jewels are infinite, he said: "Meditate on the virtues of these Three Jewels." Having so said, in order to point out that living beings are finite, he continued: "Finite are creeping things, —snakes, scorpions, centipedes, spiders, lizards, rats and mice!"

Having so said, the Future Buddha declared: "Since lust, ill-will, and delusion, which exist in these creatures, are the qualities which make creatures finite, therefore these creeping things are finite." And he said: "By the supernatural power of the Three Jewels, which are infinite, let those of us who are finite, obtain protection for ourselves both by night and by day." And he said: "Thus meditate on the virtues of the Three Jewels." Having so said, in order to point out what more must yet be done, he recited this stanza:

> I have wrought defense for myself!
> I have wrought protection for myself!
> Begone, living beings!
> I here do homage to the Exalted One
> And to the Seven Supreme Buddhas!

Said the Future Buddha: "In the very act of rendering homage, meditate on the Seven Buddhas." Thus the Future Buddha composed this protective charm for the company of ascetics and gave it to them.

From that time on the company of ascetics, abiding steadfast in the admonition of the Future Buddha, cultivated friendliness, meditated on the virtues of the Buddhas. Even as they thus meditated on the virtues of the Buddhas, all of the reptiles disappeared. As for the Future Buddha, through the cultivation of the Exalted States, he attained the goal of the World of Brahmā.

19. DRAGON JEWEL-NECK

Nobody loves a beggar.

A. Canonical version.

Vinaya iii. 145-147.

On a certain occasion the Exalted One reproved the monks for begging. Said he:

In olden times two ascetics, brothers, lived by the Ganges river. Now Jewel-neck, a dragon-king, came out of the Ganges, approached the younger ascetic, and having approached, encircled the younger ascetic seven times with his coils and rose and spread his huge hood over his head. And the younger ascetic, for fear of that dragon, became lean, dried-up, pale, yellow as ever was yellow, his body strewn with veins.

The older ascetic saw the younger ascetic lean, dried-up, pale, yellow as ever was yellow, his body strewn with veins. Seeing, he said this to the younger ascetic: "Why are you lean, dried-up, pale, yellow as ever was yellow, your body strewn with veins?" "While I was here, Jewel-neck, a dragon-king, came out of the Ganges river, approached me, and having approached, encircled me seven times with his coils and rose and spread his huge hood over my head. For fear of him I am lean, dried-up, pale, yellow as ever was yellow, my body strewn with veins."

"But do you wish that dragon never to come back again?" "I wish that dragon never to come back again." "Well, but do you see anything on that dragon?" "I see he wears a jewel on his neck." "Well then, ask that dragon for the jewel, saying: 'Give me the jewel! I want the jewel!' "

Now Jewel-neck the dragon-king came out of the Ganges river, approached the younger ascetic, and having approached, stood aside. As he stood aside, the younger ascetic said this to Jewel-neck the dragon-king: "Give me the jewel! I want the jewel!" Thereupon Jewel-neck the dragon-king, reflecting, "The monk begs the jewel, the monk wants the jewel," quickly enough departed.

Three times did the younger ascetic beg the jewel of Jewel-neck the dragon-king, and three times did Jewel-neck the dragon-king depart. The third time, Jewel-neck the dragon-king addressed the younger ascetic with stanzas:

> My food and drink, abundant, choice,
> I get by the power of this jewel.
> This I will not give you,—you ask too much;
> Nor will I even come back again to your hermitage.
>
> Like a lad with sand-washed sword in hand,
> You frighten me, asking for the stone.
> This I will not give you,—you ask too much;
> Nor will I even come back again to your hermitage.

Thereupon Jewel-neck the dragon-king, reflecting, "The monk begs the jewel, the monk wants the jewel," departed. When he departed, he departed indeed, and never came back again. And the younger ascetic, because he saw no more that dragon so fair to see, became more than ever lean, dried-up, pale, yellow as ever was yellow, his body strewn with veins.

When the older ascetic saw the younger ascetic altered in appearance, he inquired the reason. The younger ascetic told him. Then the older ascetic addressed the younger ascetic with a stanza:

> One should not beg or seek to get what is dear to another.
> Odious does one become by asking overmuch.
> When the Brahman asked the dragon for the jewel,
> Never again did the dragon let himself be seen.

"For, monks, to living beings in the form of animals, begging is said to have been offensive, hinting is said to have been offensive. How much more so must it be to human beings!"

B. Uncanonical version.

Jātaka 253: ii. 283-286.

On a certain occasion the Exalted One reproved the monks for begging. Said he: "Monks, begging is offensive even to dragons, though the World of Dragons wherein they dwell is filled to overflowing with the Seven Jewels. How much more so must it be to human beings, from whom it is as difficult to wring a penny as it is to skin a flint!" So saying, he related the following Story of the Past:

In times past, when Brahmadatta ruled at Benāres, the Future Buddha was reborn in a Brahman household of great wealth. When he was old enough to walk and could run hither and thither, another being of merit also received a new conception in the womb of his mother. When both brothers reached manhood, their mother and father died. In agitation of heart over their death, both brothers adopted the life of ascetics, and building leaf-huts on the bank of the Ganges, took up their residence there. The older brother's hut was up the Ganges; the younger brother's hut was down the Ganges.

Now one day a dragon-king named Jewel-neck came forth from the World of Dragons, walked along the bank of the Ganges disguised as a Brahman youth, came to the hermitage of the younger ascetic, bowed, and sat down on one side. The dragon-king and the younger ascetic greeted each other in a cordial manner, and became fast friends and inseparable companions.

Every day Jewel-neck would come to the hermitage of the younger ascetic and sit down and talk and converse with him.

When it was time for him to go, out of affection for the ascetic he would lay aside his human form, encircle the ascetic with his coils, and embrace him, holding his huge hood over his head. Having remained in this position for a time, and having dispelled his affection, he would unwind his body, bow to the ascetic, and go back again to his own abode.

The ascetic, for fear of him, became lean, dried-up, pale, yellow as ever was yellow, his body strewn with veins. One day he went to visit his brother. The latter asked him: "Why are you lean, dried-up, pale, yellow as ever was yellow, your body strewn with veins?" He told him the facts. The older ascetic asked: "But do you or do you not wish that dragon never to come back again?" The younger ascetic said: "I do not." "But when that dragon-king comes to your hermitage, what ornament does he wear?" "A jewel."

"Well then, when that dragon-king comes to your hermitage, before he has a chance to sit down, ask, saying: 'Give me the jewel.' If you do so, that dragon-king will depart without so much as encircling you with his coils. On the next day you must stand at the door of your hermitage and ask him just as he approaches. On the third day you must stand on the bank of the Ganges and ask him just as he comes out of the water. If you do so, he will not come back to your hermitage."

"Very well," assented the ascetic, and went to his own leaf-hut. On the next day the dragon-king came and stopped at the hermitage. The moment he stopped, the ascetic asked: "Give me this jewel you wear." Without so much as sitting down, the dragon-king fled. On the second day the ascetic, standing at the door of the hermitage, said to the dragon-king just as he approached: "Yesterday you would not give me the jewel; to-day I must have it." Without so much as entering the hermitage, the dragon-king fled. On the third day the ascetic said to the dragon-king just as he came out of the water: "This is the third day I have asked; give me this jewel now." The dragon-king, still remaining in the water, refused the ascetic, reciting these two stanzas:

My food and drink, abundant, choice,
I get by the power of this jewel.
This I will not give you,—you ask too much;
Nor will I even come back again to your hermitage.

Like a lad with sand-washed sword in hand,
You frighten me, asking for the stone.
This I will not give you,—you ask too much;
Nor will I even come back again to your hermitage.

So saying, that dragon-king plunged into the water, went back to his own World of Dragons, and never came back again. And that ascetic, because he saw no more that dragon-king so fair to see, became more than ever lean, dried-up, pale, yellow as ever was yellow, his body strewn with veins.

Now the older ascetic, thinking, "I will find out how my younger brother is getting on," went to visit him. Seeing that he was suffering more than ever from jaundice, he said: "How comes it that you are suffering more than ever from jaundice?" "Because I see no more that dragon so fair to see." "This ascetic cannot get along without the dragon-king," concluded the older ascetic, and recited the third stanza:

One should not beg or seek to get what is dear to another.
Odious does one become by asking overmuch.
When the Brahman asked the dragon for the jewel,
Never again did the dragon let himself be seen.

Having thus addressed him, the older ascetic comforted him, saying: "Henceforth grieve not;" and went back again to his own hermitage.

Said the Teacher: "Thus, monks, even to dragons, though the World of Dragons wherein they dwell is filled to overflowing with the Seven Jewels, begging is offensive. How much more so must it be to human beings!" And having completed this parable, he identified the personages in the Birth-story as follows: "At that time the younger brother was Ānanda, but the older brother was I myself."

CHAPTER V

PARABLES FROM EARLY SOURCES ON DIVERS SUBJECTS

20. THE BIRDS

Nobody loves a beggar.

Vinaya iii. 147-148.

On a certain occasion the Exalted One reproved the monks for begging. Said he:

In olden times a certain monk dwelt on a slope of Himavat in a certain forest-grove. Not far from that forest-grove was a great marsh, a swamp. Now a large flock of birds sought food in that swamp in the daytime, returning to that forest-grove at eventide to roost. Now that monk, driven away by the noise of that flock of birds, approached me, and having approached, saluted me and sat down on one side. And as he sat on one side, I said this to that monk:

"I trust, monk, that you have suffered no discomfort. I trust that you have received sufficient sustenance. I trust that you have made your journey without fatigue. And, monk, whence have you come?"

"I have suffered no discomfort, Exalted One. I have received sufficient sustenance. I have made my journey without fatigue. Reverend Sir, on a slope of Himavat is a large forest-grove. And not far from that forest-grove is a great marsh, a swamp. Now a large flock of birds seek food in that swamp in the daytime, returning to that forest-grove at eventide to roost. Thence, Reverend Sir, do I come, driven away by the noise of that flock of birds."

"But, monk, do you wish that flock of birds never to come back again?" "I wish that flock of birds never to come back again."

"Well then, monk, go there, plunge into that forest-grove, and throughout the watches of the night cry out: 'Let the pretty birds hear me, as many as roost in this forest-grove! I want feathers! Let the pretty birds each give me a feather!' "

So that monk went there, plunged into that forest-grove, and throughout the watches of the night cried out: "Let the pretty birds hear me, as many as roost in this forest-grove! I want feathers! Let the pretty birds each give me a feather!"

Thereupon that flock of birds, reflecting, "The monk begs feathers, the monk wants feathers," departed from that forest-grove. When they departed, they departed indeed, and never came back again.

"For, monks, to living beings in the form of animals, begging is said to have been offensive, hinting is said to have been offensive. How much more so must it be to human beings!"

21. THE MONKEY

Walk not in forbidden ground.

Saṁyutta v. 148-149.

[Introduction and Conclusion identical with Canonical version of Parable 17.]

Monks, there are regions of Himavat king of mountains that are rough and uneven, where neither monkeys go nor men. Monks, there are regions of Himavat king of mountains that are rough and uneven, where monkeys go but men do not. Monks, there are portions of Himavat king of mountains that are smooth and delightful, where monkeys go and also men.

There, monks, cruel men spread lime in the monkey-trails to torment the monkeys. There, monks, monkeys that are not foolish and greedy, seeing that lime, keep far away. But the monkey that is foolish and greedy, on approaching that lime, grasps it with the hand; there he sticks! "I will free my hand," says he, and grasps with his other hand; there he sticks! "I will free both hands," says he, and grasps with the foot; there he sticks! "I will free both hands and foot," says he and grasps with the other foot; there he sticks! "I will free both hands and feet," says he, and grasps with the snout; there he sticks!

Thus, monks, that monkey, smeared with lime five times, lies on his breast, having met with misfortune, having met with disaster, the sport of the cruel man. Then, monks, the cruel man impales him, disposes of him on that very bed of coals prepared with sticks of wood, and goes wherever he pleases.

22. BLIND MEN AND ELEPHANT

Avoid vain wrangling.

Udāna vi. 4: 66-69.

Thus have I heard: Once upon a time the Exalted One was in residence at Sāvatthi, at Jetavana, in Anāthapiṇḍika's Grove. Now at that time there entered Sāvatthi for alms a company of heretics, both monks and Brahmans, wandering ascetics, holding heretical views, patient of heresy, delighting in heresy, relying upon the reliance of heretical views. There were some monks and Brahmans who held this doctrine, who held this view: "The world is eternal. This view alone is truth; any other is folly." But there were other monks and Brahmans who held this view: "The world is not eternal. This view alone is truth; any other is folly." Some held that the world is finite, others that the world is infinite. Some held that the soul and the body are identical, others that the soul and the body are distinct. Some held that the Tathāgata exists after death, others that the Tathāgata does not exist after death. Some held that the Tathāgata both exists and does not exist after death, others that the Tathāgata neither exists nor does not exist after death.

They quarreled and brawled and wrangled and struck one another with the daggers of their tongues, saying: "This is right, that is not right;" "This is not right, that is right."

Now in the morning a company of monks put on their under-garments, took bowl and robe, and entered Sāvatthi for alms. And when they had made their alms-pilgrimage in Sāvatthi, they returned from their pilgrimage. And when they had eaten their breakfast, they approached the Exalted One. And having approached, they saluted the Exalted One and sat down on one side. And sitting on one side, those monks reported the matter to the Exalted One.

"The heretics, O monks, the wandering ascetics, are blind, without eyes; know not good, know not evil; know not right, know not wrong. Knowing not good, knowing not evil, knowing not right, knowing not wrong, they quarrel and brawl and wrangle and strike one another with the daggers of their tongues, saying: 'This is right, that is not right;' 'This is not right, that is right.' "

In olden times, in this very city of Sāvatthi, there was a certain king. And that king ordered a certain man: "Come, my man, assemble in one place all the men in Sāvatthi who are blind from birth." "Yes, your majesty," said that man to that king. And when, in obedience to the king's command, he had laid hands on all the men in Sāvatthi who were blind from birth, he approached that king. And having approached, he said this to that king: "Your majesty, the blind from birth in Sāvatthi are assembled for you." "Very well! Now let the blind men feel of the elephant." "Yes, your majesty," said that man to that king. And in obedience to the king's command he let the blind men feel of the elephant, saying: 'This, O blind men, is what an elephant is like.' "

Some of the blind men he let feel of the elephant's head, saying: "This, O blind men, is what an elephant is like." Some of the blind men he let feel of the elephant's ears, saying: "This, O blind men, is what an elephant is like." Some of the blind men he let feel of the elephant's tusks, saying: "This, O blind men, is what an elephant is like." Others he let feel of the trunk, saying the same. Others he let feel of the belly, others of the legs, others of the back, others of the member, others of the tail, saying to each and to all: "This, O blind men, is what an elephant is like."

Now when that man had let the blind men feel of the elephant, he approached that king. And having approached, he said this to that king: "Your majesty, those blind men have felt of the elephant; do as you think fit."

Then that king approached those blind men. And having approached, he said this to those blind men: "Blind men, have you felt of the elephant?" "Yes, your majesty, we have felt of the elephant." "Tell me, blind men, what is an elephant like?"

The blind men who had felt of the elephant's head, said: "Your majesty, an elephant is like a water-pot." The blind men who had felt of the elephant's ears, said: "Your majesty, an elephant is like a winnowing-basket." The blind men who had felt of the elephant's tusks, said: "Your majesty, an elephant is like a plowshare." Those who had felt of the trunk, said: "An elephant is like a plow-pole." Those who had felt of the belly, said: "An eleplant is like a granary." Those who had felt of the legs, said: "An elephant is like pillars." Those who had felt of the back, said: "An elephant is like a mortar." Those who had felt of the member, said: "An elephant is like a pestle." The blind men who had felt of the elephant's tail, said: "Your majesty, an elephant is like a fan."

And they fought among themselves with their fists, saying:

"This is what an elephant is like, that is not what an elephant is like;" "This is not what an elephant is like, that is what an elephant is like." And thereat that king was delighted.

"Precisely so, O monks, the heretics, the wandering ascetics, are blind, without eyes; know not good, know not evil; know not right, know not wrong. Knowing not good, knowing not evil, knowing not right, knowing not wrong, they quarrel and brawl and wrangle and strike one another with the daggers of their tongues, saying: 'This is right, that is not right;' 'This is not right, that is right.' "

23. THE ANGER-EATING OGRE

Refrain from anger.

Saṁyutta i. 237-238.

Thus have I heard: Once upon a time the Exalted One was in residence at Sāvatthi, at Jetavana, in Anāthapiṇḍika's Grove. At that time the Exalted One addressed the monks: "Monks!" "Reverend Sir!" said those monks to the Exalted One in reply. The Exalted One said this:

In former times, monks, a certain ogre, ill-favored, dwarfish, sat in the seat of Sakka king of gods. Thereat, monks, the gods of the Thirty-three became annoyed, offended, indignant: "O how wonderful, O how marvelous, that this ogre, ill-favored, dwarfish, should sit in the seat of Sakka king of gods!"

The more, monks, the gods of the Thirty-three became annoyed, offended, indignant, the more did that ogre become handsome and pleasing to look upon and gracious. Then, monks, the gods of the Thirty-three approached Sakka king of gods. And having approached, they said this to Sakka king of gods:

"Here, Sire, a certain ogre, ill-favored, dwarfish, sits in your seat. Thereat, Sire, the gods of the Thirty-three are annoyed, offended, indignant: 'O how wonderful, O how marvelous, that this ogre, ill-favored, dwarfish, should sit in the seat of Sakka king of gods!' The more, Sire, the gods of the Thirty-three become annoyed, offended, indignant, the more does that ogre become handsome and pleasing to look upon and gracious. For, Sire, of a surety he must be an anger-eating ogre!"

Thereupon, monks, Sakka king of gods approached that anger-eating ogre. And having approached, he adjusted his upper robe so as to cover one shoulder only, touched his right kneepan to the ground, bent his joined hands in reverent salutation before that anger-eating ogre, and thrice proclaimed his name: "Sire, I am Sakka king of gods! Sire, I am Sakka king of gods! Sire, I am Sakka king of gods!"

The more, monks, Sakka king of gods proclaimed his name, the more did that ogre become ill-favored and dwarfish. And having become more ill-favored and dwarfish, he then and there disappeared.

Then, monks, Sakka king of gods sat down in his own seat, and appealing to the gods of the Thirty-three, uttered at that time the following stanzas:

I am not easily vexed in spirit,
I am not easily led into a turning,
I do not cherish anger long, be sure;
Anger has no abiding-place in me.

I speak no harsh words in anger,
I do not praise my own virtues,
I restrain myself,
Intent on my own good.

CHAPTER VI

HUMOROUS PARABLES FROM EARLY AND LATE SOURCES

24. MISTRESS VEDEHIKĀ

Patient is as patient does.

Majjhima i. 125-126.

On a certain occasion the Exalted One addressed the monks as follows: "Monks, put away evil; devote yourselves to good works: so shall you obtain increase, growth, development, in this Doctrine and Discipline."

In olden times, in this very city of Sāvatthi, lived a house-mistress named Vedehikā. Of Mistress Vedehikā prevailed the following excellent reputation: "Gentle is Mistress Vedehikā, meek is Mistress Vedehikā, tranquil is Mistress Vedehikā." And Mistress Vedehikā had a servant named Blackie who was capable and industrious and performed her duties well.

Now to Servant Blackie occurred the following thought: "Of my lady mistress prevails the following excellent reputation: 'Gentle is Mistress Vedehikā, meek is Mistress Vedehikā, tranquil is Mistress Vedehikā.' But has her ladyship, in point of fact, an inward temper which she does not reveal, or has she not? Or is it solely because I have performed these duties well that her ladyship does not reveal an inward temper which, in point of fact, she does possess;—not because she does not possess it? Suppose I were to test her ladyship!"

Accordingly Servant Blackie got up late in the day. And Mistress Vedehikā said this to Servant Blackie: "See here, Blackie!" "What is it, my lady?" "Why did you get up so late?" "For no reason at all, my lady." "For no reason at all, worthless servant, you got up so late!" And Mistress Vedehikā frowned in anger and displeasure.

Then to Servant Blackie occurred the following thought: "Her ladyship does, in point of fact, possess an inward temper which she does not reveal;—it is not because she does not possess it. It is solely because I have performed these duties well that her ladyship does not reveal an inward temper which, in point of fact, she does possess;—it is not because she does not possess it. Suppose I were to test her ladyship further!"

Accordingly Servant Blackie got up later in the day. And Mistress Vedehikā said this to Servant Blackie: "See here, Blackie!" "What is it, my lady?" "Why did you get up so late?" "For no reason at all, my lady." "For no reason at all, worthless servant, you got up so late!" And in anger and displeasure Mistress Vedehikā gave vent to her displeasure in words.

Then to Servant Blackie occurred the following thought: "Her ladyship does, in point of fact, possess an inward temper which she does not reveal;—it is not because she does not possess it. It is solely because I have performed these duties well that her ladyship does not reveal an inward temper which, in point of fact, she does possess;—it is not because she does not possess it. Suppose I were to test her ladyship further!"

Accordingly Servant Blackie got up even later in the day. And Mistress Vedehikā said this to Servant Blackie: "See here, Blackie!" "What is it, my lady?" "Why did you get up so late?" "For no reason at all, my lady." "For no reason at all, worthless servant, you got up so late!" And in anger and displeasure Mistress Vedehikā seized the pin of the door-bolt and gave her a blow on the head, breaking her head.

Thereupon Servant Blackie, with broken head streaming with blood, complained to the neighbors: "See, my lady, the work of the gentle woman! See, my lady, the work of the meek woman! See, my lady, the work of the tranquil woman! For this is the way a lady acts who keeps but a single servant: 'You got up too late!' says she. So what must she do but seize the pin of the door-bolt and give you a blow on the head and break your head!"

The result was that after a time Mistress Vedehikā acquired the following evil reputation: "Cruel is Mistress Vedehikā, no meek woman is Mistress Vedehikā, no tranquil woman is Mistress Vedehikā!"

"Precisely so, monks, here in this world, many a monk is ever so gentle, ever so meek, ever so tranquil, so long as unpleasant remarks do not reach him. But when, monks, unpleasant remarks reach a monk, that is the time to find out whether he is really gentle, really meek, really tranquil."

25. MONKEY AND DYER

The Doctrine of the Buddha wears well.

Majjhima i. 384-385.

On a certain occasion the householder Upāli, contrasting the teachings of the Buddha with those of the Jains, spoke as follows:

In former times there was a certain Brahman, and he was decrepit, grown old, aged, and he had a young woman to wife, and she was pregnant, about to give birth to a child. And that young woman said this to that Brahman: "Go you, Brahman, buy a young monkey in the shop and fetch him hither, that he may be a little playmate for my little boy." Hearing these words, that Brahman said this to that young woman: "Just wait, wife, until you give birth to your child. If, wife, you give birth to a boy, I will buy a young male monkey in the shop and fetch him hither, that he may be a little boy-playmate for your little boy. On the other hand, wife, if you give birth to a girl, I will buy a young female monkey in the shop and fetch her hither, that she may be a little girl-playmate for your little girl."

Twice and thrice that young woman said this to that Brahman, and twice and thrice that Brahman made the same reply.

But that Brahman was deeply attached to that young woman, deeply in love with her. Accordingly he bought a young male monkey in the shop, carried him home, and said this to that young woman: "Here, wife, is a young male monkey I bought in the shop and brought home to you, that he may be a little boy-playmate for your little boy." Hearing these words, that young woman said this to that Brahman: "Go you, Brahman, take this young male monkey and go to Redhand the dyer, and having gone, say this to Redhand the dyer: 'I desire, Master Redhand, to have this young male monkey colored and dyed with yellow dye, beaten up and beaten down, rubbed dry on both sides.' "

Now that Brahman was deeply attached to that young woman,

deeply in love with her. Accordingly he took that young male monkey and went to Redhand the dyer, and having gone, said this to Redhand the dyer: "I desire, Master Redhand, to have this young male monkey colored and dyed with yellow dye, beaten up and beaten down, rubbed dry on both sides." Hearing these words, Redhand the dyer said this to that Brahman: "As for this young male monkey of yours, revered sir, he will of course stand dyeing, but he won't stand beating and rubbing!"

"Precisely so," said Upāli, "the doctrine of the foolish Jains will stand dyeing, for it is a doctrine of foolish folk,—not of wise men,—but it will not stand working or rubbing."

Now after a time that Brahman took a new pair of cloths and went to Redhand the dyer, and having gone, said this to Redhand the dyer: "I desire, Master Redhand, to have this new pair of cloths colored and dyed with yellow dye, beaten up and beaten down, rubbed dry on both sides." Hearing these words, Redhand the dyer said this to that Brahman: "As for this new pair of cloths of yours, revered sir, they will stand not only dyeing but also beating and rubbing."

"Precisely so," concluded Upāli, "the Doctrine of that Exalted One, the All-Holy, the Supremely Enlightened, the Buddha, will stand dyeing, for it is a doctrine of wise men,—not of foolish folk,—and it will also stand working and rubbing."

26. HOW NOT TO HIT AN INSECT

Better an enemy with sense than a friend without it.

A. Boy and mosquito.

Jātaka 44: i. 246-248.

Better an enemy. This parable was related by the Teacher while he was journeying from place to place in the country of the Magadhas, in a certain little village, with reference to some foolish villagers.

The story goes that once upon a time the Tathāgata went from Sāvatthi to the kingdom of Magadha, and journeying about from place to place in that kingdom, arrived at a certain little village. Now that village was inhabited for the most part by men who were utter fools. There one day those utter fools of men assembled and took counsel together, saying: "Folks, when we enter the forest and do our work, the mosquitoes eat us up, and because of this our work is interrupted. Let us, every one, take bows and weapons, go and fight with the mosquitoes, pierce and cut all the mosquitoes, and thus make way with them." They went to the forest with the thought in their minds, "We'll pierce the mosquitoes." But they pierced and hit one another and came to grief, and on their return, lay down within the boundaries of the village, in the village-square, and at the village-gate.

The Teacher, surrounded by the Congregation of Monks, entered that village for alms. The rest of the inhabitants, being wise men, seeing the Exalted One, erected a pavilion at the village-gate, gave abundant alms to the Congregation of Monks presided over by the Buddha, saluted the Teacher, and sat down. The Teacher, seeing wounded men lying here and there, asked those lay disciples: "Here are many men who are in a bad way. What have they done?" "Reverend Sir, these men started out with the thought in their minds, 'We'll have a fight with the mosquitoes.' But they pierced one another and returned themselves the worse for wear." Said the Teacher: "Not only in their present state of existence have utter fools of men, with the thought in their minds, 'We'll hit mosquitoes,' hit themselves; in a previous state of existence also they were the very men who, with the thought in their minds, 'We'll hit a mosquito,' hit something very different." Then, in response to a request of those men, he related the following Story of the Past:

In times past, when Brahmadatta ruled at Benāres, the Future Buddha made his living by trading. At that time, in the kingdom of Kāsi, in a certain frontier village, dwelt many carpenters. There a certain grey-haired carpenter was planing a tree. Now a mosquito settled on his head,—his head looked like the surface of a copper bowl!—and pierced his head with his stinger, just as though he were sticking him with a spear. Said he to his son who sat beside him: "Son, a mosquito is stinging me on the head,—it feels just as if he were sticking me with a spear! Shoo him away!" "Father, wait a moment! I'll kill him with a single blow!"

At that time the Future Buddha also, seeking wares for himself, having reached that village, was sitting in that carpenter's hut. Well, that carpenter said to his son: "Shoo this mosquito off!" "I'll shoo him off, father!" replied the son. Taking his stand immediately behind his father, the son, with the thought in his mind, "I'll hit the mosquito!" raised aloft a big, sharp axe, and split the skull of his father in two. The carpenter died on the spot. The Future Buddha, seeing what the son had done, thought: "Even an enemy, if he be a wise man, is better; for an enemy, though it be from fear of human vengeance, will not kill." And he uttered the following stanza:

> Better an enemy with sense
> Than a friend without it,
> For with the words, "I'll kill a mosquito!"
> A son,—both deaf and dumb!—
> Split his father's skull!

Having uttered this stanza, the Future Buddha arose and passed away according to his deeds. As for the carpenter, his kinsfolk did their duty by his body.

Said the Teacher: "Thus, lay disciples, in a previous state of existence also they were the very men who, with the thought in their minds, 'We'll hit a mosquito,' hit something very different." Having related this parable, he joined the connection and identified the personages in the Birth-story as follows: "But the wise man who uttered the stanza and departed on that occasion was I myself."

B. Girl and fly.

Jātaka 45: i. 248-249.

Better an enemy. This parable was related by the Teacher while he was in residence at Jetavana with reference to a certain slave-girl belonging to Treasurer Anāthapiṇḍika.

Anāthapiṇḍika, we are told, had a certain slave-girl named Rohiṇī. Where she was pounding rice, her old mother came in and lay down. Flies buzzed round her and ate her up, just as though they were piercing her with needles. She said to her daughter: "My dear, the flies are eating me up. Shoo them off!" "I'll shoo them off!" replied the daughter. Raising her pestle aloft, intending to kill the flies, with the thought in her mind, "I'll make way with them!" she struck her mother with the pestle and killed her. When she saw what she had done, she began to weep: "Mother! Mother!"

They reported that incident to the treasurer. The treasurer had her body attended to, and went to the monastery and reported the whole incident to the Teacher. Said the Teacher: "Verily, householder, not only in her present state of existence has this girl, with the thought in her mind, 'I'll kill the flies on my mother's head!' struck her mother with a pestle and killed her; in a previous state of existence also she killed her mother in the very same way." And in response to the treasurer's request, he related the following Story of the Past:

In times past, when Brahmadatta ruled at Benāres, the Future Buddha was reborn in a treasurer's household, and on the death of his father, succeeded to the post of treasurer. He also had a slave-girl named Rohiṇī. She also, when her mother came to the place where she was pounding rice and said to her, "My dear, shoo the flies away from me!"—she also, in the very same way, struck her mother with a pestle and killed her and began to weep. The Future Buddha, hearing of that incident, thought: "For even an enemy in this world, if only he be a wise man, is better!" And he uttered the following stanza:

> Better an enemy who is intelligent
> Than a well-disposed person who is a fool!
> Look at that wretched little Rohiṇī!
> She killed her mother, and now,—she weeps!

With this stanza did the Future Buddha preach the Doctrine, praising the man of wisdom.

Said the Teacher: "Verily, householder, not only in her present state of existence has this girl, with the thought in her mind, 'I'll kill flies!' caused the death of her mother; in a previous state of existence also she caused the death of her mother in the very same way." Having related this parable, he joined the connection and identified the personages in the Birth-story as follows: "At that time that very mother was the mother, that very daughter was the daughter, but the Great Treasurer was I myself."

27. MONKEY-GARDENERS

Misdirected effort spells failure.

A. One-stanza version.

Jātaka 46: i. 249-251.

Never, in the hands of one who knows not what is good. This parable was related by the Teacher in a certain little village in the country of the Kosalas with reference to one who spoiled a garden.

The story goes that the Teacher, while journeying from place to place in the country of the Kosalas, arrived at a certain little village. There a certain householder invited the Tathāgata, provided seats in his garden, gave alms to the Congregation of Monks presided over by the Buddha, and said: "Reverend Sirs, walk about in this garden according to your pleasure."

The monks arose, and accompanied by the gardener, walked about the garden. Seeing a certain bare spot, they asked the gardener: "Disciple, everywhere else this garden has dense shade, but in this spot there is not so much as a tree or a shrub. What, pray, is the reason for this?" "Reverend Sirs, when this garden was planted, a certain village boy watered it. In this spot he pulled up the young trees by the roots, and according as the roots were large or small, watered them plentifully or sparingly. Those young trees withered and died. That's how this spot comes to be so bare!"

The monks approached the Teacher and reported that matter to him. Said the Teacher: "Not only in his present state of existence has that village boy spoiled a garden; in a previous state of existence also he did naught but spoil a garden." So saying, he related the following Story of the Past:

In times past, when Brahmadatta ruled at Benāres, a holiday was proclaimed. From the moment they heard the holiday drum, the residents of the entire city went about making holiday.

At that time many monkeys lived in the king's garden. The gardener thought: "A holiday has been proclaimed in the city. I'll tell these monkeys to water the garden, and then I'll go make holiday." Approaching the leader of the monkeys, he said: "Master monkey-leader, this garden is of great use even to you. Here you eat flowers and fruits and shoots. A holiday has been proclaimed in the city. I'm going to make holiday." And he asked him the question: "Can you water the young trees in this garden until I come back?" "Yes, indeed, I'll water them." "Very well," said the gardener; "be heedful." So saying, he gave those monkeys water-skins and wooden water-pots to use in watering the trees, and departed. The monkeys took the water-skins and wooden water-pots and watered the young trees.

Now the leader of the monkeys said to the monkeys: "Master-monkeys, the water must not be wasted. When you water the young trees, pull them up by the roots, every one; look at the roots; water plentifully the roots that strike deep, but sparingly the roots that do not strike deep; later on we shall have a hard time getting water." "Very well," said the monkeys, promising to do as he told them to. And they did so.

At that time a certain wise man saw those monkeys working away in the king's garden, and said to them: "Master-monkeys, why are you pulling up by the roots every one of those young trees and watering them plentifully or sparingly according as the roots are large or small?" The monkeys replied: "That's what the monkey who is our leader told us to do." When the wise man heard that reply, he thought: "Alas! alas! Those that are fools, those that lack wisdom, say to themselves: 'We'll do good.' But harm's the only thing they do!" And he uttered the following stanza:

> Never, in the hands of one who knows not what is good,
> Does a good undertaking turn out happily.
> A man who lacks intelligence spoils what is good
> Like the monkey who worked in the garden.

Thus, with this stanza, did that wise man censure the leader of the monkeys. Having so done, he departed from the garden with his followers.

Said the Teacher: "Not only in his present state of existence has that village boy spoiled a garden; in a previous state of existence also he did naught but spoil a garden." Having related this parable, he joined the connection and identified the personages in the Birth-story as follows: "At that time the leader of the monkeys was the village boy who spoiled a garden, but the wise man was I myself."

B. Three-stanza version.

Jātaka 268: ii. 345-347.

If the monkey considered the best of the crowd. This parable was related by the Teacher in the South Mountain region with reference to a certain gardener's son.

The story goes that the Teacher, after keeping residence for the period of the rains, departed from Jetavana and journeyed from place to place in the South Mountain region. Now a certain lay disciple invited the Congregation of Monks presided over by the Buddha, provided seats in his garden, delighted them with rice-gruel and hard food, and said: "Noble sirs, if you desire to take a walk about the garden, go with this gardener." And he gave orders to the gardener: "Pray give the noble monks fruits and other such-like edibles."

As the monks walked about, they saw a certain cleared space, and asked: "This space is cleared, without growing trees; what, pray, is the reason for this?" Then the gardener told them: "The story goes that a certain gardener's son once watered the saplings. 'I'll water them plentifully or sparingly according as the roots are large or small,' thought he. So he pulled them up by the roots and watered them plentifully or sparingly according as the roots were large or small. That's how this space comes to be cleared!"

The monks went to the Teacher and reported that matter to him. Said the Teacher: "Not only in his present state of existence has that youth spoiled a garden; in a previous state of existence also he did naught but spoil a garden." So saying, he related the following Story of the Past:

In times past, when Vissasena ruled at Benāres, a holiday was proclaimed. Thought the gardener: "I'll go make holiday;" and said to the monkeys who lived in the garden: "This garden is of great use to you. I'm going to make holiday for seven days. You must water the saplings on the seventh day." "Very well," said they, consenting. He gave them little water-skins and departed.

The monkeys did as they were told and watered the saplings. Now the leader of the monkeys said to the monkeys: "Wait a moment! Water is at all times hard to get; it must not be wasted. What you must do is to pull up the saplings by the roots, note the length of the roots, water plentifully the saplings that have long roots, but sparingly those that have short roots." "Very well," said the monkeys, and went about watering the saplings, some of them pulling the saplings up by the roots and others planting them again.

At that time the Future Buddha was the son of a certain notable in Benāres. Having occasion, for some purpose or other, to go to the garden, he saw those monkeys working away, and asked them: "Who told you to do this?" "The monkey who is our leader." "Well! if this is the wisdom of your leader, what must yours be like!" And explaining the matter, he uttered the first stanza:

> If the monkey considered the best of the crowd
> Has wisdom like this,
> Then what in the world must the others be like?

Hearing this remark, the monkeys uttered the second stanza:

> Brahman, you don't know what you are talking about
> When you blame us like this;
> For how, unless we see the roots,
> Can we know whether the tree stands firm?

Hearing their reply, the Future Buddha uttered the third stanza:

> It isn't you I blame,—not I,—
> Nor the other monkeys in the wood;
> Vissasena alone is the one to blame,
> Who asked you to tend his trees for him.

When the Teacher had related this parable, he identified the personages in the Birth-story as follows: "At that time the leader of the monkeys was the youth who spoiled the garden, but the wise man was I myself."

28. BOAR AND LION

Touch not pitch lest ye be defiled.

Jātaka 153: ii. 9-12.

A conceited old monk annoys the Chief Disciples with foolish questions, runs away, falls into a privy, and emerges all covered with dung. The Teacher, remarking that in a previous state of existence also he measured strength with the mighty and was covered with dung, relates the following Story of the Past:

In times past, when Brahmadatta ruled at Benāres, the Future Buddha, reborn as a lion, made his home in a mountain cave in the Himālaya country. Not far off, near a certain lake, lived many boars. Near that same lake ascetics also dwelt.

Now one day the lion killed a buffalo or an elephant or some other such animal and ate his fill of its flesh. Then he descended into that lake, drank water, and started to come out again. At that moment a fat boar was feeding near that lake. The lion, seeing him, reflected: "Some other day I'll eat him. But if he sees me, he may not come back again." So for fear that the boar might not come back again, the lion, on coming up out of the water, started to steal around by one side.

The boar watched him and reflected: "That fellow, when he saw me, was afraid of me, and therefore dared not come up to me. He is fleeing in fear. Now's the time for me to measure strength with that lion." So lifting his head, he challenged the lion to do battle with him, reciting the first stanza:

I am a beast, master; you also, master, are a beast.
Come, lion, turn around. Why do you flee in fear?

When the lion heard his talk, he replied: "Master boar, to-day there will be no battle between me and you; but seven days hence the battle shall take place at this very spot." So saying, he went his way.

The boar, pleased and delighted at the thought, "I shall do battle with a lion," told the news to his kinsfolk. When they heard his story, they were frightened and terrified. Said they: "Now you will cause the destruction of every one of us. Not knowing how slight is your strength, you desire to do battle with a lion.

The lion will come and kill every one of us. Do not commit an act of violence."

The boar, frightened and terrified, asked: "What shall I do now?" Said the other boars: "Go to the dunghill of these ascetics, wallow in the muck for seven days, and let your body dry off. On the seventh day, having moistened your body with drops of dew, go to the battleground ahead of the lion, and noting the direction of the wind, stand to the windward. The cleanly lion, smelling the odor of your body, will give you the victory and depart." The boar did so. On the seventh day, there he stood!

The lion, smelling the odor of his body, and knowing that he was covered with dung, said: "Master boar, that was a beautiful stratagem you devised. Had you not covered yourself with dung, I should have killed you on the spot. But as it is, it is quite impossible for me either to crush you with my jaws or to strike you with my paws. I give you the victory." So saying, he recited the second stanza:

> You are filthy, you bristle with muck,
> With bad smells you reek, boar.
> If you wish to fight, I give you the victory, master.

The lion turned around, got himself a meal, drank water in the lake, and went back to his mountain cave. The boar informed his kinsfolk: "I conquered the lion!" They were frightened and terrified. Said they: "The lion will come back again one of these days and kill every one of us." So saying, they scampered off to another place.

29. BEETLE AND ELEPHANT

Pride goeth before a fall.

Jātaka 227: ii. 211-212.

A monk, annoyed by a youth, pelts him with dung. The Teacher, remarking that the monk attacked the youth in similar fashion in a previous state of existence, relates the following Story of the Past:

One day in the olden time some dwellers in Añga and Magadha, on their way to each other's country, put up at a house on the boundary, drank liquor, and ate fish and flesh. Early next morning they harnessed their wagons and continued their journey.

When they had gone, a certain wretched little dung-beetle, attracted by the smell of dung, drew near. Seeing liquor poured out on the ground where the travelers had drunk, and being thirsty, he drank thereof, and becoming drunk, climbed up on a dunghill. When he had climbed to the top, the moist dung gave way a little. Thereupon he exclaimed: "The earth cannot support my weight!"

At that very moment an elephant in rut came into the vicinity, but detecting the odor of dung, retreated. The beetle, seeing him, concluded: "That fellow is fleeing in fear." And saying to himself: "I must do battle with that fellow!" he challenged him, reciting the first stanza:

> A hero has met a hero who is strong and can deal a blow.
> Come, elephant, turn around. Why do you flee in fear?
> Let Aṅgas and Magadhas see my prowess and yours.

The elephant pricked up his ears when he heard the beetle's words, turned around, went up to him, and treating him as an outcast, recited the second stanza:

> I'll kill you not with foot nor tusks nor trunk;
> With dung I'll kill you; let filth be slain with filth.

So saying, the elephant let drop on top of the beetle a great mass of dung, made water on him, and thus killed him on the spot. Then he made off into the forest again, trumpeting the Heron's Call.

CHAPTER VII

PARABLES FROM VARIOUS SOURCES ON DEATH

30. KISĀ GOTAMĪ

There is no cure for death.

Aṅguttara Commentary 225-227.

GOTAMĪ was her family name, but because she tired easily, she was called Kisā Gotamī, or Frail Gotamī. She was reborn at Sāvatthi in a poverty-stricken house. When she grew up, she married, going to the house of her husband's family to live. There, because she was the daughter of a poverty-stricken house, they treated her with contempt. After a time she gave birth to a son. Then they accorded her respect.

But when that boy of hers was old enough to play and run hither and about, he died. Sorrow sprang up within her. Thought she: "Since the birth of my son, I, who was once denied honor and respect in this very house, have received respect. These folk may even seek to cast my son away." Taking her son on her hip, she went about from one house-door to another, saying: "Give me medicine for my son!"

Wherever people encountered her, they said: "Where did you ever meet with medicine for the dead?" So saying, they clapped their hands and laughed in derision. She had not the slightest idea what they meant.

Now a certain wise man saw her and thought: "This woman must have been driven out of her mind by sorrow for her son. But medicine for her,—no one else is likely to know,—the Possessor of the Ten Forces alone is likely to know." Said he: "Woman, as for medicine for your son,—there is no one else who knows,—the Possessor of the Ten Forces, the foremost individual in the world of men and the Worlds of the Gods, resides at a neighboring monastery. Go to him and ask."

"The man speaks the truth," thought she. Taking her son on her hip, when the Tathāgata sat down in the Seat of the Buddhas, she took her stand in the outer circle of the congregation and said: "O Exalted One, give me medicine for my son!"

The Teacher, seeing that she was ripe for conversion, said: "You did well, Gotamī, in coming hither for medicine. Go enter the city, make the rounds of the entire city, beginning at the beginning, and in whatever house no one has ever died, from that house fetch tiny grains of mustard-seed."

"Very well, Reverend Sir," said she. Delighted in heart, she entered within the city, and at the very first house said: "The Possessor of the Ten Forces bids me fetch tiny grains of mustard-seed for medicine for my son. Give me tiny grains of mustard-seed." "Alas! Gotamī," said they, and brought and gave to her.

"This particular seed I cannot take. In this house some one has died!"

"What say you, Gotamī! Here it is impossible to count the dead!"

"Well then, enough! I'll not take it. The Possessor of the Ten Forces did not tell me to take mustard-seed from a house where any one has ever died."

In this same way she went to the second house, and to the third. Thought she: "In the entire city this alone must be the way! This the Buddha, full of compassion for the welfare of mankind, must have seen!" Overcome with emotion, she went outside of the city, carried her son to the burning-ground, and holding him in her arms, said: "Dear little son, I thought that you alone had been overtaken by this thing which men call death. But you are not the only one death has overtaken. This is a law common to all mankind." So saying, she cast her son away in the burning-ground. Then she uttered the following stanza:

> No village-law, no law of market-town,
> No law of a single house is this,—
> Of all the world and all the Worlds of Gods
> This only is the law, that all things are impermanent.

Now when she had so said, she went to the Teacher. Said the Teacher to her: "Gotamī, did you get the tiny grains of mustard-seed?" "Done, Reverend Sir, is the business of the mustard-seed!

Only give me a refuge!" Then the Teacher recited to her the following stanza in the Dhammapada:

> That man who delights in children and cattle,
> That man whose heart adheres thereto,
> Death takes that man and goes his way,
> As sweeps away a mighty flood a sleeping village.

At the conclusion of the stanza, even as she stood there, she became established in the Fruit of Conversion, and requested admission to the Order. The Teacher granted her admission to the Order. She thrice made rightwise circuit of the Teacher, bowed to him, and going to the nuns' convent, entered the Order. Later on she made her full profession, and in no very long time, by the Practice of Meditation, developed Insight. And the Teacher recited to her this Apparition-stanza:

> Though one should live a hundred years,
> Not seeing the Region of the Deathless,
> Better were it for one to live a single day,
> The Region of the Deathless seeing.

At the conclusion of the stanza she attained Sainthood.

31. PAṬĀCĀRĀ

Kinsfolk are no refuge.

Aṅguttara Commentary 213-215.

PAṬĀCĀRĀ was reborn at Sāvatthi in the house of a merchant. Later on, when she had grown to womanhood, she formed an intimacy with a certain laborer. Later on, about to marry a man of birth equal to her own, she hinted to that man with whom she had been intimate: "From to-morrow on you will not succeed in seeing me even with the help of a hundred doorkeepers. If you mean business, take me right now and go."

"So be it!" said he. Taking such proper and necessary things as could be carried in the hand, and taking her with him, he retired three or four leagues from the city, and took up his residence in a certain hamlet. Later on she conceived a child in her womb. When her unborn child reached maturity, she said: "This is a forlorn place for us, husband; let's go home." "We'll go to-day; we'll go to-morrow," said he. Not daring to go, he let the time slip by. She knew his object. Thought she: "This simpleton does not intend to take me home." When he had gone out, she made up her mind: "I'll go home all by myself;" and started out on the road.

When he returned and saw her nowhere in the house, he asked the neighbors. Hearing, "She has gone home," he reflected, "Because of me the daughter of a respectable family is without a protector," and following in her footsteps, came up with her. Right there on the road she gave birth to her child. Then she said: "What we would have gone home for, has happened right on the road. If we go now, what shall we do?" They turned back.

Again she conceived a child in her womb. (All is to be related in detail precisely as before.) Only,—the very moment she gave birth to her child on the road, great clouds arose in the four quarters. She said to her husband: "Husband, clouds have arisen in the four quarters out of due season. Try to make me a place of shelter from the rain." "So will I do," said he. Having made a hut of sticks, he resolved, "I will fetch grass for a thatch," and started to cut grass at the base of an ant-hill. A black snake lurking in the ant-hill bit him on the leg. In that very spot he fell.

She spent the whole night thinking: "Now he will come! now he will come!" Finally she concluded: "He must certainly have abandoned me on the road, thinking, 'She is without a protector,' and made off." When it was light, she followed his footsteps, looking about, and saw him fallen at the base of the ant-hill. "On account of me my husband perished," thought she, and wept.

Taking the younger boy on her hip, and giving the older boy her fingers to hold, she proceeded along the road. On the way seeing a certain shallow riverlet, she reflected: "If now I take both boys at the same time, I shall not be able to cross." Causing the older boy to stand on the near bank, she carried the younger boy to the far bank and laid him in a cloth head-coil. Then, thinking, "I will get the other and cross," she turned back again and descended into the river.

Now when she reached the middle of the river, a certain hawk, thinking, "There's a tiny lump of meat!" approached to strike the boy with his beak. Stretching out her arm, she drove the hawk away. The older boy, seeing that movement of her arm, concluded,

"She's calling me!" descended into the river, fell into the stream, and was swept downstream. That hawk, before ever she could reach him, seized that boy and made off. Overcome with profound sorrow, she made her way along the road, singing this little song of lamentation:

Both my sons are dead;
On the road lies my husband dead.

Even as she thus lamented, she reached Sāvatthi. Though she went to the quarter of the better class, solely because of her sorrow she was unable to fix the site of her own house. She asked people by turns: "In this place there is such-and-such a family. Which is their house?" "What can you mean by asking for that family? The house where they lived was blown down by the wind, and in it they all met destruction. Indeed, the young and old of that family they are burning at this very moment. Look! don't you see the smoke roll up yonder?"

At the mere hearing of those words, she could no longer endure the cloak she wore, but naked as ever at birth she went to the spot where stood the pyre of her kinsfolk, stretching out her arms and lamenting. And completing that song of lamentation, she wailed:

Both my sons are dead;
On the road lies my husband dead.
Mother and father and brother
Burn on one funeral-pyre.

Although some one gave her a cloth, she tore it and tore it and threw it away. And wherever she was seen, a crowd flocked about her and followed her. And because they said: "This woman goes about neglecting cloth-practice, cloth-usage (*paṭācāra*)," therefore they gave her the name Paṭācārā.

One day, while the Teacher was preaching the Doctrine to the multitude, she entered the monastery and stood in the outer circle of the congregation. The Teacher suffused her with a suffusion of loving-kindness: "Return to your right mind, sister! return to your right mind, sister!" On hearing these words of the Teacher, deep shame and fear of sin came to her. She sat down right there on the ground. A man who stood not far off tossed her his outer cloak. She put it on as an undergarment and hearkened to the

Doctrine. The Teacher, by reason of her conduct, recited the following stanzas found in the Dhammapada:

Sons are no refuge, nor a father, nor relatives;
To one who has been assailed by death, there is no refuge in kinsfolk.

Knowing this power of circumstances, the wise man, restrained by the moral precepts,
Should straightway clear the path that leads to Nibbāna.

At the conclusion of the stanzas, even as she stood there, she became established in the Fruit of Conversion.

32. THE HEAVENLY MESSENGERS

Prepare for death.

Majjhima 83: ii. 74-83.

Thus have I heard: Once upon a time the Exalted One was in residence at Mithilā, in Makhādeva Mango Grove. Now at a certain spot the Exalted One smiled. And to Venerable Ānanda occurred the following thought: "What, pray, is the cause, what is the reason, for the Exalted One's smiling? Not without cause do the Tathāgatas smile." Accordingly Venerable Ānanda adjusted his robe so as to cover one shoulder only, bent his joined hands in reverent salutation before the Exalted One, and said this to the Exalted One: "What, pray, Reverend Sir, is the cause, what is the reason, for the Exalted One's smiling? Not without cause do the Tathāgatas smile."

Part 1. Makhādeva.

In olden times, Ānanda, in this very city of Mithilā, there was a king named Makhādeva. He was a righteous king, a king of righteousness, abiding steadfast in righteousness, a mighty king. He dealt righteously with Brahmans and householders, with country folk and city folk. He kept Fast-day on the fourteenth day, on the fifteenth day, and on the eighth day of the half-month.

Now, Ānanda, after many years, many hundreds of years, many thousands of years had gone by, King Makhādeva addressed his barber: "When, master barber, you see grey hairs growing on my head, pray be good enough to tell me." "Yes, your majesty," said the barber to King Makhādeva, giving him his word.

Ānanda, after many years, many hundreds of years, many thousands of years had gone by, the barber saw grey hairs growing on King Makhādeva's head. When he saw them, he said this to King Makhādeva: "The heavenly messengers have appeared to your majesty. Grey hairs are visible growing on your head." "Well then, master barber, extract these grey hairs carefully with a pair of tongs and place them in the hollow of my joined hands."

"Yes, your majesty," said the barber to King Makhādeva. And in obedienee to his command the barber extracted those grey hairs carefully and placed them in the hollow of King Makhādeva's joined hands. And, Ānanda, King Makhādeva gave the barber a splendid village. Then, addressing his eldest son, the royal prinee, he said this:

"Dear prinee, the heavenly messengers have appeared to me. Grey hairs are visible growing on my head. But I have enjoyed the pleasures of earth; it is time for me to seek the pleasures of heaven. Come, dear prince, enter upon this kingdom. As for me, I will shave off my hair and beard, put on yellow robes, and retire from the house-life to the houseless life. Now then, dear prinee, when you also see grey hairs growing on your head, then you must give your barber a splendid village, thoroughly instruct your eldest son, the royal prinee, in the duties of a king, shave off your hair and beard, put on yellow robes, and retire from the house-life to the houseless life. Inasmuch as I have established this splendid sueeession, it is your duty to keep it going; you must not be the last man to follow me. If ever, dear prince, in the lifetime of two men, one uproots the suceession, he is the last man of the line. Therefore, dear prince, I say this to you: Inasmuch as I have established this splendid succession, it is your duty to keep it going; you must not be the last to follow me."

Aeeordingly, Ānanda, King Makhādeva, having given his barber a splendid village, having thoroughly instructed his eldest son, the royal prince, in the duties of a king, in this very Makhādeva Mango Grove shaved off his hair and beard, put on yellow robes, and retired from the house-life to the houseless life. He dwelt suffusing with thoughts of friendliness, compassion, sympathy, and indifferenee, one quarter, likewise a second, likewise a third, likewise a fourth. So likewise above, below, across,—everywhere,—

identifying himself with all things, he dwelt suffusing the all-embracing earth with thoughts of friendliness, compassion, sympathy, and indifference,—ample, far-reaching, boundless, free from enmity, free from ill-will.

Now, Ānanda, King Makhādeva for eighty-four thousand years diverted himself with the diversions of a royal prince; for eighty-four thousand years exercised the functions of a viceroy; for eighty-four thousand years exercised the functions of a king; for eighty-four thousand years, in this very Makhādeva Mango Grove, having retired from the house-life to the houseless life, led the Holy Life. He cultivated the Four Exalted States, and after death, upon dissolution of the body, was reborn in the Brahmā World.

Now, Ānanda, King Makhādeva's son and his son and his son, to the number of eighty-four thousand Warrior princes descended from him, in this very Makhādeva Mango Grove, shaved off hair and beard, put on yellow robes, and retired from the house-life to the houseless life. They cultivated the Four Exalted States, and after death, upon dissolution of the body, were reborn in the Brahmā World.

Part 2. Nimi.

Nimi was the last of these kings. He was a righteous king, a king of righteousness, abiding steadfast in righteousness, a mighty king. He dealt righteously with Brahmans and householders, with country folk and city folk. He kept Fast-day on the fourteenth day, on the fifteenth day, and on the eighth day of the half-month.

In former times, Ānanda, among the gods of the Thirty-three, assembled and met together in the mote-hall Goodness, arose the following desultory talk: "O how fortunate are the Videhas, O how very fortunate are the Videhas, that they should have Nimi for their king! He is a righteous king, a king of righteousness, abiding steadfast in righteousness, a mighty king. He deals righteously with Brahmans and householders, with country folk and city folk. He keeps Fast-day on the fourteenth day, on the fifteenth day, and on the eighth day of the half-month."

Thereupon, Ānanda, Sakka king of gods addressed the gods of the Thirty-three: "Would you wish, sirs, to see King Nimi?"

"We wish, sir, to see King Nimi." Now at that time, on that very day, on Fast-day, on the fifteenth day of the half-month, King Nimi bathed his head, took upon himself the obligations of Fast-day, and went up on the terrace of his splendid palace and sat down. And, Ānanda, Sakka king of gods, just as a strong man might straighten his bent arm or bend his straightened arm, precisely so disappeared from among the gods of the Thirty-three and appeared before King Nimi. And, Ānanda, Sakka king of gods said this to King Nimi: "You are fortunate, great king! you are very fortunate, great king! Great king, the gods of the Thirty-three say thus and so. Great king, the gods of the Thirty-three desire to see you. Great king, I will send to you here a chariot drawn by a thousand thoroughbreds. Great king, you may mount the heavenly vehicle with never a tremor of fear."

And, Ānanda, King Nimi gave consent by remaining silent. Then, Ānanda, Sakka king of gods, perceiving that King Nimi had given his consent, just as a strong man might straighten his bent arm or bend his straightened arm, precisely so disappeared from the presence of King Nimi and appeared among the gods of the Thirty-three. And, Ānanda, Sakka king of gods addressed the charioteer Mātali: "Come, friend Mātali, harness a thousand thoroughbreds to a chariot, and approach King Nimi and speak as follows: 'Here, great king, is a chariot drawn by a thousand thoroughbreds, sent to you by Sakka king of gods. Great king, you may mount the heavenly vehicle with never a tremor of fear.' " "So be it! My best wishes!"

Thereupon, Ānanda, the charioteer Mātali, in obedience to the command of Sakka king of gods, harnessed a thousand thoroughbreds to a chariot, approached King Nimi, and spoke as follows: "Here, great king, is a chariot drawn by a thousand thoroughbreds, sent to you by Sakka king of gods. Great king, mount the heavenly vehicle with never a tremor of fear. But, great king, by what road shall I conduct you? Where those who have done evil deeds experience the fruition of evil deeds? Or where those who have done good deeds experience the fruition of good deeds?" "By all means conduct me by both roads, Mātali."

Thereupon, Ānanda, the charioteer Mātali escorted King Nimi to the mote-hall Goodness. Now, Ānanda, Sakka king of gods saw King Nimi approaching even from afar. Seeing, he said this to

King Nimi: "Come now, great king; you are welcome, great king. Great king, the gods of the Thirty-three, assembled in the mote-hall Goodness, uttered your praises: 'O how fortunate are the Videhas, O how very fortunate are the Videhas, that they should have Nimi for their king! He is a righteous king, a king of righteousness, abiding steadfast in righteousness, a mighty king. He deals righteously with Brahmans and householders, with country folk and city folk. He keeps Fast-day on the fourteenth day, on the fifteenth day, and on the eighth day of the half-month.' Great king, the gods of the Thirty-three desire to see you. Great king, take your pleasure among the gods and exercise the supernatural power of a god."

"Enough, Sire! Let Mātali conduct me right back there to Mithilā. There would I deal righteously with Brahmans and householders, with country folk and city folk; there would I keep Fast-day on the fourteenth day, on the fifteenth day, and on the eighth day of the half-month."

Thereupon, Ānanda, Sakka king of gods addressed the charioteer Mātali: "Come, friend Mātali, harness a thousand thoroughbreds to a chariot and conduct King Nimi right back there to Mithilā." "So be it! My best wishes!" And in obedience to the command of Sakka king of gods, the charioteer Mātali harnessed a thousand thoroughbreds to a chariot and conducted King Nimi right back there to Mithilā.

And there, Ānanda, King Nimi dealt righteously with Brahmans and householders, with country folk and city folk. There he kept Fast-day on the fourteenth day, on the fifteenth day, and on the eighth day of the half-month.

Now, Ānanda, after many years, many hundreds of years, many thousands of years had gone by, King Nimi addressed his barber: "When, master barber, you see grey hairs growing on my head, pray be good enough to tell me." "Yes, your majesty," said the barber to King Nimi, giving him his word.

Ānanda, after many years, many hundreds of years, many thousands of years had gone by, the barber saw grey hairs growing on King Nimi's head. When he saw them, he said this to King Nimi: "The heavenly messengers have appeared to your majesty. Grey hairs are visible growing on your head." "Well then, master barber, extract these grey hairs carefully with a pair of tongs and place them in the hollow of my joined hands."

"Yes, your majesty," said the barber to King Nimi. And in obedience to his command the barber extracted those grey hairs carefully and placed them in the hollow of King Nimi's joined hands. And, Ānanda, King Nimi gave the barber a splendid village. Then, addressing his eldest son, the royal prince, he said this:

"Dear prince, the heavenly messengers have appeared to me. Grey hairs are visible growing on my head. But I have enjoyed the pleasures of earth; it is time for me to seek the pleasures of heaven. Come, dear prince, enter upon this kingdom. As for me, I will shave off my hair and beard, put on yellow robes, and retire from the house-life to the houseless life. Now then, dear prince, when you also see grey hairs growing on your head, then you must give your barber a splendid village, thoroughly instruct your eldest son, the royal prince, in the duties of a king, shave off your hair and beard, put on yellow robes, and retire from the house-life to the houseless life. Inasmuch as I have established this splendid succession, it is your duty to keep it going; you must not be the last man to follow me. If ever, dear prince, in the lifetime of two men, one uproots the succession, he is the last man of the line. Therefore, dear prince, I say this to you: Inasmuch as I have established this splendid succession, it is your duty to keep it going; you must not be the last to follow me."

Accordingly, Ānanda, King Nimi, having given his barber a splendid village, having thoroughly instructed his eldest son, the royal prince, in the duties of a king, in this very Makhādeva Mango Grove shaved off his hair and beard, put on yellow robes, and retired from the house-life to the houseless life. He dwelt suffusing with thoughts of friendliness, compassion, sympathy, and indifference, one quarter, likewise a second, likewise a third, likewise a fourth. So likewise above, below, across,—everywhere,—identifying himself with all things, he dwelt suffusing the all-embracing earth with thoughts of friendliness, compassion, sympathy, and indifference,—ample, far-reaching, boundless, free from enmity, free from ill-will.

Now, Ānanda, King Nimi for eighty-four thousand years diverted himself with the diversions of a royal prince; for eighty-four thousand years exercised the functions of a viceroy; for eighty-four thousand years exercised the functions of a king; for eighty-four thousand years, in this very Makhādeva Mango Grove, having retired from the house-life to the houseless life, led the Holy Life. He cultivated the Four Exalted States, and after death, upon dissolution of the body, was reborn in the Brahmā World.

Now, Ānanda, King Nimi had a son named Kaḷārajanaka. He did not retire from the house-life to the houseless life. He uprooted that splendid succession. He was the last man of the line.

"Now, Ānanda, it may be that the thought has occurred to you: 'At that time some one other than the Exalted One was King Makhādeva, by whom that splendid succession was established.' But, Ānanda, this is not the proper view to take. I, at that time, was King Makhādeva. I established that splendid succession. By me that splendid succession was founded. Those who came after me kept it going. But, Ānanda, that splendid succession conduces, not to utter disgust, not to detachment, not to cessation, not to tranquillity, not to higher wisdom, not to enlightenment,—only to rebirth in the World of Brahmā.

"However, Ānanda, this splendid succession which I have now founded, does conduce to utter disgust, to detachment, to cessation, to tranquillity, to higher wisdom, to enlightenment,—to Nibbāna. But Ānanda, what is this splendid succession which I have now founded, which conduces to utter disgust, to detachment, to cessation, to tranquillity, to higher wisdom, to enlightenment,—to Nibbāna? It is this alone: the Noble Eightfold Path; to wit, Right Views, Right Resolution, Right Speech, Right Conduct, Right Means of Livelihood, Right Exertion, Right Mindfulness, Right Concentration. This, Ānanda, is the splendid succession which I have now founded, which conduces to utter disgust, to detachment, to cessation, to tranquillity, to higher wisdom, to enlightenment,—to Nibbāna.

"Therefore, Ānanda, I say this to you. Inasmuch as I have founded this splendid succession, it is your duty to keep it going; you must not be the last man to follow me. If ever, Ānanda, in the lifetime of two men, one uproots the succession, he is the last man of the line. Therefore, Ānanda, I say this to you: Inasmuch as I have founded this splendid succession, it is your duty to keep it going; you must not be the last man to follow me."

Thus spoke the Exalted One. Venerable Ānanda, pleased, applauded the words of the Exalted One.

33. UPASĀḶHAKĀ

Cremated fourteen thousand times in one place!

Jātaka 166: ii. 54-56.

Of men named Upasāḷhaka. This parable was related by the Teacher while he was in residence at Jetavana with reference to a certain Brahman who requested that his body be burned in an unpolluted burning-ground.

This Brahman, we are told, was rich, possessed of great wealth, but because of the views which he held, although the Buddhas were in residence at a neighboring monastery, withheld from them his bounden duty and service. But he had a son who was wise, endowed with knowledge.

When this Brahman was an old man, he said to his son: "Son, on no account permit my body to be burned in a burning-ground where any other man, an outcaste perhaps, has ever been burned; instead, cause my body to be burned in an absolutely unpolluted burning-ground." "Father, for my part, I know of no place corresponding to your description. The best plan would be for you to take me with you to some such place as you have in mind, and for you yourself to point it out to me, saying: 'This is the place where you must have my body burned.' "

"Very well, son," said the Brahman, and taking his son with him, departed from the city and climbed to the top of Vulture Peak. "Son," said he, "here is a place where no other man, an outcaste perhaps, has ever been burned; here is the place where you must have my body burned." So saying, he began the descent from the mountain, accompanied by his son.

But the Teacher, that very day, at time of dawn, surveying his kinsmen who were ripe for conversion, saw that these two, father and son, were capable of attaining the Path of Conversion. Accordingly, taking the road, he went to the foot of the mountain like a hunter on the scent, and sat down and waited for the two to descend from the top of the mountain.

As father and son descended, they saw the Teacher. The Teacher exchanged friendly greetings with them and asked: "Where have you been, Brahmans?" The Brahman youth told him all about it. Said the Teacher: "Well then, come along; let's go to the place your father pointed out." And taking father and son, he climbed to the top of the mountain and asked: "Which is the place?" Said the Brahman youth: "Reverend Sir, he pointed out the hollow between these three mountains."

Said the Teacher: "Youth, not only in this present state of existence has your father sought an unpolluted burning-ground; in a previous state of existence also he sought an unpolluted burning-ground. Not only in this present state of existence has he pointed out a place to you and said: 'This is the only place where you may have my body burned;' in a previous state of existence also he pointed out a place where he would have his body burned." Then, in response to a request of the Brahman youth, the Teacher related the following Story of the Past:

In times past, in this very city of Rājagaha, this very Upasāḷhaka was a Brahman, and this very youth was his son. At that time the Future Buddha was reborn in the kingdom of Magadha in the household of a Brahman. After perfecting himself in the various arts and crafts, he adopted the life of an ascetic and developed the Higher Powers and the Attainments. For a long time he resided in the region of Himavat diverting himself with the diversion of the Trances. Afterwards, in order that he might obtain salt and vinegar, he took up his residence in a leaf-hut on Vulture Peak.

At that time this Brahman addressed his son in the very same way, and when the son said, "You yourself point out to me the kind of place you have in mind," the father pointed out this very place. And when the father, descending from the mountain, saw the Future Buddha, he approached the Future Buddha. And when the Future Buddha, in the very same way, questioned the Brahman and the Brahman youth, and heard the Brahman youth's reply, he said: "Come along! we'll find out whether the place your father pointed out is polluted or unpolluted!" And having climbed to the top of the mountain with them, when the Brahman youth remarked, "Here is the unpolluted place, between these three mountains," the Future Buddha said:

"Youth, there is no counting the number of those whose bodies have been burned in this very place. Your very father, reborn in this very city of Rājagaha, in this very Brahman household, called by this very name Upasāḷhaka, in this very hollow among the mountains, was burned in fourteen thousand previous states of existence! For on the earth it is impossible to find a place where human bodies have not been burned, a place which has not served as a burning-ground, a place which has not been heaped and covered with human heads!" And encompassing the facts with his knowledge of previous states of existence, he recited the following pair of stanzas:

Of men named Upasāḷhaka, fourteen thousand
Were burned in this place.
There is no place in this world
Which has never been touched by death.

But in what man be truth and righteousness
And non-injury and self-restraint and self-control,—
This is the goal of the Noble,—
This, in this very world
Is Deathless Absolute.

34. UBBIRĪ

Why weep for eighty-four thousand daughters?

Therī-gāthā Commentary No. 33.

Ubbirī was reborn in the dispensation of the present Buddha at Sāvatthi, in the family of a wealthy householder, and she was exceedingly beautiful and fair to see. When she reached womanhood, she was conducted to the house of the king of Kosala, and after a few years had passed, obtained an only daughter. To the latter they gave the name Jīvantī, or Living. The king, seeing her daughter, was pleased at heart, and conferred upon Ubbirī the ceremonial sprinkling of a queen.

But when her daughter was old enough to walk and to run hither and yon, she died. Every day the mother went to the burning-ground where her body was laid, and wept. One day she went to the Teacher, saluted him, sat down for a short while, and then departed. Standing on the bank of the river Aciravatī, she wept for her daughter.

Seeing her, the Teacher, just as he sat in the Perfumed Chamber, manifested himself to her, and asked her: "Why do you lament?" "I lament for my daughter, Exalted One." "In this burning-ground have been burned eighty-four thousand daughters of yours. For which one of these do you lament?" And pointing out the spot where this one had been burned, where that, he uttered the first half of a stanza:

You cry in the wood: "O Jīvā dear!"
Come to yourself, O Ubbirī!
In all, eighty-four thousand
Daughters of yours named Jīvā
Have been burned in this burning-ground.
For which one of these do you lament?

After the Teacher had taught her this lesson, she extended her knowledge in conformity with the lesson, laid hold on Insight, and both by the charm of the Teacher's lesson and by her own accumulation of causes in previous states of existence, became established in the highest of the Fruits, Sainthood. And having attained Sainthood, she made known the Specific Attainment she had attained by uttering the second half of the stanza:

Ah! he has drawn out the arrow,
So hard to find, that was in my heart.
For when I was overcome with sorrow,
He banished my sorrow for my daughter.

I here to-day am one from whom an arrow has been drawn,
I am cut off from the world, I am gone to Nibbāna.
I seek refuge in the Sage,—the Buddha,
And in the Doctrine, and in the Order.

35. VISĀKHĀ'S SORROW

So many dear ones, so many sorrows.

Udāna viii. 8: 91-92.

THUS have I heard: Once upon a time the Exalted One was in residence at Sāvatthi, in Eastern Grove, in Visākhā Mother of Migāra's mansion. Now at that time Visākhā Mother of Migāra's granddaughter had died, and she was Visākhā's darling and delight. And Visākhā Mother of Migāra, garments wet, hair wet, at an untimely hour approached the Exalted One. And having approached, she saluted the Exalted One and sat down on one side. And as she sat there on one side, the Exalted One said this to Visākhā Mother of Migāra: "Well, Visākhā, how is it that you come here at such an untimely hour, approaching with garments wet, with hair wet?" "Reverend Sir, my granddaughter has died, and she was my darling and delight. That is why I approach at such an untimely hour, with garments wet, with hair wet."

"Should you like, Visākhā, to have as many children and grandchildren as there are human beings in Sāvatthi?" "I should like, Reverend Sir, to have as many children and grandchildren as there are human beings in Sāvatthi." "But, Visākhā, how many human beings die every day in Sāvatthi?" "Reverend Sir, ten human beings die every day in Sāvatthi, nine . . . eight . . . seven . . . six . . . five . . . four . . . three . . . two . . . one. My granddaughter, Reverend Sir, is in no class by herself, apart from the other human beings who die in Sāvatthi." "What think you, Visākhā? Should you ever, at any time, be without garments wet, without hair wet?" "No indeed, Reverend Sir."

"Verily, Visākhā, they that hold a hundred dear, have a hundred sorrows; . . . ninety . . . eighty . . . seventy . . . sixty . . . fifty . . . forty . . . thirty . . . twenty . . . ten . . . nine . . . eight . . . seven . . . six . . . five . . . four . . . three . . . two . . . one. They that hold nothing dear, have no sorrow. Free from grief are they,—free from passion, free from despair. So say I."

Whatsoever griefs or lamentations or sorrows
Are in the world, of whatsoever sort or kind,
Arise because of something that is held dear.
If nothing be held dear, these arise not.

Therefore they only are happy, they only are free from grief,
Who hold absolutely nothing in this world dear.
Therefore whoever desires to be free from grief, free from passion,
Should hold absolutely nothing in this world dear.

CHAPTER VIII

PARABLES FROM THE LONG DISCOURSES ON THE SUBJECT: "IS THERE A LIFE AFTER DEATH?"

Dīgha 23: ii. 319-352.

On a certain occasion Pāyāsi the Warrior said to Venerable Kumāra Kassapa: "I, my lord Kassapa, hold this doctrine, this view: 'There is no life after death; there are no living beings reborn without the intervention of parents; there is no fruition, no ripening, of good and evil deeds.' " "Warrior, I never encountered or heard such a view. For how can a man say such a thing as this: 'There is no life after death; there are no living beings reborn without the intervention of parents; there is no fruition, no ripening, of good and evil deeds'? Have you any reason for this view?" "My lord Kassapa, I have a reason for this view." "Warrior, what is it like?"

The wicked do not return to earth.

"Here, my lord Kassapa, I have friends and companions, kinsmen and relatives, who are murderers, thieves, fornicators and adulterers, liars, backbiters, calumniators, triflers, covetous, malevolent of spirit, holders of false views. Sometimes they fall sick, suffer pain, are in a bad way. When I feel certain that these men will not recover from that sickness, I go to them and speak thus: 'There are some monks and Brahmans who hold this doctrine, this view: "Men who are murderers, thieves, fornicators and adulterers, liars, backbiters, calumniators, triflers, covetous, malevolent of spirit, holders of false views,—such men, on dissolution of the body, after death, go to a state of punishment, to a state of pain, to a state of suffering, to hell." You, sirs, are such men. If the words of these reverend monks and Brahmans are true, you, sirs, on dissolution of the body, after death, will go to a state of punishment, to a state of pain, to a state of suffering, to hell. If, on dissolution of the body, after death, you should be reborn in a state of punishment, in a state of pain, in a state of suffering, in hell, pray return and say to me: "There is a life after death; there are living beings reborn without the intervention of parents; there is a fruition, a ripening, of good and evil deeds." ' Now my friends are trustworthy and reliable. If my friends saw anything and said they had seen it, such a thing would necessarily be true. 'Very well,' say they, giving me their word. But for all that, they never return and say it, nor do they send a messenger either. This, my lord Kassapa, is one reason why I hold the view: 'There is no life after death; there are no living beings reborn without the intervention of parents; there is no fruition, no ripening, of good and evil deeds.' "

"Well, Warrior, I will reply by asking you a question on the subject. You may answer it in any way you please. Warrior, what have you to say to the following?"

36. THE CONDEMNED CRIMINAL

Suppose your men were to capture a brigand, a criminal, and arraign him here before you, saying: "Here, lord, is a brigand, a criminal. Inflict upon him whatever punishment you desire." And you were to say: "Well, take this fellow, bind his arms tight behind his back with a stout rope, shave his head, and to the loud beating of a drum lead him about from street to street, from crossing to crossing, conduct him out of the South gate, and cut off his head in the place of execution south of the city." And they were to say: "Very well;" and in obedience to your command were to take that fellow, bind his arms tight behind his back with a stout rope, shave his head, and to the loud beating of a drum lead him about from street to street, from crossing to crossing, conduct him out of the South gate, and make him sit down in the place of execution south of the city. And suppose that brigand were to say to his executioners: "Let my lord-executioners wait,—in such-and-such a village or market-town I have friends and companions, kinsmen and relatives,—until I show myself to them and return." Would he obtain his request? Would not the executioners rather, even as he babbled, cut off his head?

"Quite right, my lord Kassapa."

"Suppose, Warrior, your friends reborn in hell say to the warders of hell: 'Let our lord-warders of hell wait until we go and say to Pāyāsi the Warrior: "There is a life after death; there are living beings reborn without the intervention of parents; there is a fruition, a ripening, of good and evil deeds." ' Are they likely to obtain their request?"

But Pāyāsi the Warrior remained unconvinced. Said he:

The virtuous do not return to earth.

"Here, my lord Kassapa, I have friends and companions, kinsmen and relatives, who refrain from murder, theft, fornication and adultery, lying, backbiting, calumny, trifling, covetousness, malevolence of spirit, holders of orthodox views. Sometimes they fall sick, suffer pain, are in a bad way. When I feel certain that these men will not recover from that sickness, I go to them and speak thus: 'There are some monks and Brahmans who hold this doctrine, this view: "Men who refrain from murder, theft, fornication and adultery, lying, backbiting, calumny, trifling, covetousness, malevolence of spirit, holders of orthodox views, —such men, on dissolution of the body, after death, go to a state of bliss, to heaven." You, sirs, are such men. If the words of these reverend monks and Brahmans are true, you, sirs, on dissolution of the body, after death, will go to a state of bliss, to heaven. If, on dissolution of the body, after death, you should be reborn in a state of bliss, in heaven, pray return and say to me: "There is a life after death; there are living beings reborn without the intervention of parents; there is a fruition, a ripening, of good and evil deeds." ' Now my friends are trustworthy and reliable. If my friends saw anything and said they had seen it, such a thing would necessarily be true. 'Very well,' say they, giving me their word. But for all that, they never return and say it, nor do they send a messenger either. This, my lord Kassapa, is another reason why I hold the view: 'There is no life after death; there are no living beings reborn without the intervention of parents; there is no fruition, no ripening, of good and evil deeds.' "

"Well, Warrior, I will compose a parable for you. Even by a parable does many a man of intelligence in this world comprehend the meaning of a statement."

37. THE MAN IN THE DUNG-PIT

Warrior, it is precisely as though a man were submerged in a dung-pit, head and all. And you were to order your men: "Now then, pull that man out of that dung-pit." And they were to say: "Very well;" and in obedience to your command were to pull that man out of that dung-pit. And you were to say to them: "Now then, scrape the dung from off the body of that man, and scrape it well." And they were to say: "Very well;" and in obedience to your command were to scrape the dung from off the body of that man, and were to scrape it well. And you were to say to them: "Now then, massage the body of that man three times with yellow clay, and massage it well." And they were to massage the body of that man three times with yellow clay, and were to massage it well. And you were to say to them: "Now then, anoint that man with oil and bathe him well three times with soft bath-powder." And they were to anoint that man with oil and to bathe him well three times with soft bath-powder. And you were to say to them: "Now then, dress that man's hair and beard." And they were to dress that man's hair and beard. And you were to say to them: "Now then, present that man with costly garlands and costly perfumes and costly garments." And they were to present that man with costly garlands and costly perfumes and costly garments. And you were to say to them: "Now then, escort that man into a palace and furnish him with the Five Pleasures of Sense." And they were to escort that man into a palace and to furnish him with the Five Pleasures of Sense.

What think you, Warrior? Would that man, well bathed, well anointed, with hair and beard dressed, decked with garlands and ornaments, dressed in clean garments, aloft in a splendid palace, supplied and provided with the Five Pleasures of Sense, ministered unto,—would that man desire to plunge once more into that dung-pit?

"No, indeed, my lord Kassapa." "Why not?" "A dung-pit, my lord Kassapa, is a filthy place; filthy in fact, and so regarded; foul-smelling in fact, and so regarded; disgusting in fact, and so regarded; repulsive in fact, and so regarded."

"Precisely so, Warrior, to the gods, human beings are filthy and so regarded, foul-smelling and so regarded, disgusting and so regarded, repulsive and so regarded. Indeed, Warrior, the stench of human beings drives the gods a hundred leagues away! How can you expect your virtuous friends, reborn in a state of bliss, in heaven, to return and say to you: 'There is a life after death; there are living beings reborn without the intervention of parents; there is a fruition, a ripening, of good and evil deeds'?"

The virtuous do not return to earth.

But Pāyāsi the Warrior, still unconvinced, repeated once more what he had said before regarding his virtuous friends, remarking that those of his friends who had refrained from murder, theft, fornication and adultery, lying, and occasions of heedlessness through the use of intoxicating liquor and spirits, and who therefore, according to the monks and Brahmans, must have been reborn in the heaven of the Thirty-three gods, had never returned to earth.

"Well, Warrior," said Venerable Kumāra Kassapa, "I will reply by asking you a question on the subject. You may answer it in any way you please. Warrior, what have you to say to the following?"

38. TIME IN HEAVEN

WARRIOR, a hundred of our years are equivalent to a night and a day in the heaven of the Thirty-three gods. Thirty of these nights make up a month, and twelve of these months make up a year. The term of life of the Thirty-three gods is a thousand of these celestial years. Your friends have indeed been reborn in the heaven of the Thirty-three gods. Now suppose the thought has occurred to them: "We are supplied and provided with the Five Pleasures of Sense. After we have been ministered to for two or three celestial nights and days, we will go and say such-and-such to Pāyāsi the Warrior." Have they, in fact, had time to do so?

How do we know that the gods exist?

"No, indeed, my lord Kassapa. The fact is, my lord Kassapa, we should be dead and gone long before they returned. But who told my lord Kassapa that the Thirty-three gods exist, or that they live as long as this? I, my lord Kassapa, do not believe that the Thirty-three gods exist, or that they live as long as this."

39. THE BLIND MAN

WARRIOR, it is precisely as though a blind man could not see black and white objects, could not see blue objects, could not see yellow objects, could not see red objects, could not see pink objects, could not see even and uneven, could not see the stars, could not see the moon and the sun. And that man were to say: "There are no black and white objects; there is no one who can see black and white objects. There are no blue objects; there is no one who can see blue objects. There are no yellow objects; there is no one who can see yellow objects. There are no red objects; there is no one who can see red objects. There are no pink objects; there is no one who can see pink objects. There is no even and uneven; there is no one who can see even and uneven. There are no stars; there is no one who can see the stars. Moon and sun do not exist; there is no one who can see the moon and the sun. I do not know them, I do not see them; therefore they do not exist." Warrior, would that man speak correctly were he to speak thus?

"No, indeed, my lord Kassapa. There *are* black and white objects; there are those who can see black and white objects. There *are* blue objects; there are those who can see blue objects. There *are* yellow objects; there are those who can see yellow objects. There *are* red objects; there are those who can see red objects. There *are* pink objects; there are those who can see pink objects. Even and uneven *do* exist; there are those who can see even and uneven. There *are* stars; there are those who can see the stars. Moon and sun *do* exist; there are those who can see the moon and the sun. 'I do not know them, I do not see them; therefore they do not exist!' No, indeed, my lord Kassapa! That man would not speak correctly were he to speak thus."

"Warrior, you are just like the blind man in the parable when you speak thus: 'But who told my lord Kassapa that the Thirty-three gods exist, or that they live as long as this? I, my lord Kassapa, do not believe that the Thirty-three gods exist, or that they live as long as this.'

"By no means, Warrior, can the next world be seen in the way you imagine it can,—with this Eye of Flesh. But, let me tell you, Warrior, there are monks and Brahmans who resort to forest-hermitages in the wilderness, remote lodgings where there is little sound, little noise; and there, living heedful, ardent, resolute, they clarify the Heavenly Eye; with the Heavenly Eye, transcending any mere human eye, clarified, they behold not only this world, but the next, and living beings reborn without the intervention of parents."

But Pāyāsi the Warrior remained unconvinced. Said he:

Why do not the virtuous commit suicide?

"Here, my lord Kassapa, I see monks and Brahmans observing the Precepts, doing good works, desiring to live, not desiring to die, desiring happiness, avoiding suffering. When, my lord Kassapa, I see them, the following thought occurs to me: 'If these reverend monks and Brahmans really knew, "Better than this would it be were we dead," immediately these reverend monks and Brahmans, observing the Precepts, doing good works, would either eat poison, or draw the sword, or kill themselves by hanging, or jump off a jumping-off place.' But since evidently these reverend monks and Brahmans do not know, "Better than this would it be were we dead," therefore these reverend monks and Brahmans, observing the Precepts, doing good works, desiring to live, not desiring to die, desiring happiness, avoiding suffering, do not kill themselves. This, my lord Kassapa, is another reason why I hold the view: 'There is no life after death; there are no living beings reborn without the intervention of parents; there is no fruition, no ripening, of good and evil deeds.'"

"Well, Warrior, I will compose a parable for you. Even by a parable does many a man of intelligence in this world comprehend the meaning of a statement."

40. THE WOMAN WITH CHILD

IN olden times, Warrior, a certain Brahman had two wives. One had a son about ten or twelve years old; the other was with child, about to bring forth. Now that Brahman died. And that youth said this to his mother's fellow: "My lady, whatever money or grain or silver or gold there is, all this is mine. You have no part in this; turn over to me, my lady, the inheritance of my father." Upon this, that Brahman's wife said this to that youth: "Just wait, my dear, until I bring forth. If it is a boy, he also will have one portion; if it is a girl, she also will be yours to be enjoyed."

The second time also the youth said this to his mother's fellow: "My lady, whatever money or grain or silver or gold there is, all this is mine. You have no part in this; turn over to me, my lady, the inheritance of my father." The second time also that Brahman's wife said this to that youth: "Just wait, my dear, until I bring forth. If it is a boy, he also will have one portion; if it is a girl, she also will be yours to be enjoyed."

The third time also that youth said this to his mother's fellow: "My lady, whatever money or grain or silver or gold there is, all this is mine. You have no part in this; turn over to me, my lady, the inheritance of my father."

Thereupon that Brahman's wife took a sword, went into an inner room, and plunged the sword into her belly: "Until I know whether it is a boy or a girl!" She destroyed herself, her living child, and her property. She met destruction and ruin, like the foolish, short-sighted woman she was, seeking an inheritance otherwise than in the right way.

"Precisely so, Warrior, you, a foolish, short-sighted man, will meet destruction and ruin by seeking the next world otherwise than in the right way, just as that Brahman's wife, that foolish, short-sighted woman, also met destruction and ruin by seeking an inheritance otherwise than in the right way.

"No, indeed, Warrior! Monks and Brahmans who observe the Precepts, who do good works, permit what is not yet ripe to become fully ripe. What is more, being wise men, they wait patiently for it to become fully ripe. For, Warrior, there is need of monks and Brahmans who observe the Precepts, who do good works, continuing alive. Warrior, in the same proportion as monks and Brahmans who observe the Precepts, who do good works, remain alive for a long long time, in the same proportion they generate much merit and act for the welfare of many, for the happiness of many, out of tender compassion for the world, for the weal and welfare and happiness of angels and men."

But Pāyāsi the Warrior remained unconvinced. Said he:

We cannot see the soul after death.

"Here, my lord Kassapa, my men capture a brigand, a criminal, and arraign him before me, saying: 'Here, lord, is a brigand, a criminal. Inflict upon him whatever punishment you desire.' And I say to them: 'Well, place this man, alive as ever, in a jar; put the lid on the jar; cover it with a wet skin; seal it with a thick paste of wet clay; lift it up on the oven; start a fire.' 'Very well,' they say to me. In obedience to my command they place that man, alive as ever, in a jar, put the lid on the jar, cover it with a wet skin, seal it with a thick paste of wet clay, lift it up on the oven, start a fire. When we know, 'That man is dead,' then we lift that jar down, break the seal, take off the lid, and look down with bated breath: 'Perhaps we may see his soul coming out!' But no! We do not see his soul coming out."

"Well, Warrior, I will reply by asking you a question on the subject. You may answer it in any way you please."

41. WE CANNOT SEE THE SOUL DURING LIFE

Warrior, do you not recollect, while taking a siesta, seeing in a dream the delights of the grove, the delights of the woods, the delights of cleared ground, the delights of the lotus-pond?—I do recollect, my lord Kassapa, while taking a siesta, seeing in a dream the delights of the grove, the delights of the woods.—Were people watching you at that time?—Yes.—Did they see your soul coming in or going out?—No, indeed, my lord Kassapa.—So then, Warrior, although you were alive, living persons did not see your soul coming in or going out. How then, after your death, could they be expected to see your soul coming in or going out?

But Pāyāsi the Warrior remained unconvinced. Said he:

The dead are heavier than the living.

"Here, my lord Kassapa, my men capture a brigand, a criminal, and arraign him before me, saying: 'Here, lord, is a brigand, a criminal. Inflict upon him whatever punishment you desire.' And I say to them: 'Well, weigh this man, while yet alive, in the balances; strangle him to death with a bow-string; then weigh him again in the balances.' 'Very well,' they say to me. In obedience to my command they weigh that man, while yet alive, in the balances, strangle him to death with a bow-string, and then weigh him again in the balances. When he is alive, then he is lighter and softer and more pliable. But when he is dead, then he is heavier, more rigid, less pliable."

"Well then, Warrior, I will compose a parable for you."

42. HEAT MAKES THINGS LIGHT

Suppose, Warrior, a man were to weigh in the balances an iron ball which had been heated all day until it was red-hot, glowing, gleaming, flaring; and suppose, afterwards, he were to weigh in the balances that same iron ball, cold, extinguished. When would that iron ball be lighter, softer, more pliable,—when it was glowing, gleaming, flaring,—or when it was cold, extinguished?

When, my lord Kassapa, that iron ball was connected with heat, was connected with wind, when it was glowing, gleaming, flaring, then it was lighter and softer and more pliable. But when that iron ball was not connected with heat, was not connected with wind, when it was cold, extinguished, then it was heavier, more rigid, less pliable.

"Precisely so, Warrior, when this body is connected with life, and connected with heat, and connected with consciousness, then it is lighter and softer and more pliable. But when this body is not connected with life, is not connected with heat, is not connected with consciousness, then it is heavier, more rigid, less pliable."

But Pāyāsi the Warrior remained unconvinced. Said he:

We cannot see the soul.

"Here, my lord Kassapa, my men capture a brigand, a criminal, and arraign him before me, saying: 'Here, lord, is a brigand, a criminal. Inflict upon him whatever punishment you desire.' And I say to them: 'Well, batter this man,—cuticle and skin and flesh and sinews and bones and marrow,—and deprive him of life.' 'Very well,' they say to me. In obedience to my command they batter that man,—cuticle and skin and flesh and sinews and bones and marrow,—and deprive him of life. When he is half-dead, I say to them: 'Now then, fling this man down on his back. Perhaps we may see his soul coming out!' They fling that man down on his back. But no! We do not see his soul coming out!

"I say to them: 'Now then, fling this man down bent double . . . on one side . . . on the other side . . . ; stand him right side up . . . up side down . . . ; beat him with the hand . . . with clods . . . with a stick . . . with a sword; shake him down . . . shake him together . . . shake him out. Perhaps we may see his soul coming out!' They do so. But no! We do not see his soul coming out!

"Now he has that same organ of sight, the eye; but that organ does not sense these visible objects. He has that same organ of hearing, the ear; but that organ does not sense these sounds. He has that same organ of smell, the nose; but that organ does not sense these odors. He has that same organ of taste, the tongue; but that organ does not sense these flavors. He has that same organ of touch, the body; but that organ does not sense these objects of touch."

"Well then, Warrior, I will compose a parable for you."

43. VILLAGERS AND TRUMPET

In olden times, Warrior, a certain trumpeter went to a frontier district with his trumpet. He approached a certain village, and having approached, stood in the centre of the village, blew the trumpet three times, set the trumpet on the ground, and sat down on one side.

Now, Warrior, to those frontiersmen occurred the following thought: "What is it that makes that sound,—so charming, so delightful, so intoxicating, so fascinating, so infatuating?" Assembling, they said this to that trumpet-blower: "Sir, what is it that makes that sound,—so charming, so delightful, so intoxicating, so fascinating, so infatuating?" "Friends, it is that trumpet which makes that sound,—so charming, so delightful, so intoxicating, so fascinating, so infatuating."

They flung that trumpet down on its bottom. "Speak, O trumpet! Speak, O trumpet!" But no! That trumpet made not a sound! They flung that trumpet down bent double . . . on one side . . . on the other side . . . ; they stood it right side up . . . up side down . . . ; they beat it with the hand . . . with clods . . . with a stick . . . with a sword . . . ; they shook it down . . . shook it together . . . shook it out. "Speak, O trumpet! Speak, O trumpet!" But no! That trumpet made not a sound!

Then, Warrior, to that trumpet-blower occurred the following thought: "How foolish these frontiersmen are! How can they hope to hear the sound of the trumpet by seeking otherwise than in the right way?" With the frontiersmen watching him, he picked up the trumpet, blew the trumpet three times, and walked off with the trumpet.

Then, Warrior, to those frontiersmen occurred the following thought: "Ah! When this trumpet is connected with a human being, and is connected with exertion, and is connected with wind, then this trumpet makes a sound! But when this trumpet is not connected with a human being, is not connected with exertion, is not connected with wind, then this trumpet makes no sound!"

"Precisely so, Warrior, when this body is connected with life, and is connected with heat, and is connected with consciousness, then it advances and retires and stands and sits and lies down; then it sees visible objects with the eye, and hears sounds with the ear, and smells odors with the nose, and tastes flavors with the tongue, and touches objects of touch with the body, and understands the Doctrine with the mind. But when this body is not connected with life, and is not connected wth heat, and is not connected with consciousness, then it does not advance, does not retire, does not sit, does not lie down; then it does not see visible objects with the eye, and does not hear sounds with the ear, and does not smell odors with the nose, and does not taste flavors with the tongue, and does not touch objects of touch with the body, and does not understand the Doctrine with the mind."

But Pāyāsi the Warrior remained unconvinced. Said he:

We cannot see the soul.

"Here, my lord Kassapa, my men capture a brigand, a criminal, and arraign him before me saying: 'Here, lord, is a brigand, a criminal. Inflict upon him whatever punishment you desire.' And I say to them: 'Well, cut this man's cuticle. Perhaps we may see his soul coming out!' They cut that man's cuticle. But no! We do not see that man's soul coming out! I say to them: 'Now then, cut this man's skin . . . flesh . . . sinews . . . bones . . . marrow. Perhaps we may see his soul coming out!' But no! We do not see his soul coming out!"

"Well then, Warrior, I will compose a parable for you."

44. THE SEARCH FOR FIRE

In olden times, Warrior, a fire-worshipper, a Jaṭila, dwelt in a forest-abode, in a leaf-hut. Now, Warrior, a certain country district rose in revolt. And that multitude spent one night near the hermitage of that fire-worshipper, that Jaṭila, and departed. Now, Warrior, to that fire-worshipper, that Jaṭila, occurred the following thought: "Suppose I were to approach that encampment! Perhaps I may find something of use there!"

Accordingly that fire-worshipper, that Jaṭila, arose betimes and approached that encampment. Having approached, he saw in that encampment, abandoned, a slip of a young boy lying on his back. When he saw him, the following thought occurred to him: "It would ill become me were a human being to die with me looking on. Suppose I were to lead this boy to my hermitage, and to bring him up and feed him and rear him!" Accordingly that fire-worshipper, that Jaṭila, led that boy to his hermitage, and brought him up and fed him and reared him.

When that boy was about ten or twelve years old, that fire-worshipper, that Jaṭila, had occasion to go to the country on some business or other. Now that fire-worshipper, that Jaṭila, said this to that boy: "I desire, my son, to go to the country. Please tend the fire, and do not let it go out on you. Only, if the fire should go out on you,—here is a hatchet, here are sticks of wood, here is a fire-drill,—please kindle the fire and tend it." And having thus instructed that boy, that fire-worshipper, that Jaṭila, went to the country.

Now while that boy was absorbed in play, the fire went out. Thereupon to that boy occurred the following thought: "My father said this to me: 'My son, please tend the fire, and do not let it go out on you. Only, if the fire should go out on you,—here is a hatchet, here are sticks of wood, here is a fire-drill,—please kindle the fire and tend it.' Suppose I were to kindle the fire and tend it!"

Accordingly that boy began to chop up the fire-drill with his hatchet: "Perhaps I may produce fire!" But no! He did not produce fire! He split the fire-drill into two pieces . . . into three pieces . . . into four pieces . . . into five pieces . . . into ten pieces . . . into a hundred pieces. He reduced it to so many bits; having reduced it to so many bits, he pounded them in a mortar; having pounded them in a mortar, he winnowed them in a strong wind: "Perhaps I may produce fire!" But no! He did not produce fire!

Now that fire-worshipper, that Jaṭila, having transacted that business in the country, approached his own hermitage. Having approached, he said this to that boy: "My son, did the fire go out on you?" "Father, while I was absorbed in play here, the fire went out on me." So saying, the boy told his foster-father what he had done.

Then to that fire-worshipper, that Jaṭila, occurred the following thought: "How foolish this boy is! how short-sighted! How could he hope to produce fire by seeking otherwise than in the right way?" With the boy watching him, he picked up a fire-drill, produced fire, and said this to that boy: "This, my son, is the way to produce fire; not, as you, a foolish, short-sighted boy, tried to produce it, by seeking otherwise than in the right way."

"Precisely thus, Warrior, are you, a foolish, short-sighted man, seeking the next world otherwise than in the right way. Renounce, Warrior, this wicked heresy! Renounce, Warrior, this wicked heresy! Let it not be to your disadvantage and sorrow for a long time to come."

Wilful persistence in error.

"No matter how emphatically my lord Kassapa says this, yet, for all that, I cannot bring myself to renounce this wicked heresy. Even King Pasenadi Kosala knows, even kings outside know regarding me: 'Pāyāsi the Warrior holds this doctrine, holds this view: "There is no life after death; there are no living beings reborn without the intervention of parents; there is no fruition, no ripening, of good and evil deeds." ' If, my lord Kassapa, I were to renounce this wicked view, there would be those who would say of me: 'How foolish is Pāyāsi the Warrior! how short-sighted! how ready to accept what is hard to accept!' Even with anger will I hold to this view, even with hypocrisy will I hold to this view, even with conceit will I hold to this view."

"Well then, Warrior, I will compose a parable for you. Even by a parable does many a man of intelligence in this world comprehend the meaning of a statement."

45. TWO CARAVAN-LEADERS

In olden times, Warrior, a great caravan of a thousand carts went from the eastern country to the western country. Wherever it went, very quickly were consumed grass, sticks, water, and pot-herbs. Now over that caravan were two caravan-leaders, one over five hundred carts, one over five hundred carts. And to these caravan-leaders occurred the following thought: "This is a great caravan of a thousand carts. Wherever we go, very quickly are consumed grass, sticks, water, and pot-herbs. Suppose we were to divide this caravan into two caravans of five hundred carts each!" They divided that caravan into two caravans, one of five hundred carts, one of five hundred carts. One caravan-leader only loaded his carts with abundant grass and sticks and water, and started his caravan forward.

Now when he had proceeded a journey of two or three days,

that caravan-leader saw coming in the opposite direction in a chariot drawn by asses, a black man with bloodshot eyes, with ungirt quiver, wearing a garland of lilies, his garments wet, the hair of his head wet, the wheels of his chariot smeared with mud. Seeing, he said this: "Whence, sir, do you come?" "From such-and-such a country." "Whither do you intend to go?" "To such-and-such a country." "Evidently, sir, farther on in the wilderness a heavy rain has been in progress." "Yes, indeed, sir. Farther on in the wilderness a heavy rain has been in progress. The roads are drenched with water; abundant are grass and sticks and water. Throw away, sir, the old grass, sticks, and water; with lightly burdened carts go ever so quickly; do not overburden the conveyances."

Now that caravan-leader told his drivers what that man had said, and gave orders as follows: "Throw away the old grass, sticks, and water; with lightly burdened carts start the caravan forward." "Yes, sir," said those drivers to that caravan-leader. And in obedience to his command they threw away the old grass, sticks, and water, and with lightly burdened carts started the caravan forward. Neither in the first stage of the journey, nor in the second, nor in the third, nor in the fourth, nor in the fifth, nor in the sixth, nor in the seventh, did they see grass or sticks or water; they all met destruction and death. And all that were in that caravan, whether men or beasts, did that ogre, that demon, devour, leaving only the bare bones.

When the second caravan-leader knew, "It is now a long time since that caravan started out," he loaded his carts with abundant grass and sticks and water, and started his caravan forward. Now when he had proceeded a journey of two or three days, this caravan-leader saw coming in the opposite direction in a chariot drawn by asses, a black man with bloodshot eyes, with ungirt quiver, wearing a garland of lilies, his garments wet, the hair of his head wet, the wheels of his chariot smeared with mud. Seeing, he said this: "Whence, sir, do you come?" "From such-and-such a country." "Whither do you intend to go?" "To such-and-such a country." "Evidently, sir, farther on in the wilderness a heavy rain has been in progress." "Yes, indeed, sir. Farther on in the wilderness a heavy rain has been in progress. The roads are drenched with water; abundant are grass and sticks and water.

Throw away, sir, the old grass, sticks, and water; with lightly burdened carts go ever so quickly; do not overburden the conveyances."

Now that caravan-leader told his drivers what that man had said, adding: "This man surely is no friend of ours, no kinsman or blood-relative. How can we trust him on our journey? On no account must the old grass, sticks, and water, be thrown away. Start the caravan forward, leaving the things just as they are. I will not permit you to throw away the old." "Yes, sir," said those drivers to that caravan-leader. And in obedience to his command they started the caravan forward, leaving the things just as they were. Neither in the first stage of the journey, nor in the second, nor in the third, nor in the fourth, nor in the fifth, nor in the sixth, nor in the seventh, did they see grass or sticks or water; but they saw that caravan in destruction and ruin. And of those that were in that caravan, whether men or beasts, they saw only the bare bones, for they had been eaten by that ogre, by that demon.

Thereupon that caravan-leader addressed his drivers: "This caravan here met destruction and ruin solely through the folly of that foolish caravan-leader who acted as its guide. Now then, throw away those wares in our own caravan which are of little worth, and take those wares in this other caravan which are of great worth." "Yes, sir," said those drivers to that caravan-leader. And in obedience to his command they threw away all those wares in their own caravan which were of little worth, and took those wares in that other caravan which were of great worth. And they passed in safety through that wilderness solely through the wisdom of that wise caravan-leader who acted as their guide.

"Precisely so, Warrior, you, a foolish, short-sighted man, will meet destruction and ruin by seeking the next world otherwise than in the right way, just as did that man in the parable, that caravan-leader. And those who fondly imagine that they must listen to you, that they must put their trust in you, they also will meet destruction and ruin, just as did those drivers. Renounce, Warrior, this wicked heresy! Renounce, Warrior, this wicked heresy! Let it not be to your disadvantage and sorrow for a long time to come."

But Pāyāsi the Warrior remained obstinate. "I cannot bring myself," said he, "to renounce this wicked heresy." "Well then, Warrior, I will compose a parable for you."

46. DUNG FOR FODDER

In olden times, Warrior, a certain swineherd went from his own village to another village. There he saw much dry dung thrown away. When he saw it, the following thought occurred to him: "Here I have much dry dung thrown away which would make fodder for my pigs. Suppose I were to take the dry dung away from here!" He spread out his upper robe, took much dry dung, wrapped it up in a bundle, put the bundle on his head, and went his way.

When he was half-way home, a great cloud rained out of season. He went on with the load of dung oozing and trickling, smeared with dung to his finger-tips. People saw him going along in this manner and spoke as follows: "Aren't you crazy, sir? aren't you out of your mind? Otherwise how can you be carrying a load of dung, oozing and trickling, smeared with dung to your finger-tips?" "You, sirs, are crazy; you, sirs, are out of your mind. Why, what I am carrying is fodder for my pigs!"

"Warrior, you are just like the man in the parable who carried dung. Renounce, Warrior, this wicked heresy!" "That will I not." "Well then, Warrior, I will compose a parable for you."

47. TWO DICERS

In olden times, Warrior, two dicers played at dice. The first dicer swallowed every ace. The second dicer saw that dicer swallow every ace. Seeing, he said this to that dicer: "You, sir, have it all your own way. Give me the dice, sir; I must hurry away." "Yes, sir," said that dicer, and handed over the dice to that dicer.

Now that dicer painted the dice with poison, and said this to that dicer: "Come, sir, let us play at dice." "Yes, sir," said that dicer in assent to that dicer.

A second time also those dicers played at dice; a second time also that dicer swallowed every ace. The second dicer saw that dicer swallow for the second time also every ace. Seeing, he said this to that dicer:

> Smeared with the strongest poison
> Was the die the man swallowed, but knew it not.
> Swallow, O swallow, wicked dicer!
> Later it will taste bitter to you.

"Warrior, you are just like the dicer in the parable. Renounce, Warrior, this wicked heresy! Renounce, Warrior, this wicked heresy! Let it not be to your disadvantage and sorrow for a long time to come."

Wilful persistence in error.

"No matter how emphatically my lord Kassapa says this, yet, for all that, I cannot bring myself to renounce this wicked heresy. Even King Pasenadi Kosala knows, even kings outside know regarding me: 'Pāyāsi the Warrior holds this doctrine, holds this view: "There is no life after death; there are no living beings reborn without the intervention of parents; there is no fruition, no ripening, of good and evil deeds." ' If, my lord Kassapa, I were to renounce this wicked view, there would be those who would say of me: 'How foolish is Pāyāsi the Warrior! how short-sighted! how ready to accept what is hard to accept!' Even with anger will I hold to this view, even with hypocrisy will I hold to this view, even with conceit will I hold to this view."

"Well then, Warrior, I will compose a parable for you."

48. GIVING UP BETTER FOR WORSE

In olden times, Warrior, a certain district rose in revolt. And friend said to friend: "Let's go, sir; let's go to that district; there, perhaps, we may come by some spoils." "Yes, sir," said friend to friend in assent. They went to that country, to some village or other where there was an uproar. There they saw much hemp thrown away. Seeing, friend addressed friend: "Here, sir, is much hemp thrown away. Now then, sir, you pack up a load of hemp, and I'll pack up a load of hemp; we'll both carry off a load of hemp." "Yes, sir," said friend to friend in assent, and packed up a load of hemp.

They both went with their loads of hemp to some village or other where there was an uproar. There they saw much hempen thread thrown away. Seeing, friend addressed friend: "The very thing, sir, for which we should have wanted hemp! Here is much hempen thread thrown away! Now then, sir, you throw away your load of hemp, and I'll throw away my load of hemp; we'll both carry off a load of hempen thread." "This load of hemp I have has been carried a long way and is well tied together. Let me alone! Decide for yourself!" And that friend threw away his load of hemp and took a load of hempen thread.

They went to some village or other where there was an uproar.

There they saw many hempen cloths thrown away. Seeing, friend addressed friend: "The very thing, sir, for which we should have wanted hemp or hempen thread! Here are many hempen cloths thrown away! Now then, sir, you throw away your load of hemp, and I'll throw away my load of hempen thread; we'll both carry off a load of hempen cloths." "This load of hemp I have, has been carried a long way and is well tied together. Let me alone! Decide for yourself!" And that friend threw away his load of hempen thread and took a load of hempen cloths.

They went to some village or other where there was an uproar. There they saw an abundance of flax . . . linen thread . . . linen cloths; . . . cotton . . . cotton thread . . . cotton cloths; . . . iron; . . . copper; . . . tin; . . . lead; . . . silver; . . . gold thrown away. Seeing, friend addressed friend: "The very thing, sir, for which we should have wanted hemp or hempen thread or hempen cloths, or flax or linen thread or linen cloths, or cotton or cotton thread or cotton cloths, or iron or copper or tin or lead or silver! Here, sir, is gold in abundance thrown away! Now then, sir, you throw away your load of hemp and I'll throw away my load of silver; we'll both carry off a load of gold." "This load of hemp I have, has been carried a long way and is well tied together. Let me alone! Decide for yourself!" And that friend threw away his load of silver and took a load of gold.

They approached their own village. That friend who went there with a load of hemp, was welcomed neither by mother and father, nor by children and wife, nor by friends and companions. Nor from them did he obtain happiness and satisfaction. But that friend who went there with a load of gold, was welcomed by mother and father, and by children and wife, and by friends and companions. And from them he obtained happiness and satisfaction.

"Warrior, you are just like the man in the parable who carried a load of hemp. Renounce, Warrior, this wicked heresy! Renounce, Warrior, this wicked heresy! Let it not be to your disadvantage and sorrow for a long time to come."

Conversion of the unbeliever.

"Even with your former parables, my lord Kassapa, have I been pleased and delighted. Moreover, I like to hear your picturesque and quick-witted answers. Only I should have realized sooner the importance of identifying myself with you. It is delightful, my lord Kassapa! It is delightful, my lord Kassapa! It is precisely, my lord Kassapa, as if one were to set upright what has been thrown down, or were to reveal what is hidden, or were to point out the way to a bewildered person, or were to carry a lamp into the darkness so that persons with eyes might see things;—precisely so has my lord Kassapa illustrated the Doctrine in manifold ways. Lo! my lord Kassapa, I seek refuge in that Exalted One, Gotama, and in the Doctrine, and in the Congregation of Monks. Let my lord Kassapa keep me, who have sought the Refuges, as his disciple from this day forth, so long as I shall live."

CHAPTER IX

PARABLES FROM BUDDHAGHOSA'S LEGENDS OF THE SAINTS

49. GHOSAKA

He that diggeth a pit shall fall into it.

Añguttara Commentary 249-255.

A. Story of the Past: A father casts away his son.

BEFORE the rebirth of our Teacher, the plague broke out in the kingdom of the Vajjians. In one house after another, at a single stroke, ten or twenty persons died, but those who went out of the kingdom saved their lives. Knowing this, a certain man took his own son and wife and departed from that kingdom with the intention of going to another kingdom. Now while they were on their way, and before they had got clear of the wilderness, the provisions for the journey which the man had obtained in his house became exhausted, and the strength of their bodies gave out. First the mother would carry the child, and then the father.

Now the father of the child thought: "The strength of our bodies is exhausted. If we carry the child with us as we go, we shall not be able to complete our journey." Accordingly, taking care that the child's mother should not know what he was doing, pretending that he had fallen behind for the purpose of making water, he set the child down on the road and resumed his journey quite alone.

Now his wife, who stood watching for him to approach, not seeing the child in his arms, ran towards him screaming. "Husband, where is my child?" said she. "What need have you of a child? If we live, we shall have a child." Said she: "This man is indeed an utter brute!" And she said to him: "Begone! I will not go with such as you!" After thinking the matter over, he said:

"Wife, pardon me for what I have done." And taking the child, he continued the journey.

In the evening, when they had got clear of the wilderness, they reached a certain cowherd's house. Now that day the members of the cowherd's household had cooked rich rice-porridge. On seeing the travelers, they reflected: "These travelers are excessively hungry." So filling a great bowl with rice-porridge, and sprinkling the porridge with a ladleful of ghee, they gave it to them. Husband and wife ate that porridge, and the woman ate only a reasonable amount. But the man ate far more than was good for him, was unable to digest what he had eaten, and died at midnight.

When the man died, he received, because of his attachment for the cowherds, a new conception in the womb of a bitch that lived in the cowherds' house. In no very long time the bitch gave birth to a pup. The cowherd, observing that that pup was a very handsome dog, coaxed him with morsels of food, got the dog very fond of him, and took him with him wherever he went.

Now one day, at the usual time for making the rounds for alms, a certain Private Buddha arrived at the door of the cowherd's house. The cowherd, seeing him, gave him alms and obtained his promise to enter upon residence as his own guest. The Private Buddha entered upon residence at a spot not far from the cowherd's house, in a certain forest-grove. Whenever the cowherd went to pay his respects to the Private Buddha, he always took that dog along. Now on the way, in the lairs of wild beasts, he would rap on a tree or a rock to drive the wild beasts away, and that dog came to understand what he did and why he did it.

Now one day that cowherd, while sitting in the company of that Private Buddha, said: "Reverend Sir, we cannot come here every time. But here is a dog that is highly intelligent. When he comes here, you will understand that you are expected to come to our house-door."

One day the cowherd sent the dog, saying: "Get the Private Buddha and come back with him." The dog, hearing his words, went at the usual time for making the rounds for alms, and lay down on his belly at the Private Buddha's feet. The Private Buddha, perceiving, "The dog has come to me," took bowl and robe and started out on the path.

The Private Buddha, for the purpose of testing the dog, left the path on which he was walking and took a different path. The dog went and stood in front of him, but withdrew when the Private Buddha entered upon the path to the cowherd's house. Here and there, where, for the purpose of driving the wild beasts away, the cowherd was in the habit of rapping on a tree or a rock, on reaching any such spot, the dog barked very loud. At sound of him, the wild beasts fled away. Moreover, when it was time to make the rounds for alms, the Private Buddha gave the dog a big, greasy morsel. As a result of getting this morsel, the dog conceived deep affection for the Private Buddha.

When the Private Buddha had kept residence for the three months, the cowherd gave him a cloth sufficient for a set of robes, and said: "Reverend Sir, if it so please you, remain right here; if not, go according to your good pleasure." The Private Buddha intimated by his manner that it was his intention to depart. That cowherd accompanied the Private Buddha a little way, and then turned back. So great was the affection of the dog for the Private Buddha, that when he perceived that the Private Buddha was going away, he was overwhelmed with profound sorrow, his heart broke, and he died and was reborn in the World of the Thirty-three Gods.

Now because, in the days when he used to accompany the Private Buddha, he used to drive the wild beasts away by making a loud noise, therefore, in the World of the Thirty-three Gods, when he talked with the deities, the sound of his voice echoed and reëchoed throughout the entire City of the Gods. Through this very circumstance he came to be called Deity Ghosaka (He-of-the-voice).

Now while Ghosaka was enjoying this glory in the World of the Thirty-three Gods, in the Path of Men, in the city of Kosambi, a king by the name of Udena entered upon his kingdom. The story of Udena is to be understood precisely as it is written in the Commentary on the Bodhi-rājakumāra Sutta in the Middle Fifty of the Majjhima Nikāya.

B. Story of the Present: Ghosaka is cast away seven times.

Now while Udena was ruling in Kosambi, the deity Ghosaka fell from the City of the Gods and receive a new conception in Kosambi, in the womb of a certain courtezan.

1. Ghosaka is cast away on a refuse-heap.

That courtezan, on the expiration of ten lunar months, brought forth a child, and learning that it was a boy, caused him to be cast away on a rcfuse-heap.

At that moment a workman of the Treasurer of Kosambi, on his way, very early in the morning, to the Treasurer's house, exclaimed: "What can that be, surrounded by crows?" Approaching, and seeing that it was a boy, he exclaimed: "That boy must be a person of great merit!" Sending the boy to his own home by the hand of a certain man, he went to the Treasurer's house.

As for the Treasurer, when it was time for him to wait upon the king, he set out for the king's house. On the way he saw the house-priest. "What is the constellation in the moon's path to-day?" asked he. The house-priest, standing just where he was, took a reckoning, and said: "Such-and-such is the constellation in the moon's path to-day. A boy born under this constellation will obtain the post of Treasurer in this city."

The Treasurer, hearing these words of the house-priest, quickly sent messengers to his house. Thought he: "This house-priest never makes a mistake in his predictions, and my wife is pregnant." And he said to the messengers: "Just find out whether my wife has given birth to a child or not." They went, found out, and said: "Noble sir, she has not yet given birth to a child."

"Well then," said the Treasurer, "go seek for the boy that was born in this city to-day." They sought for that boy, and seeing him in the house of that Treasurer's workman, reported the fact. "Well then, summon that workman." They summoned him. And the Treasurer asked him: "In your house they say there is a boy." "Yes, Noble sir." "Give that boy to us." "I will not give him to you, Noble sir." "Here! take a thousand pieces of money and give him to us." Said the workman: "This boy may live or die! he's base-born!" And taking the thousand pieces of money, he gave the boy to the Treasurer.

2. Ghosaka is cast away in a cattle-pen.

Then thought the Treasurer: "If my wife gives birth to a daughter, I will make this very boy my heir; if she gives birth to a son, I will cause this boy to be killed." His wife gave birth to a son. Then thought the Treasurer: "Thus the cattle will trample him under foot and kill him." And he said to his men: "Lay this boy in the doorway of the cattle-pen." They laid him there.

Now the leader of the herd, the bull, coming out first and seeing the boy, thought: "Thus the other cattle will not trample him under foot." And he inclosed him with his four feet and stood still. And the herdsmen, seeing him, thought: "That boy must be a person of great merit, for even the animals know his virtues! We will take care of him!" They carried him home.

3. Ghosaka is cast away in a burning-ground.

As for that Treasurer, learning that the boy was not dead, hearing that he had been carried off by herdsmen, he gave a thousand pieces of money a second time, had the boy brought to him, and had him cast away in a burning-ground.

Now at that time a goatherd belonging to the Treasurer's household was tending some she-goats near the burning-ground. And a certain milch-goat, by reason of the boy's merit, left the path and went and gave suck to the boy. And although the goatherd drove her out, she went right back there and gave him suck. Thought the goatherd: "This she-goat, ever so early in the morning, left this spot and went elsewhere. What can this mean?" Going thither and looking, he saw the boy. Thought he: "That boy must be a person of great merit, for even the animals know his virtues! I will take care of him!" And picking him up, he carried him home.

4. Ghosaka is cast away on a caravan-trail.

On the following day the Treasurer thought: "Is the boy dead, or is he not dead?" Causing his men to look, and learning that the boy had been carried off by a goatherd, he gave a thousand pieces of money and had the boy brought to him. Said he: "To-morrow a certain caravan-leader will enter this city. Carry this boy and lay him in the track of the wheels. Thus, as the carts pass, the wheels will crush him."

They laid the boy there. As he lay there, the oxen harnessed to the foremost cart, that of the caravan-leader, saw him. When they saw him, they planted their legs about him like pillars and stood still. Thought the caravan-leader: "What can this mean?" Looking to see what made them stand still, and seeing the boy, he thought: "The boy must be a person of great merit! I must take care of him!" And picking him up, he carried him off.

5. Ghosaka is thrown down a precipice.

As for the Treasurer, he caused his men to look and see whether or not the boy had been killed on the caravan-trail; and learning that he had been carried off by a caravan-leader, he gave him also a thousand pieces of money, had the boy brought to him, and caused him to be thrown down a precipice.

As the boy fell, he fell where some reed-makers were working, on a reed-maker's hut. Through the supernatural power of his merit, it felt exactly like cotton beaten a hundred times. And the leader of the reed-makers thought: "That boy must be a person of great merit! I must take care of him!" And picking him up, he carried him home.

The Treasurer caused a search to be made in the place where the boy had fallen from the precipice, to discover whether or not he was dead; and learning that he had been carried off by the leader of the reed-makers, he gave him also a thousand pieces of money and caused the boy to be brought to him.

6. Ghosaka is sent to the potter's.

After a time both the Treasurer's own son and Ghosaka reached manhood. The Treasurer, once more bethinking himself of some way to effect the youth Ghosaka's death, went to the house of his own potter and said to him secretly: "Master, in my house there is such-and-such a certain base-born youth. By some means or other he must be gotten out of the way!" Thereupon the potter closed both his ears and said: "Such terrible words as those should never be uttered!" Thereupon the Treasurer thought: "This fellow will not do it gratis." So he said to him: "Here, Master, take a thousand pieces of money and do this job!"

There is a proverb: "A bribe breaks the unbroken;" and so it was in this case. The potter immediately took the thousand pieces of money and agreed to the bargain, saying: "I intend, Noble sir, on such-and-such a day, to fire my bake-house. On that day, at such-and-such a time, send him!" The Treasurer, on his part, hearing the words of the potter, agreed to the bargain. And from that moment on, he counted the days.

When the day appointed by the potter arrived, he knew it, and summoning the youth Ghosaka, he said to him: "Son, on such-and-such a day we have need of many vessels. You must go to our potter's and say to him: 'My father tells me that he gave you a certain job to do. Finish it up to-day!'" "Very well," said Ghosaka, promising to do as he was told. So saying, he set out.

When Ghosaka was part way to the potter's, the Treasurer's own son, who was playing marbles, saw him; and going quickly to him, said: "I, dear brother, playing with these youths, have lost ever so much money. Win it back and give it to me." Said Ghosaka: "I have no time now; father has sent me to the potter's on a very important errand." Said his foster-brother: "I, dear brother, will go to the potter's; you recover my stake and give it to me." "Very well, then," said Ghosaka; "go ahead!" So he told his foster-brother the message he himself had been directed to carry, and started playing with the youths.

The Treasurer's own son went to the potter's and delivered that message. "Very well, son," said the potter, "I'll finish up the job!" He took that youth into an inner room, chopped him to pieces with a sharp axe, threw the pieces into a chatty, put the lid on the chatty, set the chatty among his other vessels, and fired the bake-house.

The youth Ghosaka, having won a big stake, sat watching for the return of his younger brother. Observing that the latter was tarrying a long time, he thought: "Why, pray, does he tarry so long?" and went to the potter's common. Seeing him nowhere about, he concluded: "He must have gone home." So he turned around and went home.

The Treasurer saw him approaching even from afar. Thought he: "What, pray, can be the matter? I sent that fellow to the potter's to get him out of the way. But here he is now, coming back again to the very place he started from!" Even as Ghosaka approached, the Treasurer said to him: "Son, didn't you go to the potter's?" "No, father," replied Ghosaka, "I didn't go." "How's that, son?" Then Ghosaka told the Treasurer the reason why he himself turned back, and the reason why his younger brother went to the potter's.

From the moment the Treasurer heard those words, it was as though he had been overwhelmed by the great earth. Thought he: "Can this that you tell me be true!" His heart palpitating with fear, because it was impossible for him to confide the facts to others, he went ever so quickly to the potter's, and said to him: "Watch out, sir! watch out, sir!" Said the potter: "Why do you tell me to watch out? The particular job you gave me to do is done!" The Treasurer immediately turned back from the potter's and went home. And from that time on he suffered from mental disease.

7. Ghosaka is sent to a village-treasurer's.

Even at that time unwilling to eat with him, the Treasurer thought: "I must devote all of my energies to the task of accomplishing, by some means or other, the ruin of the enemy of my son."

He wrote a leaf, summoned the youth Ghosaka, gave him the leaf, and said to him: "In such-and-such a village lives a workman of ours. You are to take this leaf, go to his house, give him the leaf, and say to him: 'My father says that you are to comply immediately with the message on this leaf.' " And he gave him the following message by word of mouth: "On the way lives a certain treasurer who is a friend of ours,—a village-treasurer. You are to go to his house, take your meal there, and then continue your journey."

The youth Ghosaka bowed to the Treasurer, took the leaf, and started out. On the way he went to the place of residence of the village-treasurer. Having inquired the way to his house, he found him seated in a room outside of the gate, shaving himself. He bowed to him and stood waiting. "Whence do you come, youth?" "I am the son of the Treasurer of Kosambi, sir." The village-treasurer was pleased and delighted. Thought he: "He is the son of a treasurer who is a friend of ours!"

Now at that moment a slave-woman belonging to the daughter of that treasurer was on the point of starting out to fetch flowers for the treasurer's daughter. But the treasurer said to her: "Let this errand wait. Bathe the feet of the youth Ghosaka, and spread a bed and give it to him." She did so. Having so done, she went to the shop and brought back flowers for the treasurer's daughter.

The treasurer's daughter, seeing her, said: "You've been wasting a lot of time out of the house to-day!" And becoming provoked at her, she said: "What have you been up to all of this time?"

"Say not a word, my lady! I never saw such a handsome youth before in my life! I hear he's the son of a treasurer who's a friend of your father's. I can't begin to describe the beauty he possesses! I was on my way to get flowers for you, when, all of a sudden, your father says to me: 'Bathe the feet of this youth and spread a bed and give it to him.' That's why I was out of the house so long."

Now that treasurer's daughter, in her fourth previous existence, had been the wife of that youth. Therefore from the moment she heard those words, she knew not whether she was standing or sitting. Taking that very slave-woman with her, she went to the place where he lay, and gazed at him as he slept. Seeing a leaf fastened to the hem of his garment, she thought: "What can that leaf mean?" Without awakening the youth, she took the leaf and read it. Then she exclaimed: "This youth is going about carrying his own death-warrant on his very person!" Breaking that leaf in pieces, she wrote another leaf as follows:

"I am sending my son to you. My friend the village-treasurer has a daughter who has reached marriageable age. I command you with all speed to make a levy throughout our jurisdiction, with a hundred each of all kinds of gifts to obtain the daughter of this village-treasurer for my son, to make arrangements for the wedding-ceremonies, and when the wedding-ceremonies are over, to send me word, saying: 'I have done thus and so.' And I shall devise means of doing for you what ought to be done in this matter."

Having written this leaf, she affixed that same seal to it, and before ever that youth had awakened, fastened it to the hem of his garment precisely as the first leaf had been fastened. And that youth, having spent that night in that house, on the following day took leave of the treasurer, went to the village where the workman lived, and gave him the leaf.

The workman, on reading the leaf, gathered the villagers together and said to them: "As for you, you have a way of not taking me into your reckoning. But my master has just sent word to me, telling me to obtain, with a hundred each of all kinds of gifts, a maiden to be the wife of his eldest son. See to it that the amount of the levy is speedily collected and brought together in this place!"

The workman, having made all of the preparations for the wedding-festival, sent a message to the village-treasurer, obtained his consent, completed the wedding-ceremonies with a hundred each of all kinds of gifts, and sent the following leaf to the Treasurer of Kosambi: "I, on hearing the message on the leaf which you sent, did thus and so."

The Treasurer, on hearing that message, was as if burnt with fire. "Now," thought he, "I am ruined!" Worry brought on an attack of dysentery. Thought he: "By some means or other I will summon him and disinherit him." From the time when the wedding-festival was completed, he kept thinking: "Why does my son remain without?" And he sent the following message: "Let him come quickly!"

The youth Ghosaka, on hearing the message, started to go. The Treasurer's daughter thought: "This simpleton does not know who it is through whom he obtained this success. By employing some stratagem or other, I must find some means of preventing him from going." So she said to him: "Youth, don't hurry too fast! When one goes to one's home-village, one should make proper preparations beforehand."

As for the Treasurer of Kosambi, when he perceived that the youth Ghosaka was tarrying, he sent a message a second time: "Why does my son tarry? I am suffering from an attack of dysentery. My son ought to come and see me while I yet remain alive."

At that time the Treasurer's daughter informed him: "That's not your father! you only imagine it's your father! That man sent a leaf to his workman, commanding him to put you out of the way. By removing that leaf and writing a different message, I enabled you to obtain this success. He summons you with this thought in mind: 'I will disinherit him.' Wait until he dies!"

Now when the youth Ghosaka heard that his foster-father was dead (although at that very time he was still alive), he went to the city of Kosambi. As for the Treasurer's daughter, she gave him the peremptory order: "When you enter, post your guards throughout the house; then enter." She herself, entering the house in the immediate company of the Treasurer's son, lifted up both her hands and pretended to weep. The Treasurer of Kosambi lay where it was dark. She went up to him and smote him in the heart with her very head. So weak was he that as the result of that very blow he died.

As for the Treasurer's son, after he had done his duty by his foster-father's body, he gave a bribe to the women-servants, saying: "Say that I am the Great Treasurer's own son." On the seventh day following, the king thought: "I must find some one worthy of the post of Treasurer." And he sent out his men, saying: "Find out whether the Treasurer had a son or not." The Treasurer's women-servants told the king that the youth Ghosaka was the Treasurer's own son. "Very well," said the king, accepting their statement, and gave Ghosaka the post of Treasurer. He became known as Treasurer Ghosaka.

Now his wife said to him: "Noble sir, not only are you base-born, but I also was reborn in a poverty-stricken house. But as a result of good deeds performed in previous states of existence, we have obtained all this glory. Now also let us perform good deeds." "Very well, wife," said Ghosaka, consenting. And Ghosaka instituted almsgiving, expending each day a thousand pieces of money.

50. LITTLE WAYMAN

The last shall be first.

Aṅguttara Commentary 130-135.

A. Birth of Little Wayman.

AT Rājagaha, they say, the daughter of the household of a rich merchant actually formed an intimacy with her own slave. Frightened at the thought: "Others also may know what I have done," she spoke thus: "It is out of the question for us to live in this place. If my mother and father come to know of this misdeed, they will rend us limb from limb. Let us go elsewhere and live."

Taking such necessary things as they could carry in their hand, they left the house by the principal door. "No matter where it is," said they both with one accord, "let us go to some place unknown to others," and so they did. They took up their residence in a certain place, and after they had lived together, she conceived a child.

When her unborn child reached maturity, she took counsel with her husband, saying: "My unborn child has reached maturity. If I bring forth my child in a place removed from kith and kin, it will bring naught but pain to both of us alike. Let's go right home!" "We'll go to-day! we'll go to-morrow!" said he, and let the days slip by.

Thought she: "This simpleton, because of the greatness of his own misdeed, has not the courage to go. Mother and father are one's best friends. Let this fellow go or not; I must go." When he left the house, she put the household utensils away, and having informed her next-door neighbors that she was going home, she started out on the road.

Now when that man returned to the house and saw her not, he asked the neighbors. Hearing, "She has gone home," he followed after her quickly and came up with her on the road. And right there she gave birth to her child. "What is it, wife?" asked he. "Husband, a son is born." "Now what shall we do?" "What we are going home for has happened by the way. If we go there, what shall we do? Let's go back." With one accord the two turned back.

To that boy, because he was born by the way, they gave the name Wayman. In no very long time she conceived yet another child in her womb. (All is to be related in detail precisely as before.) To that boy also, because he was born by the way, they gave the name Wayman, calling the first born Big Wayman, and the other Little Wayman. Taking the two boys with them, they went back again to their own place of residence.

While they were living there, this boy Wayman heard other boys speak of their uncles and grandfathers and grandmothers. He asked his mother: "Mother, other boys speak of their grandfathers and grandmothers. Haven't we any relatives?" "Yes, my son. You have no relatives here. In Rājagaha City you have a grandfather who is a rich merchant. There you have many relatives." "Why don't we go there, mother?" She did not tell her son why she would not go. Since her sons asked repeatedly, she said to her husband: "These children weary me excessively. Will my mother and father eat us alive if they see us? Come, let us show the children their grandfather's household." "I shall not dare be present, but I will conduct you." "Very well, good sir; by some means or other the children must see their grandfather's household."

Husband and wife, taking the children, in due course reached Rājagaha, and found lodging for the night in a certain rest-house at the city-gate. The mother of the children sent word to her mother and father that she had arrived with the two children. When they heard that message, they said: "As we have passed to and fro in the round of existences, we have not hitherto had a son or a daughter. They have done us a great wrong; it is out of the question for them to stand in our sight. But let the two take such-and-such a sum of money and go and live in a pleasant place. The children, however, they may send here." The merchant's daughter took the money sent her by her mother and father, placed the children in the hands of the very messengers that came, and sent them. The children grew up in the household of their grandfather.

Of the two boys, Little Wayman was very young, but Big Wayman used to go with his grandfather to hear the Possessor of the Ten Forces preach the Doctrine. As a result of listening regularly to religious discourse from the lips of the Teacher, his thoughts inclined to the adoption of the Religious Life. Said he to his grandfather: "If you agree, I should like to become a monk." "What say you, my son? Were you alone to adopt the Religious Life, it would please me more than it would were even the whole world so to do. If, my son, you are able so to do, by all means become a monk." So saying, he gave his consent, and went to the Teacher.

B. Little Wayman as a monk.

Said the Teacher: "Great merchant, you have a boy?" "Yes, Reverend Sir, this boy is a grandson of mine; I give my consent for him to become a monk under you." The Teacher bade a certain monk on his round for alms: "Make a monk of this boy." The Elder assigned to him as a Subject of Meditation the first five of the Constituent Parts of the Body, and made a monk of him. He learned much of the Word of the Buddha, and after completing residence during the season of the rains, made his full profession.

After making his full profession, by the Practice of Meditation he obtained the Four Trances leading to the Realm of Formlessness, and arising therefrom, attained Sainthood. Thus did he become *foremost of those who are skilled in the development of perception.*

As he diverted himself with the Bliss of the Trances, with the Bliss of the Path, with the Bliss of the Fruit, and with the Bliss of Nibbāna, he thought: "Assuredly it is possible to bestow this Bliss on Little Wayman." Accordingly, going to his grandfather the merchant, he said: "Great merchant, if you agree, I should like to make a monk of Little Wayman." "Make a monk of him, Reverend Sir." The Elder made a monk of the boy Little Wayman, and established him in the Ten Precepts. The novice Little Wayman received from his brother the following stanza:

> Even as the lotus, the red lotus, of fragrant perfume,
> Appears at early morn full-blown, with fragrance unimpaired,
> Behold the Buddha, resplendent as the blazing sun in the sky.

Every verse he learned put the preceding verse out of his mind; while he was striving merely to learn this one stanza, four months passed. Now Big Wayman said to him: "Wayman, you are incapable of mastering this Religion. In four months you are unable to learn even one stanza. How then do you expect to bring your religious duties to a head? Depart hence."

Little Wayman, bowed out by the Elder, stood weeping on the outskirts of the monastery. At that time the Teacher was in residence at Jīvaka's Mango Grove near Rājagaha. Jīvaka sent a man, saying: "Invite the Teacher with five hundred monks." Now at that time Big Wayman was steward of the Order. When Jīvaka's man said, "Reverend Sir, accept food in alms for five hundred monks," Big Wayman replied, "I accept for all except Simpleton Wayman." When Little Wayman heard this speech, he felt worse yet.

The Teacher, seeing Little Wayman's distress, thought: "Little Wayman will awaken if I go to him." He went, allowed himself to be seen no great distance off, and said: "Little Wayman, you are weeping?" "Reverend Sir, my brother bowed me out." "Wayman, your brother has no knowledge of the disposition and inclination of other individuals. You are an individual susceptible of treatment by a Buddha." So saying, he created by magic a clean rag and gave it to him. "Wayman," said he, "take this and develop [Concentration] by repeating the words: 'Removal of Impurity! Removal of Impurity.' "

Little Wayman sat down and rubbed with his hand the rag given him by the Teacher, saying as he did so: "Removal of Impurity! Removal of Impurity!" As he did so, the fibres became soiled. As he continued to rub it, it got to look like a pot-wiper. Having attained Ripeness of Knowledge, he established thereon the concept of Decay and Death, and reflected: "This rag, naturally white and perfectly clean, by reason of a body which has the Attachments, has become soiled. Precisely so does it fare with the thoughts also." He developed Concentration, and employing as props the Four Trances leading to the Realm of Form, attained Sainthood together with the [Four] Analytical Powers. Having obtained Knowledge of a Spiritual Body, he was able, being one man, to become many men; and, being many men, to become one man. By the Path of Sainthood merely, he acquired both the Tepiṭaka and the Six Supernatural Powers.

On the following day the Teacher, accompanied by five hundred monks less one, went and sat down in Jīvaka's residence. But Little Wayman, for the simple reason that food in alms had not been accepted for himself, did not go. Jīvaka started to give gruel. The Teacher covered his bowl with his hand. "Why, Reverend Sir, do you not take it?" "There is one monk left in the monastery, Jīvaka." Jīvaka sent a man, saying: "Go get the noble monk who sits in the monastery and fetch him back with you."

As for the Elder Little Wayman, before ever that man arrived, he created a thousand monks. Not a single one did he make like any other. Of not a single one did he make the monk's labor,—examination of robes, for example,—like any other. That man, seeing the multiplicity of monks in the monastery, went and said to Jīvaka: "Reverend Sir, the Congregation of Monks in the monastery is larger than this Congregation of Monks here. I do not know which reverend monk I ought to summon."

Jīvaka in turn asked the Teacher: "Reverend Sir, what is the name of the monk who sits in the monastery?" "His name is Little Wayman, Jīvaka." "Go sir, ask, 'Which is the monk named Little Wayman?' and fetch him back with you." The man went to the monastery and asked: "Which is the monk named Little Wayman?" "I am Little Wayman! I am Little Wayman!" cried the thousand monks as one monk. Again he went and said to Jīvaka: "Monks to the number of a thousand, each and every one, cry out: 'I am Little Wayman!' I do not know: 'Such-and-such a monk is the one to summon.' " Jīvaka, knowing by inference that the monks were created by magical power acquired through Penetration of Truth, said: "Friend, say to the very first monk who speaks: 'The Teacher summons you;' and take him by the hem of his robe and fetch him back with you." The man went to the monastery and did so. Immediately monks to the number of a thousand disappeared. That man returned with the Elder. The Teacher at that moment took gruel.

When the Possessor of the Ten Forces had finished his meal and had returned to the monastery, the following talk began in the Hall of Truth: "How mighty, indeed, are the Buddhas! They have endowed with magical power so great as this, a monk who in the space of four months could not learn a single stanza." The Teacher, knowing the course of the thoughts of those monks, seated himself in the Seat of the Buddhas and asked: "Monks, what are you saying?" "Exalted One, naught but this are we saying: 'Little Wayman has received rich gain from you.' Of your virtues only are we talking."

"It is no wonder, monks, that just now, by obeying my admonition, he obtained an inheritance which transcends the world. This youth in a former existence also, when my knowledge was not yet fully ripened, by obeying my admonition obtained a worldly inheritance." "When was that, Reverend Sir?" said the monks, requesting to know more about it. The Teacher explained the matter to those monks by relating the following

C. Story of the Past: The mouse-merchant

Monks, in times past a king named Brahmadatta ruled in Benāres City. At that time a wise, far-sighted youth named Merchant Little knew all the signs. One day, as he was on his way to wait upon the king, he saw a decayed mouse in the street. Comparing the positions of the constellations at the moment, he said this: "It is possible for a youth who has his eyes open, by picking up this mouse, both to support a wife and to carry on business."

A certain poverty-stricken youth, hearing those words of the merchant, thought: "It cannot be that this man does not know what he is talking about." He picked up the mouse, offered it in a certain shop for cat's food, and received a farthing. With that farthing he obtained raw sugar, and water in a water-pot. At dawn, seeing garland-makers approaching, he presented ever so small a fragment of sugar, and presented water in a ladle. They gave him each a handful of flowers. With those flowers as capital, on the following day also he obtained raw sugar and a jar of water, and went to the same flower garden. That day the garland-makers gave him half-plucked stalks of flowers as they went by. In no very long time he obtained in this way eight pieces of money. Again, one windy rainy day, he went to the refuse-yard, piled up the sticks that had fallen, and sat down. From the king's potter he received sixteen pieces of money.

Having thus accumulated twenty-four pieces of money, he thought: "This is the way for me!" At a point not far from the city he set a chatty of water and served five hundred grass-carriers with water. Said they: "You, sir, are doing much for us. What can we do for you?" Said he: "When I have something to do, please help me out." Going about here and there, he made friends with a landsman and a seaman. The landsman told him: "To-morrow a horse-dealer will arrive with five hundred horses." Hearing his words, he gave the sign to the grass-carriers and had them fetch twice as many bundles of grass. And when the horses entered the city, having piled up a thousand bundles of grass in the gateway, he sat down. The horse-dealer, unable to get feed for his horses anywhere in the city, gave him a thousand pieces of money and took that grass.

A few days after that, his friend the seaman told him: "A big ship has arrived in port." He thought: "This is the way!" With eight pieces of money he hired a covered chariot for so much an hour, went to the ship's port, and pledged a seal-ring for the ship. Not far off he had a tent set up, and seating himself therein, gave orders to his men: "When merchants arrive from abroad, have them announced by three porters."

Hearing, "A ship has arrived in port," a hundred merchants

came from Benāres, saying, "Let us have wares." "Wares you will not get; in such-and-such a place is a great merchant who has given a pledge for the lot." Hearing this, they went to him. Attendants, at a sign from the first porter, sent announcement of their arrival by three porters. Those hundred merchants, giving each a thousand pieces of money, acquired possession of the ship with him as partner; and again giving him each a thousand pieces of money, acquired his interest in the ship and made the wares their own property.

That youth, having gained two hundred thousand pieces of money, returned to Benāres. Thinking, "One should show his gratefulness," he went to Merchant Little, causing one hundred thousand pieces of money to be carried with him. The merchant asked him: "Friend, what did you do to get this wealth?" The youth replied: "By following the suggestion which you made, I got this in only four months' time." The merchant, hearing his reply, thought: "Now I must not let such a youth get into the hands of another." So when the youth grew up, the merchant gave him his daughter in marriage and made him master of all his wealth. That youth, on the death of the merchant, succeeded to the rank of principal merchant in that city, and having remained on earth during the term of life allotted to him, passed away according to his deeds. *End of Story of the Past.*

The Teacher, having related the two stories, joined the connection, and speaking as One Fully Enlightened, uttered the following stanza:

> Even with little wealth, a man who is wise and intelligent
> Can elevate himself to high position in the world,
> Just as by blowing a tiny flame one can start a great fire.

Thus did the Teacher explain this matter to the monks seated in the Hall of Truth. But subsequently, the Teacher, surrounded by the Company of the Noble, seated in the Seat of Truth, assigned to Elder Little Wayman the rank of *foremost of those who have power to create a spiritual body, and of those who are skilled in the development of thought;* and to Big Wayman the rank of *foremost of those who are skilled in the development of perception.*

51. NANDA THE ELDER

Giving up worse for better.

A. Canonical version.

Udāna iii. 2: 21-24.

THUS have I heard: Once upon a time the Exalted One was in residence at Sāvatthi, at Jetavana, in Anāthapiṇḍika's Grove. Now at that time Venerable Nanda, cousin of the Exalted One, son of his mother's sister, informed numerous monks as follows: "In discontent, brethren, am I living the Religious Life; I cannot stand the Religious Life; I intend to renounce the Vows and to return to the lower life, the life of a layman."

Now a certain monk approached the Exalted One; having approached, he saluted the Exalted One and sat down on one side. And as he sat there on one side, that monk said this to the Exalted One: "Reverend Sir, Venerable Nanda, cousin of the Exalted One, son of his mother's sister, informs numerous monks as follows: 'In discontent, brethren, am I living the Religious Life; I cannot stand the Religious Life; I intend to renounce the Vows and to return to the lower life, the life of a layman.' "

Now the Exalted One addressed a certain monk: "Come you, monk, in my name address Nanda the monk: 'The Teacher summons you, brother Nanda.' " "Yes, Reverend Sir," said that monk to the Exalted One. And in obedience to the Teacher's command that monk approached Venerable Nanda. And having approached, he said this to Venerable Nanda: "The Teacher summons you, Venerable Nanda."

"Yes, brother," said Venerable Nanda to that monk. And in obedience to that monk's command he approached the Exalted One. And having approached, he saluted the Exalted One and sat down on one side. And as he sat there on one side, the Exalted One said this to Venerable Nanda: "Is it true, Nanda, as they say, that you said this and that?" "Yes, Reverend Sir." "But, Nanda, what is the matter?"

"Reverend Sir, as I was coming out of the house, my noble wife Belle-of-the-land, with hair half-combed, took leave of me, saying: 'As soon as ever you can, Noble Sir, please come back again.' Reverend Sir, it is because I keep remembering her that I am living the Religious Life in discontent; that I cannot stand the Religious Life; that I intend to return to the lower life, the life of a layman."

Thereupon the Exalted One, taking Venerable Nanda by the arm, just as a strong man might straighten his bent arm or bend his straightened arm, precisely so disappeared from Jetavana and appeared among the gods of the Thirty-three. Now at that time five hundred pink-footed celestial nymphs were come to wait upon Sakka king of gods. Accordingly the Exalted One addressed Venerable Nanda: "Nanda, do you see these five hundred pink-footed celestial nymphs?" "Yes, Reverend Sir." "What is your opinion, Nanda?—Which are the more beautiful and fair to look upon and handsome, your noble wife Belle-of-the-land, or these five hundred pink-footed celestial nymphs?"

"Reverend Sir, as far inferior as is a greedy female monkey with ears and nose cut off to my noble wife Belle-of-the-land, even so far inferior, Reverend Sir, is my noble wife Belle-of-the-land to these five hundred pink-footed celestial nymphs. In comparison with them, she does not even come into the count, she does not even come within a fractional part of them, she cannot even be compared with them. Of course these five hundred pink-footed celestial nymphs are more beautiful and fair to look upon and handsome!"

"Cheer up, Nanda! Cheer up, Nanda! I guarantee that you shall win these five hundred pink-footed celestial nymphs!" "If, Reverend Sir, the Exalted One guarantees that I shall win these five hundred pink-footed celestial nymphs, in that case, Reverend Sir, Exalted One, I shall take the greatest pleasure in living the Religious Life."

Then the Exalted One, taking Venerable Nanda by the arm, just as a strong man might straighten his bent arm or bend his straightened arm, precisely so disappeared from among the gods of the Thirty-three and appeared at Jetavana. Now the monks heard: "It appears that it is in hope of winning celestial nymphs that Venerable Nanda, cousin of the Exalted One, son of his mother's sister, is living the Religious Life. It appears that the

Exalted One has guaranteed that he shall win five hundred pink-footed celestial nymphs."

And Venerable Nanda's fellow-monks accosted Venerable Nanda with the epithets "hireling" and "bought-with-a-price," saying: "It appears that Venerable Nanda is a hireling; it appears that Venerable Nanda is one bought with a price. It appears that it is in hope of winning celestial nymphs that Venerable Nanda is living the Religious Life; it appears that the Exalted One has guaranteed that he shall win five hundred pink-footed celestial nymphs."

Now Venerable Nanda, although his fellow-monks despised him, were ashamed of him, and tormented him by calling him "hireling" and "bought-with-a-price," nevertheless, living in solitude, withdrawn from the world, heedful, ardent, resolute, proficient, in no long time, even in this life, himself abode in the knowledge, realization, and attainment of that supreme goal of the Religious Life for the sake of which goodly youths retire once and for all from the house-life to the houseless life. This did he know: "Rebirth is at an end, lived is the Holy Life, duty is done; I am no more for this world." And Venerable Nanda was numbered among the Saints.

Now when the night was past, a certain deity of wondrous beauty approached the Exalted One, illuminating the entire Jetavana. And having approached, he saluted the Exalted One and stood on one side. And as he stood on one side, that deity said this to the Exalted One: "Reverend Sir, Venerable Nanda, cousin of the Exalted One, son of his mother's sister, by extinction of the Contaminations, even in this life, himself abides in the knowledge, realization, and attainment of freedom from the Contaminations, emancipation of the heart, emancipation of the intellect." And there arose within the Exalted One also knowledge of the following: "Nanda, by extinction of the Contaminations, even in this life, himself abides in the knowledge, realization, and attainment of freedom from the Contaminations, emancipation of the heart, emancipation of the intellect."

Now when that night was past, Venerable Nanda approached the Exalted One. And having approached, he saluted the Exalted One and sat down on one side. And as he sat there on one side, Venerable Nanda said this to the Exalted One: "Reverend Sir, I release the Exalted One from the promise which he made when he, the Exalted One, guaranteed that I should win five hundred pink-footed celestial nymphs." "Nanda, I also grasped your mind with my own mind, and saw: 'Nanda, by extinction of the Contaminations, even in this life, himself abides in the knowledge, realization, and attainment of freedom from the Contaminations, emancipation of the heart, emancipation of the intellect.' Likewise a deity informed me of the fact, saying: 'Nanda, by extinction of the Contaminations, even in this life, himself abides in the knowledge, realization, and attainment of freedom from the Contaminations, emancipation of the heart, emanicaption of the intellect.' When, therefore, Nanda, you ceased to cling to the things of the world, and your heart was released from the Contaminations, at that moment I was released from that promise."

B. Uncanonical version.

Aṅguttara Commentary 190-192.

Nanda obtained a new conception in Kapila City in the womb of Mahā Pajāpatī Gotamī. On his name-day he gave *joy* and pleasure to his assembled kinsfolk; therefore they named him Prince Nanda, or Joy.

The Great Being, having attained Omniscience, having set in motion the glorious Wheel of the Doctrine, in gracious condescension to mankind proceeded from Rājagaha to Kapila City. At first sight he established his father in the Fruit of Conversion. On the following day he went to his father's residence, gave admonition to the Mother of Rāhula, and preached the Doctrine to the rest of the people besides.

On the following day, while the ceremonies of Prince Nanda's sprinkling, house-warming, and marriage were in progress, he went to his residence, permitted the Prince to take his bowl, and for the purpose of making a monk of him, set out in the direction of the monastery. The sprinkling-ceremony did not thus weigh heavily upon Prince Nanda. He took the bowl. As he departed with the Teacher, Belle-of-the-land, on an upper floor of the splendid mansion, opened a window and screamed: "As soon as ever you can, Noble Sir, please come back!" Nanda heard this, and overmastered with desire and lust, gazed at her. But out of reverence for the Teacher he did not dare take the hint and do as he wished to do. Therefore his heart burned.

"He will turn around here! he will turn around here!" thought Nanda. But for all his thinking, the Teacher conducted him to the monastery and made a monk of him. Even while the Teacher was making a monk of him, he did not dare resist, but consented by remaining silent.

But from the day when he became a monk, he remembered only the words which Belle-of-the-land had spoken. And to him she seemed to come and stand not far off. Oppressed with discontent, he would go a little way, and every time he passed a shrub or a bush, the Possessor of the Ten Forces seemed to stand before him. As a cock's feather is tossed into the fire, even so he would whirl around and go back again into his own place of residence.

Thought the Teacher: "Nanda is excessively unheedful; he cannot suppress discontent. I must extinguish his passion." So he said to him: "Come, Nanda, let's make a journey to heaven!" "Exalted One, how am I to go to a place to which only those can go who possess magical power?" "You just make up your mind to go! Go, and you will see!"

By the supernatural power of the Possessor of the Ten Forces, Nanda made the journey to heaven with the Tathāgata himself. Looking at the abode of Sakka king of gods, he saw five hundred celestial nymphs. The Teacher saw Nanda looking at those nymphs with pleasure as his aim. Seeing, he asked: "Nanda, do these nymphs please you, or does Belle-of-the-land?" "Reverend Sir, in comparison with these nymphs, Belle-of-the-land looks like a female monkey blind of one eye, with ears and nose cut off!" "Nanda, nymphs like these are not hard to win for those who practice meditation!" "If, Reverend Sir, the Exalted One is my surety, I will practice meditation." "You trust me, Nanda! Practice meditation with confidence. *In case you die with rebirth as your lot,* I guarantee that you will win them." So!

The Teacher, having journeyed to heaven as he pleased, returned once more to Jetavana. From that time on, Elder Nanda practiced meditation night and day in the hope of winning the nymphs. The Teacher gave orders to the monks: "You walk about and say here and there: 'In Nanda's place of residence, a certain monk,—so they say!—having made the Possessor of the Ten

Forces his surety, is practicing meditation in the hope of winning celestial nymphs!' "

The monks, having promised to do as the Teacher said, walked about within earshot of the Elder and said: "Venerable Nanda is a hireling,—so they say! Venerable Nanda is one bought-with-a-price,—so they say! He is leading the Holy Life in the hope of winning celestial nymphs! The Exalted One,—so they say!—has guaranteed that he shall win five hundred pink-footed celestial nymphs!"

Elder Nanda, hearing that talk, thought: "These monks are talking about nobody else,—they are talking about me. Improper is the deed I have done!" And applying himself to meditation, he developed Insight and attained Sainthood.

Now the instant he attained Sainthood, a certain deity informed the Exalted One of that fact. Moreover the Exalted One himself was fully aware of it. On the following day Elder Nanda approached the Exalted One and spoke thus: "Reverend Sir, I release the Exalted One from the promise which he made when he, the Exalted One, guaranteed that I should win five hundred pink-footed celestial nymphs."

52. BHADDĀ KUṆḌALAKESĀ

Quick is the wit of woman.

Aṅguttara Commentary 220-224.

In Section Nine, by the words *Of those who are quick to obtain the* [*Six*] *Supernatural Powers,* the Teacher declares Bhaddā Kuṇḍalakesā to be *foremost of nuns who are quick to obtain the* [*Six*] *Supernatural Powers.*

For she also, reborn in the dispensation of the Buddha Padumuttara in the city Haṁsavatī in a respectable family, hearing the Teacher preach the Doctrine, seeing him assign preëminence among those who were quick to obtain the [Six] Supernatural Powers to a certain nun, made an Earnest Wish, aspiring to that rank.

After following the stream of the Round of Existences in the Worlds of the Gods and the world of men for a hundred thousand cycles of time, she was reborn in the dispensation of the Buddha

Kassapa in the household of Kiki, king of Kāsi, as one of seven sisters. For twenty thousand years she took upon herself the Ten Precepts, lived the Holy Life of a princess, caused cells of residence to be erected for the Order, and after following the stream of the Round of Existences in the Worlds of the Gods and the world of men during the interval between the Buddha Kassapa and the Buddha Gotama, was reborn in the dispensation of the Buddha Gotama in the city of Rājagaha in the household of a rich merchant. They gave her the name Bhaddā, or Felicia, or Blessed.

That same day moreover, in that city, the house-priest of the king had a son born. At the time of his birth, throughout the city, beginning with the king's residence, weapons flashed light. The house-priest, very early in the morning, went to the king's residence and inquired of the king whether he had slept well. Said the king: "How, master, could you expect Us to sleep well? All last night the weapons in the royal residence flashed light; We saw them and were stricken with fear."

"Great king, don't worry about that. Not in your residence only did weapons flash light; it was the same all over the city." "What was the cause, master?" "In our house a boy was born under the constellation of a robber. He has come into existence as an enemy of the entire city. That was his sign; you have nothing to fear. But if you wish, we'll get rid of him." "So long as we suffer no injury, there is no necessity of getting rid of him."

Said the house-priest: "My son has actually brought his own name with him!" Accordingly he gave the boy simply the name Little Enemy. In the merchant's house Bhaddā grew up, and likewise in the house-priest's house Little Enemy grew up. From the time he was old enough to play and run hither and yon, wherever he went, he laid hands on everything he saw, and filled the house of his mother and father. His father gave him a thousand reasons, but for all that could not stop him. But later on, when the boy had grown to manhood, the father, realizing that by no means in his power could he stop him, gave him two dark blue garments to wear, placed in his hands a housebreaking outfit and a block-and-tackle, and dismissed him, saying: "Get a living this way anyhow."

From that day on he would throw his block-and-tackle, climb the face of houses, make a breach in the wall, and taking goods deposited in other people's houses with as much assurance as though he had himself deposited them, go his way. In the entire city there was not a single house he didn't plunder.

One day the king, driving through the city in a chariot, asked his charioteer: "How comes it that the houses in this city are everywhere nothing but holes?" "Your majesty, in this city is a robber named Little Enemy who is breaking through walls and robbing people's houses." The king had the city watchman summoned: "In this city, I am told, is a robber who does this and that. Why don't you catch him?" "Your majesty, we can't get that robber with the goods!" "If you don't catch that robber to-day, I will do for you as does a king."

"Very well, your majesty," said the city watchman. He had men patrol the entire city, and catching that robber in the act of breaking through a wall and robbing other people of their property, arraigned him, goods and all, before the king. Said the king: "Conduct this robber out of the South gate and have him executed." The city watchman, in obedience to the king's command, having given that robber a thousand lashes at every cross-roads, went out of the South gate with him.

At that time this maiden Bhaddā, daughter of the rich merchant, hearing the hubbub of the multitude, opened a window, looked out, and saw Little Enemy the robber being led along in this manner. Seeing, she pressed both hands to her heart and went and laid herself down on her splendid couch with upturned face. Now she was the sole dearly beloved daughter of that house, wherefore her kinsfolk could not bear even the slightest alteration for the worse in her facial expression. So when they saw her lying on her couch, they asked her: "What are you doing, dear girl?" "Did you see that robber being led to execution for committing a capital offense?" "Yes, dear girl, we saw him." "*If I can have him, I will live; if I cannot have him,—death only for me!*"

By no means whatever could they quiet her. "Life is better than death!" they concluded. So her father went to the city watchman, gave him a thousand pieces of money as a bribe, and said to him: "My daughter is in love with a robber. Get him off the best way you can." "Very well," said the city watchman. In obedience to the merchant's command he took the robber, dilly-dallied here and there until the sun was about to set, and when the sun was about to set, removing a certain man from the prison, freed Little Enemy from his bonds, sent Little Enemy to the merchant's house, bound the other man with bonds, conducted him out of the South gate, and slew him. Moreover slaves of the merchant escorted Little Enemy to the merchant's residence.

When the merchant's daughter saw him, she thought: "I will fulfil my desire." So she caused Little Enemy to bathe in perfumed water, caused him to be adorned with all the adornments, and sent him to the mansion. Bhaddā, thinking, "Fulfilled is my aspiration," adorned herself with the adornments that were left over, and spent her time ministering to him. After spending a few days thus, Little Enemy thought: "This woman's ornaments must be mine; by hook or crook I must get hold of them." Accordingly, when they were seated together happily, he said to Bhaddā: "There is something I have to say."

The merchant's daughter was as pleased at heart as though she had gained a thousand pieces of money. "Speak freely, Noble Sir," said she. Said Little Enemy: "You think: 'Through me this man has received his life.' But as a matter of fact, the instant I was caught, I made the following vow to the deity residing on the mountain called Robbers' Cliff: 'If I receive my life, I will make an offering to you.' Make haste and prepare an offering."

Bhaddā, thinking, "I will fulfil his desire," prepared the offering, adorned herself with all her adornments, mounted the same conveyance, accompanied her husband to the mountain called Robbers' Cliff, and with the thought in her mind, "I will make an offering to the spirit of the mountain," started to climb the mountain.

Little Enemy thought: "If all climb the mountain, there will be no chance for me to get this woman's jewels." Accordingly he caused Bhaddā alone to take the vessel containing the offering; having so done, he climbed the mountain. He talked with Bhaddā, but the words he spoke were not friendly words. She knew, merely by his manner of acting, what he was up to.

Then said he to her: "Bhaddā, take off your cloak and wrap up in it the jewels you have on." "Husband, what wrong have I done?" "You imagine: 'Why! but I came here for the purpose of making an offering!' But for my part, I could tear out the liver of this deity and devour it! As a matter of fact, the offering was only a pretext by which I got you here with the intention of taking your jewels." "But, Noble Sir, to whom the jewels belong, to him I also belong." "I don't admit anything of the sort. Your property is one thing, my property is another."

"Very well, Noble Sir. But fulfil this one wish of mine: Permit me, adorned just as I am, to embrace you both before and behind." "Very well," said he, consenting. She, knowing that he had consented, made a pretense of embracing him before and behind, and —flung him over the cliff. He fell through the air, and while yet in the air, was reduced to powder and dust. The deity residing on the mountain, realizing what a brilliant thing she had done, uttered these stanzas in praise of her good qualities:

Not under all circumstances is that male wise,—
Woman too is wise, wary of this, wary of that.
Not under all circumstances is that male wise,—
Woman too is wise, though she have but an instant to think.

Then Bhaddā thought: "It is out of the question, as matters stand, for me to go back home again. I will leave this place, at any rate, retire from the world, and enter some religious order." So she went to the monastery of the Jains and asked the Jains to admit her to the religious life. Now they said to her: "What mode of religious life shall it be?" She replied: "Admit me to the very highest plane of your religious life." "Very well," said they. And tearing out her hair with a palmyra comb, they admitted her to the religious life.

When her *hair* came in again, it grew so thick that it hung in *curls* and ringlets. Solely through this circumstance she received the name Curly-hair, Kuṇḍalakesā.

In the place where she had adopted the religious life, there she learned all the branches of religious knowledge they had to teach. But coming to the conclusion that beyond these they had nothing of any special worth, she wandered through villages, market-towns, and royal cities, visiting all the places where there were wise men, and learning all the branches of religious knowledge they had to teach. In fact, so learned did she become that in many places men were unable to answer her questions.

Finding no one who could match question and answer with her, whenever she entered a village or a market-town, she would make a pile of sand at the gate, plant a rose-apple branch on it, and give the sign to the boys standing near: "Whoever has the courage to argue with me,—let him trample this branch under his feet!" For seven whole days there were none who trampled the branch under their feet. So she took it and departed.

At this time our Exalted One, reborn in the world of men, was in residence at Jetavana near Sāvatthi. Kuṇḍalakesā in due course reached Sāvatthi, and entering within the city, planted the branch on a pile of sand precisely as before, and gave the sign to the boys standing near. At this time Sāriputta, Commander of the Faith, entered the city quite alone, having permitted the Congregation of Monks to precede him, and seeing the rose-apple branch on the pile of sand, asked: "How does this come to be planted here?" The boys told him what there was about it, omitting none of the details. "If that's the case, boys, take it and trample it under your feet." When the boys heard the Elder say this, there were some who did not dare trample it under their feet; but others, the very instant the Elder gave the word, trampled it under their feet and reduced it to powder and dust.

Kuṇḍalakesā, having finished her breakfast, came out. Seeing the branch trampled to dust, she asked: "Whose is this work?" Then the boys told her that they themselves had done it, and that Sāriputta, Commander of the Faith, had put them up to it. Thought she: "Had he not known his own strength, he would never have dared tell these boys to trample this branch under their feet. He must certainly be some great man. But as for me, since I am a person of no consequence, I shall not appear to advantage. The best thing for me to do is to go right back into the town and give the sign to my followers." She did so. (We are to understand that of the eighty thousand families who resided in the city, since they had all things in common, every one of them knew.)

As for the Elder, when he had finished his breakfast, he sat down at the foot of a tree. Now this nun Kuṇḍalakesā, surrounded by a great throng of people, went to the Elder, exchanged friendly greetings with him, took her stand on one side, and asked: "Reverend Sir, was it you who told those boys to trample that branch under their feet?" "Yes, it was I who told those boys to trample that branch under their feet." "That being the case, Reverend

Sir, I should like to engage in a disputation with you." "All right, my lady."

"Whose privilege is it to ask questions, and whose to answer?" "As for asking questions, it is my privilege to do that; but you ask questions on whatever subject you are acquainted with." In accordance with the direction of the Elder, she asked him questions about every single doctrine she knew. The Elder answered every question she asked. When she had asked all of her questions, she became silent. Then said the Elder to her: "You have asked a great deal. Let me too ask a single question." "Ask it, Reverend sir." "What is One?"

Said Kuṇḍalakesā: "I don't know, Reverend Sir." "If you don't know that little bit, what else can you be supposed to know?" Then and there she fell at the Elder's feet, saying: "In you, Reverend Sir, do I seek refuge." "There is no such thing as seeking refuge in me. Residing at a neighboring monastery is the foremost individual in the world of men and the Worlds of the Gods. Seek refuge in him." "I will do so," said she. So at even-tide, when it was time for the Teacher to preach the Doctrine, she went to him, and saluting him with the Five Rests, took her stand on one side. The Teacher, knowing that by the course she had adopted she had trampled under her feet all existing things, uttered this stanza:

> Even if there were a hundred stanzas
> Composed of verses devoid of meaning,
> A single verse of a stanza were better,
> By the hearing of which a man attains peace.

At the conclusion of the stanza, even as she stood there, she attained Sainthood together with the [Four] Analytical Powers, and requested admission to the Order. The Teacher granted her admission to her. She went to the Nuns' Convent and was admitted.

On a later occasion the following talk began in the midst of the Fourfold Assembly: "Great indeed is this Bhaddā Kuṇḍalakesā, who attained Sainthood at the conclusion of a stanza of four verses!" The Teacher, taking advantage of this opportunity, assigned to the nun Kuṇḍalakesā *preëminence among those who are quick to obtain the [Six] Supernatural Powers.*

53. VISĀKHĀ'S MARRIAGE

Honor the household divinity.

Aṅguttara Commentary 241-249.

In the Second Sutta, with the words *of almsgivers*, the Buddha declares Visākhā Mother of Migāra to be *foremost of female lay disciples who delight in almsgiving.*

She, we are told, was reborn in the dispensation of the Buddha Padumuttara in the city of Haṁsavatī, in a respectable family. Later on, hearing the Teacher preach the Doctrine, and seeing him assign a certain female lay disciple to the rank of foremost of almsgivers, she made an Earnest Wish, aspiring to that distinction.

Passing from birth to birth in the Worlds of the Gods and the world of men for a period of one hundred thousand cycles of time, she was reborn in the dispensation of the Buddha Kassapa in the household of Kiki king of Kāsi as the youngest of seven sisters. For at that time

Samaṇī and Samaṇaguttā and Bhikkhunī and Bhikkhadāyikā
And Dhammā and Sudhammā and Saṅghadāsī as seventh

were seven sisters. In the present dispensation, as

Khemā and Uppalavaṇṇā and Paṭācārā and Gotamī
And Dhammadinnā and Mahā Māyā and Visākhā as seventh

have they been reborn.

The seventh of these, Saṅghadāsī, after passing from birth to birth during the interval between the Buddha Kassapa and the Buddha Gotama, received a new conception in the dispensation of the Buddha Gotama in the kingdom of Aṅga, in the city of Bhaddiya, in the womb of Lady Flower, chief consort of Treasurer Wealth-winner, son of Treasurer Ram. They gave her the name Visākhā.

Conversion of Visākhā.

When she was seven years old, the Possessor of the Ten Forces, seeing that the Brahman Sela and other of his kinsmen in the faith possessed the faculties requisite for Conversion, journeying from place to place in that kingdom with a great company of monks, came to that city. Now at that time Householder Ram held the post of treasurer in that city, being the chief of five persons of great merit.

(The five persons of great merit were Treasurer Ram, Moon-lotus his principal wife, his son Wealth-winner, his wife Lady Flower, and Treasurer Ram's slave Puṇṇa. Treasurer Ram possessed limitless wealth; but not he alone,—in the jurisdiction of the great king Bimbisāra there were five possessors of limitless wealth: Jotiya, Jaṭila, Ram, Puṇṇaka, and Kākavaliya.)

When Treasurer Ram heard that the Possessor of the Ten Forces had come to his own city, he sent for the maiden Visākhā, daughter of Treasurer Wealth-winner, and spoke thus: "Dear girl, both for you and for me this is an auspicious day. With the five hundred maidens who are your fellows, mount five hundred chariots, and accompanied by five hundred slave-maidens, go forth to meet the Possessor of the Ten Forces."

Hearing the words of her grandfather, she did so. Now because she well knew both what to do and what not to do, she proceeded in a vehicle as far as there was room for a vehicle to go; then, descending from the vehicle, she approached the Teacher on foot, bowed to him, and took her stand on one side. Pleased with her conduct, the Teacher preached the Doctrine to her, and at the conclusion of his discourse both she and her five hundred maidens were established in the Fruit of Conversion.

Treasurer Ram also went to the Teacher, bowed to the Teacher, and sat down on one side. The Teacher also, because of his conduct, preached the Doctrine. At the conclusion of the discourse he was established in the Fruit of Conversion. Thereupon he invited the Teacher to be his guest on the morrow. On the following day he entertained in his own house the Congregation of Monks presided over by the Buddha, serving them with the choicest food, both hard and soft, and in like manner during the following fortnight provided them with abundant food. When the Teacher had remained in the city of Bhaddiya during his good pleasure, he departed.

Betrothal of Visākhā.

From this point on, the story should be confined to the career of Visākhā, to the exclusion of all other topics.

For the king of Kosala at Sāvatthi sent word to Bimbisāra: "In my jurisdiction there is no personage possessed of limitless wealth; let him send us a personage possessed of limitless wealth!" The king took counsel with his ministers. His ministers said: "It is impossible to send a great personage, but we will send a single treasurer's son." And they mentioned Treasurer Wealth-winner, son of Treasurer Ram. The king, hearing their answer, sent him. And the king of Kosala gave him the post of treasurer in the city of Sāketa, seven leagues from Sāvatthi, and provided him with a residence there.

Now there lived at Sāvatthi a treasurer named Migāra, and he had a son named Puṇṇavaddhana Kumāra, who had just reached manhood. Now his father, knowing, "My son has reached manhood; it is time for me to get him married," sent out men who knew both what to do and what not to do, saying: "Seek out a maiden in a family of birth equal to our own." Seeing at Sāvatthi no maiden who pleased them, they went to Sāketa.

Now that day Visākhā, accompanied by five hundred maidens of age equal to her own, went to a certain pool to make holiday. As for those men, after making a tour of the city and seeing no maiden who pleased them, they stood outside of the city-gate. Now at that time the god began to rain. Accordingly those maidens who set out with Visākhā, for fear of getting wet, entered the rest-house. Those men saw among those maidens also none that pleased them. Last of all those maidens, Visākhā, not so much as recking of the rain, drenched though she was, entered the rest-house.

Those men, even when they saw her, thought: "In beauty there may be some other besides even superior to her; but this beauty of hers is like the ripe fruit of a pomegranate-tree which is all one mass of shade. By starting up a conversation and talking with her we shall find out whether her voice is sweet or not." So they said to her: "Dear girl, you act like a woman that has long since reached her maturity." "What do you see that makes you say this, friends?" "The other maidens who are your playfellows, for fear of getting wet, came quickly and entered the rest-house. But you act like an old woman; you do not come with quickened pace; although your robe is wet, you reck not of it. Would you act thus if an elephant or a horse were pursuing you?" "Friends, robes are not hard to get; indeed, in my house, robes are easy to get. But women are like goods offered for sale; if a woman breaks an arm or a leg, people are repelled by her bodily defects and spit upon her. That is why I came slowly."

Thought those men: "Like this maiden is no other maiden in this Land of the Rose-apple. Such as she is in beauty, such is she also in speech. She knows both what to do and what not to do; and as she knows, she talks." And they threw over her head a mass of garlands. Now Visākhā thought: "Before, I was possessed by none other; but now I am possessed by another." Accordingly, in the manner prescribed by the rules of good breeding, she seated herself on the ground. And as she sat there, they drew a curtain around her. When she was fully clothed, she went home, accompanied by her retinue of slave-maidens. Those emissaries of Treasurer Migāra also went right with her to the house of Treasurer Wealth-winner.

"Friends, in what village do you live?" they were asked. "We are emissaries of Treasurer Migāra, who lives in the city of Sāvatthi," they replied. "Our treasurer heard, 'In your house there is a maiden who has reached marriageable age,' and sent us." "Well done, friends! your treasurer may not be our equal in wealth, but he is our equal in birth. A man with all of the qualifications is hard to find! You tell your treasurer that we accept."

Hearing his reply, they went to Sāvatthi and gave joy and delight to the heart of Treasurer Migāra. "Master," said they, "in Sāketa, in the house of Treasurer Wealth-winner, we found a maiden!" Hearing this, Treasurer Migāra was delighted in heart. "In the house of a great personage," thought he, "we have found a maiden!" He immediately sent word to Treasurer Wealth-winner: "We will straightway fetch the maiden; let them do what they should do!" Treasurer Wealth-winner sent back word to him: "This is no hard matter for us; but let the treasurer himself do what he should do!"

Migāra and the king visit Wealth-winner.

Treasurer Migāra went to the king of Kosala and reported: "Sire, I have a wedding-festival in hand. I would fetch hither Visākhā, daughter of Treasurer Wealth-winner, to be the wife of your slave Puṇṇavaddhana. Give me leave to go to Sāketa." "Very well, great treasurer. But ought We too to go?" "Sire, how is it possible to prevail upon personages like yourself to go?" The king, desiring to bestow favor on the son of a great personage, assented, saying: "Let be, great treasurer, I will go." So the king accompanied Treasurer Migāra to the city of Sāketa.

Treasurer Wealth-winner, hearing, "Treasurer Migāra, they say, has arrived with the king of Kosala," went forth to meet the king, and escorted him to his own residence. Forthwith he ordered for Pasenadi Kosala and for the king's force and for Treasurer Migāra both lodgings and requisites,—garlands, perfumes, garments, and the rest. "This, this man must have! this, this woman must have!"—of himself, he knew all. Severally, those people thought: "To us alone the treasurer is doing honor!"

Now one day the king sent a message to Treasurer Wealth-winner: "It is impossible for the treasurer to provide maintenance and support for us for a very long time. Let him appoint a time for the maiden's departure." The treasurer sent a message to the king: "The season of the rains has now arrived. It is impossible for four months to travel. Whatever your army should have, that it will be my duty to provide. Let your majesty depart only at such time as I may send him."

From that time on, the city of Sāketa was like a village engaged in perpetual holiday. Thus three months passed. But the great-creeper parure for the daughter of Treasurer Wealth-winner was not yet completed. Now his foremen came and reported: "As for aught else, nothing is lacking,—but there is not enough firewood to cook food for the army." "Go, friends, take down the elephant-stables and horse-stables and cow-stables and cook food." The firewood they thus obtained and used for cooking lasted only a fortnight. Then they reported again: "Master, there is not enough firewood." "Friends, at this time of year it is impossible to procure firewood; therefore open the storehouse where the cloths are kept, take all the coarse cloths you can find, make wicks of them, soak them in a vessel of oil, and thus cook the food." The firewood they thus obtained and used for cooking lasted four full months.

Wealth-winner gives Visākhā Ten Admonitions.

Then Treasurer Wealth-winner, knowing that his daughter's great-creeper parure was completed, resolved: "To-morrow I will send my daughter." Accordingly, causing his daughter to sit close by, he admonished her, saying: "Dear girl, thus and so must a woman school herself to behave when she lives in her husband's family." That other treasurer, Migāra, also, lying in the chamber immediately adjoining, heard the Admonitions which Treasurer Wealth-winner addressed to his daughter. And these were the Admonitions which Treasurer Wealth-winner addressed to his daughter:

"Dear daughter, so long as you live in the house of your father-in-law, *The indoor fire is not to be carried outside; The outdoor fire is not to be carried inside; Give only to him that gives; Give not to him that gives not; Give both to him that gives and to him that gives not; Sit happily; Eat happily; Sleep happily; Tend the fire; Honor the household divinity.*"

These Ten Admonitions did Treasurer Wealth-winner give to his daughter. On the following day he assembled all the guilds of artisans, and standing in the midst of the king's army, appointed eight householders to be sponsors for his daughter, saying to them: "If to my daughter, in the place to which she is going, any fault is charged, you are to clear her of the charge."

Wealth-winner sends Visākhā away.

Then he caused his daughter to be adorned with her great-creeper parure which cost nine crores of treasure, and gave her fifty-four cartloads of treasure to buy aromatic powders for the bath, five hundred slave-maidens to accompany her always, five hundred chariots drawn by thoroughbreds, of all manner of presents a hundred each; and having so done, dismissed the king of Kosala and Treasurer Migāra.

When it was time for his daughter to go, he summoned the men who had charge of the cattle-pens and said to them: "Friends, in the place to which my daughter is going, she will need milch-cows to provide her with milk to drink, and bulls to yoke to her conveyances. Therefore open the gates of the cattle-pen on the road which my daughter takes, allow a space eight leagues in width to become filled with a multitude of cattle,—three-quarters of a league distant there is such-and-such a cave,—when the herd of cattle reaches that point, give a signal on a drum and close the gates of the cattle-pen." "Very well," said they, promising to do as the treasurer said. And so they did. When the gates were opened, those splendid cattle came out one after another; and even after the gates were closed, through the merit of Visākhā, both the older powerful cattle and the younger untamed cattle leaped over the fence, one after another, and struck into the road.

Visākhā enters Sāvatthi.

Now when Visākhā reached the gate of the city, she thought to herself: "Shall I enter the city sitting in a closed carriage or standing up in a chariot?" Thereupon the following thought occurred to her: "If I enter the city sitting in a closed carriage, the splendor and magnificence of my great-creeper parure will be visible to none." Accordingly she entered the city standing up in a chariot, showing herself to all the city. When the residents of Sāvatthi beheld Visākhā's state, they said: "This, they say, is Visākhā! this beauty and this state become her alone!" Such was the splendid state in which she entered Treasurer Migāra's house. On the very day of her arrival, the residents of the entire city said: "Treasurer Wealth-winner did us high honors when we visited his own city." Therefore they sent presents to Visākhā according to their power and ability. And all the presents which were sent to her, Visākhā distributed among the various families throughout the city.

Visākhā offends Migāra.

Now in the middle of the night Visākhā's thoroughbred mare gave birth to a foal. Visākhā went to the stable with slave-maidens carrying torches, and having gone there, caused the mare to be bathed with hot water and anointed with oil. Having so done, she went back to her own quarters again.

For seven days Treasurer Migāra presided over the festivities in honor of his son's marriage, and during all this time, although the Tathāgata was in residence at a neighboring monastery, he completely ignored him. On the seventh day, having first provided seats, he filled his entire residence with Naked Ascetics, and sent the following message to Visākhā: "Let my daughter come and salute the Saints!"

Now Visākhā had attained the Fruit of Conversion and was one of the Noble Disciples, and was therefore pleased and delighted when she heard the word "Saints." But when she entered the hall where the Naked Ascetics were sitting, and looked at them, she said: "Such as they,—Saints! Why did my father-in-law summon me into the presence of men so utterly lacking sense of modesty and fear of sin? Fie! fie!" Thus reproaching him, she went back to her own quarters again.

When the Naked Ascetics saw Visākhā, they all reproached the treasurer with one accord, saying: "Householder, could you get no other woman? Why did you introduce into your house this disciple of the monk Gotama,—this Jonah of Jonahs? Remove her from this house immediately!" At this the treasurer thought: "It is impossible for me to remove this woman from the house on the mere say-so of these ascetics; this woman is the daughter of a great personage." Accordingly he dismissed the Naked Ascetics, saying: "Teachers, young women are likely to do all sorts of things, whether knowingly or unknowingly. Hold your peace."

The treasurer caused a high couch to be prepared for him, seated himself thereon, took a golden spoon, and waited on by Visākhā, began to eat rich rice porridge flavored with honey out of a golden bowl. At this time a certain monk who was going his round for alms, in the course of his round, came to the door of the treasurer's house. When Visākhā saw him, she thought: "It is not proper for me to announce this monk to my father-in-law." So she stepped aside, that her father-in-law might not see the Elder. But that simpleton, although he saw the Elder, pretended not to see him, and with bowed head kept right on eating rice porridge. Visākhā perceived within herself: "Although my father-in-law sees the Elder, yet he makes no sign." And approaching the Elder, she said: "Pass on, Reverend Sir. My father-in-law is eating stale fare!"

Now up to this time Treasurer Migāra had resisted the importunities of the Naked Ascetics. But the very instant he heard Visākhā say: "My father-in-law is eating stale fare!" he removed his hand from the bowl and said: "Take away this rice porridge and remove this woman from this house! To think that at a time of festivity she should accuse such a man as I am of eating unclean food!" But in this house all the slaves and servants belonged to

Visākhā. Who, therefore, would take hold of her hands and her feet? There was no one who dared even open his mouth!

Visākhā is tried by her sponsors.

Now when Visākhā heard the words of her father-in-law, she said: "Dear father-in-law, this is no sufficient reason why I should leave your house. It is not as if I were a common wench brought hither by you from some bathing-place on the river. Daughters who have mothers and fathers living do not leave the house of their father-in-law for any such reason as this. Indeed, for this very reason, when I set out to come hither, my father summoned eight householders and placed me in their hands, saying: 'If against my daughter any fault is charged, you are to clear her of the charge.' Send, therefore, for my sponsors and let them clear me of the charge."

"What she says is right," said the treasurer. Accordingly he summoned the eight householders and said to them: "This young woman, even before the seventh day was over, said of me as I was sitting in the house of festivity: 'My father is eating unclean food!' " "Is what he says true, dear girl?"

"Dear friends, it is of course true that my father did desire to eat unclean food. But I did not say that he had so done. The facts are these: A certain Elder on his round for alms stopped at the door of the house. My father-in-law here was eating rich rice porridge and did not notice him. For that reason I said to the Elder: 'Pass on, Reverend Sir. My father-in-law in his present state of existence is storing up no new merit, but is consuming old merit.' That is all I said." "Noble sir, here is no fault. Our daughter talks reason. Why do you get angry?"

"Noble sirs, granted that there is no fault to be found with her for that! But on the very day she came, without so much as making a sign to my son, she went where she pleased." "Is what he says true, dear girl?" "Dear friends, I did not go where I pleased. The facts are these: My thoroughbred mare had given birth to a foal in the stable attached to this house. I thought to myself: 'It is not right that I should sit here and make no sign.' So I ordered my slaves to procure torches, and accompanied by my slaves, both male and female, I went to the stable and saw to it that proper care was given to the mare." "Noble sir, our daughter does work in your house which is not fit even for female slaves to do. What fault do you find in this?"

Interpretation of the Ten Admonitions.

"Noble sirs, let it be granted that this was to her credit. But on the day when she came hither, her father gave her certain admonitions. *The indoor fire is not to be carried outside,* said he. But could we live without giving fire to the neighbors who live on both sides of us?" "Is what he says true, dear girl?" "Dear friends, my father was not speaking with reference to that fire. What he meant was this: If your mother-in-law or other female members of the household engage in private conversation within the house, their conversation is not to be communicated to slaves, whether female or male; for such conversation becomes gossiped about and leads to quarrels. It was with reference to that that my father spoke, friends."

"Noble sirs, let this be as it may. But her father said to her: *The outdoor fire is not to be carried inside.* When the fire in the house is extinguished, what else can we do than to bring fire in from without?" "Is what he says true, dear girl?" "Dear friends, my father was not speaking with reference to that fire. What he meant was this: The conversation of slaves and servants is not to be communicated to persons within the household; for such conversation becomes gossiped about and leads to quarrels. It was with reference to that that my father spoke, dear friends."

Thus she was found free from fault in this matter, and as in this so also in the others. And this is the true meaning of the remaining admonitions: *Give only to him that gives* means that one should give only to those that return borrowed articles. *Give not to him that gives not* means that one should not give to those who do not return borrowed articles. *Give both to him that gives and to him that gives not* means that when poor kinsfolk and friends seek assistance, one should give to them, whether or not they are able to repay.

Sit happily means that when a wife sees her mother-in-law or her father-in-law, she should stand and not remain sitting. *Eat happily* means that a wife should not eat before her mother-in-law and her father-in-law and her husband have eaten. She should serve them first, and when she is sure that they have had all they care for, then and not until then may she herself eat. *Sleep happily* means that a wife should not go to bed before her mother-in-law and her father-in-law and her husband. She should first perform the major and minor duties which she owes them, and when she has so done, then she may herself lie down to sleep. *Tend the fire* means that a wife should regard her mother-in-law and her father-in-law and her husband as a flame of fire or as a serpent-king.

"Granted that all these things are to her credit. But her father bade her *reverence the household divinity.* What is the meaning of that?" "Is what he says true, dear girl?" "Yes, dear friends, my father said that also. But this is what he meant: 'Dear girl, when a monk, after keeping residence in a remote lodging, comes to the door of your house, and you see him, you must first give to such monks of whatever food there is in the house, both hard and soft; only after you have so done, may you yourself eat.'" Then said those sponsors to the treasurer: "But you, great treasurer, when you see monks, are satisfied to give them nothing at all. Is not that so?" The treasurer, seeing no other answer to make, sat with bowed head.

Then the householders asked him: "Treasurer, is there any other fault in our daughter?" "Noble sirs, there is not." "But why, if she is without fault, do you seek without cause to remove her from your house?" At this moment Visākhā said: "At first, of course, it would not have been proper for me to leave at the command of my father-in-law. But on the day when I came hither my father entrusted me to your care and placed me in your hands, to determine my guilt or my innocence. Now it is my pleasure to go." And she gave orders to her slaves both female and male: "Make ready my carriages and other conveyances."

Visākhā as almsgiver.

Thereupon the treasurer detained those householders and said to Visākhā: "Dear daughter-in-law, it was through ignorance that I spoke. Pardon me." "Dear father-in-law, I pardon you freely so far as in me lies. But I am the daughter of a house which has firm faith in the Religion of the Buddha, and we cannot exist without the Congregation of Monks. If I may be permitted to minister to the Congregation of Monks according to my inclination, I will remain." "Dear daughter-in-law, you may minister to your monks to your heart's content."

Visākhā caused an invitation to be sent to the Possessor of the Ten Forces, and on the following day, having first caused seats to be prepared, filled the house with the Congregation of Monks presided over by the Buddha. The Naked Ascetics also, hearing that the Teacher had gone to Treasurer Migāra's house, went there and seated themselves in a circle about the house. Visākhā gave Water of Donation, and sent the following message to her father-in-law: "The feast is all ready. Let my father-in-law come and wait upon the Possessor of the Ten Forces."

Treasurer Migāra listened to the words of the Naked Ascetics and said: "Let my daughter wait upon the Supremely Enlightened One." Visākhā served the Possessor of the Ten Forces with food flavored with all manner of choice flavors, and when the meal was over, again sent word: "Let my father-in-law come and hear the Possessor of the Ten Forces preach the Doctrine." Thought the treasurer: "Now it would be quite unjustifiable for me not to go;" and because of his desire to hear the Doctrine, set out. The Naked Ascetics said to him: "If you are determined to hear the monk Gotama, sit outside of a curtain and hear him." And preceding him, they drew a curtain around. Treasurer Migāra went and sat outside of the curtain.

Said the Tathāgata: "You may sit beyond a curtain or beyond a wall or beyond a mountain, or you may sit beyond the range of mountains that encircles the earth; I am the Buddha, and can make you hear my voice." And as though laying hold of a mango-tree laden with golden fruit by the trunk and shaking it, he preached the Doctrine. At the conclusion of the discourse the Treasurer was established in the Fruit of Conversion. Raising the curtain, he reverenced the feet of the Teacher with the Five Rests, and saying to Visākhā, "Under the Teacher, you, dear girl, are henceforth my mother," he adopted Visākhā as his own mother. From that time on Visākhā was known as Mother of Migāra.

One day, while a holiday was in progress in the city, Visākhā reflected, "Within the city is no goodness," and accompanied by her slave-maidens, set out to hear the Teacher preach the Doctrine. On the way she reflected, "To go into the presence of the Buddhas proudly dressed is not fitting." So she took off her great-creeper parure and placed it in the hands of a slave-maiden. Then she approached the Teacher, saluted him, and sat down on one side. The Teacher preached the Doctrine. Visākhā, at the conclusion of the discourse, saluted the Possessor of the Ten Forces and set out in the direction of the city.

Now as that female slave walked along, she remembered that she had left somewhere or other the parure she received from her mistress, and turned back for the parure. Thereupon Visākhā asked her: "But where did you leave it?" "In the apartment of the Perfumed Chamber, my lady." "Very well,—go and get it. From the moment it was left in the apartment of the Perfumed Chamber, it has been improper for us to take it back again. Therefore we will do penance by giving it up. But if it be left there, it will be an obstacle to the Noble Monks."

On the following day the Teacher, accompanied by the Congregation of Monks, came to the door of Visākhā's house. Now in her house seats were always ready. Visākhā took the Teacher's bowl, escorted the Teacher into the house, and caused him to sit down on a seat already prepared. When the Teacher had finished his meal, Visākhā brought that parure, laid it at the Teacher's feet, and said: "This, Reverend Sir, I give to you." The Teacher declined to accept it, saying: "Adornment is not permitted to monks." "I know, Reverend Sir; but I will have this appraised and with the money I will have built a Perfumed Chamber as a place of residence for you." Then the Teacher graciously accepted.

Visākhā had the parure appraised, and with the nine crores of treasure it brought caused a Perfumed Chamber to be erected as a place of residence for the Tathāgata in Pubbārāma monastery,—a monastery adorned with a thousand cells. Now in the morning Visākhā's residence was ablaze with yellow robes, a very eddy of the breezes of holy men. As in the house of Anāthapiṇḍika, so also in her house, all the foods were always ready. In the morning she did honor to the Congregation of Monks with worldly gifts; after breakfast, causing both the medicaments and the eight varieties of drinks to be carried with her, she went to the monastery and gave alms to the Congregation of Monks. Afterwards, having heard the Teacher preach the Doctrine, she went home.

Subsequently, when the Teacher assigned the female lay disciples, one after another, to their respective positions of preëminence, he assigned Visākhā Mother of Migāra to the rank of *foremost of almsgivers.*

54. KING KAPPINA AND QUEEN ANOJĀ

Behold the fruit of faith!

Aṅguttara Commentary 193-195.

EVEN before the rebirth of our Teacher, this Kappina obtained a new conception in a frontier district, in a city named Kukkuṭavatī, in the king's household. The rest of the men [who in a previous state of existence had been his companions and had performed works of merit with him] were reborn in that same city in the families of ministers of the king. Prince Kappina on the death of his father raised the royal parasol and became known as King Kappina the Great.

The woman who had been the mistress of his household in the former state of existence in which each had performed works of merit, was reborn in a royal household of birth equal to his own, and became the chief consort of King Kappina the Great. And because her body was of the hue of the anojā flower, she became known as Queen Anojā.

King Kappina the Great was versed in sacred lore and right conduct. He rose very early in the morning and despatched messengers quickly from the four gates, saying: "Where you encounter men who have heard much sacred lore, who retain what sacred lore they have heard, there turn back and bring me word."

Now at that time our Teacher, reborn in the world of men, was in residence near Sāvatthi. At that time traders residing in the city of Sāvatthi, obtaining in Sāvatthi goods confiscated from rebels, went to the city of Kukkuṭavatī. Having put away their goods, they went to the gate of the king's residence, carrying presents in their hands, with the thought in their minds: "We will see the king." "The king has gone to the pleasure-garden." Hearing this, they went to the pleasure-garden, stopped at the gate, and announced themselves to the guard.

When announcement was made to the king, he caused them to be summoned. They handed over their presents, bowed, and stood upright. "Friends, whence come you?" asked he. "From Sāvatthi, your majesty." "I trust that your country is well supplied with food, and that you have a righteous ruler for your king." "Yes, your majesty." "But is there any news at all in your district?" "There is, your majesty. But we cannot tell it with leavings of food in our mouths."

The king caused water to be given them in a golden ewer. They rinsed out their mouths, faced in the direction of the Possessor of the Ten Forces, stretched out their joined hands towards him in an attitude of reverent salutation, and said: "Your majesty, in our district has arisen the Jewel of the Buddha!" The very instant the king heard that word, joy sprang up within him, suffusing his entire body. Then he said: "Friends, do you say 'The Buddha'?" "Your majesty, we say 'The Buddha.'" Three times in this manner did he cause them to say the word. (The word "Buddha" is not to be compassed; it was impossible for him to compass it.)

In that very word reposing faith, he caused them to be given a hundred thousand pieces of money. "What news have you besides?" asked he. "Your majesty, the Jewel of the Doctrine has arisen!" Hearing that word also, in the same manner did he obtain assurance from them three times, and give them another thousand pieces of money besides. Again he asked: "What other news have you?" "The Jewel of the Order, your majesty, has arisen!" Hearing that word also, in the same manner did he obtain assurance from them three times, and give them another thousand pieces of money besides.

Having so done, the king scratched on a palm-leaf a record of his gifts, and despatched them with it, saying: "Friends, go to the queen." When they had gone, he asked his ministers: "Friends, the Buddha has arisen in the world. What do you intend to do?" "Your majesty, what do you desire to do?" "I intend to retire from the world and become a monk." "We also will retire from the world and become monks." They all, with never a look at either house or treasure, retired from the world on the very same horses on which they were mounted.

The dealers went to Queen Anojā and showed her the palm-leaf. She read it and asked: "Friends, the king has given you many pieces of money. What did you do?" "Your majesty, we brought him news which pleased him." "Friends, may we also ask to hear you?" "You may, your majesty. But we cannot speak with leavings of food in our mouths." She caused them to be given water in a golden ewer. They rinsed out their mouths and made announcement to the queen in precisely the same terms as they had made announcement to the king. In her case also, when she heard the words, delight sprang up within her. Just as had the king, so also did the queen, at each several word, obtain assurance from them three times, and each time she received assurance from them, give them three hundred thousand pieces of money, making nine hundred thousand pieces of money in all. Thus the dealers received in all twelve hundred thousand pieces of money.

Then she asked them: "The king,—where is he, friends?" "Your majesty, he has retired from the world with the intention of becoming a monk." Then she dismissed them, saying: "Very well, friends, you may go." Having summoned the wives of the ministers in the retinue of the king, she asked: "Ladies, do you know where your husbands went?" "We know, your majesty. They went with the king to divert themselves in the pleasure-garden." "True, ladies, so they did. But when they got there, they heard: 'The Buddha has arisen; the Doctrine has arisen; the Order has arisen;' and hearing, they resolved: 'We will retire from the world and become monks under the Possessor of the Ten Forces;' and resolving, they departed. What do you intend to do?" "But, your majesty, what do you desire to do?" "I intend to retire from the world and become a nun. The vomit they have vomited I will not put on the tip of my tongue." "If that is the case, we also will retire from the world and become nuns." And causing chariots to be harnessed, they retired from the world.

Now the king, with his thousand ministers, reached the bank of the Ganges. But at this time the Ganges was full. When the king saw this, he said: "The Ganges here is full, and swarms with savage fish. Moreover we have with us no slaves or men to make boats or rafts for us. But of this Teacher the virtues extend from the Avīci Hell beneath to the Peak of Existence above. If this Teacher be the Supremely Enlightened Buddha, may not the tips of the hoofs of these horses be wetted!"

They caused the horses to spring forward on the surface of the water. Of not a single horse was so much as the tip of the hoof wetted. On a king's highway proceeding, as it were, they went to the far shore. Farther on they reached another river. There, was needed no other Act of Truth. By that same Act of Truth, that river also,—half a league in breadth, did they cross over. Then they reached the third river, the mighty river Candabhāgā. That river also, by that same Act of Truth, did they cross over.

Now the Teacher, arising on that day at time of dawn from a Trance of Great Compassion, and surveying the world, saw the following: "To-day Kappina the Great, having renounced a kingdom three hundred leagues in extent, with a retinue of a thousand ministers, will come hither to retire from the world and become a monk under me." And he reflected: "It is proper that We should go forth to meet them."

Accordingly, very early in the morning, having made his toilet, accompanied by the Congregation of Monks, he made his round for alms in Sāvatthi; and when he had returned from his round for alms and had eaten his breakfast, he himself, alone, taking bowl and robe, flew up into the air. Now on Candabhāgā's bank, at a spot facing the landing-place on the river where they crossed, stood a giant banyan tree. There he sat down cross-legged, setting Mindfulness before him, diffusing the six-colored rays of a Buddha.

The king and his thousand ministers, crossing at that landing-place, beheld the rays of a Buddha darting hither and thither, saw the countenance of a Buddha resplendent with the glory of the full moon, and at the mere seeing, said: "This must certainly be the Teacher for whose sake we have retired from the world." And coming to the landing-place, and bowing low all the way from the place where they had seen what they saw, until they reached the Candabhāgā, they saluted the Teacher. The king, grasping the Teacher by the ankles, saluted him, and seated himself on one side, surrounded by his thousand ministers.

The Teacher preached the Doctrine to them. At the conclusion of the discourse every one of them became established in Sainthood, and asked the Teacher for admission to the Order. The

Teacher, knowing, "Because in a previous state of existence these men gave the gift of robes, therefore they have come with robes of their own," stretched forth his arm, whose hue was as the hue of gold, and said: "Come, monks! Well taught is the Doctrine. Lead the Holy Life to the utter extinction of suffering." And this formula sufficed both for the admission and for the full profession of these Venerables as members of the Order. Elders of a hundred years' residence, as it were, they surrounded the Teacher.

Queen Anojā, surrounded by a thousand chariots, reaching the bank of the Ganges and seeing no boat or raft brought for the king, by her own intuition concluded: "The king must have crossed by making an Act of Truth. But this Teacher was reborn not for them alone. If this Teacher be the Supremely Enlightened Buddha, may our chariots not sink into the water!"

She caused the chariots to spring forward on the surface of the water. Of the chariots not even so much as the outer rims of the wheels was wetted. The second river also, the third river also, she crossed by the same Act of Truth. Even in the act of crossing, she saw the Teacher at the foot of the banyan tree.

As for the Teacher, he reflected: "If these women see their own husbands, desire and lust will spring up within them, and will impede their attainment of the Paths and the Fruits. It shall not have the power so to do!" And he so wrought that they saw not each other.

All of those women, on leaving the landing-place, saluted the Possessor of the Ten Forces and sat down. The Teacher preached the Truth to them. At the conclusion of the discourse, all of those women were established in the Fruit of Conversion, and wives and husbands saw each other. The Teacher thought: "Let Uppalavaṇṇā come nigh!" The nun Uppalavaṇṇā approached, made nuns of all those women, and presented them. They then went to the Nuns' Convent. The Teacher took the Congregation of Monks and went through the air to Jetavana.

Now this Elder Kappina the Great, knowing that his own duty had come to a head, living at ease, passing his time in the Bliss of the Attainment of the Fruits, dwelling in the forest, dwelling at the foot of a tree, dwelling in solitude, constantly breathed forth the utterance: "O happiness! O happiness!" The monks began to talk about this, saying: "It is because Elder Kappina remembers the happiness he enjoyed as a king, that he breathes forth this utterance."

They reported the matter to the Tathāgata. Said the Tathāgata: "It is with reference to the Bliss of the Paths, with reference to the Bliss of the Fruits, that my son breathes forth this utterance." So saying, he recited the following stanza found in the Dhammapada:

> He that drinks Truth sleeps happily, with mind serene;
> In Truth made known by holy men, ever delights the wise man.

55. KHEMĀ

Beauty is but skin-deep.

Aṅguttara Commentary 205-206.

KHEMĀ was reborn in the kingdom of Madda, in the city of Sāgalā, in the household of the king. The hue of her body was the yellow of fine gold. But when she grew up, she married King Bimbisāra and went to live in the royal household at Rājagaha. Near Rājagaha, at Veḷuvana, resided the Tathāgata. Thought Khemā: "The Teacher, they say, finds fault with beauty of form." And becoming intoxicated with the intoxication of her beauty of form, fearing, "In my own case also he may find fault with beauty of form," she refrained from going to see the Possessor of the Ten Forces.

Thought the king: "I am the principal supporter of the Teacher. Yet the principal consort of a Noble Disciple like me refrains from going to see the Possessor of the Ten Forces." Accordingly he had court-poets compose songs in praise of Veḷuvana Gardens, and said to them: "Sing them within hearing of Queen Khemā." The queen, hearing the praises of the Gardens, became desirous of going, and asked permission of the king. Said the king: "Go to the Gardens. But unless you see the Teacher, you shall not have the privilege of returning." The queen, making no reply to the king, started out on the road. The king said to the men who acted as her escort: "If the queen, on her way back from the Gardens, sees the Possessor of the Ten Forces,—well and good! If, however, she does not see him, force her to see him by royal authority."

Now that queen, having spent the daytime walking about the Gardens, started to return without so much as having seen the Possessor of the Ten Forces. But the king's men, despite her unwillingness, conducted her to the Teacher. The Teacher, seeing her coming, put forth his magical power and created a single celestial nymph, causing the nymph, as it were, to take a palm-leaf fan and fan him.

Queen Khemā, seeing her, thought: "Alas, my vanity has ruined me! To think that such women as these, the very counterparts of celestial nymphs, stand close beside the Possessor of the Ten Forces! I am not worthy so much as to wait upon these women. In my vanity, for no reason at all, I have permitted evil thoughts to ruin me." Spell-bound, she stood gazing only at that woman.

Now as she gazed, that woman, by command of the Tathāgata, passed from youth to middle age, as it were; and from middle age to old age, as it were; standing there with wrinkled skin, faded hair, and teeth broken and loose. Finally, even as the queen gazed, that woman collapsed and fell to the ground, fan and all.

Then Khemā, as that object, through the accumulation of causes in previous states of existence, came within range of her mental vision, thought thus: "Even a body like this,—so beautiful as this,—comes finally to destruction. My body also will of necessity come to just such an end." Now the instant her thoughts took this turn, the Teacher recited the following stanza found in the Dhammapada:

> They that are reddened with lust follow a stream,
> As a spider a web, made by self.
> Cleaving this, men go forth from the world,
> Free from Craving, renouncing the Pleasures of Sense.

At the conclusion of the stanza, standing just where she had planted her feet, she attained Sainthood together with the [Four] Analytical Powers.

Now a lay person who attains Sainthood must on that very day either pass into Nibbāna or adopt the religious life. So Queen Khemā, knowing the direction her own Aggregates of Life were taking, resolved: "I will ask for myself permission to adopt the religious life." Accordingly she bowed to the Teacher, went to the king's residence, and stood there without so much as saluting the king. The king, even by her manner of acting, knew: "She must have attained the Noble Estate of Sainthood." So he said to her: "O queen, did you go to see the Teacher?" "Great king, the seeing you have seen is the merest trifle. I, however, have seen the Possessor of the Ten Forces and have seen him well! Give me permission to adopt the religious life." "Very well," said the king in assent. He sent her to the Nuns' Convent and had her admitted to the Order. Now because Khemā, even as a lay person, attained Sainthood, she became renowned for her great wisdom. So much for the story.

But subsequently the Teacher, sitting in Jetavana monastery, assigning to the nuns their respective ranks, assigned to the nun Khemā the rank of *foremost of those who possess great wisdom.*

56. NANDĀ

Beauty is but skin-deep.

Aṅguttara Commentary 217-218.

NANDĀ was reborn, even before the rebirth of our Teacher, as the daughter of Mahā Pajāpatī Gotamī. She was also called Beauty-Nandā, Rūpa-Nandā. Later on, because of her surpassing beauty, she became known as Belle-of-the-land, Janapada-Kalyāṇī.

Our Possessor of Ten Forces, having attained Enlightenment, came in due course to Kapila City, made monks of Nanda and Rāhula, and departed. After the great king Suddhodana had passed into Nibbāna, Mahā Pajāpatī Gotamī and Mother of Rāhula retired from the world and became nuns under the Teacher.

From the time when Mahā Pajāpatī Gotamī and Mother of Rāhula retired from the world, Nandā reflected: "What is there for me to do here?" So she went to Mahā Pajāpatī Gotamī and became a nun.

From the day when she retired from the world, she heard it said: "The Teacher finds fault with beauty of form." Therefore she refrained from going to wait upon the Teacher. When the time came for the Teacher to give admonition, she sent another in her place, saying: "Fetch me home the admonition."

The Teacher, knowing that she was intoxicated solely with the intoxication of her own beauty, said: "Let her come all by herself and get her own admonition. No nun is permitted to send any other person in her place."

So Rūpa-Nandā, seeing no other way, much against her will, went to receive admonition. The Teacher, by reason of her conduct, put forth his magical power and created a single woman's form, causing her to take a palm-leaf fan and fan him, as it were. Rūpa-Nandā, seeing that form, thought: "I have refrained from coming here because I have been intoxicated with my own beauty, —and for no reason at all! To think that such women as these walk on terms of intimacy with the Teacher! I have refrained from coming here all this time, not knowing that my own beauty does not come within a fractional part of their beauty!" Spellbound by that very woman, she stood gazing at her. Because of her accumulation of causes in previous states of existence, the Teacher recited to her the following stanza found in the Dhammapada:

> It is a city made of bones, plastered with flesh and blood,
> Where lodge old age and death and pride and deceit.

Also the Sutta:

> Whether walking or standing or sitting or lying,
> Whoever thinks thoughts of evil, of the world,
> A blind path has such a monk entered,
> By confusion is he confounded;
> Unable is such a monk to attain Supreme Enlightenment.
>
> Whoever, walking or standing or sitting or lying,
> Tranquillizes his thoughts,
> Delights in tranquillity of thought,
> Able is such a monk to attain Supreme Enlightenment.

Rūpa-Nandā, concentrating her attention on that very form, set going the mental reflex of Decay and Death and attained Sainthood.

CHAPTER X

PARABLES FROM EARLY SOURCES ON THE DOCTRINE

57. THE SOWER

Like the soil of the earth is the soil of the heart.

Saṁyutta iv. 315-317.

On a certain occasion, while the Exalted One was in residence at Nālandā, he addressed the village headman Asibandhakaputta as follows:

HERE a farmer, a householder, has three fields: one field with good soil, one field with fair soil, one field with poor soil,—a jungle, barren land impregnated with salt, poor land. What think you of this, headman? Suppose that farmer, that householder, wished to sow seed,—where would he sow seed first,—in that field with good soil? or in that field with fair soil? or in that field with poor soil,—that jungle, that barren land impregnated with salt, that poor land?

Reverend Sir, if that farmer, that householder, wished to sow seed, he would first sow seed in that field with good soil; having sown seed there, he would sow seed in that field with fair soil; having sown seed there, he would sow no seed at all in that field with poor soil,—that jungle, that barren land impregnated with salt, that poor land. Why not? "Without fail, I must have feed for my cattle!"

Headman, just like that field with good soil are my monks and nuns. To them I preach the Doctrine, beautiful in its beginning, beautiful in its middle, beautiful in its end, in the spirit and in the letter; I proclaim the Holy Life in all its fulness, in all its purity. Why is this? Because, headman, they abide possessing Me for an island of retirement, Me for a cave of retreat, Me for an armor of defense, Me for a refuge.

Headman, just like that field with fair soil are my lay disciples, both male and female. To them I preach the Doctrine, beautiful in its beginning, beautiful in its middle, beautiful in its end, in the spirit and in the letter; I proclaim the Holy Life in all its fulness, in all its purity. Why is this? Because, headman, they abide possessing Me for an island of retirement, Me for a cave of retreat, Me for an armor of defense, Me for a refuge.

Headman, just like that field with poor soil,—that jungle, that barren land impregnated with salt, that poor land, are the teachers of perverse doctrines opposed to me,—the wandering ascetics, both monks and Brahmans. To them I preach the Doctrine, beautiful in its beginning, beautiful in its middle, beautiful in its end, in the spirit and in the letter; I proclaim the Holy Life in all its fulness, in all its purity. Why is this? "Perhaps, were they to know but a single word, it would be to their welfare and happiness for a long time to come!"

Suppose, headman, a man had three waterpots: one waterpot uncracked, unattractive, not very attractive; one waterpot uncracked, attractive, very attractive; one waterpot cracked, attractive, very attractive. What think you of this, headman? Suppose that man wished to put water into a waterpot,—into which waterpot would he put it first,—into that waterpot which was uncracked, unattractive, not very attractive? or into that waterpot which was uncracked, attractive, very attractive? or into that waterpot which was cracked, attractive, very attractive?

Reverend Sir, if that man wished to put water into a waterpot, he would first put it into that waterpot which was uncracked, unattractive, not very attractive; having put water into that waterpot, he would put water into that waterpot which was uncracked, attractive, very attractive; having put water into that waterpot, he would put no water at all into that third waterpot. Why not? "Without fail, I must have water to wash my utensils!"

Headman, just like that waterpot which is uncracked, unattractive, not very attractive, are my monks and nuns. To them I preach the Doctrine. . . . Headman, just like that waterpot which is uncracked, attractive, very attractive, are my lay disciples, both male and female. To them I preach the Doctrine. . . . Headman, just like that waterpot which is cracked, attractive, very attractive, are the teachers of perverse doctrines opposed to me,—the wandering ascetics, both monks and Brahmans. To them

I preach the Doctrine, beautiful in its beginning, beautiful in its middle, beautiful in its end, in the spirit and in the letter; I proclaim the Holy Life in all its fulness, in all its purity. Why is this? "Perhaps, were they to know but a single word, it would be to their welfare and happiness for a long time to come!"

58. THE BUDDHA AND ĀNANDA

Whoever walks in righteousness, honors the Buddha.

Dīgha ii. 138.

As the Buddha lay on his death-bed, he addressed Venerable Ānanda as follows:

All one mass of blossoms blown, O Ānanda, the twin Sāl-trees, with flowers out of season, besprinkle, bestrew, overspread, the body of the Tathāgata, to the honor of the Tathāgata. Moreover heavenly Mandārava flowers fall from the sky; these besprinkle, bestrew, overspread, the body of the Tathāgata, to the honor of the Tathāgata. Moreover heavenly sandal-powder falls from the sky; this besprinkles, bestrews, overspreads, the body of the Tathāgata, to the honor of the Tathāgata. Moreover heavenly instruments make music in the sky, to the honor of the Tathāgata. Moreover heavenly songs are wafted through the sky, to the honor of the Tathāgata.

But, O Ānanda, not for all this is the Tathāgata revered or reverenced or venerated or honored or esteemed. *For, O Ānanda, whoever, be it monk or nun, be it lay disciple male or female,—whoever always walks according to the Higher and the Lower Law, walks in righteousness, observes the Lower Law,—he reveres, reverences, venerates, honors, the Tathāgata with the highest honor.*

59. THE BUDDHA AND VAKKALI

Whoever sees the Truth, sees Me.
Whoever sees Me, sees the Truth.

Saṁyutta iii. 119-120.

Thus have I heard:

Once upon a time the Exalted One was in residence at Rājagaha, at Veḷuvana, at Kalandakanivāpa.

Now at that time Venerable Vakkali was in residence at the abode of a potter, afflicted with sickness, afflicted with pain, severely ill. And Venerable Vakkali addressed his attendants: "Come you, brethren, approach the Exalted One; having approached, in my name reverence with the head the feet of the Exalted One, saying: 'Reverend Sir, the monk Vakkali is afflicted with sickness, afflicted with pain, severely ill; he reverences with the head the feet of the Exalted One.' And say this further: 'It were well, Reverend Sir,' says he, 'were the Exalted One, out of compassion, to approach the monk Vakkali.' "

"Yes, brother," said those monks to Venerable Vakkali. And in obedience to his command they approached the Exalted One. And having approached, they saluted the Exalted One and sat down on one side. And sitting there on one side, those monks said this to the Exalted One: "Reverend Sir, the monk Vakkali is afflicted with sickness, afflicted with pain, severely ill; he reverences with the head the feet of the Exalted One. And he commands us to say this further: 'It were well, Reverend Sir,' says he, 'were the Exalted One, out of compassion, to approach the monk Vakkali.' "

The Exalted One gave consent by remaining silent.

Now the Exalted One put on under-garment, took bowl and robe, and approached Venerable Vakkali. Venerable Vakkali saw the Exalted One approaching from afar. Seeing, he quaked in his bed. Now the Exalted One said this to Venerable Vakkali: "Enough, Vakkali! Quake not in your bed! Seats are at hand, already prepared; there will I sit down." The Exalted One sat down on a seat already prepared. Having sat down, the Exalted One said this to Venerable Vakkali:

"I trust, Vakkali, that life is endurable, that you can support life. I trust that sensations of pain are retreating, not attacking; that a retreat for good and all is apparent, no attack."

"Not for me, Reverend Sir, is life endurable; I cannot support life. Severe sensations of pain attack me, do not retreat; an attack for good and all is apparent, no retreat."

"I trust, Vakkali, that you entertain no restlessness at all, no querulousness at all."

"On the contrary, Reverend Sir, I entertain no little restlessness, no little querulousness."

"I trust, Vakkali, that in your case the Self has no fault to find with Morality."

"No indeed, Reverend Sir, in my case the Self has no fault to find with Morality."

"If in your case, Vakkali, as you say, the Self has no fault to find with Morality, then why this restlessness of yours? why this querulousness of yours?"

"For a long time, Reverend Sir, I have desired to approach the Exalted One to look upon him; but I have not sufficient strength in my body to approach the Exalted One to look upon him."

"Enough, Vakkali! What is the use of your looking upon this foul body? *Whoever, Vakkali, sees the Truth, sees Me. Whoever sees Me, sees the Truth. For, Vakkali, seeing the Truth, one sees Me; seeing Me, one sees the Truth.*"

60. THE BUDDHA AND THE SICK MAN

He that would wait upon Me, let him wait upon the sick.

Vinaya i. 301-302.

But at that time a certain monk was sick with a disorder of the bowels, and lay sprawling in his own urine and dung. Now the Exalted One, with Venerable Ānanda as attendant monk, wandering from place to place in search of lodging, approached the dwelling-place of that monk. The Exalted One saw that monk lying sprawling in his own urine and dung. Seeing, he approached that monk, and having approached, said this to that monk: "Monk, what ails you?" "Disorder of the bowels, Exalted One." "But have you a monk to wait upon you?" "I have not, Exalted One." "Why do not the monks wait upon you?" "I, Reverend Sir, am of no use to the monks; therefore the monks do not wait upon me."

Then the Exalted One addressed Venerable Ānanda: "Go, Ānanda, fetch water; we will bathe this monk." "Very well," said Venerable Ānanda to the Exalted One, and in obedience to his command fetched water. The Exalted One poured the water; Venerable Ānanda bathed the man. The Exalted One grasped him by the head; Venerable Ānanda lifted him by the feet; they laid him on a bed.

Then the Exalted One, employing this incident as the source, as the subject, of a lesson, convoked the Assembly of Monks and asked the monks one question after another:

"Monks, is there a sick monk in yonder dwelling-place?" "There is, Exalted One."

"Monks, what ails that monk?" "That monk, Reverend Sir, is sick with a disorder of the bowels."

"But, monks, has that monk anyone to wait upon him?" "He has not, Exalted One."

"Why do not the monks wait upon him?" "That monk, Reverend Sir, is of no use to the monks; therefore the monks do not wait upon him."

"Monks, you have no mother, you have no father, to wait upon you. If you, monks, will not wait upon each other, then who, pray, will wait upon you? *Monks, he that would wait upon Me, let him wait upon the sick.*"

61. THE SNAKE

Grasp the Scriptures aright.

Majjhima i. 133-134.

"Grasped wrongly," said the Buddha on a certain occasion, "the Scriptures conduce to hurt and harm."

It is precisely as if a man, wanting a water-snake, hunting a water-snake, searching for a water-snake, were to see a big water-snake and were to grasp it by the body or by the tail, and that water-snake were to turn on him and were to bite him on the hand or on the arm or on some other major or minor member of the body, and as a result of this he were to incur death or mortal pain. And why? Because he wrongly grasped the water-snake.

"Precisely so," said the Buddha, "the Scriptures, wrongly grasped, conduce to hurt and harm."

"On the other hand," said the Buddha, "the Scriptures, rightly grasped, conduce to weal and welfare."

It is precisely as if a man, wanting a water-snake, hunting a water-snake, searching for a water-snake, were to see a big water-snake, and with a goat's foot, with a stick, were to hold it down, were to hold it down firmly; and with the goat's foot, with the stick, holding it down, holding it down firmly, were to grasp it by the neck, were to grasp it firmly;—no matter how much that water-snake were to wrap its coils about that man's hand or arm or other major or minor member of his body, nevertheless, as a result of that man's firm grasp, he would incur neither death nor mortal pain. And why? Because he rightly grasped the water-snake.

"Precisely so," said the Buddha, "the Scriptures, rightly grasped, conduce to weal and welfare."

62. WALKING ON THE WATER

Behold the fruit of faith!

Jātaka 190: ii. 111-113.

A. Story of the Present.

Behold the fruit of faith! This parable was related by the Teacher while he was in residence at Jetavana monastery with reference to a certain lay disciple possessed of faith.

THIS Noble Disciple, we are told, possessed of faith and serenity of mind, set out one day for Jetavana monastery. At eventide he reached the bank of the river Aciravatī, after the boatman had beached his boat and gone to hear the preaching of the Doctrine.

Not seeing a boat, he had recourse to the Practice of Meditation, concentrated his thoughts on the Buddha, attained the Ecstasy of Joy, and descended into the river. His feet did not sink in the water. He walked along as though he were walking on the surface of the land until he came to mid-stream. Then he saw waves. Then the Ecstasy of Joy, the result of the concentration of his thoughts on the Buddha, became weak. Then his feet began to sink. But he concentrated his thoughts anew on the Buddha, strengthened the Ecstasy of Joy, walked on the surface of the water as before, entered Jetavana monastery, bowed to the Teacher, and sat down on one side.

The Teacher exchanged greetings with him, and asked: "Lay disciple, I trust that as you came hither, you came hither without weariness." "Reverend Sir, I had recourse to the Practice of Meditation, concentrated my thoughts on the Buddha, attained the

Ecstasy of Joy, obtained support on the surface of the water, and came hither as though I were treading the earth."

Said the Teacher: "But, lay disciple, you are not the only one who has obtained support by meditating on the Merits of the Buddha. In former times also, lay disciples who were shipwrecked in mid-ocean meditated on the Merits of the Buddha, and thus obtained support." Then, in response to the layman's request, he related the following

B. Story of the Past.

In times past, in the dispensation of the Buddha Kassapa, a Noble Disciple who had attained the Fruit of Conversion, put to sea in a boat with a householder, a barber. The barber's wife put him in the hands of that lay disciple with the injunction: "Noble Sir, you are to care for him, for better, for worse."

Now on the seventh day that boat suffered shipwreck in mid-ocean. Those two persons, lying on a single plank, reached a certain little island. There that barber killed some birds and cooked and ate them, and gave some also to the lay disciple.

"None for me!" said the lay disciple, refusing to eat them. Thought he: "In this place there is no support for us except the Three Refuges: the Buddha, the Doctrine, and the Order of Monks."

Accordingly he began to meditate on the Merits of the Three Jewels. As he meditated and meditated on the Merits of the Three Jewels, a dragon-king reborn on that little island, formed and created out of his own body a great ship. A sea-spirit was pilot. The ship was filled with the seven kinds of jewels. The three masts were of sapphire, the anchor of gold, the ropes of silver, the planks of gold.

The sea-spirit, standing on the ship, called out: "Any passengers for the Land of the Rose-apple?" Said the lay disciple: "We are going!" "Well then, come along! get on board ship!" The lay disciple embarked on the ship, and called to the barber. Said the sea-spirit: "You alone may come,—that fellow may not!" "Why not?" "That fellow does not walk in the moral virtues,—that is why. I brought this ship for you,—not for that fellow." "Never mind! I give to him the fruit of the merit which I have acquired by the alms which I have given, by the moral precepts which I have kept, by the supernatural powers which I have developed by the Practice of Meditation." Said the barber: "I thank you, master." Said the spirit: "Now I will take him!"

And him the spirit took on board. And departing from the ocean with those two persons, the spirit went by river to Benāres. And by his own supernatural power having stored wealth in the house of those very two, he addressed them as follows: "Only with the wise should one associate. For had this barber not associated with this lay disciple, he would have perished right there in mid-ocean." And extolling the advantages of association with the wise, he pronounced the following stanzas:

Behold the fruit of faith and goodness and generosity!
As 'twere a ship, a dragon bears a layman who has faith!

With good men only should ye sit, with good men only friendly be!
For through association with the good, the barber goes to safety!

Thus the sea-spirit, poised in mid-air, preached the Doctrine by way of admonition. Then, taking the king of the dragons along, he went back again to his own abode.

The Teacher, having related this parable, proclaimed the Truths, and interpreted the Birth-Story: (At the conclusion of the Truths, the lay disciple was established in the Fruit of the Second Path.)

"At that time the lay disciple who had attained the Fruit of Conversion passed to Nibbāna; the king of the dragons was Sāriputta. The sea-spirit was I myself."

63. THE BEGINNINGLESS ROUND OF EXISTENCES.

Uproot Craving, the Eye of Existence.

Synopsis of Saṁyutta 15: ii. 178-193.

Thus have I heard: Once upon a time the Exalted One was in residence at Sāvatthi, at Jetavana, in Jīvaka's Mango Grove. At that time the Exalted One addressed the monks: "Monks!" "Reverend Sir!" replied those monks to the Exalted One. The Exalted One said this:

Without conceivable beginning, monks, is this Round of Existences. Unknown is a starting-point in the past of beings impeded by the Impediment of Ignorance, fettered by the Fetter of Craving, hasting, hurrying, from birth to birth. The ancestors of a man are more numerous than all the blades of grass and sticks and branches and leaves in India; more numerous than all the particles of dust that compose the earth. The tears shed, the mother's milk drunk by a man in his previous states of existence, are more abundant than all the water contained in the four great oceans.

How long is a cycle of time?—Longer than would be required for a range of mountains a league in length, a league in breadth, a league in height, of solid rock, without a cleft, without a crack, to waste and wear away, were it to be wiped once in a century with a silken cloth; longer than would be required for a heap of mustard-seed of the same dimensions to disappear, were but a single seed to be removed once in a century. Of cycles of time as long as this, there have elapsed many hundreds of cycles, many thousands of cycles, many hundreds of thousands of cycles. Indeed, it is impossible to count them in terms of cycles or hundreds of cycles or thousands of cycles or hundreds of thousands of cycles. For example, were each of four centenarians to call to mind a hundred thousand cycles of time every day of his life, all four would die or ever they could count them all.

The cycles of time that have elapsed are more numerous than all the sands that lie between the source and the mouth of the Ganges. The bones left by a single individual in his passage from birth to birth during a single cycle of time would form a pile so huge that were all the mountains of Vepulla-range to be gathered up and piled in a heap, that heap of mountains would appear as naught beside it. The head of every man has been cut off so many times in his previous states of existence, either as a human being or as an animal, as to cause him to shed blood more abundant than all the water contained in the four great oceans. For so long a time as this, you have endured suffering, you have endured agony, you have endured calamity. In view of this, you have every reason to feel disgust and aversion for all existing things and to free yourselves from them.

Thus spoke the Exalted One. When he, the Happy One, had thus spoken, he, the Teacher, spoke thus further:

Impermanent are all existing things:
Birth and decay inhere therein;
They come to exist and cease to exist;
It is well when they have ceased to exist.

64. THE RELAYS

The religious life is only a means to an end.

Majjhima 24: i. 147-148.

On a certain occasion Venerable Sāriputta said this to Venerable Mantāṇiputta:

"Is the religious life lived under our Exalted One?" "Yes."

"Is the religious life lived under the Exalted One for the sake of purity of conduct?" "No indeed."

"Is the religious life lived under the Exalted One for the sake of purity of heart?" "No indeed."

"Is the religious life lived under the Exalted One for the sake of purity of belief?" "No indeed."

"Is the religious life lived under the Exalted One for the sake of purity of certitude?" "No indeed."

"Is the religious life lived under the Exalted One for the sake of purity of insight through knowledge of what is the Way and what is not the Way?" "No indeed."

"Is the religious life lived under the Exalted One for the sake of purity of insight through knowledge of the Path?" "No indeed."

"Is the religious life lived under the Exalted One for the sake of purity of insight through knowledge?" "No indeed."

"Brother, when I ask you: 'Is the religious life lived under the Exalted One for the sake of purity of conduct?—for the sake of purity of heart?—for the sake of purity of belief?—for the sake of purity of certitude?—for the sake of purity of insight through knowledge of what is the Way and what is not the Way?—for the sake of purity of insight through knowledge of the Path?—for the sake of purity of insight through knowedge?'—you say: 'No indeed.' For the sake of what, pray, *is* the religious life lived under the Exalted One?"

"Brother, the religious life is lived under the Exalted One that we may, through detachment from the things of earth and heaven, attain Supreme Nibbāna."

"Is purity of conduct detachment,—Supreme Nibbāna?" "No indeed."

"Is purity of heart detachment,—Supreme Nibbāna?" "No indeed."

"Is purity of belief detachment,—Supreme Nibbāna?" "No indeed."

"Is purity of certitude detachment,—Supreme Nibbāna?" "No indeed."

"Is purity of insight through knowledge of what is the Way and what is not the Way, detachment,—Supreme Nibbāna?" "No indeed."

"Is purity of insight through knowledge of the Path, detachment,—Supreme Nibbāna?" "No indeed."

"Is purity of insight through knowledge, detachment,—Supreme Nibbāna?" "No indeed."

"Then is some state other than these detachment,—Supreme Nibbāna?" "No indeed."

"Brother, when I ask you: 'Does detachment,—Supreme Nibbāna, consist of purity of conduct?—of purity of heart?—of purity of belief?—of purity of certitude?—of purity of insight through knowledge of what is the Way and what is not the Way?—of purity of insight through knowledge of the Path?—of purity of insight through knowledge?—of some state other than these?'—you say: 'No indeed.' What interpretation, pray, am I to put on your words?"

"Brother, if the Exalted One had taught that Supreme Nibbāna, whose essence is detachment, is purity of conduct,—purity of heart,—purity of belief,—purity of certitude,—purity of insight through knowledge of what is the Way and what is not the Way,—purity of insight through knowledge of the Path,—purity of insight through knowledge,—if, I say, the Exalted One had taught that Supreme Nibbāna, whose essence is *de*tachment, is any one of these, the Exalted One might just as well have taught that the essence of Supreme Nibbāna is *at*tachment. Moreover, if Supreme Nibbāna, whose essence is detachment, were some state other than these, an unconverted person might attain Nibbāna, for an unconverted person is in some state other than these.

"Therefore, brother, I will compose a parable for you. Even by a parable does many a man of understanding here in this world comprehend the meaning of a statement."

Suppose, brother, while King Pasenadi Kosala is residing in Sāvatthi, some business or other of a pressing nature were to come up, requiring his presence in Sāketa, and suppose his men were to place in readiness for him, between Sāvatthi and Sāketa, seven relays of chariots. And, brother, suppose King Pasenadi Kosala were to depart from Sāvatthi, and at the gate of his palace were to mount the first relay of chariots, and in the first relay of chariots were to go as far as the second relay of chariots. He would dismiss the first relay of chariots and mount the second relay of chariots, and in the second relay of chariots would go as far as the third relay of chariots. In this manner he would go until he reached the seventh relay of chariots. When he reached the seventh relay of chariots, he would dismiss the sixth relay of chariots, mount the seventh relay of chariots, and go in the seventh relay of chariots until he reached Sāketa, until he reached the gate of his palace.

And suppose, when he reached the gate of his palace, his friends and companions, his kinsmen and blood-relatives were to ask him this question: "Great king, was it in this chariot that you traveled all of the way from Sāvatthi to Sāketa, all of the way to the gate of your palace?" With what manner of answer, brother, would King Pasenadi Kosala answer, were he to answer correctly? With this manner of answer, brother, would King Pasenadi Kosala answer, were he to answer correctly:

"Lo! while I was residing in Sāvatthi, some business or other of a pressing nature came up, requiring my presence in Sāketa. My men placed in readiness for me, between Sāvatthi and Sāketa, seven relays of chariots. So I departed from Sāvatthi, and at the gate of my palace mounted the first relay of chariots, and in the first relay of chariots came as far as the second relay of chariots. I dismissed the first relay of chariots and mounted the second relay of chariots, and in the second relay of chariots came as far as the third relay of chariots. In this manner came I until I reached the seventh relay of chariots. When I reached the seventh relay of chariots, I dismissed the sixth relay of chariots, mounted the seventh relay of chariots, and came in the seventh relay of chariots until I reached Sāketa, until I reached the gate of my palace."

With this manner of answer, brother, would King Pasenadi Kosala answer, were he to answer correctly.

"Precisely so, brother, purity of conduct leads straight to purity of heart. Purity of heart leads straight to purity of belief. Purity of belief leads straight to purity of certitude. Purity of certitude leads straight to purity of insight through knowledge of what is the Way and what is not the Way. Purity of insight through knowledge of what is the Way and what is not the Way, leads straight to purity of insight through knowledge of the Path. Purity of insight through knowledge of the Path, leads straight to purity of insight through knowledge. Purity of insight through knowledge leads straight to detachment,—Supreme Nibbāna.

"Brother, the religious life is lived under the Exalted One that we may, through detachment from the things of earth and heaven, attain Supreme Nibbāna."

65. THE GREAT OCEAN

The Doctrine tastes only of Deliverance.

Aṅguttara iv. 197-204.

Once upon a time the Exalted One was in residence at Verañjā, at Naḷerupucimaṇḍamūla. Now Pahārāda king of Asuras approached the Exalted One, and having approached, saluted the Exalted One and stood aside. And as Pahārāda king of Asuras stood aside, the Exalted One said this to him: "But, Pahārāda, do the Asuras delight in the Great Ocean?" "Reverend Sir, the Asuras do delight in the Great Ocean." "But, Pahārāda, how many are the wonderful and marvelous properties possessed by the Great Ocean, perceiving which the Asuras delight in the Great Ocean?" "Eight in number, Reverend Sir, are the wonderful and marvelous properties possessed by the Great Ocean, perceiving which the Asuras delight in the Great Ocean. What are the Eight?"

Eight properties of the Great Ocean.

THE Great Ocean, Reverend Sir, lowers gradually, slopes gradually, hollows gradually, and there is no steep declivity. Inasmuch, Reverend Sir, as the Great Ocean lowers gradually, slopes gradually, hollows gradually, and inasmuch as there is no steep declivity, this, Reverend Sir, is the first wonderful and marvelous property possessed by the Great Ocean, perceiving which the Asuras delight in the Great Ocean.

But again further, Reverend Sir, the Great Ocean ever abides steadfast and never overpasses its bounds. This is the second property.

But again further, Reverend Sir, the Great Ocean will not brook association with a dead body. If there be a dead body in the Great Ocean, quickly enough does the Great Ocean wash that dead body up on the shore, cast it up on dry land. This is the third property.

But again further, Reverend Sir, all the Great Rivers, to wit, Gaṅgā, Yamunā, Aciravatī, Sarabhū, Mahī, on reaching the Great Ocean, renounce their former personal and family names, and are called "The Great Ocean." This is the fourth property.

But again further, Reverend Sir, although all the streams that are in the world flow into the Great Ocean, and all the showers that are in the atmosphere fall into it, not therefore does the

Great Ocean appcar to be either diminished or replenished. This is the fifth property.

But again further, Reverend Sir, the Great Ocean has but one taste, the taste of salt. This is the sixth property.

But again further, Reverend Sir, the Great Ocean contains many jewels, numerous jewels; therein are these jewels, to wit: pearls, gems, lapis lazuli, conch, rock, coral, silver, gold, rubies, cat's eye. This is the seventh property.

But again further, Reverend Sir, the Great Ocean is the abode of mighty beings; therein dwell the following beings: Timitimiñgalas, Timiramiñgalas, Asuras, Nāgas, Gandhabbas; there are in the Great Ocean monsters a hundred leagues in measure, monsters two hundred leagues in measure, monsters three hundred leagues in measure, monsters four hundred leagues in measure, monsters five hundred leagues in measure. Inasmuch, Reverend Sir, as the Great Ocean is the abode of mighty beings; inasmuch as therein dwell the following beings: Timitimiñgalas, Timiramiñgalas, Asuras, Nāgas, Gandhabbas; inasmuch as there are in the Great Ocean monsters a hundred leagues in measure, monsters two hundred leagues in measure, monsters three hundred leagues in measure, monsters four hundred leagues in measure, monsters five hundred leagues in measure, this, Reverend Sir, is the eighth wonderful and marvelous property possessed by the Great Ocean, perceiving which the Asuras delight in the Great Ocean.

"These, Reverend Sir, are the eight wonderful and marvelous properties possessed by the Great Ocean, perceiving which the Asuras delight in the Great Ocean."

"But, Reverend Sir, do the monks delight in this Doctrine and Discipline?"

"Pahārāda, the monks do delight in this Doctrine and Discipline."

"But, Reverend Sir, how many are the wonderful and marvelous properties possessed by this Doctrine and Discipline, perceiving which the monks delight in this Doctrine and Discipline?"

"Eight in number, Pahārāda, are the wonderful and marvelous properties possessed by this Doctrine and Discipline, perceiving which the monks delight in this Doctrine and Discipline. What are the Eight?"

Eight properties of the Doctrine and Discipline.

Just as the Great Ocean lowers gradually, slopes gradually, hollows gradually, and there is no steep declivity, so also in this

Doctrine and Discipline the training is graduated, the labor is graduated, the Path is graduated, and there is no sudden attainment of Knowledge. Inasmuch as in this Doctrine and Discipline the training is graduated, the labor is graduated, the Path is graduated, and there is no sudden attainment of Knowledge, this is the first wonderful and marvelous property possessed by this Doctrine and Discipline, perceiving which the monks delight in this Doctrine and Discipline.

Just as the Great Ocean ever abides steadfast and never overpasses its bounds, so also my disciples, on their lives, do not transgress the body of precepts which I have enjoined upon them. This is the second property.

Just as the Great Ocean will not brook association with a dead body, but, if there be a dead body in the Great Ocean, the Great Ocean quickly enough washes that dead body up on the shore, casts it up on dry land, so also, if there be an individual who is immoral, of bad character, of impure and doubtful conduct, of hidden deeds,—not really a monk, although he may have taken the monastic vows,—not really chaste, although he may have taken the vow of chastity,—foul within, lustful,—a worthless fellow, the Order will not brook association with him, but quickly enough assembles and casts him out. And even if that monk be seated in the midst of the Order of Monks, yet, for all that, he is far indeed from the Order, and the Order from him. This is the third property.

Just as all the Great Rivers, to wit, Gaṅgā, Yamunā, Aciravatī, Sarabhū, Mahī, on reaching the Great Ocean, renounce their former personal and family names, and are called "The Great Ocean," so also these four castes, to wit, Khattiyas, Brāhmaṇas, Vessas, Suddas, on going forth from the house-life to the houseless life under the Doctrine and Discipline proclaimed by the Tathāgata, renounce their former personal and family names, and are called "Sons of the Sakya Prince." This is the fourth property.

Just as, although all the streams that are in the world flow into the Great Ocean, and all the showers that are in the atmosphere fall into it, not therefore does the Great Ocean appear to be either diminished or replenished, so also, although many monks pass to Supreme Nibbāna, to that form of Nibbāna in which no traces of the Elements of Being remain, not therefore does that form of

Nibbāna in which no traces of the Elements of Being remain appear to be either diminished or replenished. This is the fifth property.

Just as the Great Ocean has but one taste, the taste of salt, so also this Doctrine and Discipline has but one taste, the taste of Deliverance. This is the sixth property.

Just as the Great Ocean contains many jewels, numerous jewels; just as therein are these jewels, to wit: pearls, gems, lapis lazuli, conch, rock, coral, silver, gold, rubies, cat's eye, so also this Doctrine and Discipline contains many jewels, numerous jewels; therein are these jewels, to wit: the Four Intent Contemplations, the Four Right Exertions, the Four Means of Attaining Magical Power, the Five Moral Senses, the Five Powers, the Seven Requisites for Attaining Supreme Knowledge, the Noble Eightfold Path. This is the seventh property.

Just as the Great Ocean is the abode of mighty beings; just as therein dwell the following beings: Timitimiñgalas, Timiramiñgalas, Asuras, Nāgas, Gandhabbas; just as there are in the Great Ocean monsters a hundred leagues in measure, monsters two hundred leagues in measure, monsters three hundred leagues in measure, monsters four hundred leagues in measure, monsters five hundred leagues in measure, so also this Doctrine and Discipline is the abode of mighty beings; therein are the following beings: He-who-has-entered-the-stream, he who has entered the Path of Conversion, he who has entered the Path that leads to the realization of the Fruit of Conversion; He-who-will-be-reborn-but-once, he who has entered the Path that leads to the realization of the Fruit of One-who-will-be-reborn-but-once; He-who-will-be-reborn-no-more, he who has entered the Path that leads to the realization of the Fruit of One-who-will-be-reborn-no-more; the Saint, he who has entered upon Sainthood.

Inasmuch as this Doctrine and Discipline is the abode of mighty beings; inasmuch as therein are the following beings: He-who-has-entered-the-stream, he who has entered the Path of Conversion, he who has entered the Path that leads to the realization of the Fruit of Conversion; He-who-will-be-reborn-but-once, he who has entered the Path that leads to the realization of the Fruit of One-who-will-be-reborn-but-once; He-who-will-be-reborn-no-more, he who has entered the Path that leads to the realization of the Fruit of One-who-will-be-reborn-no-more; the Saint, he who has entered upon Sainthood, this is the eighth wonderful and marvelous property possessed by this Doctrine and Discipline, perceiving which the monks delight in this Doctrine and Discipline.

"These are the eight wonderful and marvelous properties possessed by this Doctrine and Discipline, perceiving which the monks delight in this Doctrine and Discipline."

66. THE BUDDHA AND THE HERDSMAN DHANIYA

So if thou wilt, rain, O god!

Sutta Nipāta No. 2.

Herdsman: Boiled is my rice, milked are my cows,
Along the bank of the river Grand I dwell with equals;
Covered my hut, kindled my fire:
So if thou wilt, rain, O god!

Buddha: Free from anger, free from stubbornness am I,
Along the bank of the river Grand I dwell for a single night;
Uncovered my hut, extinguished my fire:
So if thou wilt, rain, O god!

Herdsman: Fireflies and mosquitoes are non-existent;
In marshy land overgrown with grass my cattle roam;
Even should rain come, they could stand it:
So if thou wilt, rain, O god!

Buddha: I have fashioned a swimming-girdle of twisted grass;
It was put together with care.
I have crossed and gone to the farther shore,
Having overcome the flood.
I need the girdle no more:
So if thou wilt, rain, O god!

Herdsman: My wife is obedient, not wanton;
Long has she lived with me; she is dear to my heart;
I hear no evil at all of her:
So if thou wilt, rain, O god!

Buddha: My thoughts are obedient, completely delivered,
In the course of a long period of time
Developed to perfection, well-tamed;
Moreover evil is not found in me:
So if thou wilt, rain, O god!

Herdsman: On my earnings I support myself,
And my children are healthy, one and all;
I hear no evil at all of them:
So if thou wilt, rain, O god!

Buddha: I am nobody's hireling;
With what I have acquired I go all over the world;
I need no hire:
So if thou wilt, rain, O god!

Herdsman: I have cows, I have calves,
I have also young cows for breeding,
And I also have a bull for lord of the herd:
So if thou wilt, rain, O god!

Buddha: I have no cows, I have no calves,
Nor have I young cows for breeding,
Nor have I here a bull for lord of the herd:
So if thou wilt, rain, O god!

Herdsman: The stakes are driven in, unshakable;
The ropes of muñja-grass are new, in good condition;
Not even calves will be able to burst them:
So if thou wilt, rain, O god!

Buddha: Like a bull I have burst the Bonds,
As an elephant sunders a galoci-creeper;
I shall not again enter the couch of the womb:
So if thou wilt, rain, O god!

Filling both marshy land and dry,
A mighty cloud rained down straightway.
Hearing the god raining,
Dhaniya spoke these words:

Herdsman: It is indeed our very great privilege
To have seen the Exalted One;
We come to thee for Refuge, O Far-seeing One!
Be thou our Teacher, O Mighty Sage!

Both my wife and I will be obedient,
We will live the Holy Life under the Happy One,
We will go to the farther shore of Birth and Death,
We will make an end of Suffering.

Evil One: He that has sons rejoices in sons,
The cowherd likewise rejoices in cows,
For increase is the joy of a man,
Nor does he rejoice who is without increase.

Buddha: He that has sons rejoices in sons,
The cowherd likewise rejoices in cows,
For increase is the sorrow of a man,
Nor does he sorrow who is without increase.

67. THE AXE IN THE MOUTH

Every man is born with an axe in his mouth.

Sutta Nipāta No. 36.

On a certain occasion a monk named Kokāliya reviled the two Chief Disciples, and in consequence of that evil deed, died of a loathsome disease and was reborn in Hell. On that occasion the Buddha preached the Doctrine, concluding as follows:

For when a human being is born,
An axe is born in his mouth
Wherewith he cuts himself,—the fool!
By speaking evil words.

He that praises the blameworthy
Or blames the praiseworthy,
Accumulates an ace in his mouth
Whereby he gets no happiness.

The merest trifle is that ace
Which costs a man his wealth at dice;
But this is a bigger ace by far:
Corrupting men's minds against the Buddhas.

He who tells what never happened, goes to Hell;
And also he who, having done, declares: "I did it not."
They both are equal after death,
In the world beyond,—men of base deeds!

He that offends against the offenseless,
Against the man that is free from impurity, free from lust,
Unto that very fool returns that evil deed again,
Like fine dust tossed against the wind.

He that is given to the vice of cupidity,
Will revile others in his speech;
He will be faithless, miserly, ungenerous,
Niggardly, given to backbiting.

O thou foul-mouthed, false, ignoble fellow!
Destroyer of increase! wicked fellow!
Lowest of men! ace! base-born!
Speak not much in this world! thou art a denizen of Hell!

Thou dost scatter dust to thy hurt;
The good, thou dost reproach,—thou wrongdoer!
Now, forasmuch as many are the evil deeds that thou hast done,
Thou hast gone to Hell to remain for long.

For no man's deeds are ever lost;
They always come straight back to him;
The owner gets his very own.
The foolish wrongdoer, in the next world,
Experiences suffering in his own person.

CHAPTER XI

SIMILES AND SHORT PARABLES FROM THE QUESTIONS OF MILINDA

§1. THERE IS NO PERMANENT INDIVIDUALITY

Milindapañha 25-28.

Now King Milinda approached Venerable Nāgasena. Having approached, he greeted Venerable Nāgasena in a friendly manner. Having completed the usual friendly greetings, he sat down on one side. Venerable Nāgasena returned the compliment, thereby delighting the heart of King Milinda. Then King Milinda said this to Venerable Nāgasena: "How is your Reverence known? what is your name, Reverend Sir?"

"As 'Nāgasena,' great king, am I known; 'Nāgasena,' great king, is what my fellow-religious are accustomed to call me. However, although mothers and fathers give such names as 'Nāgasena' or 'Sūrasena' or 'Vīrasena' or 'Sīhasena,' yet, great king, this 'Nāgasena' is only a conventional epithet, designation, appellation, style,—a mere name. For no 'individual' is thereby assumed to exist."

Then King Milinda spoke as follows: "Give ear to me, you five hundred Greeks and you eighty thousand monks! Nāgasena here speaks as follows: 'For no "individual" is thereby assumed to exist.' Is it reasonable to accept this?"

Then King Milinda said this to Venerable Nāgasena: "If, Reverend Nāgasena, an 'individual' is not assumed to exist, who, pray, gives you the Requisites,—robes, alms, lodging, medicines for the relief of the sick? Who enjoys them? Who keeps the Precepts? Who applies himself to the Practice of Meditation? Who realizes the Paths and the Fruits and Nibbāna? Who kills living beings? Who takes what is not given? Who misconducts himself in the matter of the Pleasures of Sense? Who speaks falsehood? Who drinks intoxicants? Who does the five evil deeds which bring immediate retribution? Ergo,—there is no good, there is no evil; there is no one who either does or causes to be done either good or evil deeds; there is no fruition, no ripening, of good and evil deeds. If, Reverend Nāgasena, he that kills you does not exist, then it is also true that he does not take life; it is also true, Reverend Nāgasena, that you have no teacher, no preceptor, no reception into the Order of Monks.

"Now you say: '"Nāgasena" is what my fellow-religious are accustomed to call me.' What is this 'Nāgasena' you speak of? Pray,

Reverend Sir, is the hair of the head 'Nāgasena'?" "No indeed, great king." "Is the hair of the body 'Nāgasena'?" "No indeed, great king." "Are the nails, the teeth, the skin, the flesh, the sinews, the bones, the marrow of the bones, the kidneys, the heart, the liver, the peritoneum, the spleen, the lungs, the intestines, the mesentery, the stomach, the faeces, the bile, the phlegm, the pus, the blood, the sweat, the fat, the tears, the serum, the saliva, the mucus of the nose, the synovial fluid, the urine, the grey matter in the skull,—are any or all of these 'Nāgasena'?" "No indeed, great king."

"Pray, Reverend Sir, is Form 'Nāgasena'?" "No indeed, great king." "Is Sensation 'Nāgasena'?" "No indeed, great king." "Is Perception 'Nāgasena'?" "No indeed, great king." "Are the States of Mind 'Nāgasena'?" "No indeed, great king." "Is Consciousness 'Nāgasena'?" "No indeed, great king." "Well, Reverend Sir! Is the sum total of Form, Sensation, Perception, the States of Mind, and Consciousness, —is this 'Nāgasena'?" "No indeed, great king." "Well, Reverend Sir! Is something other than the sum total of Form, Sensation, Perception, the States of Mind, and Consciousness,—is this 'Nāgasena'?" "No indeed, great king." "Reverend Sir, I have asked you every question I can think of, but I cannot discover 'Nāgasena'! Apparently 'Nāgasena' is nothing but a sound! But, Reverend Sir, what is there about all this that is 'Nāgasena'? Reverend Sir, you utter untruth, you utter falsehood, when you say: 'There is no "Nāgasena."'" Then Venerable Nāgasena said this to king Milinda:

68. CHARIOT

You, great king, are a delicate prince, an exceedingly delicate prince. If you, great king, being the kind of man you are, travel on foot in the middle of the day, when the earth has become heated, when the sand is hot, treading on sharp pebbles and gravel and sand, your feet ache, your body grows weary, your mind is distressed, and a body-consciousness associated with pain arises within you. Tell me,—did you come on foot or in a vehicle?—

Reverend Sir, I do not travel on foot; I came in a chariot.—

If, great king, you came in a chariot, tell me about the chariot. Pray, great king, is the pole the "chariot"?—No indeed, Reverend Sir.

Is the axle the "chariot"?—No indeed, Reverend Sir.

Are the wheels the "chariot"?—No indeed, Reverend Sir.

Is the chariot-body the "chariot"?—No indeed, Reverend Sir.

Is the flagstaff of the chariot the "chariot"?—No indeed, Reverend Sir.

Is the yoke the "chariot"?—No indeed, Reverend Sir.

Are the reins the "chariot"?—No indeed, Reverend Sir.

Is the goad-stick the "chariot"?—No indeed, Reverend Sir.

Well, great king! Is the sum total of pole, axle, wheels, chariot-body, flagstaff, yoke, reins, and goad,—is this the "chariot"?—No indeed, Reverend Sir.

Well, great king! Is something other than the sum total of pole, axle, wheels, chariot-body, flagstaff, yoke, reins, and goad,—is this the "chariot"?—No indeed, Reverend Sir.

Great king, I have asked you every question I can think of, but I cannot discover the "chariot"! Apparently the "chariot" is nothing but a sound! But, great king, what is there about all this that is the "chariot"? Great king, you utter untruth, you utter falsehood, when you say: "There is no 'chariot.'" You, great king, are the foremost king in all the Land of the Rose-apple. Of whom, pray, are you afraid that you utter falsehood?

Give ear to me, you five hundred Greeks and you eighty thousand monks! King Milinda here speaks as follows: "I came in a chariot." But when I say to him: "If, great king, you came in a chariot, tell me about the chariot!" he cannot prove that there is any chariot. Is it reasonable to accept this?

Hearing this, the five hundred Greeks applauded Venerable Nāgasena, and said this to King Milinda: "Now, great king, answer if you can!" Then King Milinda said this to Venerable Nāgasena: "Reverend Nāgasena, I do not utter falsehood. Because of the pole, and because of the axle, and because of the wheels, and because of the chariot-body, and because of the flagstaff, the epithet, designation, appellation, style, name—'chariot'—comes into use."

"Great king, you understand perfectly what a chariot is. And precisely the same thing, is true with reference to me also. Because of the hair of the head, and because of the hair of the body, and because of the nails, and because of the teeth, and because of the skin, and because of the flesh, and because of the sinews, and because of the bones, and because of the marrow of the bones, and because of the kidneys, and because of the heart, and because of the liver, and because of the peritoneum, and because of the spleen, and because of the lungs, and because of the intestines, and because of the mesentery, and because of the stomach, and because of the faeces, and because of the bile, and because of the phlegm, and because of the pus, and because of the blood, and because of the sweat, and because of the fat, and because of the tears, and because of the serum, and because of the saliva, and because of the mucus of the nose, and because of the synovial fluid, and because of the urine, and because of the grey matter in the skull,—and because of Form, and because of Sensation, and because of Perception, and because of the States of Mind, and because of Consciousness,—because of all these, there comes into use the epithet, designation, appellation, style, name,—but name only,—'Nāgasena.' In the highest sense of the word, however, no 'individual' is thereby assumed to exist. Moreover, great king, listen to what the nun Vajirā said in the presence of the Exalted One:

For just as for an assemblage of parts
The term "chariot" is employed,
So, when the Aggregates are present,
The expression "living being" is employed.

"It is wonderful, Reverend Nāgasena! it is marvelous, Reverend Nāgasena! Brilliant beyond measure, highly illuminating, are the answers you have given to these questions! If the Buddha were standing here, he would give his applause. Well done, well done, Nāgasena! Brilliant beyond measure, highly illuminating, are the answers you have given to these questions!"

§2. THERE IS NO CONTINUOUS PERSONAL IDENTITY

Milindapañha 40-41.

Said the king: "Reverend Nāgasena, is the person who is reborn the same person, or a different person?" Said the Elder: "He is neither the same person nor a different person." "Give me an illustration."

69. EMBRYO AND CHILD

What do you think about this, great king? You are now big. You were once young, tender, weak, lying on your back. Are you the same person now that you were then?

No indeed, Reverend Sir. He that was young, tender, weak, lying on his back, was one person; I, big as I am now, am a different person.

If this be true, great king, then it must also be true that you never had a mother, that you never had a father, that you never had a teacher, that you never acquired the arts and crafts, that you never took upon yourself the Precepts, that you never acquired a store of merit. Can it possibly be true, great king, that the mother of the embryo in the first stage of development is one person, that the mother of the embryo in the second stage is another, that the mother of the embryo in the third stage is another, that the mother of the embryo in the fourth stage is another? Is the mother of the little child one person, and the mother of the grown man another? Is it one person who acquires the arts and crafts, and another person who has acquired them? Is it one person who does evil deeds, and another person whose hands and feet are cut off?

No indeed, Reverend Sir. But how about you, Reverend Sir? suppose that same question were put to you; what would you have to say to it?

It was I myself, great king, who was once young, tender, weak, lying on my back; it is I myself who am now big. Solely because of dependence on this body, all these are embraced in one.—Give me an illustration.

70. LAMP AND FLAME

SUPPOSE, great king, some man or other were to light a lamp. Would that lamp burn all night long?—Yes, Reverend Sir, it would burn all night long.

Well, great king, is the flame that burns in the first watch the same as the flame that burns in the middle watch?—No indeed, Reverend Sir.

Is the flame that burns in the middle watch the same as the flame that burns in the last watch?—No indeed, Reverend Sir.

Well, great king, was the lamp one thing in the first watch, something different in the middle watch, and something still different in the last watch?—No indeed, Reverend Sir. The lamp was only the cause of the flame that burned all night long.

"Precisely so, great king, there is an uninterrupted succession of mental and physical states. One state ceases to exist and another comes to exist. The succession is such that there is, as it were, none that precedes, none that follows. Thus it is neither that same person nor yet a different person which goes to the final summation of consciousness." "Give me another illustration."

71. MILK AND BUTTER

TAKE the case of sweet milk, great king. Let it stand for a time after it has been drawn, and it will turn into sour milk; from sour milk, it will turn into fresh butter, and from fresh butter into clarified butter. Suppose, great king, a man were to say: "The sweet milk is the same thing as the sour milk, and the sour milk is the same thing as the fresh butter, and the fresh butter is the same thing as the clarified butter." Great king, would a man speak correctly who said such a thing as that?

No indeed, Reverend Sir. The milk is only the cause of the butter which comes.

"Precisely so, great king, there is an uninterrupted succession of mental and physical states. One state ceases to exist and another comes to exist. The succession is such that there is, as it were, none that precedes, none that follows. Thus it is neither that same person nor yet a different person which goes to the final summation of consciousness."

"You are a clever man, Reverend Nāgasena!"

§3. WHAT, THEN, IS REBORN?

Name-and-Form is reborn.

Milindapañha 46-49.

Said the king: "Reverend Nāgasena, what is reborn?" Said the Elder: "Name-and-Form, great king, is reborn." "Is it this same Name-and-Form that is reborn?" "No, great king, it is not this same Name-and-Form that is reborn. On the contrary, great king, with one Name-and-Form Kamma is wrought, a man does good or evil deeds, and by the power of this Kamma another Name-and-Form is reborn." "If, Reverend Sir, it is not this same Name-and-Form that is reborn, surely the man must be released from his evil deeds." Said the Elder: "If he were *not* reborn, he *would* be released from his evil deeds; but since, great king, he *is* reborn, therefore he is *not* released from his evil deeds." "Give me an illustration."

72. THEFT OF MANGOES

Great king, it is precisely as if some man or other were to steal mangoes belonging to a certain man, and the owner of the mangoes were to catch that thief and were to arraign him before the king and were to say, "This man, your majesty, stole my mangoes," and the thief were to say, "Your majesty, I didn't steal this man's mangoes; the mangoes this man planted are one thing, and the mangoes I stole are another; I am not guilty." In point of fact, great king, would not that man be guilty?

Yes, Reverend Sir, he would be guilty.

For what reason?

No matter what that man might say, Reverend Sir, he would not he able to deny that the last mango came from the first, and therefore he would be guilty of the theft of the last mango.

"Precisely so, great king, with one Name-and-Form Kamma is wrought, a man does good or evil deeds, and by the power of this Kamma another Name-and-Form is reborn. Therefore he is not released from his evil deeds." "Give me another illustration."

Great king, it is precisely as if some man were to steal another man's rice . . . sugar-cane . . .

73. FIRE IN A FIELD

Great king, it is precisely as if some man, in the winter-time, were to light a fire and warm himself and then go away without putting it out, and that fire were to set fire to a certain man's field, and the owner of the field were to catch that man and were to arraign him before the king and were to say, "This man, your majesty, set fire to my field," and the man were to say, "Your majesty, I didn't set fire to this man's field; the fire I failed to put out is one thing, and the fire that set fire to this man's field is another; I am not guilty." In point of fact, great king, would not that man be guilty?

Yes, Reverend Sir, he would be guilty.

For what reason?

No matter what that man might say, Reverend Sir, he would not be able to deny that the last fire came from the first, and therefore he would be guilty of setting the last fire.

74. LAMP UNDER A THATCH

Great king, it is precisely as if some man or other were to take a lamp and were to climb to the attic of a thatched house and were to eat, and the lamp as it burned were to set fire to the thatch, and the thatch as it burned were to set fire to the house, and the house as it burned were to set fire to the village, and the village-folk were to catch that man and were to say, "Why, Master man, did you set fire to the village?" and the man were to say, "Friends,

I didn't set fire to the village; the fire of the lamp by whose light I ate is one thing, but the fire that burned the village is another." Suppose they carried the dispute to you. Whose side, great king, would you take?

The side of the village-folk, Reverend Sir.

Why?

That man might say whatever he would, but all the same, that last fire came straight from the first.

75. GIRL AND WOMAN

Great king, it is precisely as if some man or other were to choose a young girl to be his wife and were to pay the purchase-money and were to go his way, and after a time that young girl were to become a grown woman, were to attain her majority, and then a second man were to pay the purchase-money and were to marry her, and the first man were to come and say, "But why, Master man, are you carrying off my wife?" and the second man were to say, "I am not carrying off your wife; that young girl of tender years whom you chose to be your wife and for whom you paid the purchase-money is one person; this grown woman who has attained her majority, whom I chose to be my wife and for whom I paid the purchase-money, is another person." Suppose they carried the dispute to you. Whose side, great king, would you take?

The side of the first man, Reverend Sir.

Why?

That man might say whatever he would, but all the same, that grown woman came straight from that young girl.

76. MILK AND CURDS

Great king, it is precisely as if some man or other were to buy a pot of milk from the hands of a cowherd, and were to place it in the hands of that same cowherd and were to go his way, saying, "To-morrow I'll come and get it," and on that morrow that milk were to turn to curds, and that man were to come and say, "Give me the pot of milk," and the cowherd were to show him the curds, and the man were to say, "I didn't buy curds at your hands; give me the pot of milk!" and the cowherd were to say, "I didn't know your milk had turned to curds!" Suppose they carried the dispute to you. Whose side, great king, would you take?

The side of the cowherd, Reverend Sir.

Why?

That man might say whatever he would, but all the same, those curds came straight from that milk.

"Precisely so, great king, although one Name-and-Form comes to an end at death, and another Name-and-Form comes into existence at rebirth, nevertheless the second comes straight from the first. Therefore that man is not released from his evil deeds."

"You are a clever man, Reverend Nāgasena!"

What is Name and what is Form?

Said the king: "Reverend Nāgasena,—but as for this expression which you employ,—Name-and-Form:—in this complex, what is Name? what is Form?" "Whatever in this complex, great king, is gross and coarse, this is Form; whatever entities in this complex are fine, of the mind, mental, these are Name." "Reverend Nāgasena, why is it that Name, all by itself, is not reborn? or Form, all by itself?" "Dependent one upon the other, great king, are these entities; they invariably come into existence together." "Give an illustration."

77. GERM AND EGG

Suppose, great king, a hen had no germ of new life in her. In that case neither would there be any egg. Of these two,—germ and egg,—both are absolutely dependent the one upon the other; they invariably come into existence together.

"Precisely so, great king, if in this complex there were no Name, neither would there be any Form. Of these two,—Name and Form,—both are absolutely dependent the one upon the other; they invariably come into existence together. Thus has Name-and-Form been brought into existence for a long time."

"You are a clever man, Reverend Nāgasena!"

§4. TIME HAS NO BEGINNING

Milindapañha 50-51.

Said the king: "Reverend Nāgasena,—but as for this expression which you employ,—'long time': what do you mean by this word 'time'?" "Past time, great king, future time, present time. . . . And of all this time a starting-point is unknown." . . . "But as for this statement which you make,—'a starting-point is unknown': give an illustration of this."

78. SEED AND FRUIT

Great king, it is precisely as if a man were to plant a tiny seed in the earth, and from that seed a sprout were to come up and in the course of time were to attain growth, increase, development, and were to yield fruit; and as if, from that fruit, the man were to take a seed and plant again, and from that seed a sprout were to come up and in the course of time were to attain growth, increase, development, and were to yield fruit. Is there any end to this series?

There is not, Reverend Sir.

"Precisely so, great king, is it with time also; of it no starting-point is known." "Give me another illustration."

79. EGG AND HEN

Great king, it is precisely as if you had an egg from a hen, and a hen from the egg, and an egg from the hen. Is there any end to this series?

There is not, Reverend Sir.

"Precisely so, great king, is it with time also; of it no starting-point is known." "Give me another illustration."

80. CIRCLE

The Elder drew a circle on the ground and said this to King Milinda:

Great king, is there any end to this circle?

There is not, Reverend Sir.

"Precisely so, great king, is it with time also; of it no starting-point is known."

"You are a clever man, Reverend Nāgasena!"

§5. OUT OF NOTHING COMES NOTHING

Milindapañha 52-54.

Said King Milinda to the sage Nāgasena: "Reverend Nāgasena, are there any things that exist which come out of things that did not exist?"

"There are not, great king, any things that exist which come out of things that did not exist. Only out of things that existed, great king, come things that exist." "Give me an illustration."

81. TIMBERS AND HOUSE

Well, what do you think, great king? Did this house where you are now sitting come out of things that did not exist?

There is not a single thing here, Reverend Sir, which came out of things that did not exist. Only out of things that existed did it come. For example, Reverend Sir, these timbers existed in the forest, and this clay existed in the earth. Thus, through the effort, through the exertion, of women and men, did this house come to exist.

"Precisely so, great king, there are not any things that exist which come out of things that did not exist. Only out of things that existed, great king, come things that exist." "Illustrate the point further."

82. SEEDS AND PLANTS

For example, great king, when the different varieties of seed-life and plant-life are placed in the earth, in due course they will attain increase, growth, development, and will yield flowers and fruits. But these plants do not come out of things that did not exist. Only out of things that existed do they come.

83. CLAY AND VESSELS

For example, great king, a potter takes clay out of the earth and makes various kinds of vessels. But these vessels do not come out of things that did not exist. Only out of things that existed do they come.

84. LYRE AND SOUND

For example, great king, suppose a lyre had no leaf, had no skin, had no bowl, had no handle, had no neck, had no strings, had no quill, and suppose there were no effort or exertion on the part of a human being,—would any sound come out?

No indeed, Reverend Sir.

On the other hand, great king, if the lyre had a leaf, had a skin, had a bowl, had a handle, had a neck, had strings, had a quill, and if there were effort and exertion on the part of a human being,—a sound would come out?

Yes, Reverend Sir, a sound would come out.

85. FIRE-DRILL AND FIRE

For example, great king, suppose a fire-drill had no fire-stick, had no fire-stick base, had no fire-stick cord, had no upper fire-stick, had no rag, and suppose there were no effort or exertion on the part of a human being,—could fire be produced?

No indeed, Reverend Sir.

On the other hand, great king, if the fire-drill had a fire-stick, had a fire-stick base, had a fire-stick cord, had an upper fire-stick, had a rag, and if there were effort and exertion on the part of a human being,—fire could be produced?

Yes, Reverend Sir, fire could be produced.

86. BURNING-GLASS AND FIRE

For example, great king, suppose there were no burning-glass, no heat from the sun, no cow-dung,—could fire be produced?

No indeed, Reverend Sir.

On the other hand, great king, if there were a burning-glass, if there were heat from the sun, if there were cow-dung,—fire could be produced?

Yes, Reverend Sir, fire could be produced.

87. MIRROR AND REFLECTION

For example, great king, suppose there were no mirror, no light, no face,—would any reflection appear?

No indeed, Reverend Sir.

On the other hand, great king, if there were a mirror, if there were light, if there were a face,—a reflection would appear?

Yes, Reverend Sir, a reflection would appear.

"Precisely so, great king, there are not any things that exist which come out of things that did not exist. Only out of things that existed, great king, come things that exist."

"You are a clever man, Reverend Nāgasena!"

§6. THERE IS NO SOUL

Milindapañha 54-57.

Said the king: "Reverend Nāgasena, do you assume the existence of the soul?" "But, great king, what is this thing you call the 'soul'?" "The living principle within, Reverend Sir, which with the eye sees visible objects, with the ear hears sounds, with the nose smells odors, with the tongue tastes flavors, with the body touches tangible objects, with the mind perceives the Doctrine:—just as we here, sitting in this palace, may look out of whatever window we please,—east, west, north, south,—so also, Reverend Sir, this living principle within looks out of whatever door it pleases." Said the Elder: "Let me tell you, great king, about the Five Doors of the Senses. Hearken to this! give close attention!"

88. SIX DOORS OF THE SENSES

If there is a living principle within which sees visible objects with the eye, just as we, sitting in this palace, may look out of whatever window we please,—east, west, north, south,—can this living principle within, in like manner, see visible objects equally well with the ear, the nose, the tongue, the body, and the mind? Can it hear sounds equally well with the eye, the nose, the tongue, the body, and the mind? Can it smell odors equally well with the eye, the ear, the tongue, the body, and the mind? Can it taste flavors equally well with the eye, the ear, the nose, the body, and the mind? Can it touch tangible objects equally well with the eye, the ear, the nose, the tongue, and the mind? Can it perceive the Doctrine equally well with the eye, the ear, the nose, the tongue, and the body?

No indeed, Reverend Sir.

But, great king, what you said last does not agree with what you said first, nor does what you said first agree with what you said last.

89. MEN IN PALACE

But again, great king, take ourselves for example. You and I, sitting in this palace, with these lattice-windows flung open, in broad daylight, with our faces turned outward, see visible objects perfectly. Can this living principle within, also, in like manner, when the doors of the eyes are flung open, in broad daylight, see visible objects perfectly? When the doors of the ears are flung open, when the door of the nose is flung open, when the door of the tongue is flung open, when the door of the body is flung open, in broad daylight, can it hear sounds perfectly, smell odors, taste flavors, touch tangible objects?

No indeed, Reverend Sir.

But, great king, what you said last does not agree with what you said first, nor does what you said first agree with what you said last.

90. MAN OUTSIDE OF GATEWAY

But again, great king, suppose Dinna here were to go out and stand outside of the gateway. Would you, great king, know: "Dinna here has gone out and stands outside of the gateway"?

Yes, Reverend Sir, I should know.

But again, great king, suppose Dinna here were to come in and stand in front of you. Would you, great king, know: "Dinna here has come in and is standing in front of me"?

Yes, Reverend Sir, I should know.

In just the same way, great king, in case a flavor were placed on the tongue, would this living principle within know whether it was sour or salt or bitter or pungent or astringent or sweet?

Yes, Reverend Sir, it would know.

But after that flavor has passed into the stomach, would the living principle then know whether it was sour or salt or bitter or pungent or astringent or sweet?

No indeed, Reverend Sir.

But, great king, what you said last does not agree with what you said first, nor does what you said first agree with what you said last.

91. MAN IN TROUGH OF HONEY

Suppose, great king, some man or other were to fetch a hundred pots of honey and were to fill a trough of honey and were to seal some man's lips and were to throw that man into the trough of honey. Great king, would that man know whether he was in honey or not?

No indeed, Reverend Sir.

Why?

Because, Reverend Sir, the honey could not get into his mouth.

But, great king, what you said last does not agree with what you said first, nor does what you said first agree with what you said last.

"I am no match for you in an argument. Be good enough to explain the matter to me."

The Elder enlightened King Milinda with a discourse on Abhidhamma: "Here in this world, great king, because of the eye and because of visible objects arises the sense of sight; simultaneously are produced contact, sensation, perception, thought, focussing of thoughts, vitality, attention. Thus do these physical and mental states originate from a cause, *for there is no soul involved in any of them.* Because of the ear and because of sounds arises the sense of sound; because of the nose and because of odors arises the sense of smell; because of the tongue and because of flavors arises the sense of taste; because of the body and because of tangible objects arises the sense of touch. Because of the mind and because of objects of thought arises mental consciousness; simultaneously are produced contact, sensation, perception, thought, focussing of thoughts, vitality, attention. Thus do these physical and mental states originate from a cause, *for there is no soul involved in any of them.*"

"You are a clever man, Reverend Nāgasena!"

§7. WHY DOES NOT THE FIRE OF HELL DESTROY THE DENIZENS OF HELL?

Because of the Power of Kamma.

Milindapañha 67-68.

Said the king: "Reverend Nāgasena, you Buddhists say: 'Far hotter than any ordinary fire is the Fire of Hell. A tiny stone, cast into any ordinary fire, will smoke for a whole day and not crumble. But a rock as big as a pagoda, cast into the Fire of Hell, will crumble in an instant.' But on the other hand you also say this: 'As for the living beings that are reborn in Hell, no matter how many thousands of years they are tormented therein, they go not to destruction.' That is something I do not believe."

Said the Elder:

92. EMBRYO OF REPTILES AND BIRDS

What do you think about this, great king? Do not female sharks and crocodiles and tortoises and peacocks and pigeons swallow hard stones and gravel?

Yes, Reverend Sir, they do.

Now these hard substances, once inside of their abdomen, once in their belly, go to destruction; do they not?

Yes, Reverend Sir, they do.

But does the embryo in their belly also go to destruction?

No indeed, Reverend Sir.

For what reason?

I suppose, Reverend Sir, it is because of the Power of Kamma that it does not go to destruction.

"Precisely so, great king, because of the Power of Kamma, the denizens of Hell, no matter how many thousands of years they are tormented in Hell, go not to destruction. Right there are they born, right there do they grow up, right there do they die. Moreover, great king, this was said by the Exalted One: 'He shall not die so long as that Evil Kamma is not exhausted.' "

"Give me another illustration."

93. EMBRYO OF BEASTS OF PREY

WHAT do you think about this, great king? Do not lionesses and tigresses and leopardesses and bitches eat meat with hard bones in it? . . .

94. HUMAN EMBRYO

WHAT do you think about this, great king? Do not the delicate princesses of the Greeks and of the Warriors and of the Brahmans and of the householders eat pieces of meat that are hard and tough?

Yes, Reverend Sir, they do.

Now these hard substances, once inside of their abdomen, once in their belly, go to destruction; do they not?

Yes, Reverend Sir, they do.

But does the embryo in their belly also go to destruction?

No indeed, Reverend Sir.

For what reason?

I suppose, Reverend Sir, it is because of the Power of Kamma that it does not go to destruction.

"Precisely so, great king, because of the Power of Kamma, the denizens of Hell, no matter how many thousands of years they are tormented in Hell, go not to destruction. Right there are they born, right there do they grow up, right there do they die. Moreover, great king, this was said by the Exalted One: 'He shall not die so long as that Evil Kamma is not yet exhausted.' "

"You are a clever man, Reverend Nāgasena!"

§8. NIBBĀNA IS UNALLOYED BLISS

Milindapañha 313-315.

"Reverend Nāgasena, is Nibbāna unalloyed bliss, or is it alloyed with pain?" "Nibbāna, great king, is unalloyed bliss; it is not alloyed with pain." "I, Reverend Nāgasena, do not believe that statement: 'Nibbāna is unalloyed bliss.' This, Reverend Nāgasena, is my firm conviction on the subject: 'Nibbāna is alloyed with pain.' Now I have a reason to give for this statement: 'Nibbāna is alloyed with pain.' What is the reason for this?

"Reverend Nāgasena, in the case of all those who seek after Nibbāna, plainly evident are their effort and exertion of body and mind, their self-restraint in standing and walking and sitting and lying and eating, their suppression of sleep, their repression of the Organs of Sense, their renunciation of goods and grain and of dear kinsfolk and friends.

"Now persons in the world who are happy, who are endowed with happiness, all with one accord please and increase their Organs of Sense: the eye with all manner of delightful visible objects which yield pleasurable reflexes; the ear with songs and strains; the nose with odors of flowers, fruits, leaves, bark, roots, essences; the tongue with flavors of hard and soft food and of sippings and drinkings and tastings; the body with contacts with objects both delicate and fine, both soft and mild; the mind by fixing the attention of the thoughts on all manner of delightful objects of thought, both good and evil, both pure and impure.

"But you strike at and strike down, hew at and hew down, obstruct and impede, the increase of eye, ear, nose, tongue, body, and mind. Therefore both the body suffers and the mind suffers. When the body suffers, sensations of bodily pain are experienced; when the mind suffers, sensations of mental pain are experienced. Did not also Māgandiya the wandering ascetic, in railing at the Exalted One, say this: 'A Destroyer of Increase is the monk Gotama'? This is my reason for saying: 'Nibbāna is alloyed with pain.' "

"No indeed, great king, Nibbāna is not alloyed with pain; Nibbāna is unalloyed bliss. Now, great king, as to your statement that Nibbāna is pain,—this pain is not Nibbāna at all; this is only the beginning of the realization of Nibbāna, this is only the seeking after Nibbāna. Nibbāna, great king, is unalloyed bliss, pure and simple; it is not alloyed with pain. Let me explain what I mean."

95. BLISS OF SOVEREIGNTY

GREAT king, do kings enjoy the bliss of sovereignty?—Yes, Reverend Sir, kings enjoy the bliss of sovereignty.

Now, great king, is this bliss of sovereignty alloyed with pain? —No indeed, Reverend Sir.

But, great king, what have you to say to this? When a border-province breaks into insurrection, in order to quell those border-inhabitants, kings go afield with their retinues of ministers and captains and soldiers and servants, permit themselves to be tormented by gnats and mosquitoes, by wind and sun, hurry this way and that over even and uneven ground, wage mighty battles, and risk their lives!

Reverend Nāgasena, this is not the bliss of sovereignty; this is only a preliminary to the quest of the bliss of sovereignty. With pain, Reverend Nāgasena, do kings seek after sovereignty; then they enjoy the bliss of sovereignty. Thus, Reverend Nāgasena, the bliss of sovereignty is not alloyed with pain. Bliss of sovereignty is one thing; pain is quite another.

"Precisely so, great king, Nibbāna is unalloyed bliss . . ."

96. BLISS OF KNOWLEDGE

GREAT king, do teachers who know the arts and crafts enjoy the bliss of the arts and crafts?—Yes, Reverend Sir, teachers who know the arts and crafts enjoy the bliss of the arts and crafts.

Now, great king, is this bliss of the arts and crafts alloyed with pain?—No indeed, Reverend Sir.

But, great king, what have you to say to this? They torture their bodies with services to teachers,—by rising to greet, by rising to meet, by fetching water and sweeping houses and presenting toothsticks and water for rinsing the mouth, by accepting remnants of food and shampooing and bathing and dressing the feet, by submission of their own wills, by compliance with the wills of others, by sleeping in discomfort, by eating all kinds of food!

Reverend Nāgasena, this is not the bliss of the arts and crafts; this is only a preliminary to the quest of the arts and crafts. With pain, Reverend Nāgasena, do teachers seek to acquire the arts and crafts; then they enjoy the bliss of the arts and crafts. Thus,

Reverend Nāgasena, the bliss of the arts and crafts is not alloyed with pain. The bliss of the arts and crafts is one thing; pain is quite another.

"Precisely so, great king, Nibbāna is unalloyed bliss; it is not alloyed with pain. But those who are seeking after this Nibbāna, torture both body and mind. They restrain themselves in standing and walking and sitting and lying and eating; they suppress sleep; they repress the Organs of Sense; they renounce both body and life. However, having sought Nibbāna with pain, they enjoy a Nibbāna which is unalloyed bliss, just as teachers enjoy the bliss of the arts and crafts. Thus, great king, Nibbāna is unalloyed bliss; it is not alloyed with pain. Pain is one thing; Nibbāna is quite another."

"Good, Reverend Nāgasena! So it is! I agree absolutely!"

§9. NIBBĀNA IS UNLIKE ANYTHING ELSE

Milindapañha 315-323.

"Reverend Nāgasena, you are continually talking about Nibbāna. Now is it possible to make clear the form or figure or age or dimensions of this Nibbāna, either by an illustration or by a reason or by a cause or by a method?" "Nibbāna, great king, is unlike anything else; it is impossible." "This, Reverend Nāgasena, I cannot admit,—that if Nibbāna really exists, it should be impossible to make known its form or figure or age or dimensions, either by an illustration or by a reason or by a cause or by a method. Tell me why." "Let be, great king; I will tell you why."

97. UNLIKE ANYTHING ELSE IS THE GREAT OCEAN

Is there, great king, such a thing as the great ocean?—Yes, Reverend Sir, there is such a thing as the great ocean.

If, great king, some man were to ask you: "Great king, how much water is there in the great ocean? And how many living creatures dwell in the great ocean?"—if, great king, some man were to ask you this question, how would you answer him?

If, Reverend Sir, some man were to ask me: "Great king, how much water is there in the great ocean? And how many living creatures dwell in the great ocean?" I, Reverend Sir, should say this to him: "The question you ask, Master man, is a question you have no right to ask; that is no question for anybody to ask; that question must be set aside. The hair-splitters have never gone into the subject of the great ocean. It is impossible to measure the water in the great ocean, or to count the living beings that make their abode there." That is the reply I should give him, Reverend Sir.

But, great king, if the great ocean really exists, why should you give him such a reply as that? Surely you ought to measure and count, and then tell him: "There is so much water in the great ocean, and there are so many living beings dwelling in the great ocean!"

It's impossible, Reverend Sir. That question isn't a fair one.

"Great king, just as, although the great ocean exists, it is impossible to measure the water or to count the living beings that make their abode there, precisely so, great king, although Nibbāna really exists, it is impossible to make clear the form or figure or age or dimensions of Nibbāna, either by an illustration or by a reason or by a cause or by a method. Great king, a person possessed of magical power, possessed of mastery over mind, could estimate the quantity of water in the great ocean and the number of living beings dwelling there; but that person possessed of magical power, possessed of mastery over mind, would never be able to make clear the form or figure or age or dimensions of Nibbāna, either by an illustration or by a reason or by a cause or by a method.

"Yet again, great king, hear one more reason why this is impossible:"

98. UNLIKE ANYTHING ELSE ARE THE GODS WITHOUT FORM

Are there, great king, among the gods, gods that are called the Formless Gods?—Yes, Reverend Sir, according to sacred lore, there are, among the gods, gods that are called the Formless Gods.

Now, great king, in the case of these Formless Gods, is it possible to make clear their form or figure or age or dimensions, either by an illustration or by a reason or by a cause or by a method?—No indeed, Reverend Sir.

Well then, Reverend Sir, there are no Formless Gods!

Reverend Sir, there are Formless Gods! But it is not possible to make clear their form or figure or age or dimensions, either by an illustration or by a reason or by a cause or by a method.

"Great king, just as, although the Formless Gods are beings that really exist, it is not possible to make clear their form or figure or age or dimensions, either by an illustration or by a reason or by a cause or by a method, precisely so, great king, although Nibbāna really exists, it is not possible to make clear its form or figure or age or dimensions, either by an illustration or by a reason or by a cause or by a method."

Nibbāna, however, has certain qualities.

"Reverend Nāgasena, granted that Nibbāna is unalloyed bliss, and that it is impossible to make clear its form or figure or age or dimensions, either by an illustration or by a reason or by a cause or by a method. But, Reverend Sir, has Nibbāna any qualities in common with other things,—something that might serve as an illustration or example?"

"In the matter of form, great king, it has not. But in the matter of qualities, there are some illustrations and examples which might be employed."

"Good, Reverend Nāgasena! And that I may receive, even with reference to the qualities of Nibbāna, some little light on a single point, speak quickly! Quench the fever in my heart! Subdue it with the cool, sweet breezes of your words!"

Great king, Nibbāna has one quality in common with the lotus.
Two qualities of water.
Three qualities of medicine.
Four qualities of the great ocean.
Five qualities of food.
Ten qualities of space.
Three qualities of the wishing-jewel.
Three qualities of red-sandalwood.
Three qualities of the cream of ghee.
Nibbāna has five qualities in common with a mountain-peak.

99. ONE QUALITY OF THE LOTUS

Just as the lotus is not polluted by water, so also Nibbāna is not polluted by any of the Depravities.

100. TWO QUALITIES OF WATER

Just as water is cool and quenches fever, so also Nibbāna is cool and quenches every one of the Depravities.

But again further,—water subdues the thirst of the races of men and animals when they are tired and weary and thirsty and overcome with the heat. Precisely so Nibbāna subdues the thirst of Craving for the Pleasures of Sense, of Craving for Existence, of Craving for Power and Wealth.

101. THREE QUALITIES OF MEDICINE

JUST as medicine is the refuge of living beings oppressed by poison, so also Nibbāna is the refuge of living beings oppressed by the poison of the Depravities.

But again further,—medicine puts an end to bodily ills. Precisely so Nibbāna puts an end to all sufferings.

But again further,—medicine is deathess. Precisely so Nibbāna is the Deathless.

102. FOUR QUALITIES OF THE GREAT OCEAN

JUST as the great ocean is free from any corpses, so also Nibbāna is free from any of the Depravities.

But again further,—the great ocean is vast, boundless, fills not up for all of the streams [that flow into it]. Precisely so Nibbāna is vast, boundless, fills not up for all of the living beings [that pass thereunto].

But again further,—the great ocean is the abode of mighty beings. Precisely so Nibbāna is the abode of mighty beings,—the mighty Saints, in whom there is no stain, in whom the Contaminations are extinct, who have attained unto power, who have become masters of self.

But again further,—the great ocean is all in blossom, as it were, with the flowers of its waves,—mighty, various, unnumbered. Precisely so Nibbāna is all in blossom, as it were, with the Flowers of Purity, Knowledge, and Deliverance,—mighty, various, unnumbered.

103. FIVE QUALITIES OF FOOD

JUST as food is the support of life of all living beings, so also Nibbāna, once realized, is the support of life, for it destroys old age and death.

But again further,—food increases the strength of all living beings. Precisely so Nibbāna, once realized, increases the strength of the Power of Magic of all living beings.

But again further,—food is the source of the beauty of all living beings. Precisely so Nibbāna, once realized, is the source of the beauty of the virtues of all living beings.

But again further,—food relieves the wear and tear to which all living beings are subject. Precisely so Nibbāna, once realized, relieves the wear and tear to which all living beings are subject because of the Depravities, one and all.

But again further,—food dispels the weakness of hunger in all living beings. Precisely so Nibbāna, once realized, dispels the weakness of hunger produced by all manner of sufferings in all living beings.

104. TEN QUALITIES OF SPACE

Just as space is not produced, does not age, does not suffer death, does not pass out of existence, does not come into existence, cannot be forcibly handled, cannot be carried away by thieves, rests on nothing, is the pathway of birds, presents no obstacles, is endless,—so also Nibbāna is not produced, does not age, does not suffer death, does not pass out of existence, does not come into existence, cannot be forcibly handled, cannot be carried away by thieves, rests on nothing, is the pathway of the Noble, presents no obstacles, is endless.

105. THREE QUALITIES OF THE WISHING-JEWEL

Just as the wishing-jewel fulfils desires, so also Nibbāna fulfils desires.

But again further,—the wishing-jewel provokes a smile of satisfaction. Precisely so Nibbāna provokes a smile of satisfaction.

But again further,—the wishing-jewel diffuses lustre. Precisely so Nibbāna diffuses lustre.

106. THREE QUALITIES OF RED-SANDALWOOD

Just as red-sandalwood is difficult to obtain, so also Nibbāna is diffcult to obtain.

But again further,—red-sandalwood exhales fragrance which is unequalled. Precisely so Nibbāna exhales fragrance which is unequalled.

But again further,—red-sandalwood is praised by the well-born. Precisely so Nibbāna is praised by the Noble.

107. THREE QUALITIES OF THE CREAM OF GHEE

Just as the cream of ghee possesses beauty, so also Nibbāna possesses beauty of quality.

But again further,—the cream of ghee possesses fragrance. Precisely so Nibbāna possesses the Fragrance of Morality.

But again further,—the cream of ghee possesses flavor. Precisely so Nibbāna possesses flavor.

108. FIVE QUALITIES OF A MOUNTAIN-PEAK

Just as a mountain-peak is exceedingly lofty, so also Nibbāna is exceedingly lofty.

But again further,—a mountain-peak is immovable. Precisely so Nibbāna is immovable.

But again further,—a mountain-peak is difficult of ascent. Precisely so Nibbāna is difficult of ascent for the Depravities, one and all.

But again further,—on a mountain-peak seeds, any and all, will not grow. Precisely so, in Nibbāna the Depravities, any and all, will not grow.

But again further,—a mountain-peak is free from cringing and repulsion. Precisely so Nibbāna is free from cringing and repulsion.

"Good, Reverend Nāgasena! It is even so! I agree absolutely!"

§10. NIBBĀNA IS NEITHER PAST NOR FUTURE NOR PRESENT

It is neither produced nor not produced nor to be produced. Yet it exists, and may be realized.

Milindapañha 323-326.

"Reverend Nāgasena, you Buddhists say: 'Nibbāna is neither past nor future nor present; it is neither produced nor not produced nor to be produced.' With reference to this point, Reverend Nāgasena,—does the person who, by ordering his walk aright, realizes Nibbāna, realize something which has already been produced?—or does he first produce it and then realize it?"

"Whoever, great king, by ordering his walk aright, realizes Nibbāna, neither realizes something which has already been produced, nor first produces and then realizes it. Nevertheless, great king, this element Nibbāna, which whoever orders his walk aright realizes, exists."

"Do not, Reverend Nāgasena, throw light on this question by covering it; throw light on it by uncovering it, by making it manifest. Rouse your will! rouse your effort! pour out on this very point all that you have learned from your training. On this point this people here is bewildered, perplexed, plunged in doubt. Destroy this arrow within!"

"Great king, this element Nibbāna exists,—peaceful, blissful, sublime; and whoever orders his walk aright, whoever, in accordance with the teaching of the Conquerors, through wisdom, grasps the Aggregates, realizes Nibbāna. Great king, just as a pupil, by following the instructions of his teacher, through wisdom, realizes what is to be known, precisely so, great king, a man, by ordering his walk aright, by following the teaching of the Conquerors, by wisdom, realizes Nibbāna.

"But how is Nibbāna to be viewed? By its freedom from trouble, by its freedom from adversity, by its freedom from peril, by its security, by its peace, by its bliss, by its sweetness, by its sublimity, by its purity, by its coolness."

109. ESCAPE FROM A BON-FIRE

Great king, just as a man burning in a blazing, crackling fire heaped up with many faggots, escaping therefrom with effort, entering a place free from fire, will there experience supreme bliss, precisely so, great king, whoever orders his walk aright, will, by diligent mental effort, realize Nibbāna, Supreme Bliss, from which the torment of the Three-fold Fire is absent.

"Great king, the fire of faggots is to be viewed as the Three-fold Fire; the man in the fire is to be viewed as the man who orders his walk aright; the place free from fire is to be viewed as Nibbāna."

110. ESCAPE FROM A HEAP OF CORPSES

Or again, great king, just as a man in a heap of fragments of corpses and excrement of snakes and dogs and men, enmeshed in the tangled tangles of corpses, escaping therefrom with effort, entering a place free from corpses, will there experience supreme bliss, precisely so, great king, whoever orders his walk aright, will, by diligent mental effort, realize Nibbāna, Supreme Bliss, from which the torment of the Three-fold Fire is absent.

"Great king, the corpses are to be viewed as the Five Pleasures of Sense; the man among the corpses is to be viewed as the man who orders his walk aright; the place free from corpses is to be viewed as Nibbāna."

111. ESCAPE FROM PERIL

OR again, great king, just as a man, frightened, trembling, quaking, his thoughts whirling and twirling, escaping from that peril with effort, entering a place that is firm and fast and immovable and free from peril, will there experience supreme bliss, precisely so, great king, whoever orders his walk aright, will, by diligent mental effort, realize Nibbāna, Supreme Bliss, from which the torment of the Three-fold Fire is absent.

"Great king, the peril is to be viewed as the perils which proceed forth, one after another, from Birth, Old Age, Disease, and Death; the man in a fright is to be viewed as the man who orders his walk aright; the place free from peril is to be viewed as Nibbāna."

112. ESCAPE FROM MUD

OR again, great king, just as a man fallen in a place that is foul and filthy, full of mud and mire, removing that mud and mire with effort, going to a place that is perfectly clean, free from filth, will there experience supreme bliss, precisely so, great king, whoever orders his walk aright, will, by diligent mental effort, realize Nibbāna, from which the filth and mire of the Depravities is absent.

"Great king, the mud is to be viewed as gain and honor and fame; the man in the mud is to be viewed as the man who orders his walk aright; the place that is perfectly clean, free from filth, is to be viewed as Nibbāna.

How does a man "order his walk aright"?

"Now as to the statement: 'A person, by ordering his walk aright, realizes Nibbāna.' What is meant by the expression: 'by ordering his walk aright'?"

"Whoever, great king, orders his walk aright, grasps the course of the Aggregates. Grasping their course, he sees therein Birth, he sees therein Old Age, he sees therein Disease, he sees therein Death. He sees therein nothing that is pleasant, nothing that is agreeable; from the beginning to the middle to the end he sees nothing therein which it is possible for him to lay hold of."

113. RED-HOT IRON BALL

GREAT king, just as in the case of a man who, when an iron ball has been heated all day until it blazes and glows and crackles, from the beginning to the middle to the end sees no spot which it is possible for him to lay hold of, precisely so, great king, in the case of a man who grasps the course of the Aggregates;—grasping their course, he sees therein Birth, he sees therein Old Age, he sees therein Disease, he sees therein Death; he sees therein nothing that is pleasant, nothing that is agreeable; from the beginning to the middle to the end he sees nothing which it is possible for him to lay hold of. When he sees that there is nothing which it is possible for him to lay hold of, discontent springs up and abides in his heart, a fever descends upon his body; being without protection, without a refuge, refugeless, he conceives disgust for the Existences.

114. BON-FIRE

SUPPOSE, great king, a man were to enter a mighty mass of fire of flaming flames; being without protection there, without a refuge, refugeless, he would conceive disgust for the fire. Precisely so, great king, when the man in question sees that there is nothing which it is possible for him to lay hold of, discontent springs up and abides in his heart, a fever descends upon his body; being without protection, without a refuge, refugeless, he conceives disgust for the Existences.

When he sees the perils in the course of the Aggregates, the following thought arises within him: "Red-hot, indeed, is this course of the Aggregates,—flaming and blazing, full of suffering, full of despair! If only one might obtain cessation of the course of the Aggregates,—that were good, that were excellent!—namely, quiescence of all the Aggregates, riddance of all the Conditions of Existence, destruction of Craving, freedom from Lust, Cessation, Nibbāna!" Thus indeed these thoughts of his spring forward to the cessation of the course of the Aggregates, are satisfied, bristle with joy, leap for joy: "I have indeed gained Escape from the Round of Existences!"

115. TRAVELER WHO HAS LOST HIS WAY

Great king, just as a man traveling in an unfamiliar region who has lost his way, upon seeing a path which will take him out, springs forward thereto, is satisfied, bristles with joy, leaps for joy: "I have gained a path which will take me out!" precisely so, great king, the thoughts of a man who sees the perils in the course of the Aggregates, spring forward to the cessation of the course of the Aggregates, are satisfied, bristle for joy, leap for joy: "I have indeed gained Escape from the Round of Existences!"

To cessation of the course of the Aggregates he battles, seeks, cultivates, broadens, a way. To that end mindfulness abides steadfast in him, to that end vigor abides steadfast in him, to that end joy abides steadfast in him. As he continues mental effort from one point to another, those thoughts of his leap over the course of the Aggregates and descend upon cessation of the course of the Aggregates; then he has reached cessation of the course of the Aggregates.

"This, great king, is what is meant by the statement: 'A person, by ordering his walk aright, realizes Nibbāna.' "

"Good, Reverend Nāgasena! It is just as you say! I agree absolutely!"

§11. NIBBĀNA IS NOT A PLACE

Milindapañha 326-328.

"Reverend Nāgasena, is this region in the East, or in the South, or in the West, or in the North, or above or below or across,—this region where Nibbāna is located?"

"Great king, the region does not exist, either in the East, or in the South, or in the West, or in the North, or above or below or across, where Nibbāna is located."

"If, Reverend Nāgasena, there is no place where Nibbāna is located, then there *is* no Nibbāna; and as for those who have realized Nibbāna, their realization also is vain. Let me tell you why I think so:"

116. FIELDS AND CROPS

Reverend Nāgasena, just as on earth, a field is the place of origin of crops, a flower is the place of origin of odors, a bush is the place of origin of flowers, a tree is the place of origin of fruits, a mine is the place of origin of jewels, insomuch that whoever desires anything, has but to go to the proper place and get it,—precisely so, Reverend Nāgasena, if Nibbāna really exists, it also follows that a place of origin of this Nibbāna must be postulated. But since, Reverend Nāgasena, there is no place of origin of Nibbāna, therefore I say: There is no Nibbāna; and as for those who have realized Nibbāna: Their realization also is vain.

"Great king, there is no place where Nibbāna is located. Nevertheless, this Nibbāna really exists; and a man, by ordering his walk aright, by diligent mental effort, realizes Nibbāna."

117. FIRE-STICKS AND FIRE

Great king, just as there is such a thing as fire, but no place where it is located,—the fact being that a man, by rubbing two sticks together, produces fire,—so also, great king, there is such a thing as Nibbāna, but no place where it is located,—the fact being that a man, by ordering his walk aright, by diligent mental effort, realizes Nibbāna.

118. SEVEN JEWELS OF A KING

Or again, great king, just as there are Seven Jewels of a King, to wit, the Jewel of the Wheel of Empire, the Jewel of the Elephant, the Jewel of the Horse, the Jewel of the Gem, the Jewel of the Woman, the Jewel of the Householder, the Jewel of the Captain,—but no place exists where these Jewels are located,—the fact being that a Prince, by ordering his walk aright, by a right walk, comes by these Jewels,—precisely so, great king, there is such a thing as Nibbāna, but no place where it is located,—the fact being that a man, by ordering his walk aright, by diligent mental effort, realizes Nibbāna.

"Reverend Nāgasena, let it be granted that there is no place where Nibbāna is located. But is there a place where a man must stand to order his walk aright and realize Nibbāna?"

Morality is the Place of Origin of Nibbāna.

"Yes, great king, there *is* a place where a man must stand to order his walk aright and realize Nibbāna."

"But what, Reverend Sir, is the place where a man must stand to order his walk aright and realize Nibbāna?"

"Morality, great king, is the place! Abiding steadfast in Morality, putting forth diligent mental effort,—whether in the land of the Scythians or in the land of the Greeks, whether in China or in Tartary, whether in Alexandria or in Nikumba, whether in Kāsi or in Kosala, whether in Cashmere or in Gandhāra, whether on a mountain-top or in the highest heaven,—no matter where a man may stand, by ordering his walk aright, he realizes Nibbāna."

"Good, Reverend Nāgasena! You have made it plain what Nibbāna is, you have made it plain what the realization of Nibbāna is, you have well described the Power of Morality, you have made it plain how a man orders his walk aright, you have uplifted the Banner of Truth, you have set the Eye of Truth in its socket, you have demonstrated that Right Effort on the part of those who put forth diligent effort is not barren. It is just as you say, most excellent of excellent teachers! I agree absolutely!"

§12. HOW DO WE KNOW THAT THE BUDDHA EVER EXISTED?

Milindapañha 329-341.

Now King Milinda approached Venerable Nāgasena. Having approached, he bowed to Venerable Nāgasena and sat down on one side. Sitting on one side, King Milinda, desiring to know, desiring to hear, desiring to bear in mind, desiring to see the Light of Knowledge, desiring to rend Ignorance asunder, desiring to make the Light of Knowledge rise, desiring to destroy the Darkness of Ignorance, summoning up surpassing courage and energy and mindfulness and intelligence, said this to Venerable Nāgasena:

"Reverend Nāgasena,—but did you ever see the Buddha?"—"No indeed, great king."

"But did your teachers ever see the Buddha?"—"No indeed, great king."

"Reverend Nāgasena, you say you never saw the Buddha, and you say your teachers never saw the Buddha either. Well then, Reverend Nāgasena, the Buddha never existed! for there is nothing here to show that he ever did!"

How do we know that Kings existed of old?

"But, great king, did Kings exist of old,—those who were your predecessors in the line of Kings?"—"Yes, Reverend Sir,—why doubt? Kings did exist of old,—those who were my predecessors in the line of Kings."

"Did you, great king, ever see those Kings of old?"—"No indeed, Reverend Sir."

"But, great king, did those who instructed you,—house-priests, commanders-in-chief, judges, ministers,—did they ever see those Kings of old?"—"No indeed, Reverend Sir."

"But, great king, if you never saw those Kings of old, and if, as you say, your instructors never saw those Kings of old either,—where are those Kings of old?—for there is nothing here to show that those Kings of old ever existed!"

We know that Kings existed of old by what they have left us.

"Visible, Reverend Nāgasena, are the insignia employed by Kings of old, to wit, the white parasol, the diadem, the slippers, the yak's tail fan, the jeweled sword, and the couches of great price. By these, we may know and believe: 'Kings existed of old.' "

So is it in the case of the Buddha.

"Precisely so, great king, we also, with reference to that Exalted One, may know and believe. There is a reason why we may know and believe: 'That Exalted One existed.' What is the reason? There exist, great king, the insignia employed by that Exalted One, the All-knowing One, the All-seeing One, the All-worthy, the Supremely Enlightened, the Buddha; to wit, the Four Intent Contemplations, the Four Right Exertions, the Four Bases of Magical Power, the Five Sensations, the Five Forces, the Seven Prerequisites of Enlightenment, the Noble Eightfold Path. By these, the world of men and the Worlds of the Gods know and believe: 'That Exalted One existed.' This, great king, is the reason, this is the cause, this is the way, this is the method of inference, by which it is to be known: 'That Exalted One existed.' "

"As for him who ferried a multitude over the Ocean of Rebirth,
Who, by destroying the Constituents of Being, attained Nibbāna,
By inference may it be known: 'That Best of Men existed.' "

"Reverend Nāgasena, give an illustration."

119. THE BUILDER OF A CITY IS KNOWN BY HIS CITY

Take the case, great king, of the builder of a city. Desiring to create a city, he would first of all look out a spot of ground which was smooth, without elevations, without depressions, free from stones and rocks, immune from attack, faultless, pleasing to the eye. The rough places therein, he would make smooth; stumps and brambles he would clear away. There he would create a city,—resplendent, well-proportioned, divided into parts, with trenches and ramparts thrown up, with strong gates and towers and fortifications, with broad commons and squares and junctions and crossroads, with clean, smooth-surfaced king's highways, with well-proportioned open shops, furnished with groves and gardens and lakes and lotus-pools and wells, adorned with all manner of holy places, free from all faults. When that city was complete in every way, he would go to another country. And after a time that city would become prosperous, flourishing, plentifully supplied with food, secure, highly prosperous, happy, free from trouble, immune from attack, the resort of all sorts and conditions of men. And all sorts and conditions of men . . . from all parts of the earth . . . coming to that city to live, and seeing that it was new, well-proportioned, free from defect, free from fault, pleasing to the eye, would know by inference: "Skilful indeed was that city-builder who created this city!"

120. SO IS THE BUDDHA KNOWN BY HIS CITY OF RIGHTEOUSNESS

PRECISELY so, great king, that Exalted One, without an equal, without equals, without a peer, without a similar, not to be weighed, not to be reckoned, not to be measured, not to be estimated, whose virtues were immeasurable, who attained the perfection of virtues, whose wisdom was endless, whose glory was endless, whose vigor was endless, whose power was endless, who attained the perfection of the Powers of a Buddha,—precisely so that Exalted One conquered Māra the Evil One and his host, burst asunder the Net of False Views, put down Ignorance, uplifted Knowledge, upheld the Torch of Righteousness, attained Omniscience, and unconquered and unconquerable in the fight, created the City of Righteousness.

Moreover, great king, the City of Righteousness created by the Exalted One has Morality for its ramparts, Shame for its trenches, Knowledge for its battlemented gateway, Vigor for its towers, Faith for its pillars, Mindfulness for its gate-keeper, Wisdom for its terraced heights, the Suttantas for its commons and squares, the Abhidhamma for its junctions and crossroads, the Vinaya for its court of justice, the Earnest Meditations for its street.

Seven Shops of the Buddha.

Moreover, great king, in this City of Righteousness, in the Street of the Earnest Meditations, Seven Shops are open, and these are their names: a Flower-shop, a Perfume-shop, a Fruit-shop, a Medicine-shop, an Herb-shop, an Ambrosia-shop, a Jewel-shop,—and a General shop.

121. FLOWER-SHOP OF THE BUDDHA

"Reverend Nāgasena, what is the Flower-shop of the Exalted One, the Buddha?"

THERE exist, great king, proclaimed by the Exalted One, the All-knowing One, the All-seeing One, the All-worthy, the Supremely Enlightened, Subjects of Meditation, duly systematized and classified, as follows: the Ideas of Impermanence, Unreality, Impurity, Disadvantage, Renunciation, Passionlessness, Cessation; the Idea of Dissatisfaction with any and all worlds; the Idea of the Impermanence of the Constituents of Being; Meditation on In- and Out-breathing; Ideas of the Corpses: bloated, purple, festering, fissured, gnawed, scattered, pounded-and-scattered, bloody, wormy, bony; the Ideas of Friendliness, Compassion, Joy, Indifference; Meditation on Death; Meditation on the Body. These, great king, are the Subjects of Meditation, duly systematized and classified, proclaimed by the Exalted One, the Buddha.

With reference to these,—whoever desires to be delivered from Old Age and Death, chooses one or another of these Subjects of Meditation, and by means of this Subject of Meditation obtains deliverance from Lust, Ill-will, Delusion, Pride, False Views; crosses the Ocean of the Round of Existences; stems the Stream of Craving; cleanses himself of the Threefold Stain; destroys all the Contaminations; enters that Best of Cities, the City of Nibbāna, which is free from stain, free from dust, clean white, free from Birth, free from Old Age, free from Death, which is Bliss, Coolness, Freedom from Peril,—through Sainthood obtains deliverance of the heart.

This, great king, is what is meant by the Flower-shop of the Buddha.

With Kamma as the price, go up unto the shop;
Buy a Subject of Meditation; so obtain deliverance through Deliverance.

122. PERFUME-SHOP OF THE BUDDHA

"Reverend Nāgasena, what is the Perfume-shop of the Exalted One. the Buddha?"

THERE exist, great king, proclaimed by the Exalted One, certain Precepts, duly systematized and divided; and anointed with the Perfume of these Precepts, the sons of the Exalted One fume and perfume with the Perfume of the Precepts the world of men and the Worlds of the Gods. They exhale fragrance, they exhale exceeding sweet fragrance, in the principal directions, in the intermediate directions, with the wind, against the wind; they abide ever suffusing them.

Now what are these Precepts, duly systematized and divided? The Precepts of the Refuges, the Five Precepts, the Eight Precepts, the Ten Precepts, the Precepts of Restraint contained in the Book of Confession and included in the Five Recitations thereof.

This, great king, is what is meant by the Perfume-shop of the Buddha. Moreover, great king, this has been said by the Exalted One, god over gods:

> The perfume of flowers goes not against the wind,
> Nor that of sandal, or of Tagara and Mallikā flowers;
> But the perfume of the righteous goes against the wind;
> In all directions a good man exhales fragrance.
>
> Above and beyond all varieties of perfume,
> Whether of sandal or of lotus
> Or of Tagara and Vassikī flowers,
> The perfume of virtue is preëminent.
>
> Weak is this perfume, this perfume of Tagara and of sandal;
> The perfume of the virtuous is the finest that is wafted to the gods.

123. FRUIT-SHOP OF THE BUDDHA

"Reverend Nāgasena, what is the Fruit-shop of the Exalted One, the Buddha?"

THERE are Fruits, great king, proclaimed by the Exalted One, to wit: the Fruit of Conversion, the Fruit of one-who-will-be-reborn-but-once, the Fruit of one-who-will-be-reborn-no-more-on-earth, and the Fruit of Sainthood; the Attainment of the Fruit of Freedom from the Depravities; the Attainment of the Fruit of Freedom from the Marks of Lust, Ill-will, and Delusion; the Attainment of the Fruit of Freedom from Inclination thereto. Of these, whichever Fruit a man desires, he gives Kamma as the price, and buys the Fruit he wants.

124. BUYER AND SELLER OF MANGOES

Suppose, great king, some man or other had a mango-tree which bore fruit continually, and suppose he never shook down mangoes so long as buyers did not come, but when a buyer arrived, he took the price and told him this: "Master man, this mango-tree bears fruit continually; take from it as much fruit as you want,—immature, or decayed, or hairy, or unripe, or ripe"; and suppose the buyer, for the price he had given the seller, if he wanted immature, took immature; if he wanted decayed, took decayed; if he wanted hairy, took hairy; if he wanted unripe, took unripe; if he wanted ripe, took ripe.

Precisely so, great king, whichever Fruit a man desires, he gives Kamma as the price, and buys the Fruit he wants. If he desires the Fruit of Conversion, he receives it; if he desires the Fruit of one-who-will-be-reborn-but-once, he receives it; if he desires the Fruit of one-who-will-be-reborn-no-more-on-earth, he receives it; if he desires the Fruit of Sainthood, he receives it; if he desires the Attainment of the Fruit of Freedom from the Depravities, he receives it; if he desires the Attainment of the Fruit of Freedom from the Marks of Lust, Ill-will, and Delusion, he receives it; if he desires the Attainment of the Fruit of Freedom from Inclination thereto, he receives it.

This, great king, is what is meant by the Fruit-shop of the Buddha.

People give Kamma as the price, and buy the Fruit of the Deathless;
Therefore they are in Bliss that have bought the Fruit of the Deathless.

125. MEDICINE-SHOP OF THE BUDDHA

"Reverend Nāgasena, what is the Medicine-shop of the Exalted One, the Buddha?"

There are Medicines, great king, proclaimed by the Exalted One, and with these Medicines that Exalted One frees the world of men and the Worlds of the Gods from the Poison of the Depravities. Now what are these Medicines? Great king, they are the Four Noble Truths proclaimed by the Exalted One; to wit, the Noble Truth regarding Suffering, the Noble Truth regarding the Origin of Suffering, the Noble Truth regarding the Cessation of Suffering, the Noble Truth regarding the Way to the Cessation of Suffering. Now whosoever, longing for Sublime Knowledge, hearken to the Doctrine of the Four Truths, they are delivered from Birth, they are delivered from Old Age, they are delivered from Death, they are delivered from sorrow, lamentation, suffering, dejection, and despair.

This, great king, is what is meant by the Medicine-shop of the Buddha.

Of all the medicines in the world that are antidotes for poison,
There is none equal to the Medicine of the Doctrine; drink this, O monks!

126. HERB-SHOP OF THE BUDDHA

"Reverend Nāgasena, what is the Herb-shop of the Exalted One, the Buddha?"

THERE are Herbs, great king, proclaimed by the Exalted One, with which herbs that Exalted One cures both gods and men; to wit: the Four Earnest Meditations, the Four Right Exertions, the Four Bases of Magical Power, the Five Sensations, the Five Forces, the Seven Prerequisites of Enlightenment, the Noble Eightfold Path. With these Herbs the Exalted One purges Wrong Views, purges Wrong Resolution, purges Wrong Speech, purges Wrong Conduct, purges Wrong Means of Livelihood, purges Wrong Exertion, purges Wrong Mindfulness, purges Wrong Concentration; produces vomiting of Desire, produces vomiting of Ill-will, produces vomiting of Delusion, produces vomiting of Pride, produces vomiting of False Views, produces vomiting of Doubt, produces vomiting of Arrogance, produces vomiting of Sloth-and-Torpor, produces vomiting of Shamelessness and of Fearlessness of Wrongdoing,—produces vomiting of all the Depravities.

This, great king, is what is meant by the Herb-shop of the Buddha.

Of all the herbs that are known in the world, many and various,
There are none equal to the Herbs of the Doctrine; drink these, O monks!

They that drink the Herbs of the Doctrine will no more grow old and die;
By Concentration and Insight destroying the Constituents of Being, they will attain Nibbāna.

127. AMBROSIA-SHOP OF THE BUDDHA

"Reverend Nāgasena, what is the Ambrosia-shop of the Exalted One, the Buddha?"

An Ambrosia, great king, has been proclaimed by the Exalted One, and with this Ambrosia that Exalted One sprinkles the world of men and the Worlds of the Gods; and sprinkled with this Ambrosia, both gods and men have obtained deliverance from Birth, Old Age, Disease, Death, and from sorrow, lamentation, suffering, dejection, and despair. What is this Ambrosia? It is Meditation on the Body. Moreover, great king, this has been said by the Exalted One, god over gods: "Ambrosia, O monks, do they enjoy who enjoy Meditation on the Body."

This, great king, is what is meant by the Ambrosia-shop of the Buddha.

Afflicted with disease he saw mankind, and opened an Ambrosia-shop.
"With Kamma, monks, come, buy and eat Ambrosia!"

128. JEWEL-SHOP OF THE BUDDHA

"Reverend Nāgasena, what is the Jewel-shop of the Exalted One, the Buddha?"

Jewels, great king, have been proclaimed by the Exalted One, and adorned with these Jewels, the sons of the Exalted One brighten, illuminate, irradiate, the world of men and the Worlds of the Gods, —shine, shine forth,—diffuse light above, below, across. What are these Jewels? The Jewel of the Precepts of Morality, the Jewel of Concentration, the Jewel of Wisdom, the Jewel of Deliverance, the Jewel of Insight through Knowledge of Deliverance, the Jewel of the Analytical Powers, the Jewel of the Prerequisites of Enlightenment.

Seven Jewels of the Buddha.

129. JEWEL OF MORALITY

WHAT, great king, is the Jewel of the Precepts of Morality proclaimed by the Exalted One?

It is the Precepts of Restraint contained in the Book of Confession, the Precepts of Restraint of the Organs of Sense, the Precepts regarding Purity of Means of Livelihood, the Precepts relating to the Monastic Requisites, the Lower Precepts, the Middle Precepts, the Higher Precepts, the Precepts regarding the Paths, the Precepts regarding the Fruits.

Moreover, great king, for a man adorned with the Jewel of the Precepts of Morality, all living beings, the world of men, the Worlds of the Gods, the World of Māra, the World of Brahmā, the world of monks and nuns, cherish affection, cherish longing. Moreover, great king, a monk wearing the Jewel of the Precepts of Morality, brightens, brightens exceedingly, the principal directions and the intermediate directions, above and below and across; from the Waveless Hell below to the Highest Heaven above, he abides irradiating light which exceeds, which surpasses, the light of all the jewels that are between. Such, great king, are the Jewels of the Precepts of Morality which are exposed for sale in the Jewel-shop of the Exalted One.

This, great king, is what is meant by the Jewel-shop of the Buddha.

Such are the Precepts in the Shop of the Buddha;
Buy these Jewels with Kamma, and deck yourselves therewith.

130. JEWEL OF CONCENTRATION

WHAT, great king, is the Jewel of Concentration proclaimed by the Exalted One?

Concentration with which is associated reasoning, with which is associated investigation; Concentration which is devoid of reasoning, with which investigation only is associated; Concentration which is devoid of reasoning, which is devoid of investigation; Concentration on Freedom from the Depravities; Concentration on Freedom from the Marks of Lust, Ill-will, and Delusion; Concentration on Freedom from Inclination thereto.

Moreover, great king, when a monk wears the Jewel of Concentration, thoughts of Lust, thoughts of Ill-will, thoughts of Injury, and the many and various evil thoughts which have their bases in the Depravities of Pride, Arrogance, False Views, and Doubt,—all these, on encountering Concentration, scatter, disperse, fall away, abide not, adhere not.

Precisely, great king, as water on a lotus leaf scatters, disperses, falls away, abides not, adheres not,—why is this? because of the purity of the lotus leaf,—just so, great king, when a monk wears the Jewel of Concentration, thoughts of Lust, thoughts of Ill-will, thoughts of Injury, and the many and various evil thoughts which have their bases in the Depravities of Pride, Arrogance, False Views, and Doubt,—all these, on encountering Concentration, scatter, disperse, fall away, abide not, adhere not. Why is this? Because of the purity of Concentration.

This, great king, is what is meant by the Jewel of Concentration proclaimed by the Exalted One. Such, great king, are the Jewels of Concentration exposed for sale in the Jewel-shop of the Exalted One.

> Let a monk wear the Necklace of the Jewels of Concentration,
> And the evil thoughts will not spring up,
> Nor will the thoughts suffer distraction;
> Come, deck yourselves therewith.

131. JEWEL OF WISDOM

WHAT, great king, is the Jewel of Wisdom proclaimed by the Exalted One? Great king, it is the Wisdom with which the Noble Disciple perceives aright: "This is good;" perceives aright: "That is not good;" perceives aright that this is blameworthy and that is not, that this is low and that is high, that this is dark and that is light, that this resembles dark and light; perceives aright: "This is Suffering;" perceives aright: "This is the Origin of Suffering;" perceives aright: "This is the Cessation of Suffering;" perceives aright: "This is the Path which leads to the Cessation of Suffering."

This, great king, is what is meant by the Jewel of Wisdom proclaimed by the Exalted One.

> Let a monk wear the Necklace of the Jewels of Wisdom,
> And Existence continues not for long;
> Quickly he touches the Deathless,
> Nor does he delight in Existence.

132. JEWEL OF DELIVERANCE

What, great king, is the Jewel of Deliverance proclaimed by the Exalted One? Sainthood, great king, is what is meant by the Jewel of Deliverance; and, great king, a monk who has attained Sainthood is said to wear the Jewel of Deliverance.

Precisely, great king, as a man adorned with ornaments of strings of pearls and gems and gold and coral, his limbs anointed . . . , gaily decked with flowers . . . , surpassing other folk, is resplendent, is resplendent exceedingly, shines down, shines forth, shines all about, gleams, gleams forth, overwhelms, overspreads, with his adornments of garlands and perfumes and jewels,—just so, great king, a monk who has attained Sainthood, who has rid himself of the Contaminations, who wears the Jewel of Deliverance, surpassing, far surpassing, all other monks beginning with those in the lowest grade of attainment and extending to those who have attained Deliverance, is resplendent, is resplendent exceedingly, shines down, shines forth, shines all about, gleams, gleams forth, overwhelms, overspreads, with Deliverance. Why is this? Because, great king, this Adornment is the foremost of all the adornments, —that is to say, the Adornment of Deliverance.

This, great king, is what is meant by the Jewel of Deliverance proclaimed by the Exalted One.

> To one who wears a necklace of gems,
> Housefolk look up as lord;
> But to one who wears the Jewel of Deliverance,
> Both gods and men look up.

133. JEWEL OF INSIGHT THROUGH KNOWLEDGE OF DELIVERANCE

What, great king, is the Jewel of Insight through Knowledge of Deliverance, proclaimed by the Exalted One? Knowledge through

Self-examination, great king, is what is meant by the Jewel of Insight through Knowledge of Deliverance, proclaimed by the Exalted One. For by this Knowledge the Noble Disciple examines the Paths and the Fruits and Nibbāna, the Depravities he has got rid of, and the Depravities which remain.

That Knowledge by which the Noble know their accomplishments,—
Strive, O true sons of the Conqueror, to obtain that Jewel of Knowledge!

134. JEWEL OF THE ANALYTICAL POWERS

WHAT, great king, is the Jewel of the Analytical Powers proclaimed by the Exalted One? Four in number, great king, are the Analytical Powers: Understanding of the Meaning of Words, Understanding of the Doctrine, Grammar and Exegesis, and Readiness in Speaking. Adorned, great king, with these Four Analytical Powers, a monk, no matter what manner of assemblage he approaches, whether it be an assemblage of Warriors or an assemblage of Brahmans or an assemblage of householders or an assemblage of religious, approaches confident, approaches that assemblage untroubled, unafraid, unalarmed, untrembling, with no bristling of the hair of the body.

Precisely, great king, as a warrior, a hero in battle, girded with the Five Weapons, goes into battle: "If enemies shall be far off, I will lay them low with arrows; if they shall be nearer, I will hit them with the javelin; if they shall be nearer yet, I will hit them with the spear; if an enemy shall come to close quarters with me, I will cleave him in twain with my sabre; if he shall grapple with me, I will pierce him through and through with my knife;"—just so, great king, a monk, adorned with the Jewel of the Four Analytical Powers, approaches an assemblage unafraid:

"If any man shall ask me a question involving Understanding of the Meaning of Words, I will tell him the meaning by another meaning; I will tell him the reason by another reason; I will tell him the cause by another cause: I will tell him the way by another way: I will render him free from doubt, I will dispel his perplexity, I will delight him with my handling of the question.

"If any man shall ask me a question involving Understanding of the Doctrine, to him I will explain the Doctrine by another doctrine, the Deathless by ambrosia, the Uncreate by the uncreated, Nibbāna by extinguishment, Freedom from the Depravities by freedom, Freedom from the Marks of Lust, Ill-will, and Delusion, by freedom from marks, Freedom from Inclination thereto by freedom by inclination, Freedom from Lust by freedom from lust: I will render him free from doubt, I will dispel his perplexity, I will delight him with my handling of the question.

"If any man shall ask me a question involving Grammar and Exegesis, to him I will explain one etymology by another etymology, one word by another word, one particle by another particle, one letter by another letter, one assimilation by another assimilation, one consonent by another consonant, one semi-consonant by another semi-consonant, one vowel by another vowel, one accent by another accent, one rule by another rule, one usage by another usage: I will render him free from doubt, I will dispel his perplexity, I will delight him with my handling of the question.

"If any man shall ask me a question involving Readiness in Speaking, to him I will render easy of comprehension one exposition by another exposition, one comparison by another comparison, one characteristic by another characteristic, one quality by another quality: I will render him free from doubt, I will dispel his perplexity, I will delight him with my handling of the question."

This, great king, is what is meant by the Jewel of the Analytical Powers proclaimed by the Exalted One.

Whoever, buying the Analytical Powers, touches them with Knowledge,
Unfrightened, unterrified, illuminates the worlds of men and gods.

135. JEWEL OF THE PREREQUISITES OF ENLIGHTENMENT

WHAT, great king, is the Jewel of the Prerequisites of Enlightenment proclaimed by the Exalted One? Seven in number, great king, are these Prerequisites of Enlightenment: Mindfulness, Examination of the Doctrine, Vigor, Joy, Repose, Concentration, Indifference. Adorned, great king, with these Seven Prerequisites of Enlightenment, a monk overcomes all darkness, and brightens, illuminates, and irradiates the world of men and the Worlds of the Gods.

This, great king, is what is meant by the Jewel of the Prerequisites of Enlightenment proclaimed by the Exalted One.

Before a monk wearing the Necklace of the
Jewels of the Prerequisites of Enlightenment,
Both gods and men stand up.
Buy these Jewels with Kamma, and deck yourselves therewith.

136. GENERAL SHOP OF THE BUDDHA

"Reverend Nāgasena, what is the General shop of the Exalted One, the Buddha?"

GREAT king, the General shop of the Exalted One is the Ninefold Word of the Buddha, relics of his body, relics consisting of things which he used, mounds erected over them, and the Jewel of the Order of Monks. In the General shop, great king, the Exalted One has exposed for sale the Attainments of high birth, wealth, long life, health, beauty, wisdom, worldly glory, heavenly glory, Nibbāna. Whoever desire any one of these Attainments, give Kamma as the price, and buy whatever Attainment they long for. Some buy by taking upon themselves the Precepts, some buy by keeping Fast-day; with Kamma as the price, though it be but the merest trifle, they obtain the Attainments, beginning with the lowest and extending to the highest.

Precisely, great king, as in the shop of a shop-keeper, with a very small quantity of sesame and beans or a small quantity of rice and beans as the price, men obtain what they require, beginning with the least and extending to the greatest, just so, great king, in the General shop of the Exalted One, with Kamma as the price, though it be but the merest trifle, men receive the Attainments in return, beginning with the lowest and extending to the highest.

This, great king, is what is meant by the General shop of the Exalted One.

Long life, health, beauty, heaven, high birth,
And the Uncreate, Nibbāna, are in the Conqueror's General shop.
Be it little or much, with Kamma as the price are they obtained.
With Faith as the Price, buy, and be rich, O monks!

§13. THE PURE PRACTICES

Twenty-six similes.

Milindapañha 353-355.

137. Like the earth are they in properties, for they are a firm footing to those who desire Salvation.

138. Like water are they, for they wash away all the flecks of the Depravities.

139. Like fire are they, for they burn the whole forest of the Depravities.

140. Like wind are they, for they blow away all the dust and flecks of the Depravities.

141. Like medicine are they, for they cure all the diseases of the Depravities.

142. Like ambrosia are they, for they counteract all the poisons of the Depravities.

143. Like a field are they, for therein grow crops of all the virtues of the Religious Life.

144. Like the wish-fulfiller are they, for they grant all the Attainments prayed for and longed for by those who desire Salvation.

145. Like a ship are they, for they ferry those who desire Salvation across the Great Ocean of the Round of Existences.

146. Like a shelter for the frightened are they, for they restore confidence to those who are frightened by Old Age and Death.

147. Like a mother are they, for they treat kindly those who are oppressed with the sufferings caused by the Depravities.

148. Like a father are they, for they foster all the virtues of the Religious Life in those who desire to increase in good works.

149. Like a friend are they, for they break not their word to those who seek after all the virtues of the Religious Life.

150. Like the lotus are they, for to them adhere not any of the flecks of the Depravities.

151. Like the four choice kinds of perfumes are they, for they dispel the foul odors of the Depravities.

152. Like a lofty mountain-peak are they, for they cannot be shaken by the winds of the Eight Conditions of Life.

153. Like space are they, for they are impalpable, broad, diffused, outspread, mighty.

154. Like a river are they, for they wash away the flecks of the Depravities.

155. Like a skilful guide are they, for they conduct those who desire Salvation out of the wilderness of Rebirth, out of the tangle of the forest of the Depravities.

156. Like a mighty caravan-leader are they, for they enable those who desire Salvation to reach that blessed, most blessed, City of Nibbāna, which is free from all perils, secure, without perils.

157. Like a well-polished, spotless mirror are they, for they enable those who desire Salvation to see the true nature of the Constituents of Being.

158. Like a shield are they, for they ward off the clubs and arrows and swords of the Depravities.

159. Like an umbrella are they, for they ward off the rain of the Depravities, and the heating and scorching of the Threefold Fire.

160. Like the moon are they, for they are prayed for and longed for by those who desire Salvation.

161. Like the sun are they, for they dispel the darkness and gloom of Delusion.

162. Like the ocean are they, for to those who desire Salvation they are the place of origin of the priceless jewels of the many and various virtues of the Religious Life; and they are not to be measured, not to be reckoned, not to be estimated.

CHAPTER XII

PARABLES FROM THE LONG DISCOURSES ON THE FRUITS OF THE RELIGIOUS LIFE

Dīgha 2: i. 71-85.

On a certain occasion the Buddha said to King Ajātasattu of Magadha:

If a monk would obtain the fruits of the Religious Life, he must first school himself in the Moralities.

REMOVAL OF THE FIVE OBSTACLES

He must next get rid of the Five Obstacles:

Getting rid of Longing for the World, he dwells with heart free from Longing for the World; he cleanses his heart of Longing for the World.

Getting rid of the sin of Malice, he dwells with heart free from Malice, compassionate for the welfare of all living beings; he cleanses his heart of the sin of Malice.

Getting rid of Sloth-and-Torpor, he dwells free from Sloth-and-Torpor, with perception clear, mindful, fully conscious; he cleanses his heart of Sloth-and-Torpor.

Getting rid of the impropriety of Pride, he dwells not puffed up, tranquil in heart within; he cleanses his heart of the impropriety of Pride.

Getting rid of Doubt, he dwells triumphing over Doubt, free from uncertainty regarding good ways; he cleanses his heart of Doubt.

163. PAYMENT OF A DEBT

It is precisely as if a man were to conduct his business on borrowed capital, and his business were to prosper, and he were to pay off the old debt and have a surplus left over sufficient to support a wife. The following thought would occur to him: "In the old days I used to conduct my business on borrowed capital, and my business prospered, and here I have paid off the old debt and have a surplus left over sufficient to support a wife!" Because of this, he would obtain joy, he would attain satisfaction.

164. RECOVERY FROM A SICKNESS

It is precisely as if a man were afflicted with sickness, suffering pain, severely ill, unable to digest his food, his body lacking its normal strength. After a time he would recover from that sickness and would be able to digest his food and his body would possess its normal strength. And the following thought would occur to him: "In the old days I was afflicted with sickness, I suffered pain, I was severely ill, I was unable to digest my food, my body lacked its normal strength. But here I am now, recovered from that sickness, able to digest my food, and my body possesses its normal strength!" Because of this, he would obtain joy, he would attain satisfaction.

165. RELEASE FROM PRISON

It is precisely as if a man were bound in a prison-house. After a time he would be released from those bonds. He would be safe; he would suffer no loss,—indeed, he would lose not one of his possessions. And the following thought would occur to him: "In the old days I was bound in a prison-house. But here I am now, released from those bonds! I am safe; I have suffered no loss,—indeed, I have lost not one of my possessions!" Because of this, he would obtain joy, he would attain satisfaction.

166. EMANCIPATION FROM SLAVERY

It is precisely as if a man were a slave, not his own master, having another for his master, without the right to go where he pleased. After a time he would be freed from that slavery, he would become his own master, he would have no other for his master, he would be a free man, he would have the right to go where he pleased. And the following thought would occur to him: "In the old days I was a slave, not my own master, having another for my master, without the right to go where I pleased. But here I am now, freed from that slavery, my own master, having no other for my master, a free man, having the right to go where I please!" Because of this, he would obtain joy, he would attain satisfaction.

167. RETURN FROM A JOURNEY

It is precisely as if a man with wealth and possessions were to start out on a long and hazardous journey through a country stricken with famine, beset with perils. After a time he would complete that hazardous journey; he would reach the outskirts of his village in safety; he would attain security, freedom from perils. And the following thought would occur to him: "Some time ago, with my wealth and possessions, I started out on a long and hazardous journey through a country stricken with famine, beset with perils. But here I am now, that hazardous journey completed! I have reached the outskirts of my village in safety; I have attained security, freedom from perils!" Because of this, he would obtain joy, he would attain satisfaction.

Precisely so, great king, a monk, so long as these Five Obstacles are not suppressed within himself, views them as he would a Debt, a Sickness, a Prison-house, Slavery, a Long and Hazardous Journey. But, great king, a monk, so soon as these Five Obstacles are suppressed within himself, views their suppression as he would the Payment of a Debt, Recovery from a Sickness, Release from Prison, Emancipation from Slavery, a Safe Return from a Journey.

While he views these Five Obstacles suppressed within himself, gladness springs up within him. While he is glad, joy springs up within him. While his heart is filled with joy, his body becomes calm. While his body is calm, he experiences bliss. While he is in bliss, his thoughts attain Concentration.

THE FOUR TRANCES

The First Trance.

Having utterly isolated himself from the Pleasures of Sense, having isolated himself from evil ways, he dwells, having entered upon the First Trance, with which is associated reasoning, with which is associated investigation, which has its beginning in isolation, which is full of joy and bliss. This very body, with joy and bliss originating in isolation, he drenches, he saturates, he permeates, he suffuses: there is not a single part of his whole body which is not suffused with joy and bliss originating in isolation.

168. BALL OF LATHER

It is precisely as if a dexterous bath-attendant or his assistant were to pour bath-powder into a metal bowl, and sprinkling it with water from time to time, were to mix it and knead it. It would become a ball of lather, taking up the oil, becoming enveloped with oil, becoming suffused with oil within and without, nor would there be any ooze.

Precisely so, great king, with a monk. This very body, with joy and bliss originating in isolation, he drenches, he saturates, he permeates, he suffuses: there is not a single part of his whole body which is not suffused with joy and bliss originating in isolation.

This, great king, is a fruit of the Religious Life, productive of advantage even in this world, surpassing, excelling, the former fruits of the Religious Life which are productive of advantage in this world.

The Second Trance.

But again further, great king, a monk, through the cessation of reasoning and investigation, dwells, having entered upon the Second Trance,—a trance devoid of reasoning, devoid of investigation, a tranquillization of the inner self, a focussing of the thoughts, which has its beginning in Concentration, which is full of joy and bliss. This very body, with joy and bliss originating in Concentration, he drenches . . .

169. POOL OF WATER

It is precisely as if there were a deep pool of water, with water welling up into it from a spring beneath, and there were no inlet in the eastern quarter and no inlet in the western quarter and no inlet in the northern quarter and no inlet in the southern quarter, and from time to time a cloud were to pour forth upon it copious showers of rain. Now the streams of cool water welling up out of that pool of water would drench, saturate, permeate, suffuse, that very pool of water with cool water: there would not be a single part of that whole pool of water which would not be suffused with cool water.

Precisely so, great king, with a monk. This very body, with joy and bliss originating in Concentration, he drenches . . .

This, great king, is a fruit of the Religious Life, productive of advantage even in this world, surpassing, excelling, the former fruits of the Religious Life which are productive of advantage in this world.

The Third Trance.

But again further, great king, a monk dwells indifferent both to joy and to absence of passion, and mindful, and conscious, experiencing bliss in the body,—being a monk such as he of whom the Noble say, "He is indifferent; he is mindful; he dwells in bliss;"—a monk dwells, having entered upon the Third Trance. This very body, with bliss devoid of joy, he drenches . . .

170. LOTUS-FLOWERS

It is precisely as if, within a lotus-pond containing lotus-flowers blue and red and white, some few lotus-flowers, whether blue or red or white, sprouting in the water, growing in the water, failed to lift their heads above the water, took nourishment while still submerged. Those lotus-flowers, both to the tips and to the roots, would be drenched, saturated, permeated, suffused, with water: there would not be a single part of all those lotus-flowers, whether blue or red or white, which would not be suffused with cool water.

Precisely so, great king, with a monk. This very body, with bliss devoid of joy, he drenches . . .

This, great king, is a fruit of the Religious Life, productive of advantage even in this world, surpassing, excelling, the former fruits of the Religious Life which are productive of advantage in this world.

The Fourth Trance.

But again further, great king, a monk dwells, through the putting away of bliss, through the putting away of suffering, through the destruction even of former satisfaction and dissatisfaction, having entered upon the Fourth Trance,—a trance devoid of suffering, devoid of bliss,—the perfection of indifference and mindfulness. He sits suffusing this very body with thoughts that are purified and cleansed: there is not a single part of his whole body which is not suffused with thoughts that are purified and cleansed.

171. CLEAN GARMENT

It is precisely as if a man were to sit with a clean garment drawn over his head. There would not be a single part of his whole body which would not be touched by the clean garment.

Precisely so, great king, with a monk. He sits suffusing this very body with thoughts that are purified and cleansed: there is not a single part of his whole body which is not suffused with thoughts that are purified and cleansed.

This, great king, is a fruit of the Religious Life, productive of advantage even in this world, surpassing, excelling, the former fruits of the Religious Life which are productive of advantage in this world.

INSIGHT

With thoughts thus concentrated, purified, cleansed, stainless, free from contamination, impressionable, tractable, steadfast, immovable, he inclines, he bends down, his thoughts to the attainment of Insight through Knowledge. He perceives the following: "This body of mine has material form, is made up of the Four Great Elements, springs from mother and father, increases through the eating of boiled rice and sour gruel, is by nature impermanent, subject to wear and tear, to dissolution and disintegration; moreover, this consciousness of mine is dependent on it, is bound up with it."

172. THREADED GEM

It is precisely as if there were a gem, a lapis lazuli, brilliant, of the finest quality, with eight facets, beautifully polished, translucent, clear, flawless, perfect in every particular, and that gem were strung on a thread either blue or saffron or red or white or yellow. A man with eyes, taking that gem in his hand and examining it, would reflect: "This gem, this lapis lazuli, is indeed brilliant, of the finest quality, possesses eight facets, is beautifully polished, translucent, clear, flawless, perfect in every particular, and this gem is strung on a thread either blue or saffron or red or white or yellow."

Precisely so, great king, with a monk. With thoughts thus concentrated . . .

This, great king, is a fruit of the Religious Life, productive of advantage even in this world, surpassing, excelling, the former fruits of the Religious Life which are productive of advantage in this world.

CREATION OF A SPIRITUAL BODY

With thoughts thus concentrated, purified, cleansed, stainless, free from contamination, impressionable, tractable, steadfast, immovable, he inclines, he bends down, his thoughts to the creation of a Spiritual Body. From this body of his he creates another body, possessing form, a spiritual body, endowed with all the major and minor members, lacking none of the organs of sense.

173. REED, SWORD, SNAKE

It is precisely as if a man were to draw a reed out of a reed-grass. The following thought would occur to him: "This is the reed-grass, this is the reed. The reed-grass is one thing, the reed is another. From the reed-grass indeed has the reed been drawn."

It is precisely as if a man were to draw a sword out of its sheath. The following thought would occur to him: "This is the sword, this is the sheath. The sword is one thing, the sheath is another. From the sheath indeed has the sword been drawn."

It is precisely as if a man were to pull a snake out of his skin. The following thought would occur to him: "This is the snake, this is the skin. The snake is one thing, the skin is another. Out of the skin indeed has the snake been pulled."

Precisely so, great king, with a monk. With thoughts thus concentrated . . .

This, great king, is a fruit of the Religious Life, productive of advantage even in this world, surpassing, excelling, the former fruits of the Religious Life which are productive of advantage in this world.

THE SIX SUPERNATURAL POWERS

Magical power.

With thoughts thus concentrated, purified, cleansed, stainless, free from contamination, impressionable, tractable, steadfast, immovable, he inclines, he bends down, his thoughts to the acquisition of the various kinds of Magical Power. He enjoys, one after another, the various kinds of Magical Power, the several varieties thereof:

Being one man, he becomes many men. Being many men, he becomes one man.

He becomes visible; he becomes invisible.

He passes through walls and ramparts and mountains without adhering thereto, as though through the air.

He darts up through the earth and dives down into the earth, as though in the water.

He walks on water without breaking through, as though on land.

He travels through the air cross-legged, like a bird on the wing.

He strokes and caresses with his hand the moon and the sun, so mighty in power, so mighty in strength.

He ascends in the body even to the World of Brahmā.

174. POTTER, IVORY-CARVER, GOLDSMITH

It is precisely as if a skilful potter or potter's apprentice, out of carefully prepared clay, were to make, were to produce, any kind of vessel he might wish.

It is precisely as if a skilful ivory-carver or ivory-carver's apprentice, out of carefully prepared ivory, were to make, were to produce, any kind of ivory product he might wish.

It is precisely as if a skilful goldsmith or goldsmith's apprentice, out of carefully prepared gold, were to make, were to produce, any kind of gold object he might wish.

Precisely so, great king, with a monk. With thoughts thus concentrated . . .

This, great king, is a fruit of the Religious Life, productive of advantage even in this world, surpassing, excelling, the former fruits of the Religious Life which are productive of advantage in this world.

The Heavenly Ear.

With thoughts thus concentrated, purified, cleansed, stainless, free from contamination, impressionable, tractable, steadfast, immovable, he inclines, he bends down, his thoughts to the acquisition of the Heavenly Ear. With the Heavenly Ear, purified, transcending that of man, he hears both kinds of sounds: both divine and human; both those that are far off, and those that are nigh.

175. SOUNDS OF DRUMS

It is precisely as if a man who had started out on a highway were to hear the sound of kettle-drums, the sound of tabors, the sound of chank horns and small drums. The following thought would occur to him: "Those are the sounds of kettle-drums; those are the sounds of tabors; those are the sounds of chank horns and small drums."

Precisely so, great king, with a monk. With thoughts thus concentrated . . .

This, great king, is a fruit of the Religious Life, productive of advantage even in this world, surpassing, excelling, the former fruits of the Religious Life which are productive of advantage in this world.

Mind-reading.

With thoughts thus concentrated, purified, cleansed, stainless, free from contamination, impressionable, tractable, steadfast, immovable, he inclines, he bends down, his thoughts to reading the minds of others. With his own mind embracing the minds of other living beings, of other individuals, he discerns, according to their true nature, together with their opposites, thoughts that are passionate, malevolent, deluded, attentive, extended, inferior, concentrated, emancipated.

176. REFLECTION IN A MIRROR

It is precisely as if a woman or a man or a young fellow given to self-adornment, gazing at the reflection of his face in a mirror purified and cleansed, or in a vessel of clear water, were to know that he had a mole on his face, if he had one; were to know that he had not a mole on his face, if he had not.

Precisely so, great king, with a monk. With thoughts thus concentrated . . .

This, great king, is a fruit of the Religious Life, productive of advantage even in this world, surpassing, excelling, the former fruits of the Religious Life which are productive of advantage in this world.

Recollection of previous states of existence.

With thoughts thus concentrated, purified, cleansed, stainless, free from contamination, impressionable, tractable, steadfast, immovable, he inclines, he bends down, his thoughts to the recollection and knowledge of previous states of existence. He calls to mind manifold and various previous states of existence, to wit: one birth, two births, three births, four births, five births, ten births, twenty births, thirty births, forty births, fifty births, a hundred births, a thousand births, a hundred thousand births, innumerable periods of dissolution, innumerable periods of evolution, innumerable periods of dissolution and evolution.

"There was I! Such was my name! such my family! such my appearance! such my gettings! such the pleasure and pain I experienced! such the termination of my life! Passing from this state of existence, I was reborn in that. There again was I! Such was my name! such my family! such my appearance! such my gettings! such the pleasure and pain I experienced! such the termination of my life! Passing from that state of existence, I was reborn here."

Thus does he call to mind manifold and various states of existence, together with their characteristics, together with their particulars.

177. RECOLLECTION OF A JOURNEY

It is precisely as if a man were to go from his own village to another village, were to go from that village to another village, from that village were to go back again to his own village. The following thought would occur to him: "I indeed went from my own village to that village; there I stood thus, sat thus, spoke thus, was silent thus. From this village I went to that village; there I stood thus, sat thus, spoke thus, was silent thus. Now I have returned from that village to my own village."

Precisely so, great king, with a monk. With thoughts thus concentrated . . .

This, great king, is a fruit of the Religious Life, productive of advantage even in this world, surpassing, excelling, the former fruits of the Religious Life which are productive of advantage in this world.

The Heavenly Eye.

With thoughts thus concentrated, purified, cleansed, stainless, free from contamination, impressionable, tractable, steadfast, immovable, he inclines, he bends down, his thoughts to the knowledge of the passing out of existence and the coming into existence of living beings. With the Heavenly Eye, transcending that of man, he beholds living beings passing out of existence and coming into existence:—the lowly, the high-born; the well-appearing, the ill-appearing; those in good circumstances, those in poor circumstances.

Reborn according to their deeds does he perceive all living beings: "These living beings, verily, guilty of evil deeds, guilty of evil words, guilty of evil thoughts, defamers of the Noble, holders of wrong views, followers of courses of conduct corresponding to wrong views,—these living beings, upon dissolution of the body, at death, are reborn in a state of loss, in a state of suffering, in a state of punishment, in hell.

"But those other living beings, having good deeds to their credit, having good words to their credit, having good thoughts to their credit, not being defamers of the Noble, holders of right views, followers of courses of conduct corresponding to right views,—these living beings, upon dissolution of the body, at death, are reborn in a state of bliss, in a heavenly world."

Thus, with the Heavenly Eye, purified, transcending that of man, he beholds living beings passing out of existence and coming into existence:—the lowly, the high-born; the well-appearing, the ill-appearing; those in good circumstances, those in poor circumstances. Reborn according to their deeds does he perceive all living beings.

178. MANSION AT CROSS-ROADS

It is precisely as if there were a mansion at the meeting-point of four roads, and a man with eyes, standing there, were to see human beings going into the house and coming out of the house and walking about together in the street and sitting at the centre of the cross-roads. The following thought would occur to him: "These human beings are going into the house and are coming out of the house and are walking about together in the street and are sitting at the centre of the cross-roads."

Precisely so, great king, with a monk. With thoughts thus concentrated . . .

This, great king, is a fruit of the Religious Life, productive of advantage even in this world, surpassing, excelling, the former fruits of the Religious Life which are productive of advantage in this world.

Knowledge of the means of destroying the Three Contaminations.

With thoughts thus concentrated, purified, cleansed, stainless, free from contamination, impressionable, tractable, steadfast, immovable, he inclines, he bends down, his thoughts to the knowledge of the destruction of the Contaminations. "This is Suffering!"—he comprehends Suffering in its fulness. "This is the Origin of Suffering!"—he comprehends the Origin of Suffering in its fulness. "This is the Cessation of Suffering!"—he comprehends the Cessation of Suffering in its fulness. "This is the Way to the Cessation of Suffering!"—he comprehends the Way to the Cessation of Suffering in its fulness.

"These are the Contaminations!"—he comprehends the Contaminations in their fulness. "This is the Origin of the Contaminations!"—he comprehends the Origin of the Contaminations in its fulness. "This is the Cessation of the Contaminations!"—he comprehends the Cessation of the Contaminations in its fulness. "This is the Way to the Cessation of the Contaminations!"—he comprehends the Way to the Cessation of the Contaminations in its fulness.

Nibbāna.

As he thus perceives, as he thus beholds, his thoughts are delivered from the Contamination of Craving for the Pleasures of Sense, his thoughts are delivered from the Contamination of Craving for Existence, his thoughts are delivered from the Contamination of Ignorance. The knowledge comes to him: "In the Delivered is Deliverance!" The knowledge comes to him: "Rebirth is at an end! lived is the Holy Life! done is what was to be done! I am no more for this world!"

179. POOL OF WATER

It is precisely as if, on the top of a mountain, there were a deep pool of water, clear, transparent, still; and as if a man with eyes, standing on the bank of that pool, were to see oysters and shells, pebbles and gravel, and shoals of fish, both moving and stationary. The following thought would occur to him: "Here indeed is a deep pool of water, clear, transparent, still; and in it are these oysters and shells, these pebbles and gravel, and these shoals of fish, both moving and stationary!"

Precisely so, great king, with a monk. With thoughts thus concentrated . . .

This, great king, is a fruit of the Religious Life, productive of advantage even in this world, surpassing, excelling, the former fruits of the Religious Life which are productive of advantage in this world. Than this, great king, of all the fruits of the Religious Life, there is no fruit of the Religious Life higher or more excellent!

CHAPTER XIII

PARABLES FROM THE MEDIUM-LENGTH DISCOURSES ON TWO KINDS OF HERDSMEN

180. MĀRA, THE WICKED HERDSMAN

Majjhima 25: i. 151-160.

Thus have I heard: Once upon a time the Exalted One was in residence at Sāvatthi, at Jetavana, in Anāthapiṇḍika's Grove. At that time the Exalted One addressed the monks: "Monks!" "Reverend Sir!" said those monks to the Exalted One in reply. The Exalted One said this:

THE hunter does not strew bait for the herds of deer with the thought: "Let the herds of deer, enjoying this bait which I have strewn, be long-lived, possess beauty, maintain themselves for long, for a long time!" With this thought, rather, does the hunter strew bait for the herds of deer: "The herds of deer, having nibbled this bait which I have strewn, will eat food to their confusion. Having nibbled, eating food to their confusion, they will become intoxicated. Being intoxicated, they will become heedless. Being heedless, they will come into my power to do with as I will, all by reason of this bait."

Of four herds of deer, the first, having nibbled that bait which the hunter had strewn, ate food to their confusion. Under those circumstances, having nibbled, eating food to their confusion, they became intoxicated. Being intoxicated, they became heedless. Being heedless, they came into the power of the hunter to do with as he would, all by reason of that bait. For so that first herd of deer did not escape from the power and might of the hunter.

Of four herds of deer, the second thus reflected: "The first herd of deer did thus and so, and came to such and such an end. Suppose we were to refrain altogether from eating the bait! Suppose, refraining from this perilous food, we were to plunge into forest-abodes and dwell therein!" They refrained altogether from eating the bait. Refraining from that perilous food, they plunged into forest-abodes and dwelt therein.

In the last of the hot months the grass and water gave out, and their bodies became excessively lean. Their bodies becoming excessively lean, their strength and vigor came to an end. Their strength and vigor coming to an end, they returned to that same bait which the hunter had strewn. Under those circumstances, having nibbled, they ate food to their confusion. Under those circumstances, having nibbled, eating food to their confusion, they became intoxicated. Being intoxicated, they became heedless. Being heedless, they came into the power of the hunter to do with as he would, all by reason of that bait. For so that second herd of deer also did not escape from the power and might of the hunter.

Of four herds of deer, the third thus reflected: "The first herd of deer did thus and so, and came to such and such an end. The second herd of deer also did thus and so, and came to such and such an end. Suppose we were to make our resort near this bait which the hunter has strewn! Having made our resort here, not having nibbled this bait which the hunter has strewn, we shall eat food without confusion. Not having nibbled, eating food without confusion, we shall not become intoxicated. Being unintoxicated, we shall not become heedless. Being heedful, we shall not come into the power of the hunter to do with as he will, all by reason of this bait." They did so. They came not into the power of the hunter.

Then to the hunter and his men occurred the following thought: "How cunning are the deer of this third herd! how discriminating! How marvelous are the powers of the deer of this third herd, these strangers! Not only do they enjoy this bait which has been strewn, but we know neither their coming nor their going! Suppose we were completely to surround this bait which has been strewn, ground and all, with a palisade of tall stakes! Perhaps we might see the resort of the deer of this third herd, where they go to get their food." They completely surrounded that bait which had been strewn, ground and all, with a palisade of tall stakes. The hunter and his men saw the resort of the deer of that third herd, where they went to get their food. For so that third herd of deer also did not escape from the power and might of the hunter.

Of four herds of deer, the fourth thus reflected: "The first herd of deer did thus and so, and came to such and such an end. The second herd of deer also did thus and so, and came to such and such an end. The third herd of deer also did thus and so, and came to such and such an end. Suppose we were to make our resort where the hunter and his men do not come! Having made our resort here, not having nibbled this bait which the hunter has strewn, we shall eat food without confusion. Not having nibbled, eating food without confusion, we shall not become intoxicated. Being unintoxicated, we shall not become heedless. Being heedful, we shall not come into the power of the hunter to do with as he will, all by reason of this bait." They did so. They came not into the power of the hunter.

Then to the hunter and his men occurred the following thought: "How cunning are the deer of this fourth herd! how discriminating! How marvelous are the powers of the deer of this fourth herd, these strangers! Not only do they enjoy this bait which has been strewn, but we know neither their coming nor their going! Suppose we were completely to surround this bait which has been strewn, ground and all, with a palisade of tall stakes! Perhaps we might see the resort of the deer of this fourth herd, where they go to get their food." But the hunter and his men never so much as saw the resort of the deer of that fourth herd, where they went to get their food.

Then to the hunter and his men occurred the following thought: "If we alarm the deer of this fourth herd, they, alarmed, will alarm others; and they, alarmed, will alarm others; under such circumstances the herds of deer will abandon for good and all this bait which has been strewn. Suppose we were to ignore the deer of this fourth herd!" The hunter and his men ignored the deer of that fourth herd. For so that fourth herd of deer escaped from the power and might of the hunter.

A parable, O monks, I here give unto you, that ye may understand the meaning of the matter. And this alone is the meaning of the matter: The Bait, O monks, typifies the Five Pleasures of Sense. The Hunter, O monks, typifies Māra the Evil One. The Retinue of the Hunter, O monks, typifies the Retinue of Māra the

Evil One. The Herds of Deer, O monks, typify monks and Brahmans.

Of four groups of monks and Brahmans, the first, having nibbled that bait which Māra had strewn, those allurements of the world, ate food to their confusion. Under those circumstances, having nibbled, eating food to their confusion, they became intoxicated. Being intoxicated, they became heedless. Being heedless, they came into the power of Māra to do with as he would, all by reason of that bait, those allurements of the world. For so that first group of monks and Brahmans did not escape from the power and might of Māra. Unto the first herd of deer in this parable do I liken this first group of monks and Brahmans.

Of four groups of monks and Brahmans, the second thus reflected: "The first group of monks and Brahmans did thus and so, and came to such and such an end. Suppose we were to refrain altogether from eating the bait, the allurements of the world! Suppose, refraining from this perilous food, we were to plunge into forest-abodes and dwell therein!" They refrained altogether from eating the bait, the allurements of the world. Refraining from that perilous food, they plunged into forest-abodes and dwelt therein. There their food consisted of pot-herbs, millet, paddy, wild rice, scraps, rice-dust, scum of boiled rice, cotton-seed, grass, cow-dung. There, confirmed vegetarians that they were, they subsisted on a diet of roots and fruits of the forest.

In the last of the hot months the grass and water gave out, and their bodies became excessively lean. Their bodies becoming excessively lean, their strength and vigor came to an end. Their strength and vigor coming to an end, their emancipation of heart came to an end. Their emancipation of heart coming to an end, they returned to that same bait which Māra had strewn, those allurements of the world. Under those circumstances, having nibbled, they ate food to their confusion. Under those circumstances, having nibbled, eating food to their confusion, they became intoxicated. Being intoxicated, they became heedless. Being heedless, they came into the power of Māra to do with as he would, all by reason of that bait, those allurements of the world. For so that second group of monks and Brahmans also did not escape from the power and might of Māra. Unto the second herd of deer in this parable do I liken this second group of monks and Brahmans.

Of four groups of monks and Brahmans, the third thus reflected: "The first group of monks and Brahmans did thus and so, and came to such and such an end. The second group of monks and Brahmans also did thus and so, and came to such and such an end. Suppose we were to make our resort near this bait which Māra has strewn, these allurements of the world! Having made our resort here, not having nibbled this bait which Māra has strewn, these allurements of the world, we shall eat food without confusion. Not having nibbled, eating food without confusion, we shall not become intoxicated. Being unintoxicated, we shall not become heedless. Being heedful, we shall not come into the power of Māra to do with as he will, all by reason of this bait, these allurements of the world." They did so. They came not into the power of Māra.

However, they held the following views: 'The world is eternal.' 'The world is not eternal.' 'The world is finite.' 'The world is infinite.' 'The soul and the body are identical.' 'The soul and the body are distinct.' 'The Tathāgata exists after death.' 'The Tathāgata does not exist after death.' 'The Tathāgata both exists and does not exist after death.' 'The Tathāgata neither exists nor does not exist after death.' For so that third group of monks and Brahmans also did not escape from the power and might of Māra. Unto the third herd of deer in this parable do I liken this third group of monks and Brahmans.

Of four groups of monks and Brahmans, the fourth thus reflected: "The first group of monks and Brahmans did thus and so, and came to such and such an end. The second group of monks and Brahmans also did thus and so, and came to such and such an end. The third group of monks and Brahmans also did thus and so, and came to such and such an end. Suppose we were to make our resort where the Māra and his retinue do not come! Having made our resort here, not having nibbled this bait which Māra has strewn, these allurements of the world, we shall eat food without confusion. Not having nibbled, eating food without confusion, we shall not become intoxicated. Being unintoxicated, we shall not become heedless. Being heedful, we shall not come into the power of Māra to do with as he will, all by reason of this bait, these allurements of the world." They did so. They came not into the power of Māra. For so that fourth group of monks and Brahmans escaped from the power and might of Māra. Unto the fourth herd of deer in this parable do I liken this fourth group of monks and Brahmans.

DESTRUCTION OF THE EYE OF MĀRA

The Four Trances.

"And how, O monks, does one get beyond the reach of Māra and his retinue? Here in this world, O monks, dwells a monk who has utterly isolated himself from the Pleasures of Sense, who has isolated himself from evil states of mind, who has entered upon the First Trance,—a trance with which is associated reasoning, with which is associated investigation, which has its beginning in isolation, which is full of joy and bliss. With reference to this monk, O monks, it is said of him: 'He has made Māra blind; he has destroyed the Eye of Māra, leaving not a trace; he is gone out of sight of the Evil One.'

"But again further, O monks, dwells a monk who, through the cessation of reasoning and investigation, has entered upon the Second Trance,—a trance devoid of reasoning, devoid of investigation, a tranquillization of the inner self, a focussing of the thoughts, which has its beginning in Concentration, which is full of joy and bliss. With reference to this monk, O monks, it is said of him: 'He has made Māra blind; he has destroyed the Eye of Māra, leaving not a trace; he is gone out of sight of the Evil One.'

"But again further, O monks, dwells a monk, indifferent to joy and to absence of passion, and mindful, and conscious, experiencing bliss in the body,—a monk of whom the Noble say, 'He is indifferent; he is mindful; he dwells in bliss;'—dwells a monk who has entered upon the Third Trance. With reference to this monk, O monks, it is said of him: 'He has made Māra blind; he has destroyed the Eye of Māra, leaving not a trace; he is gone out of sight of the Evil One.'

"But again further, O monks, dwells a monk who, through the putting away of bliss, through the putting away of suffering, through the destruction even of former satisfaction and dissatisfaction, has entered upon the Fourth Trance,—a trance devoid of suffering, devoid of bliss,—the perfection of indifference and mindfulness. With reference to this monk, O monks, it is said of him: 'He has made Māra blind; he has destroyed the Eye of Māra, leaving not a trace; he is gone out of sight of the Evil One.'

Knowledge of the means of destroying the Three Contaminations.

"But again further, O monks, dwells a monk who, through passing altogether beyond perceptions of form, through the sinking to rest of perceptions of obstacles, through inattention to perceptions of diversity, perceiving, 'Infinite is space,' has entered upon the realm of the infinity of space. With reference to this monk, O monks, it is said of him: 'He has made Māra blind; he has destroyed the Eye of Māra, leaving not a trace; he is gone out of sight of the Evil One.'

"But again further, O monks, dwells a monk who, having altogether passed beyond the realm of the infinity of space, perceiving, 'Infinite is consciousness,' has entered upon the realm of the infinity of consciousness. With reference to this monk, O monks, it is said of him: 'He has made Māra blind; he has destroyed the Eye of Māra, leaving not a trace; he is gone out of sight of the Evil One.'

"But again further, O monks, dwells a monk who, having altogether passed beyond the realm of the infinity of consciousness, perceiving, 'There exists nothing at all,' has entered upon the realm of nothingness. With reference to this monk, O monks, it is said of him: 'He has made Māra blind; he has destroyed the Eye of Māra, leaving not a trace; he is gone out of sight of the Evil One.'

"But again further, O monks, dwells a monk who, having altogether passed beyond the realm of nothingness, has entered upon the realm of neither perception nor non-perception. With reference to this monk, O monks, it is said of him: 'He has made Māra blind; he has destroyed the Eye of Māra, leaving not a trace; he is gone out of sight of the Evil One.'

"But again further, O monks, dwells a monk who, having altogether passed beyond the realm of neither perception nor non-perception, has entered upon cessation of perception and sensation;—when, in his wisdom, he sees this, the Contaminations fall away from him. With reference to this monk, O monks, it is said of him: 'He has made Māra blind; he has destroyed the Eye of Māra, leaving not a trace; he is gone out of sight of the Evil One. He has got beyond attachment for the world.' "

Thus spoke the Exalted One. Delighted in heart, those monks applauded the words of the Exalted One.

181-183. THE BUDDHA, THE GOOD HERDSMAN I

Majjhima 19: i. 114–118.

Thus have I heard: Once upon a time the Exalted One was in residence at Sāvatthi, at Jetavana, in Anāthapiṇḍika's Mango Grove. At that time the Exalted One addressed the monks: "Monks!" "Reverend Sir!" said those monks to the Exalted One in reply. The Exalted One said this:

How Gotama mastered his thoughts.

"Even before my Complete Enlightenment, before I became a Supreme Buddha, while I was yet a mere Buddha-to-be, the following thought occurred to me: 'Suppose, during my monastic residence, I were to separate my thoughts into two groups!' Accordingly I made this one group of these thoughts of the pleasures of sense and of ill-will and of injury, and this other group of these thoughts of the renunciation of the pleasures of sense and of good-will and of non-injury.

"So when, as I resided thus heedful, ardent, resolute, a thought of the pleasures of sense arose within me, I perceived the following: 'Arisen within me indeed is this thought of the pleasures of sense. And this thought indeed conduces both to the ruin of self and to the ruin of others,—even to the ruin both of self and of others. It is destructive of wisdom, it is in league with ruin, it does not conduce to Nibbāna.'

"Even as I considered within myself, 'This thought conduces to the ruin of self,' this thought utterly faded away. Even as I considered within myself, 'This thought conduces to the ruin of others,' this thought utterly faded away.

"Even as I considered within myself, 'This thought conduces both to the ruin of self and to the ruin of others,' this thought utterly faded away. Even as I considered within myself, 'This thought is destructive of wisdom, is in league with ruin, does not conduce to Nibbāna,' this thought utterly faded away. Thus, every single time a thought of the pleasures of sense arose within me, I absolutely rejected it, I absolutely banished it, I absolutely abolished it. So likewise with the thoughts of ill-will and the thoughts of injury.

"Whatsoever a monk considers much, ponders much, to that does his heart incline. If it be a thought of the pleasures of sense that a monk considers much, ponders much, he has rejected the thought of the renunciation of the pleasures of sense; he has made much of the thought of the pleasures of sense; to the thought of the pleasures of sense does that heart of his incline. So likewise with the thoughts of ill-will and the thoughts of injury."

181. HERD OF COWS

It is precisely as if, in the last of the months of the rains, in the autumn time, when the crops are grown thick, a herdsman were to tend his cows. That herdsman with his stick would drive those cows away from this, from that; would guide those cows away from this, from that; would restrain them, would restrict them. Why would he do so? Because that herdsman sees in this, in that, a cause of death or capture or injury or harm.

"Precisely so I saw the disadvantage, the worthlessness, the contamination, of evil ways; of good ways, I saw advantage in the renunciation of the pleasures of sense, I saw the same in league with purity.

How Gotama concentrated his thoughts.

"So when, as I resided thus heedful, ardent, resolute, the thought of the renunciation of the pleasures of sense arose within me, I perceived the following: 'Arisen within me indeed is this thought of the renunciation of the pleasures of sense. And this thought indeed does not conduce to the ruin of self, does not conduce to the ruin of others, —does not conduce either to the ruin of self or to the ruin of others. It increases wisdom, it is in league with good-will, it conduces to Nibbāna.'

"Did I by night consider this, ponder this, I saw therein no cause of fear. Did I by day consider this, ponder this, I saw therein no cause of fear. Did I by night and day consider this, ponder this, I saw therein no cause of fear. 'However,' thought I, 'should I consider this, should I ponder this, too long, my body is likely to grow weary. Should my body grow weary, my thoughts are likely to become agitated. Should my thoughts become agitated, my thoughts will be far removed from Concentration.' Accordingly I stablished my very inmost thoughts, I settled them, I focussed them, I concentrated them. Why did I do this? 'Let not my thoughts become agitated!' So likewise with thoughts of good-will and thoughts of non-injury.

"Whatsoever a monk considers much, ponders much, to that does his heart incline. If it be the thought of the renunciation of the pleasures of sense that a monk considers much, ponders much, he has rejected the thought of the pleasures of sense; he has made much of the thought of the renunciation of the pleasures of sense; to the thought of the renunciation of the pleasures of sense does his heart incline. So likewise with thoughts of good-will and thoughts of non-injury."

182. HERD OF COWS

It is precisely as if, in the last of the months of the rains, when all of the crops have been brought together on the outskirts of the village, a herdsman were to tend his cows. Whether he sits at the foot of a tree or out in the open, his business is ever and always to be mindful of the fact: "There are the cows!"

"Precisely so it was my business ever and always to be mindful of the fact: 'There are the good and the evil ways!'

HOW GOTAMA ATTAINED ENLIGHTENMENT

The Four Trances.

"Aroused indeed was my vigor, not relaxed; fixed was my attention, not distracted; tranquil was my body, not agitated; concentrated were my thoughts, focussed on a single point. Thus did I dwell, having utterly isolated myself from the pleasures of sense, having isolated myself from evil ways, having entered upon the First Trance, with which is associated reasoning, with which is associated investigation, which has its beginning in isolation, which is full of joy and bliss.

"Then did I dwell, through the cessation of reasoning and investigation, having entered upon the Second Trance,—a trance devoid of reasoning, devoid of investigation, a tranquillization of the inner self, a focussing of the thoughts, which has its beginning in Concentration, which is full of joy and bliss.

"Then did I dwell, indifferent to joy and to absence of passion, and mindful, and conscious, experiencing bliss in the body,—a monk such as he of whom the Noble say, 'He is indifferent; he is mindful; he dwells in bliss;'—I dwelt, having entered upon the Third Trance.

"Then did I dwell, through the putting away of bliss, through the putting away of suffering, through the destruction even of former satisfaction and dissatisfaction, having entered upon the Fourth Trance,—a trance devoid of suffering, devoid of bliss,—the perfection of indifference and mindfulness.

Recollection of previous states of existence.

"My thoughts thus concentrated, purified, cleansed, stainless, free from contamination, impressionable, tractable, steadfast, immovable, I bent my thoughts to the recollection and knowledge of previous states of existence. I called to mind manifold and various previous states of existence, to wit: one birth, two births, three births, four births, five births, ten births, twenty births, thirty births, forty births, fifty births, a hundred births, a thousand births, a hundred thousand births, innumerable periods of dissolution, innumerable periods of evolution, innumerable periods of dissolution and evolution.

"There was I! Such was my name! such my family! such my appearance! such my gettings! such the pleasure and pain I experienced! such the termination of my life! Passing from this state of existence, I was reborn in that. There again was I! Such was my name! such my family! such my appearance! such my gettings! such the pleasure and pain I experienced! such the termination of my life! Passing from that state of existence, I was reborn here.

"Thus did I call to mind manifold and various states of existence, together with their characteristics, together with their particulars. This, verily, in the first watch of the night, was the first knowledge I acquired,—ignorance shattered, knowledge arisen; darkness shattered, light arisen,—as I dwelt heedful, ardent, resolute.

The Heavenly Eye.

"My thoughts thus concentrated, purified, cleansed, stainless, free from contamination, impressionable, tractable, steadfast, immovable, I bent my thoughts to the knowledge of the passing out of existence and the coming into existence of living beings. With the Heavenly Eye, purified, transcending that of man, I beheld living beings passing out of existence and coming into existence:—the lowly, the high-born; the well-appearing, the ill-appearing; those in good circumstances, those in poor circumstances.

"Reborn according to their deeds did I perceive all living beings: 'These living beings, verily, guilty of evil deeds, guilty of evil words, guilty of evil thoughts, defamers of the Noble, holders of wrong views, followers of courses of conduct corresponding to wrong views,—these living beings, upon dissolution of the body, at death, are reborn in a state of loss, in a state of suffering, in a state of punishment, in hell.

" 'But these other living beings, having good deeds to their credit, having good words to their credit, having good thoughts to their credit, not being defamers of the Noble, holders of right views, followers of courses of conduct corresponding to right views,—these living beings, upon dissolution of the body, at death, are reborn in a state of bliss, in a heavenly world.'

"Thus, with the Heavenly Eye, purified, transcending that of man, I beheld living beings passing out of existence and coming into existence:—the lowly, the high-born; the well-appearing, the ill-appearing; those in good circumstances, those in poor circumstances. Reborn according to their deeds did I perceive all living beings. This, verily, in the second watch of the night, was the second knowledge I acquired,—ignorance shattered, knowledge arisen; darkness shattered, light arisen, —as I dwelt heedful, ardent, resolute.

Knowledge of the means of destroying the Three Contaminations.

"My thoughts thus concentrated, purified, cleansed, stainless, free from contamination, impressionable, tractable, steadfast, immovable, I bent my thoughts to the knowledge of the destruction of the Contaminations. 'This is Suffering!'—I comprehended Suffering in its fulness. 'This is the Origin of Suffering!'—I comprehended the Origin of Suffering in its fulness. 'This is the Cessation of Suffering!'—I comprehended the Cessation of Suffering in its fulness. 'This is the Way to the Cessation of Suffering!'—I comprehended the Way to the Cessation of Suffering in its fulness.

" 'These are the Contaminations!'—I comprehended the Contaminations in their fulness. 'This is the Origin of the Contaminations!'—I comprehended the Origin of the Contaminations in its fulness. 'This is the Cessation of the Contaminations!'—I comprehended the Cessation of the Contaminations in its fulness. 'This is the Way to the Cessation of the Contaminations!'—I comprehended the Way to the Cessation of the Contaminations in its fulness.

"Lo! as I thus perceived, as I thus beheld, my thoughts were delivered from the Contamination of Craving for the Pleasures of Sense, my thoughts were delivered from the Contamination of Craving for Existence, my thoughts were delivered from the Contamination of Ignorance. The knowledge came to me: 'In the Delivered is Deliverance!' I came to comprehend: 'Rebirth is at an end! lived is the Holy Life! done is what was to be done! I am no more for this world!' This, verily, in the last watch of the night, was the third knowledge I acquired,—ignorance shattered, knowledge arisen; darkness shattered, light arisen,—as I dwelt heedful, ardent, resolute."

183. HERD OF DEER

It is precisely as if, in a forest, in a grove, there were a great marsh, a swamp, and near it lived a great herd of deer;—and some man or other were to happen along, not desiring their weal, not desiring their welfare, not desiring their security;—and were to close the path which was secure, which was safe, which led to joy; and were to open the downward path, were to let the deer into the morass, were to set them roving in the water. For under these circumstances that great herd of deer would after a time be thinned out and would come to destruction and ruin.

But on the other hand, suppose that to that same great herd of deer there came some man or other, desiring their weal, desiring their welfare, desiring their security;—he would open the path which was secure, which was safe, which led to joy;—he would close the downward path, would cut them off from the morass, would prevent them from roving in the water. For under those circumstances that great herd of deer would after a time attain increase, growth, development.

A parable, O monks, I here give unto you, that ye may understand the meaning of the matter. And this alone is the meaning of the matter:

The great marsh, the swamp, typifies the Pleasures of Sense. The great herd of deer typifies all living beings. The man who desires not their weal, who desires not their welfare, who desires not their security, typifies Māra the Evil One. The downward path typifies the Wrong Eightfold Path, to wit: Wrong Views, Wrong Resolution, Wrong Speech, Wrong Conduct, Wrong Means of Livelihood, Wrong Exertion, Wrong Mindfulness, Wrong Concentration. The morass typifies passion for delight. Roving in the water typifies ignorance.

The Buddha, the Good Herdsman.

The man who desires their weal, who desires their welfare, who desires their security, typifies the Tathāgata, the All-worthy, the Supremely Enlightened. The path which is secure, which is safe, which leads to joy, is the Noble Eightfold Path, to wit: Right Views, Right Resolution, Right Speech, Right Conduct, Right Means of Livelihood, Right Exertion, Right Mindfulness, Right Concentration.

Thus, O monks, have I opened the path which is secure, which is safe, which leads to joy; thus have I closed the downward path, cut the deer off from the morass, prevented them from roving in the water. All that can be done by a Teacher who desires the welfare of his disciples, who has compassion for his disciples, out of compassion, all that have I done for you.

Here, O monks, are the roots of trees! here are the abodes of solitude! Meditate, O monks! be not heedless! have no regrets hereafter!

Thus spoke the Exalted One. Delighted at heart, those monks applauded the utterance of the Exalted One.

184. THE BUDDHA, THE GOOD HERDSMAN II

Majjhima 34: i. 225-227.

Thus have I heard: Once upon a time the Exalted One was in residence among the Vajjians, at Ukkācelā, on the bank of the Ganges river. At that time the Exalted One addressed the monks: "Monks!" "Reverend Sir!" said those monks to the Exalted One in reply. The Exalted One said this:

In olden times a Magadha herdsman, a stupid sort of fellow, in the last of the months of the rains, in the autumn time, without examining the near bank of the Ganges river, without examining the far bank of the Ganges river, without so much as finding a ford, drove his cattle across to the farther bank, to the territory of the Suvidehas. Now when the cattle reached the middle of the stream of the Ganges river, they formed in a circle, and then and there met destruction and death.

What was the cause of this?

It was because that Magadha herdsman, a stupid sort of fellow, in the last of the months of the rains, in the autumn time, without examining the near bank of the Ganges river, without examining the far bank of the Ganges river, without so much as finding a ford, drove his cattle across to the farther bank, to the territory of the Suvidehas.

Precisely so is it with those monks and Brahmans who know not this world, who know not the next world, who know not the realm of Māra, who know not what is not the realm of Māra, who know not the realm of Death, who know not what is not the realm of Death,—those who shall decide that they ought to listen to them, that they ought to put their trust in them,—it will be to their disadvantage and sorrow for a long time to come.

In olden times a Magadha herdsman, an intelligent kind of man, in the last of the months of the rains, in the autumn time, having examined the near bank of the Ganges river, having examined the far bank of the Ganges river, having first found a ford, drove his cattle across to the farther bank, to the territory of the Suvidehas.

He first drove across the bulls, the fathers of the cattle, the leaders of the cattle. They, crossing, cleft the stream of the Ganges and went in safety to the far bank. He then drove across the powerful cattle, the steers. They, crossing, cleft the stream of the Ganges and went in safety to the far bank. He then drove across the larger calves, the larger heifers. They, crossing, cleft the stream of the Ganges and went in safety to the far bank. He then drove across the little calves, the weaklings. They, crossing, cleft the stream of the Ganges and went in safety to the far bank.

In that olden time there was a wee bit of a calf, a youngling, that very moment born, guided by the lowing of his mother. He also, crossing, cleft the stream of the Ganges and went in safety to the far bank.

What was the cause of this?

It was because that Magadha herdsman, an intelligent kind of man, in the last of the months of the rains, in the autumn time, having examined the near bank of the Ganges river, having examined the far bank of the Ganges river, having first found a ford, drove his cattle across to the farther bank, to the territory of the Suvidehas.

Precisely so is it with those monks and Brahmans who know this world, who know the next world, who know the realm of Māra, who know what is not the realm of Māra, who know the realm of Death, who know what is not the realm of Death,—those who shall decide that they ought to listen to them, that they ought to put their trust in them,—it will be to their welfare and happiness for a long time to come.

Just as those bulls, the fathers of the cattle, the leaders of the cattle, crossing, cleft the stream of the Ganges and went in safety to the far bank, so also those monks who are Saints, who have rid themselves of the Contaminations, who have completed residence, who have done what was to be done, who have laid down their burden, who have achieved the welfare they desired, who have burst the Bonds, who have attained Deliverance through Right Knowledge,—so also these latter, crossing, have cleft the Stream of Māra and gone in safety to the Far Bank.

Just as those powerful cattle, the steers, crossing, cleft the stream of the Ganges and went in safety to the far bank, so also those monks who, by the destruction of the Five Bonds which cause rebirth in the Worlds of the Pleasures of Sense, have obtained rebirth without the intervention of parents in a heavenly world, there have attained Supreme Nibbāna, from that world are destined to return no more,—so also these latter, crossing, will cleave the Stream of Māra and go in safety to the Far Bank.

Just as those larger calves, those larger heifers, crossing, cleft the stream of the Ganges and went in safety to the far bank, so also those monks who, by the destruction of the Three Bonds, by the thinning of Lust, Ill-will, Delusion, destined to return but once, returning but once to this world, will make an end of suffering,—so also these latter, crossing, will cleave the Stream of Māra and go in safety to the Far Bank.

Just as those little calves, the weaklings, crossing, cleft the stream of the Ganges and went in safety to the far bank, so also those monks who, by the destruction of the Three Bonds, have attained the Fruit of Conversion, who are not destined to the States of Suffering, who are assured of Salvation, who will at last attain Complete Enlightenment,—so also these latter, crossing, will cleave the Stream of Māra and go in safety to the Far Bank.

Just as that wee bit of a calf, that youngling, at that very moment born, guided by the lowing of his mother, crossing, cleft the stream of the Ganges and went in safety to the far bank, so also those monks who walk in conformity with the Doctrine, who walk in conformity with the Faith,—so also these latter, crossing, will cleave the Stream of Māra and go in safety to the Far Bank.

But, O monks, I am he that knoweth this world; I am he that knoweth the next world. I am he that knoweth the realm of Māra; I am he that knoweth what is not the realm of Māra. I am he that knoweth the realm of Death; I am he that knoweth what is not the realm of Death. They that shall resolve to hearken to Me, to put their trust in Me,—it will be to their welfare and happiness for a long time to come.

CHAPTER XIV

PARABLES FROM THE MEDIUM-LENGTH DISCOURSES ON THE PLEASURES OF SENSE

185-191. SEVEN PARABLES

Majjhima i. 364-367.

On a certain occasion the Buddha discoursed to the householder Potaliya on the folly of gratifying the lusts of the flesh. Said he:

185. SKELETON

Suppose, householder, a dog overcome by hunger and weakness were to come up to a cow-killer's slaughter-house, and the dexterous cow-killer or his assistant were to throw the dog a skeleton, smeared with blood, scraped clean of flesh, not to be desired, by no means to be desired. What do you think about that, householder? Could that dog, by gnawing at that skeleton, smeared with blood, scraped clean of flesh, not to be desired, by no means to be desired, subdue his hunger and weakness?

By no means, Reverend Sir. Why not? Because, Reverend Sir, that skeleton is smeared with blood, scraped clean of flesh, not to be desired, by no means to be desired, insomuch that that dog would suffer weariness and distress.

Precisely so, householder, the Noble Disciple reflects as follows:

"With the parable of the Skeleton have the lusts of the flesh been described by the Exalted One,—full of pain, full of despair,—manifold the disadvantages thereof!"

Thus, with Right Knowledge, perceiving this truth in its fulness, he utterly abandons that form of Indifference which is associated with Diversity, which depends on Diversity, and cultivates that form of Indifference which is associated with Unity, which depends on Unity, wherein longings for the baits of the world cease utterly, without leaving a trace.

186. PIECE OF MEAT

Suppose, housholder, a vulture or a falcon or a heron were to rise up with a piece of meat, and vultures and falcons and herons, one after another, were to fly after him and peck at him and seek to make him disgusted. What do you think about that, householder? In case that vulture or falcon or heron did not very quickly let go of that piece of meat, would he not, because of it, incur death or mortal pain?

Yes indeed, Reverend Sir.

Precisely so, householder, the Noble Disciple reflects as follows: "With the parable of the Piece of Meat have the lusts of the flesh been described by the Exalted One" . . .

187. TORCH OF GRASS

Suppose, householder, a man were to carry a blazing torch of grass against the wind. What do you think about that, householder? In case that man did not very quickly let go of that blazing torch of grass, would not that blazing torch of grass burn his hand or burn his arm or burn some other major or minor member of his body? and would he not, because of it, incur death or mortal pain?

Yes indeed, Reverend Sir.

Precisely so, householder, the Noble Disciple reflects as follows: "With the parable of the Torch of Grass have the lusts of the flesh been described by the Exalted One" . . .

188. PIT OF RED-HOT COALS

Suppose, householder, there were a pit of red-hot coals, as deep as the height of a man, full of red-hot coals, free from flames, free from smoke, and a man were to approach,—desiring to live, not desiring to die,—desiring pleasure, averse to pain,—and two powerful men were to seize him with their several arms and were to drag him down to that pit of red-hot coals. What do you think about that, householder? Would not that man writhe and twist his body thus and so?

Yes indeed, Reverend Sir. And why? Because, Reverend Sir,

that man would know full well: "In case I fall into that pit of red-hot coals, because of it I shall incur death or mortal pain."

Precisely so, householder, the Noble Disciple reflects as follows: "With the parable of the Pit of Red-hot Coals have the lusts of the flesh been described by the Exalted One" . . .

189. DREAM

Suppose, householder, a man were to see in a dream the delights of the grove, the delights of the forest, the delights of cleared ground, the delights of the lotus-pond; and suppose that, upon awakening, he were to see nothing at all.

Precisely so, householder, the Noble Disciple reflects as follows: "With the parable of the Dream have the lusts of the flesh been described by the Exalted One" . . .

190. BORROWED GOODS

Suppose, householder, a man were to borrow goods,—a vehicle, a statue, a magnificent cluster of jewels,—and preceded and surrounded by those borrowed goods, were to enter among the shops; and suppose people, seeing him, were to speak thus: "A possessor indeed is that man! Thus, say we all, possessors possess possessions!" And suppose the owners, wherever they happened to see him, were to recover their own. What do you think about that, householder? Would not that man soon get his fill of acting differently from his fellows?

Yes indeed, Reverend Sir. And why? Because, Reverend Sir, owners are in the habit of recovering their own.

Precisely so, householder, the Noble Disciple reflects as follows: "With the parable of the Borrowed Goods have the lusts of the flesh been described by the Exalted One" . . .

191. FRUIT OF TREE

Suppose, householder, not far from some village or market-town there were a deep forest-grove, and in that forest-grove there were a tree abounding in fruit, laden with fruit; and suppose a man were to approach, wanting fruit, seeking fruit, searching for fruit, and were to plunge into that forest-grove and were to see that tree abounding in fruit, laden with fruit; and suppose the following thought were to occur to him: "This tree indeed abounds in fruit, is laden with fruit, but no fruit at all has fallen to the ground. However, I know how to climb a tree. Suppose I were to climb this tree, eat as much as I want, and fill a fold of my garment!" And suppose he were to climb that tree, were to eat as much as he wanted, and were to fill a fold of his garment.

Suppose then a second man were to approach, wanting fruit, seeking fruit, searching for fruit, and suppose he had a sharp axe; and suppose he were to plunge into that forest-grove and were to see that tree abounding in fruit, laden with fruit; and suppose the following thought were to occur to him: "This tree indeed abounds in fruit, is laden with fruit, but no fruit at all has fallen to the ground. Now I do not know how to climb a tree. Suppose I were to chop this tree down at the roots, eat as much as I want, and fill a fold of my garment!" And suppose he were to chop that tree down at the roots!

What do you think about that, householder? In case that man who came first and climbed the tree did not very quickly climb down, would not that tree, as it fell, break his hand or break his foot or break some other major or minor member of his body? and would he not, because of it, incur death or mortal pain?

Yes indeed, Reverend Sir.

Precisely so, householder, the Noble Disciple reflects as follows: "With the parable of the Fruit of the Tree have the lusts of the flesh been described by the Exalted One,—full of pain, full of despair, —manifold the disadvantages thereof!"

Thus, with Right Knowledge, perceiving this truth in its fulness, he utterly abandons that form of Indifference which is associated with Diversity, which depends on Diversity, and cultivates that form of Indifference which is associated with Unity, which depends on Unity, wherein longings for the baits of the world cease utterly, without leaving a trace.

192. CREEPER AND TREE

Majjhima i. 306-307.

On a certain occasion the Exalted One reprobated the view that there is no harm in the Pleasures of Sense. Said he:

Suppose, monks, in the last of the hot months, the seed-pod of a creeper were to burst, and a seed of the creeper were to fall at the roots of a certain Sāl-tree. And suppose, monks, the spirit resident in that Sāl-tree were to become frightened, agitated, terrified. And suppose, monks, the friends and companions, the kinsfolk and blood-relatives of the spirit resident in that Sāl-tree,—the spirits of the grove, the spirits of the forest, the spirits of the trees,—the spirits resident in the plants and in the grass and in the trees,—were to assemble and meet together and were to comfort that spirit as follows: "Fear not, friend! fear not, friend! Very likely either a peacock will swallow this seed of a creeper, or a deer will eat it, or a forest-fire will burn it, or woodmen will pick it up, or white ants will carry it off, or perhaps, after all, it may have no germ of life in it."

But suppose, monks, neither a peacock were to swallow that seed of a creeper, nor a deer were to eat it, nor a forest-fire were to burn it, nor woodmen were to pick it up, nor white ants were to carry it off, and suppose, after all, it did have a germ of life in it. That seed, rained on by a cloud of the rainy season, would shoot up rapidly; it would become a creeper, tender, soft, hairy, drooping; it would attach itself to that Sāl-tree.

And suppose, monks, to the spirit resident in that Sāl-tree were to occur the following thought: "What future peril did those good friends and companions of mine, those kinsfolk and blood-relatives of mine,—the spirits of the grove, the spirits of the forest, the spirits of the trees,—the spirits resident in the plants and in the grass and in the trees,—what future peril did they foresee in the seed of a creeper, that they assembled and met together and comforted me as follows: 'Fear not, friend! fear not, friend! Very likely either a peacock will swallow this seed of a creeper, or a deer will eat it, or a forest-fire will burn it, or woodmen will pick it up, or white ants will carry it off, or perhaps, after all, it may have no germ of life it it'? Pleasant is it to touch this creeper-vine,—tender, soft, hairy, drooping!"

That creeper would encircle that Sāl-tree; having encircled that Sāl-tree, it would fork above; having forked above, it would exert pressure; having exerted pressure, it would crush every one of the mighty trunks of that Sāl-tree.

And suppose, monks, to the spirit resident in that Sāl-tree were to occur the following thought: "This very future peril did those good friends and companions of mine, those kinsfolk and blood-relatives of mine,—the spirits of the grove, the spirits of the forest, the spirits of the trees,—the spirits resident in the plants and in the grass and in the trees,—this very future peril did they foresee in the seed of a creeper, that they assembled and met together and comforted me as follows: 'Fear not, friend! fear not, friend! Very likely either a peacock will swallow this seed of a creeper, or a deer will eat it, or a forest-fire will burn it, or woodmen will pick it up, or white ants will carry it off, or perhaps, after all, it may have no germ of life in it.' For indeed, because of that seed of a creeper, I am experiencing sharp, bitter sensations of pain!"

"Precisely so, monks, there are some monks and Brahmans who hold this doctrine, who hold this view: 'There is no harm in the pleasures of sense.' They fall into the slough of the pleasures of sense; they consort with nuns, with those whose hair is bound in a topknot; they speak thus: 'What future peril do those good monks and Brahmans foresee in the pleasures of sense, that they preach the renunciation of the pleasures of sense and proclaim thorough knowledge of the pleasurs of sense? Pleasant is it to touch the tender, soft, downy arm of this nun!' They fall into the slough of the pleasures of sense. Having fallen into the slough of the pleasures of sense, upon dissolution of the body, after death, they are reborn in a state of loss, in a state of suffering, in a state of punishment, in hell. They there experience sharp, bitter sensations of pain. They speak thus: 'This very future peril do those good monks and Brahmans foresee in the pleasures of sense, that they preach the renunciation of the pleasures of sense and proclaim thorough knowledge of the pleasures of sense. For here we are, because of the pleasures of sense, on account of the pleasures of sense, experiencing sharp, bitter sensations of pain!'"

CHAPTER XV

PARABLES FROM THE MEDIUM-LENGTH DISCOURSES ON THE FRUIT OF GOOD AND EVIL DEEDS

193-197. FOUR COURSES OF CONDUCT

Majjhima i. 313-317.

On a certain occasion the Exalted One addressed the monks as follows:

Four in number are the Courses of Conduct.
What are the Four?
There is a Course of Conduct which gives pain now and ripens in pain hereafter.
There is a Course of Conduct which gives pleasure now and ripens in pain hereafter.
There is a Course of Conduct which gives pain now and ripens in pleasure hereafter.
There is a Course of Conduct which gives pleasure now and ripens in pleasure hereafter.

Pain now and pain hereafter.

Here in this world many a man, with pain, with grief, is a murderer, a thief, a fornicator and adulterer, a liar, a backbiter, a calumniator, a trifler, covetous, malevolent of spirit, a holder of false views. Because of this, he experiences pain and grief. Such a man, upon dissolution of the body, after death, is reborn in a state of loss, in a state of suffering, in a state of punishment, in hell. This is what is meant by the Course of Conduct which gives pain now and ripens in pain hereafter.

Pleasure now and pain hereafter.

Here in this world many a man, with pleasure, with satisfaction, is a murderer, a thief, a fornicator and adulterer, a liar, a backbiter, a calumniator, a trifler, covetous, malevolent of spirit, a holder of false views. Because of this, he experiences pleasure and satisfaction. Such a man, upon dissolution of the body, after death, is reborn in a state of loss, in a state of suffering, in a state of punishment, in hell. This is what is meant by the Course of Conduct which gives pleasure now and ripens in pain hereafter.

Pain now and pleasure hereafter.

Here in this world many a man, with pain, with grief, refrains from murder, theft, fornication and adultery, lying, backbiting, calumny, trifling, covetousness, malevolence of spirit, and is a holder of orthodox views. Because of this, he experiences pain and grief. Such a man, upon dissolution of the body, after death, is reborn in a state of bliss, in heaven. This is what is meant by the Course of Conduct which gives pain now and ripens in pleasure hereafter.

Pleasure now and pleasure hereafter.

Here in this world many a man, with pleasure, with satisfaction, refrains from murder, theft, fornication and adultery, lying, backbiting, calumny, trifling, covetousness, malevolence of spirit, and is a holder of orthodox views. Because of this, he experiences pleasure and satisfaction. Such a man, upon dissolution of the body, after death, is reborn in a state of bliss, in heaven. This is what is meant by the Course of Conduct which gives pleasure now and ripens in pleasure hereafter.

These, monks, are the Four Courses of Conduct.

193. POISONED CALABASH

It is precisely as if there were a bitter calabash mingled with poison, and a man were to approach,—desiring to live, not desiring to die, —desiring pleasure, averse to pain,—and they were to say to that man: "Ho, fellow! here is a bitter calabash mingled with poison! if you wish, drink! But if you drink, it will not please you, either with color or with odor or with flavor. Moreover, by drinking, you will incur either death or mortal pain." He would drink it without reflecting; he would not refuse. But when he drank it, it would not please him, either with color or with odor or with flavor. Moreover, by drinking, he would incur either death or mortal pain.

This, I say, is a parable of the First Course of Conduct; namely, the Course of Conduct which gives pain now and ripens in pain hereafter.

194. POISONED CUP

It is precisely as if there were a cup of water, possessing color, possessing odor, possessing flavor, and it were mingled with poison, and a man were to approach,—desiring to live, not desiring to die, —desiring pleasure, averse to pain,—and they were to say to that man: "Ho, fellow! here is a cup of water, possessing color, possessing odor, possessing flavor, and it is mingled with poison. If you wish, drink! For if you drink, it will please you, both with color and with odor and with flavor. But by drinking, you will incur either death or mortal pain." He would drink it without reflecting; he would not refuse. For when he drank it, it would please him, both with color and with odor and with flavor. But by drinking, he would incur either death or mortal pain.

This, I say, is a parable of the Second Course of Conduct; namely, the Course of Conduct which gives pleasure now and ripens in pain hereafter.

195. FOUL-TASTING MEDICINE

It is precisely as if there were some stale urine mingled with various medicaments, and a man suffering from jaundice were to approach, and they were to say to him: "Ho, fellow! here is some stale urine mingled with various medicaments! if you wish, drink! For if you drink, it will not please you, either with color or with odor or with flavor; but by drinking, you will recover your health." He would drink it without reflecting; he would not refuse. For when he drank it, it would not please him, either with color or with odor or with flavor; but by drinking, he would recover his health.

This, I say, is a parable of the Third Course of Conduct; namely, the Course of Conduct which gives pain now and ripens in pleasure hereafter.

196. CURDS AND HONEY AND GHEE AND JAGGERY

It is precisely as if there were some curds and honey and ghee and jaggery, mingled together, and a man suffering from dysentery were to approach, and they were to say to him: "Ho, fellow! here are curds and honey and ghee and jaggery, mingled together! if you wish, drink! If you drink, it will please you, both with color and with odor and with flavor. Moreover, by drinking, you will recover your health." He would drink it without reflecting; he would not refuse. When he drank, it would please him, both with color and with odor and with flavor. Moreover, by drinking, he would recover his health.

This, I say, is a parable of the Fourth Course of Conduct; namely, the Course of Conduct which gives pleasure now and ripens in pleasure hereafter.

197. EVEN AS THE SUN, SO SHINES RIGHTEOUSNESS

Just as when, in the last of the rainy months, in the autumn time, the sun pierces the clouds and drives away the thunder-heads, and smites and overwhelms every mist of the air and every mist of the darkness, and beams and gleams and shines out, so also this Fourth Course of Conduct, which gives pleasure now and ripens in pleasure hereafter, smites all the perverse contentions of unconverted monks and Brahmans, and beams and gleams and shines out.

Thus spoke the Exalted One. Delighted in heart, those monks applauded the utterances of the Exalted One.

198-203. FIVE FUTURE STATES

Majjhima i. 73-77.

On a certain occasion the Exalted One addressed Venerable Sāriputta as follows:

Five in number are the Future States.

What are the Five?

Hell, the Animal Kingdom, the Region of the Fathers, the World of Men, the Worlds of the Gods.

Hell I know, and the road which leads to hell, and the path which leads to hell, and the path which if a man enter upon, he is reborn, upon dissolution of the body, after death, in a state of loss, in a state of suffering, in a state of punishment, in hell,—that too I know.

The animal kingdom I know, and the road which leads to the animal kingdom, and the path which leads to the animal kingdom, and the path which if a man enter upon, he is reborn, upon dissolution of the body, after death, in the animal kingdom,—that too I know.

The region of the fathers I know, and the road which leads to the region of the fathers, and the path which leads to the region of the fathers, and the path which if a man enter upon, he is reborn, upon dissolution of the body, after death, in the region of the fathers,—that too I know.

The world of men I know, and also the road which leads to the world of men, and the path which leads to the world of men, and the path which if a man enter upon, he is reborn, upon dissolution of the body, after death, in the world of men,—that too I know.

The worlds of the gods I know, and the road which leads to the worlds of the gods, and the path which leads to the worlds of the gods, and the path which if a man enter upon, he is reborn, upon dissolution of the body, after death, in a state of bliss, in a heavenly world,—that too I know.

Nibbāna too I know, and the road which leads to Nibbāna, and the path which leads to Nibbāna, and the path which if a man enter upon, he dwells, through destruction of the Contaminations, even in this present world, having himself comprehended, realized, entered upon, freedom from the Contaminations, deliverance of the mind, deliverance of the understanding,—that too I know.

Hell.

Here in this world, I, embracing mind with mind, with reference to many a man, perceive as follows: Such a path has this man entered upon, and so does he walk, and such a road has he taken, that upon dissolution of the body, after death, he will be reborn in a state of loss, in a state of suffering, in a state of punishment, in hell. And that very man I behold, after a time, with the Heavenly Eye, purified, transcending that of man, upon dissolution of the body, after death, reborn in a state of loss, in a state of suffering, in a state of punishment, in hell, experiencing sharp, bitter sensations of utter pain.

198. PIT OF RED-HOT COALS

It is precisely as if there were a pit of red-hot coals, in depth exceeding a man's height, full of red-hot coals, free from flames, free from smoke; and as if a man were to approach, overheated by the heat, overcome by the heat, weary, trembling, thirsty, and were to make a straight course for that very pit of red-hot coals; and as if a man with eyes were to see that man and were to say: "Such a path has this good man entered upon, and so does he walk, and such a road has he taken, that he will find himself in that very pit of red-hot coals;" and as if he were to behold that very man, after a time, fallen into that pit of red-hot coals, experiencing sharp, bitter sensations of utter pain.

Precisely so I, here in this world, embracing mind with mind, with reference to many a man, perceive as follows: Such a path has this man entered upon, and so does he walk, and such a road has he taken, that upon dissolution of the body, after death, he will be reborn in a state of loss, in a state of suffering, in a state of punishment, in hell. And that very man I behold, after a time, with the Heavenly Eye, purified, transcending that of man, upon dissolution of the body, after death, reborn in a state of loss, in a state of suffering, in a state of punishment, in hell, experiencing sharp, bitter sensations of utter pain.

Animal kingdom.

Here in this world, moreover, I . . . perceive as follows: Such a path has this man entered upon . . . that . . . he will be reborn in the animal kingdom. And that very man I behold . . . reborn in the animal kingdom, experiencing sharp, bitter sensations of pain.

199. DUNG-PIT

It is precisely as if there were a dung-pit, in depth exceeding a man's height, full of dung; and as if a man were to approach, overheated by the heat, overcome by the heat, weary, trembling, thirsty, and were to make a straight course for that very dung-pit; and as if a man with eyes were to see that man and were to say: "Such a path has this good man entered upon, and so does he walk, and such a road has he taken, that he will find himself in that very dung-pit;" and as if he were to behold that very man, after a time, fallen into that dung-pit, experiencing sharp, bitter sensations of pain.

Precisely so I . . . perceive . . . and behold . . .

Region of the fathers.

Here in this world, moreover, I . . . perceive as follows: Such a path has this man entered upon . . . that . . . he will be reborn in the region of the fathers. And that very man I behold . . . reborn in the region of the fathers, experiencing sensations abounding in pain.

200. TREE WITH SCANTY SHADE

It is precisely as if, on a piece of poor soil, there grew a tree with sparse leaves and foliage, with scanty shade; and as if a man were to approach, overheated by the heat, overcome by the heat, weary, trembling, thirsty, and were to make a straight course for that very tree; and as if a man with eyes were to see that man and were to say: "Such a path has this good man entered upon, and so does he walk, and such a road has he taken, that he will come to that very tree;" and as if he were to behold that very man, after a time, sitting or lying in the shade of that tree, experiencing sensations abounding in pain.

Precisely so I . . . perceive . . . and behold . . .

World of men.

Here in this world, moreover, I . . . perceive as follows: Such a path has this man entered upon . . . that . . . he will be reborn in the world of men. And that very man I behold . . . reborn in the world of men, experiencing sensations abounding in pleasure.

201. TREE WITH AMPLE SHADE

It is precisely as if, on a piece of good soil, there grew a tree with thick leaves and foliage, with ample shade; and as if a man were to approach, overheated by the heat, overcome by the heat, weary, trembling, thirsty, and were to make a straight course for that very tree; and as if a man with eyes were to see that man and were to say: "Such a path has this good man entered upon, and so does he walk, and such a road has he taken, that he will come to that very tree;" and as if he were to behold that very man, after a time, sitting or lying in the shade of that tree, experiencing sensations abounding in pleasure.

Precisely so I . . . perceive . . . and behold . . .

Worlds of the Gods.

Here in this world, moreover, I . . . perceive as follows: Such a path has this man entered upon . . . that . . . he will be reborn in a state of bliss, in a heavenly world. And that very man I behold . . . reborn in a state of bliss, in a heavenly world, experiencing sensations of perfect happiness.

202. PALACE

It is precisely as if there were a palace, and in the palace there were a pavilion with bell-shaped pinnacle, plastered within and without, sheltered from the wind, the door-bolts driven home, the windows closed, and in the pavilion there were a couch spread with coverlets, some with long fleeces, some pure white, some woven thickly with flowers, with coverings of the choicest antelope-skins, with a canopy overhead, with red cushions at both ends; and as if a man were to approach, overheated by the heat, overcome by the heat, weary, trembling, thirsty, and were to make a straight course for that very palace; and as if a man with eyes were to see that man and were to say: "Such a path has this good man entered upon, and so does he walk, and such a road has he taken, that he will come to that very palace;" and as if he were to behold that very man, after a time, in that palace, in that pavilion, sitting or lying on that couch, experiencing sensations of perfect happiness.

Precisely so I . . . perceive . . . and behold . . .

Nibbāna.

Here in this world, I, embracing mind with mind, with reference to many a man, perceive as follows: Such a path has this man entered upon, and so does he walk, and such a road has he taken, that he will dwell, through destruction of the Contaminations, even in this present world, having himself comprehended, realized, entered upon, freedom from the Contaminations, deliverance of the mind, deliverance of the understanding. And that very man I behold, after a time, dwelling, through destruction of the Contaminations, even in this present world, having himself comprehended, realized, entered upon, freedom from the Contaminations, deliverance of the mind, deliverance of the understanding,—experiencing sensations of perfect happiness.

203. LOTUS-POND

It is precisely as if there were a lotus-pond, with clear water, with pleasant water, with cool water, transparent, easy of access, full of charm,—and not far off there were a deep forest-grove; and as if a man were to approach, overheated by the heat, overcome by the heat, weary, trembling, thirsty, and were to make a straight course for that very lotus-pond; and as if a man with eyes were to see that man and were to say: "Such a path has this good man entered upon, and so does he walk, and such a road has he taken, that he will come to that very lotus-pond;" and as if he were to behold that very man, after a time, after plunging into that lotus-pond, after bathing and drinking, having quieted, having overcome, all oppression and weariness and burning, sitting or lying in that forest-grove, experiencing sensations of perfect happiness.

Precisely so I, here in this world, embracing mind with mind, with reference to many a man, perceive as follows: Such a path has this man entered upon, and so does he walk, and such a road has he taken, that he will dwell, through destruction of the Contaminations, even in this present world, having himself comprehended, realized, entered upon, freedom from the Contaminations, deliverance of the mind, deliverance of the understanding. And that very man I behold, after a time, dwelling, through destruction of the Contaminations, even in this present world, having himself comprehended, realized, entered upon, freedom from the Contaminations, deliverance of the mind, deliverance of the understanding,—experiencing sensations of perfect happiness.

These, verily, are the Five Future States.

CHAPTER XVI

PARABLES OF THE SACRED HEART OF BUDDHA

"Thou alone, O my Heart, art called to be the Saviour of All!"

A. ON THE TREASURY OF MERITS OF BUDDHA

"Thou art a Treasury of Merits!"

204. ON THE PERFECTING OF THE PERFECTIONS

"Mine eyes have I torn out! My heart's flesh have I uprooted!"

Extract from Dhammapada Commentary i. 1.

On a certain occasion, we are told, a rich merchant of Sāvatthi named Anāthapiṇḍika entertained the Buddha. But because Anāthapiṇḍika remembered that the Buddha was of royal descent, and had been reared amid wealth and luxury, it occurred to him that his guest might grow weary were he to ask him to preach the Doctrine. Therefore he refrained from asking him any questions.

But so soon as Anāthapiṇḍika took his seat, says the legend, the Buddha read his thoughts, and reflected: "This merchant protects me where I have no need to be protected. For I spent four periods of time of incalculable length, and a hundred thousand cycles of time in addition, perfecting the Perfections. My own gloriously adorned head have I cut off! Mine eyes have I torn out! My heart's flesh have I uprooted! Both son and wife, dear to me as life, have I renounced!—And all this I did that I might preach the Doctrine to others. This merchant protects me where I have no need to be protected." And straightway be preached the Doctrine.

205. ON THE ATTAINMENT OF ENLIGHTENMENT

"Blessed indeed is that mother, whose son is such a one as he!"

Extract from Dhammapada Commentary i. 8 *a*.

In one of his previous states of existence, at a time in the past so unimaginably remote that only the merest suggestion of its remoteness is conveyed by the statement that it was four periods of time of incalculable length and a hundred thousand cycles of time in addition in the past, the future Buddha performed a work of merit and formed the High Resolve thereby to attain Enlightenment, to become a Buddha. After he had fulfilled the Ten Perfections and the Ten Minor Perfections and the Ten Major Perfections, making in all Thirty Perfections, he was reborn as Vessantara. In his existence as Vessantara he *bestowed alms* so generously that the earth trembled and quaked, and in that existence also he *renounced both wife and children.* When the term of life allotted to him was come to an end, he was reborn in heaven; and when he had remained in this state of existence during the term of life allotted to him, the deities of the Ten Thousand Worlds assembled together and thus addressed him:

The time is at hand, valiant hero; descend into the womb of your mother;
Deliver the worlds of men and gods; reveal the Region of the Deathless.

Thereupon he made the Five Great Observations, and passing from that state of existence, received a new existence in the royal household of the Sākiyas, as the son of King Suddhodana and Queen Mahā Māyā. In this royal household he was brought up amid wealth and splendor, and in the course of time attained auspicious youth. He spent his youth in three mansions appropriate to the three seasons of the year, enjoying splendor and majesty of sovereignty comparable to the splendor of the World of the Gods. In the course of time it came to pass that, as he proceeded on four successive days to the garden to disport himself, he beheld the Four Heavenly Messengers: an Old Man, a Sick Man, a Corpse, and a Monk. Thereupon he resolved to become a monk. In the evening, as he entered the city, his cousin Kisā Gotamī thus saluted him:

Blessed indeed is that mother, blessed indeed is that father,
Blessed indeed is that wife, whose husband is such a one as he!

Renouncing son and wife, he adopted the Religious Life, and for six years engaged in prolonged fasts and other austerities, hoping thereby to win mastery over self and attain Supreme Enlightenment. While thus engaged, he was tempted by the Evil One. But the future Buddha rebuked the Evil One, and he departed for a season. At the end of this period of austerities, called the Great Struggle, he seated himself cross-legged in Mahāvana Grove, and spent the day in the various degrees of Ecstatic Meditation. In the evening he ascended the Throne of Enlightenment and formed the following resolution: "I will not abandon this posture until I have ceased utterly to crave the things of this world, and my heart is rid of the Depravities."

Thereupon he seated himself under a banyan-tree, facing the east, and before the sun had set, overcame the host of the Evil One. In the first watch he beheld the entire course of his past lives. In the second watch he beheld the fate after death of all living beings. At the conclusion of the third and last watch, he came to understand that the cause of human suffering is Craving for worldly pleasures and life and riches; that if this Craving be uprooted, rebirth and suffering will come to an end; that this Craving can be uprooted by right belief, right living, and the practice of meditation. And thus he became Buddha, the Awakened, the Enlightened. Thereupon he breathed forth the Song of Triumph of All the Buddhas:

CRAVING, BUILDER OF THE HOUSE OF REPEATED EXISTENCES

Through a round of countless existences have I run to no purpose,
Seeking the Builder of the House. Repeated existences involve suffering.

I see thee, Builder of the House! Thou shalt not build the House again!
Broken are all thy rafters! Shattered is thy ridge-pole!
The heart, at rest in Nibbāna, has attained Extinction of Cravings.

206. ABATEMENT OF PLAGUES AT VESĀLI

"If he but come hither, these plagues will subside."

Extract from Dhammapada Commentary xxi. 1.

ONCE upon a time the city of Vesāli was a city of splendor and magnificence and great wealth; numerous were the folk that dwelt therein, and the streets thereof were thronged with inhabitants; therein resided seven thousand and seven hundred and seven Warrior princes, who reigned by turns. For each of the seven thousand and seven hundred and seven princes was provided a separate place of residence; equal in number were the palaces and pagodas; equal in number were the parks and pools, that each might take his pleasure out of doors. But after a time the food-supply gave out and the crops failed and a famine ensued. Thus arose plagues three in number: the plague of famine, the plague of evil spirits, and the plague of disease.

Then the inhabitants of the city assembled and met together and said to the king: "One that is Supremely Enlightened, a Buddha, has arisen in the world, for he, the Exalted One, preaches a Doctrine that avails to the weal and welfare and happiness of all living beings. Moreover, he possesses great magical power and great supernatural power. If he but come hither, these plagues will instantly subside." Accordingly they approached the Exalted One, did reverence to him, and spoke thus: "Reverend Sir, three plagues have arisen at Vesāli. If you but go thither, they will subside. Come, Reverend Sir, let us go thither." The Exalted One acceded to their request.

At eventide the Buddha took his stand at the gate of the city of Vesāli and spoke thus to the Beloved Disciple Ānanda: "Ānanda, receive from me this Sutta of the Three Jewels [Buddha, Doctrine, Order of Monks], and recite it as a charm within the three walls of the city of Vesāli, making the rounds thereof with the Licchavi princes." Elder Ānada received the Sutta of the Three Jewels from the lips of the Buddha, took holy water in the Buddha's stone bowl, and went and took his stand at the gate of the city.

And standing at the gate of the city, Ānanda meditated on all the Merits of the Buddha, beginning with his High Resolve; considering in turn the Ten Perfections of the Tathāgata, the Ten Minor Perfections, and the Ten Major Perfections; the Five Great Sacrifices; the Three Meritorious Acts: in behalf of the world, in behalf of his kinsmen, and for the sake of Enlightenment; his Descent into the Womb in the last state of his existence; his Birth of Queen Māyā; the Great Retirement from the World; the Great Struggle, the Conquest of Māra the Evil One on the Throne of Enlightenment under the Bo-tree, the Attainment of Omniscience, and the Nine Transcendent Conditions.

And when he had so done, he entered the city, and during the three watches of the night went about within the walls thereof reciting the Sutta of the Three Jewels as a charm.

1. Ye spirits that are in this place assembled,
Whether in earth ye dwell, or 'twixt the earth and heaven,
Show each and all a kindly disposition,
And then attentive hark to what is uttered!

2. Therefore, O spirits, be ye all attentive,
With friendliness suffuse all human beings,
Who day and night bring unto you their offerings:
Therefore do ye with heedfulness protect them.

3. Of all the wealth in this world or the next world,
Of all the precious jewels in the heavens,
The like of the Tathāgata exists not,
This is the Precious Jewel of the Buddha:
If this be true, then let there be Salvation!

The moment he uttered the words *Of all the wealth in this world or the next world,* and threw the water upwards, it fell upon the evil spirits. From the third stanza on, drops of water resembling tiny balls of silver rose into the air and fell upon the sick men. Straightway the sickness of those men was cured, and rising to their feet in all quarters, they surrounded the Elder. And the evil spirits, with one accord, departed from the city and returned no more.

207. THE KING WHO TOOK UPON HIMSELF THE SINS AND SUFFERINGS OF HIS PEOPLE

"If there be any that hunger, it is I that have made them hungry."

From E. Chavannes, Cinq Cents Contes No. 15.

ON THE PERFECTION OF GENEROSITY

When we speak of the Perfection of Generosity, what do we mean?

To surround men and animals with benevolent care; to have compassion on the multitude of those that are in error; to rejoice that wise men have succeeded in obtaining Salvation; to protect and succor all living beings; overpassing the heavens and overstepping the earth, to cherish benevolence wide as a river or as the sea, and to exhibit liberality to all living beings; to feed those that are hungry; to relieve those that are thirsty; to clothe those that are cold; to refresh those that suffer with heat; to offer prompt assistance with medicines; when it is a matter of chariots, horses, boats, vehicles, precious substances of all kinds, including famous jewels, husbands and wives, children, or kingdom,—whatever it may be that is asked for,—to make gift thereof immediately,—even as did the crown-prince Sudāna, who exhibited his liberality towards the poor even as a father nourishes his children, and who, when he was banished by the king his father, entertained pity, but not hatred.

King Kindly-and-Silent.

Thus have I heard: Once upon a time the Buddha was keeping residence in the kingdom of Shrāvastī, at the Jetavana monastery, in Anāthapiṇḍada's Grove. The Buddha said to the monks:

ONCE upon a time there was a king named Kindly-and-Silent. This king conducted himself with goodness and fairness. He loved the people as if they had been his children. In governing his kingdom, he applied just laws, and there was no one among his people who entertained hatred for him. His kingdom was a large one, and every one that was therein was occupied with his own business.

This king always cherished sentiments of benevolence, and looked with compassion on the multitude of living beings. He was afflicted by their stupidity and by their errors, through which, in their folly, they brought only loss upon themselves. He sought after and maintained principles of wisdom, and it was his delight not to be ignorant of anything. He had pity on all living beings, and protected them as does Shakra, king of the deities.

Murder, theft, lewdness, deceit, slander, falsehood, words of double meaning, jealousy, anger,—none of all these evil things had left any trace in his heart. He exhibited filial piety and obedience to his father and mother; he respected and loved his relatives within nine degrees of kindred. He sought out the wise men and honored the holy men. He believed in the Buddha, he believed in the Law, he believed in the words of the monks. He believed that good deeds are rewarded with happiness, and that evil deeds are punished with misfortune. He kept the plain rules of the Ten Good Courses of Conduct:

Ten Commandments of the Buddha.

Sinful Acts	1. Thou shalt not take the life of any living being. 2. Thou shalt not take that which is not given. 3. Thou shalt not give way to the sins of the flesh.
Sinful Words	4. Thou shalt not speak falsehood. 5. Thou shalt not speak harshly. 6. Thou shalt not utter slander. 7. Thou shalt not speak idle words.
Sinful Thoughts	8. Thou shalt not covet. 9. Thou shalt not wish evil to another. 10. Thou shalt not entertain false doctrine.

Another List of Ten.

1-4. As above.
5. Thou shalt avoid occasions of heedlessness through the use of liquor or spirits or other intoxicants.
6-10. Rules for persons vowed to the religious life.

King Kindly-and-Silent and the thief.

It so happened that in his kingdom there was a poor man in such a state of misery that he could endure it no longer. Being at the end of his resources, he committed a theft. The owner of the stolen goods arrested him and arraigned him before the king.

The king asked him: "Did you steal?"

The thief replied that he had indeed stolen.

"Why," returned the king, "did you steal?"

The thief replied: "I was actually in terrible misery, and had no means of living; that is why, breaking your laws, so holy and plain, I walked into the fire and committed a theft."

The king, penetrated with compassion, praised him for his frank sincerity, and quite embarrassed, felt ashamed of himself. Heaving a deep sigh, he said: "If there are among my people those that suffer from hunger, it is I that have made them hungry. If there are among my people those that suffer from cold, it is I that have stripped them of their garments." Then he added: "I am so situated that I can bring it about that no one in my kingdom shall be in misery. On me alone depend the sufferings and the enjoyments of the people."

Accordingly he granted a general amnesty to his kingdom. He brought forth all the precious objects which he had in his storehouses and dispensed them in largesses. Those who were worn out with hunger and thirst, he made to eat and drink. Those who were cold, he clad. Those who were sick, he provided with medicines. Fields, gardens, dwellings, gold, silver, round pearls and irregular pearls,—of all these, each person obtained as much as he asked for. From the birds that fly and the animals that walk, to the insects, all obtained all that they wanted, in the matter of the five kinds of cereals and products of the soil.

From the moment when the king dispensed these largesses, the kingdom was prosperous and the people lived in comfort. One person drew another towards wisdom. Among the people, no one killed any more, nor stole the goods of another, nor sinned with the wife of another, nor was a cheat or a slanderer or a liar or insincere in his talk or jealous or angry: all these wicked and mean impulses subsided and disappeared. All men believed in the Buddha, believed in the Law, believed in the monks; they believed that whoever does good deeds obtains happiness, that whoever practices evil incurs misfortune. The whole kingdom was peaceful and happy; the punishments of the lash and the stick were no more administered. The enemy kingdoms made their submission; the arms of war rotted in the magazines; in the prisons no more were prisoners put in chains. The people praised this happy state of things, and said: "What happiness, that we were permitted to live at such a time!"

The deities, the dragons, the demons, and the spirits,—all, without exception, contributed to the rejoicing, and accorded their favors and their protection to this kingdom. Baneful influences disappeared; the five cereals ripened in abundance; households possessed them in abundance. But more particularly the king rejoiced; at that time he obtained the Five Blessings. These are the Five Blessings: (1) to live long; (2) to possess comeliness that grows each day; (3) to possess virtue which shakes the eight directions, the zenith and the nadir; (4) to have no sickness, and to have energy which increases each day; (5) to possess a kingdom whose four regions are at peace, and to have a heart that rejoices without ceasing.

When, finally, the king died, he was at that moment like a man in full vigor, who eats heartily and delights to sleep. Immediately he was reborn in heaven among the gods of the Thirty-three. As for the people of this kingdom, they kept the Ten Commandments which the king had given to them, and there was none of them that went to be reborn in the form of a denizen of hell, a hungry ghost, or an animal: after their death, they were all reborn in heaven among the deities.

The Buddha said to the monks: "At that time, he that was King Kindly-and-Silent was I myself."

Having heard this religious instruction, the monks rejoiced above measure; they bowed to the Buddha and then withdrew.

B. ON THE SACRIFICE OF THE BODY AND BLOOD

"I will satisfy the hunger of my friends with my own body and blood!"

208. BOAR AND LION

"Eat me, O lion!"

Adapted from C. H. Tawney, Ocean of the Streams of Story (Kathāsaritsāgara), Chapter 72.

In times past there dwelt in a cave the Vindhya mountains a wise boar, who was none other than the Buddha in a previous state of existence, and with him his friend a monkey. He was compassionate towards all living beings. One day there came to his cave a lion and a lioness and their cub. And the lion said to his mate: "Since the rains have hindered the movements of all living beings, we shall of a certainty perish for lack of some animal to eat." And the lioness said: "Of a certainty one or another of us is destined to die of hunger. Therefore do you and the cub eat me, for thus you will save your lives! Are you not my lord and master? Can you not get another mate like me? Therefore do you and the cub eat me, for thus you will save your lives!"

Now at that moment the wise boar awoke, and hearing the words of the lioness, was delighted, and thought to himself: "This is the fruit of the merit which I have acquired in previous states of existence. I will satisfy the hunger of my friends with my own body and blood." Then the wise boar arose from his bed and went out of his cave and said to the lion: "My good friend, do not despair. For here I am, ready to be eaten by you and your mate and your cub. Eat me, O lion!" Now when the lion heard these words, he was delighted, and said to his mate: "Let our cub eat first; then I will eat, and you shall eat after me." The lioness agreed.

So first the cub ate some of the flesh of the wise boar, and then the lion began to eat. And while he was eating, the wise boar said to him: "Be quick and drink my blood before it sinks into the ground, and satisfy your hunger with my flesh, and let your mate eat what is left." So the lion gradually devoured the flesh until only the bones were left. But—wonderful to relate!—the wise boar did not die, for his life remained in him, as if to see how long his endurance would endure. In the meantime the lioness died of hunger in the cave, and the lion went off somewhere or other with his cub, and so the night came to an end.

Then the monkey awoke and went out of the cave, and seeing the wise boar reduced to a heap of bones, became greatly excited and exclaimed: "What reduced you to a heap of bones? Tell me, O friend, if you can." So the wise boar told him the whole story. Then the monkey did reverence to the wise boar, and said to him: "Tell me what you wish me to do, and I will do it." The wise boar replied: "I wish only to have my body restored to me like as it was before, and to have the lioness that died of hunger restored to life again, that she may satisfy her hunger with my body and blood." Thereupon, as the fruit of the merit which the wise boar had acquired, he was transformed into a sage, and the monkey into a sage likewise.

209. FAIRY-PRINCE AND GRIFFIN

"Eat me, O griffin!"

Adapted from C. H. Tawney, Ocean of the Streams of Story (Kathāsaritsāgara), Chapters 22 and 90.

On a ridge of the Himālaya stands a city called the Golden City, for it gleams from afar like the rays of the sun. And in that city, once upon a time, lived the king of the fairies, and his name was Jīmūta-ketu. And in the garden of his palace grew a wishing-tree, and its name was Granter of Desires, for it granted all desires.

By the favor of that tree the king obtained a son, who was none other than the Future Buddha, and his name was Jīmūta-vāhana. He was valiant in generosity, of mighty courage, and compassionate towards all living beings.

When Jīmūta-vāhana was become of age, his father made him crown-prince. Thus did he become the fairy-prince. And when he had become the fairy-prince, the ministers of the kingdom came to him and said: "O fairy-prince, do reverence always to this wishing-tree, for it grants all desires, and cannot be resisted by any living creature. For so long as we possess this tree, we cannot suffer injury of any kind from any one, even from Indra, king of the gods, much less from any other."

When Jīmūta-vāhana heard these words, he thought to himself: "Alas! our forefathers, for all their possession of this noble tree, obtained by the favor of this tree naught but wealth and victory over their enemies; thus did they demean themselves, and thus did they demean this tree likewise. For no such purposes as these will I employ this tree. For I know that the good things of this world endure but for a short while, and then perish and vanish utterly. But friendliness and compassion and generosity towards all living beings yield abundant fruit, both in this world and in the next. As for wealth, if it be not used for the benefit of others, it is like lightning which for an instant stings the eye, and then flickers and vanishes. Therefore if this wishing-tree which we possess, and which grants all desires, be employed for the benefit of others, we shall reap from it all the fruit that it can give. Accordingly I will so act that by the wealth of this tree all living beings shall be delivered from poverty and distress."

Then Jīmūta-vāhana went to the wishing-tree and said: "O tree-spirit, thou that dost grant to us the fruit that we desire, fulfil to-day this one wish of mine: Deliver all living beings from poverty and distress." Straightway—wonderful to relate!—the wishing-tree showered a shower of gold upon the earth, and all living beings rejoiced thereat and became well-disposed to Jīmūta-vāhana, and the fame and glory of him spread both near and far. But the relatives of Jīmūta-ketu, seeing that his throne was firmly established by the glory of his son, were moved to jealousy and became hostile to him. And because the kingdom of Jīmūta-ketu was weak, they determined to attack it and overthrow it, and to take possession of the wishing-tree that granted all desires. And they assembled and met together and began preparations to attack the kingdom of Jīmūta-ketu and to overthrow it and to take possession of the wishing-tree that granted all desires.

Thereupon Jīmūta-vāhana the fairy-prince said to Jīmūta-ketu the fairy-king his father: "Why should we seek to obtain new wealth, or to retain the wealth that we possess? Is not this body of ours like a bubble in the water, which bursts in an instant and vanishes? Is it not like a candle, which, when it is exposed to the wind, flickers for an instant and goes out? Should a wise man desire to obtain wealth or to retain it when it is obtained, by the killing of living beings? I will not fight with my relatives. Therefore I will leave my kingdom and go to some forest-hermitage. Let these miserable wretches do as they like, but let us not kill the members of our own family."

And Jīmūta-ketu the fairy-king said to Jīmūta-vāhana the fairy-prince his son: "Then will I too go, my son. For what desire for rule can I have, who am old, when you, who are young, out of compassion towards all living beings, abandon your kingdom as though it were so much straw and stubble?" Thereupon Jīmūta-vāhana, with his father and mother, went to the Malaya mountain, and took up his abode in a forest-hermitage, the dwelling of the fairy-magicians, the Siddhas, where the brooks were hidden by the sandalwood trees, and devoted himself to the care of his father and mother.

One day, as he was roaming about with a companion, he came to a wood on the shore of the sea. There he saw many heaps of bones. And he said to his companion: "Whose bones are these?" His companion replied: "Give ear, and I will tell you the story in a few words."

Fairy-king and griffin.

In times past Kadrū and Vinatā, the two wives of Kashyapa, had a quarrel. Kadrū said that the horses of the Sun were black, and Vinatā said that they were white, and they made a wager that whichever of the two was wrong should become a slave of the other. Then Kadrū, bent on winning, actually induced her sons the snakes to defile the horses of the Sun by spitting venom over them;

and showing them to Vinatā thus defiled, she conquered her by a trick and made her her slave.

When the griffin, the son of Vinatā, heard of that, he came and tried to induce Kadrū to release Vinatā from slavery. Then the snakes, the sons of Kadrū, said to the griffin, the son of Vinatā: "O griffin, the gods have begun to churn the sea of milk. Fetch thence the drink of immortality and give it to us as a substitute, and then take your mother away with you." When the griffin heard these words, he went to the sea of milk and displayed his mighty prowess in order to obtain the drink of immortality. Then the god Vishṇu, pleased with his mighty prowess, condescended to say to him: "I am pleased with thee; choose some boon." Then the griffin, angry because his mother had been made a slave, asked the following boon of Vishṇu: "May the snakes become my food!" Vishṇu granted him this boon. Now Indra, king of the gods, listened to the conversation, and when the griffin, by his mighty prowess, had obtained the drink of immortality, he said to him: "O griffin, take steps to prevent the foolish snakes from consuming the drink of immortality, and to enable me to take it away from them again." The griffin agreed, and elated by the boon of Vishṇu, he went to the snakes with the vessel containing the drink of immortality.

And he called out from afar to the snakes: "To you have I brought the drink of immortality. Take it, and release my mother. But if you are afraid, I will put it on a bed of darbha-grass. So soon as my mother is released, I will go; therefore take the drink of immortality thence." Now the snakes were terrified by reason of the boon which Vishṇu had granted to the griffin, and at once agreed to the bargain. Then the griffin set on a bed of darbha-grass the vessel containing the drink of immortality, and the snakes released his mother from slavery, and the griffin departed with her.

But while the snakes, not suspicious of a ruse, were in the very act of taking the drink of immortality, Indra, king of the gods, suddenly swooped down, and confounding them with his mighty prowess, carried off the vessel containing the drink of immortality. Then the snakes in despair licked the bed of darbha-grass with their tongues, thinking that there might be so much as a drop of the drink of immortality spilt thereon; whereupon—wonderful to relate!—their tongues became split, and they became double-tongued for nothing.

Thus did the snakes fail to obtain the drink of immortality. And straightway their enemy the griffin, relying on the boon which he had obtained from Vishṇu, swooped down on them and began to devour them. And this he did again and again. And he wrought such havoc among them that the snakes in Pātāla were nigh unto death from sheer fright, and their females miscarried, and the whole race of the snakes was nigh unto utter destruction. Then Vāsuki, king of the snakes, fearing that the whole race of the snakes would be rooted out, begged the griffin to relent, and made the following agreement with him: "O king of birds, every day, on the hill that rises out of the sand of the sea, I will send you a single snake to eat. But you must not commit the folly of entering Pātāla, for by destroying utterly the whole race of the snakes, you will only defeat your own purpose." The griffin consented. So every day, on the hill that rises out of the sand of the sea, Vāsuki, king of the snakes, sends to the griffin, the king of the birds, a single snake to eat. And the griffin, the king of the birds, devours each day the snake which Vāsuki, king of the snakes, sends to him to eat. These heaps of bones are the bones of the snakes which the griffin has eaten, and which, gradually accumulating, have come to look like the peak of a mountain.

When Jīmūta-vāhana, the fairy-prince, embodiment of generosity and compassion towards all living beings, heard this story from the lips of his companion, he was pricked to the heart. And he said to his companion: "Of a truth, Vāsuki, king of the snakes, is to be pitied, for that, like a coward, he delivers with his own hand into the hands of his most bitter enemy the snakes that are his subjects. Since he has a thousand faces and a thousand mouths, why can he not say with one of his mouths to the griffin who is his enemy: 'Eat me first, O griffin!'" Then did the noble-hearted Jīmūta-vāhana make the following Earnest Wish: "May I, by the sacrifice of my own body and blood, obtain Supreme Enlightenment!"

At that moment a servant summoned Jīmūta-vāhana's companion to return home, and Jīmūta-vāhana, embodiment of generosity and compassion towards all living beings, was left alone.

And Jīmūta-vāhana roamed about alone, intent on carrying out the resolution which he had formed. And as he roamed about, he heard afar off a piteous sound of weeping. And drawing near, he beheld on a lofty slab of rock a youth of handsome appearance plunged in bitter grief. And by his side stood an officer of some monarch, as if he had brought him and left him there. And the youth was seeking to persuade an old woman who was weeping, to cease her weeping and return whence she had come.

And Jīmūta-vāhana stood and listened, melted with pity, eager to know who he might be, and she. And the old woman, overwhelmed with the burden of her grief, began to look again and again at the youth, and to lament her misfortune in the following words: "Alas, Shankha-chūḍa! thou that wast obtained by me at the cost of a hundred bitter pangs! Alas, virtuous youth! Alas, son, only scion of our family, where shall I behold thee again? Bereft of thee, thy father will be plunged into the darkness of sorrow, and will not for long endure to live. That body of thine, which would suffer even from the torch of the sun's rays,—how can it endure the agony of being devoured by the griffin? How comes it that Fate and the king of the snakes were able to discover thee, the only son of ill-starred me, though the world of the snakes is wide?" Thereupon the youth said: "Mother, I am afflicted enough as it is. Why do you afflict me more? Return to your home, I beg you. This is my last reverence to you. The griffin will soon be here." When the old woman heard those words, she cast her sorrowful eyes all around the horizon, and cried aloud: "Alas, I am undone! Who will deliver my son from death?"

Then Jīmūta-vāhana with joy and delight went up to the old woman and said: "Mother, I will deliver your son!"

When the old woman heard those words, she was frightened and terrified, for she thought that the griffin had come. And straightway she cried out: "Eat me, O griffin! eat me!" Then said the youth her son: "Mother, be not afraid, for this is no griffin!" Then said Jīmūta-vāhana: "Mother, I am the prince of the fairies, disguised in the garb of a man. I am come to deliver your son from death. I will give my own body and blood to the hungry griffin. Therefore return to your home, and take your son with you." But the old woman said: "By no means! for in a still higher sense you yourself are my very own son, since you have shown such a measure of compassion to me and my son at this time." Then said Jīmūta-vāhana: "I have formed a resolution, and you must not defeat my purpose."

Then said the youth: "O thou of great and noble heart! I cannot consent to save my own body at the cost of thine. Should a common stone be saved by the sacrifice of a precious stone? The world is full of those who, like myself, pity only themselves. But few in number are those who entertain sentiments of compassion for the whole world and for all the living beings that are therein." At that moment the trees began to sway with the wind of the wings of the griffin, and seemed to utter a cry of dissuasion. And the sea, churned by the wind, seemed with the eyes of its bright-flashing jewels to be gazing in wonder and astonishment at the greatness of his courage and the depth of his compassion. Then came the griffin, hiding the heavens with his outspread wings. And swooping down, he smote the valiant hero Jīmūta-vāhana with his beak, and gripping him with his talons, carried him off from that slab of rock; and soaring aloft, flew quickly with him to a peak of the Malaya mountain, to eat him there. And Jīmūta-vāhana's crest-jewel was torn from his head, and drops of blood fell from his body, as the griffin carried him through the air. And while the griffin was devouring his body and blood, he uttered the following Earnest Wish: "May my body and blood be offered thus in every state of my existence, and may I not obtain rebirth in heaven or deliverance from the round of existences if thereby I shall be deprived of the opportunity of doing good to my neighbor!"

But afterwards, through the finding of his crest-jewel, his kinsfolk and friends effected his deliverance from the power of the griffin, and a goddess sprinkled him with a potion, whereupon he arose more glorious than before, with all his limbs made whole again. And the goddess said to him: "My son, I am pleased with this sacrifice of thy body and blood. Therefore I sprinkle thee king of the fairies, and thy reign shall endure for a cycle of time." Thereupon a rain of flowers fell from the sky, and the drums of the gods resounded with approbation. And the griffin repented of his evil deeds, and said: "From this day henceforth I will not again eat snakes. As for those which I have already eaten, let them return to life again!" Then—wonderful to relate!—all the snakes that he had previously eaten returned to life again. Then Jīmūta-vāhana was escorted to the Himālaya, and was sprinkled king over all the kings of the fairies, and his reign endured for a cycle of time.

210. JEWELER, MONK, AND GOOSE

"I am ready to sacrifice my body to preserve the life of this goose!"

Moreover, one should observe the Precepts strictly; it is better to renounce one's life than to violate them.

From E. Huber, Açvaghosha's Sūtrālaṁkāra, No. 63.

Thus have I heard: A monk was making his round for alms from door to door. He reached the house of a jeweler, and stopped before the door. At that moment the jeweler was preparing to pierce a pearl for the king. The color of the monk's robe was reflected on the pearl, which thus took on a red color. The jeweler went into his house to seek food for the monk. At that moment a goose saw this pearl, red in color, similar in appearance to a piece of meat; immediately she swallowed it. Then the jeweler returned with the food and gave it to the monk. When he looked for the pearl, nowhere could he find it again. This pearl was of great value and belonged to the king. The jeweler, who was poor, and who had just lost the king's precious pearl, addressed the monk excitedly and said to him: "Give me back the pearl!" Then the monk thus reflected: "This pearl has just been swallowed by a goose. If I say that to this man, he will kill the goose to get the pearl. I am in a very painful situation. What should I do to avert this calamity?" Then he uttered the following stanzas:

If I respect the life of this living being, my body will endure sufferings;
But I have no other means,—my life alone can redeem hers.

If I say to this man that the goose has swallowed [the pearl],
He will not believe me, and he will kill this goose.

Why should I use this means?
I am going to give my own body to save her.

Now, to prevent this goose from being killed,
Shall I say that some one has taken it and carried it off?

No more may this be said.
For if one desires to keep oneself free from sins,
One must refrain from words of falsehood.

I have indeed heard the Brahmans say:
Recoil not from falsehood to save your life.

But I have also heard this saying of an ancient sage:
It is better to abandon one's life than ever to make a lie.

The Buddha has related the story of a thief
Whose body was mutilated with a saw.

But even in the midst of his sufferings,
He was altogether unwilling to violate the Law.

Even though by a lie one might save himself,
It is not proper to make it.

It is better to remain faithful to the Precepts
And to renounce your own life.

If I should make myself guilty of a lie,
All those who are vowed to the religious life
Could accuse me of having violated the Precepts.

Such an accusation, and their contempt,
Would, of a surety, be calculated to burn my heart.

It is for this reason
That it does not become me to violate the Precepts.

In the midst of my sorry plight,
I should imitate geese,
Which, when drinking a mixture of water and milk,

Are able to drink all of the milk,
And leave only the water.

It is thus that I should act:
I should flee the evil, and choose only the good.

Here are the words of a Sūtra:
When a wise man and a simpleton
Find themselves in the same difficulty,
The former does not imitate the bad conduct of the latter.

The man who adheres to the good,
Knows how to leave the evil alone,
Like a goose that drinks a mixture of water and milk.

I am ready to sacrifice my body and my life
To preserve the life of this goose.

This faithful observance of the Precepts
Will bring me to Deliverance.

When the jeweler had heard these stanzas, he said to the monk: "Give me back my pearl! If you don't give it back, I will make you endure many sufferings, and will show you no pity." The monk replied to him: "Do you think I would remain silent, if I had stolen your pearl?" The jeweler said to him: "Nevertheless, there was no other person who would have been able to rob me of this pearl." And immediately the jeweler closed his door and said to the monk: "You are mighty obstinate!" Then the monk turned his eyes in the four directions, but found a refuge nowhere,—like a stag taken in an enclosure, knowing no way to get out: thus was the monk, deprived of help. Then the monk tightened and adjusted his robes. This man said to the monk: "Are you getting ready to fight with me?" The monk replied to him: "I will not fight with you. I fight only with the Contaminations and the Bonds. What I have just done, was for a different reason: I fear that my body may be stripped naked when you strike me. For we monks, when we are about to endure sufferings, when our end is at hand, cover ourselves with our robes to prevent the stripping of our body." And the monk uttered these stanzas further:

The Exalted One was full of modesty;
I am obedient to his teaching.

When I reach the termination of my life,
I wish not to have my body remain naked.

Then the jeweler said to the monk: "Have you not, then, the least concern for your life?" The monk replied to him: "The Law of us religious requires us to preserve our life until we have attained Deliverance. Even in the midst of the greatest dangers, it is necessary to protect your own life. But now I know in advance that I ought to abandon this body; and for this deed the congregation of those who have retired from the world will glorify my name." Then he uttered these stanzas:

When I quit life,
I shall fall as a dry branch falls.

But that will be in order that I may be glorified
For having given my life to save a goose.

And that will cause all who come after me
To be inspired with disgust [for the world]
And to be ready to sacrifice their body.

Those who hear the story of it told
Will redouble their zeal;
They will follow the Noble Path;
They will keep the Precepts faithfully.

And those who violate the Precepts
Will form the resolution to keep them with all their heart.

Then the jeweler said to the monk: "What you have just said is only sham and falsehood. You wish simply to win the praises of men." The monk replied to him: "Then you believe me to be capable of staining myself with a falsehood? Pray, what good would these praises do me? I am not shamming when I say that I am joyful. I am not anxious to have men glorify my name, but I desire the Exalted One to know my devoted heart." Then he uttered these stanzas:

The disciples of the Great Sage,
In order to remain faithful to the Precepts,

Abandon life, which is difficult to abandon:
They do so in order that the inhabitants of the whole world

And all those that have retired from the world
May form high resolutions.

Though they may not have formed them,
They will surely form them in the future.

Then the jeweler bound the monk and beat him with a stick. He asked the monk: "Where is the pearl? Give me back my pearl!" The monk replied to him: "I haven't the pearl." The jeweler began to weep, for his heart was full of remorse; and the fact that the pearl belonged to the king added yet more to his despair. The monk uttered these stanzas:

Alas! how poor this man is!
I know good and evil deeds.
His heart is filled with remorse.
Alas! this poor man
Does evil because he is poor.

Then the jeweler, shedding tears, prostrated himself on his face before the feet of the monk, and said to him: "Make me glad, and give me back my pearl. Then you will cease to suffer, and you will not make me suffer any more." The monk replied: "I have not, in reality, taken it." Then the jeweler said: "This monk is very obstinate; notwithstanding his sufferings, he denies having the pearl."

The jeweler, who was very poor, and who could not find his pearl, commenced once more, insane with anger, to beat [the monk]. The monk, who had his two hands and his neck bound, turned his eyes in the four directions; he saw no one whom he could call; death for him was inevitable. Then the monk said to himself: "In the round of existences, one is always in danger of such sufferings. One must stoutly refuse to violate the Precepts. For if one violates the Precepts, one is smitten with the punishments of hell, which are indeed more terrible than my present evils." And he pronounced these stanzas:

With constancy I call to mind the All-knowing,
The Merciful, the Compassionate,
My venerated Master;
I remember his teaching,
And the words of Fou-na-kia,
And I call to mind
The sage Kshānti who resided in the forest:
They mutilated his feet and his hands,
They cut off his ears and his nose,
Without making him angry.

A monk ought also to call to mind
That which is said in the Sūtra:
Thus the Buddha enjoins upon the monks:
If with a saw they mutilate you,
All your members, your hands and your feet,
You must not get angry.
You must think solely of the Buddha;
You must call to mind the Precepts!

In my previous states of existence
I have been put to death for adultery or for theft
So many times that they cannot be counted.
As deer, as stag, or as one of the six domestic animals,
I have been put to death innumerable times,
But in these occurrences I suffered without profit to myself.

To die for the keeping of the Precepts
Is better than to live and violate them.

Even if one desires to preserve his life,
He will end by dying just the same.
It is far better to keep the Precepts

And to preserve one's life for the profit of others.
Let us renounce this body, exposed to dangers,
To obtain life in Deliverance.

Among those who renounce life,
There are those who reap merit therefrom,
And there are those who derive no profit therefrom.
The wise man, while preserving his life,
Reaps glory and merit;
The man without intelligence, when he abandons his life,
Suffers in vain, and gains no advantage.

At that moment the monk said to the jeweler: "Do not forget sentiments of pity! Oh, how I suffer!" Then the jeweler, weeping and sad, pronounced these stanzas:

Even in the act of beating you,
I suffer horribly;
And when I think of the king
Who will demand of me an accounting for my pearl,
Renewed is my inclination to torture you.

Escape, then, from these sufferings,
And cause my sufferings to cease.
You have renounced the world;
You should renounce covetousness.
Drive covetousness from your heart!
Give me back my pearl!

The monk smiled feebly, and pronounced these stanzas:

Yes! my heart is full of covetousness,
But never have I desired this pearl.
Hearken to what I shall say to you:
What I covet is the good opinion
And the admiration of the sages;
What I covet is the Precepts
And the Law which procures final Deliverance.
The supreme object of my covetousness
Is the Way of the Deathless [Nirvāṇa].

Never has my heart desired your pearl.
I clothe myself with robes from a dust-heap,
I live on food received by way of alms,
I have established my residence under the trees:
All that suffices me.
What reason should I have
To make myself a thief?
Consider this well!

The jeweler said to the monk: "What is the good of all these words?" Then he garroted him further, beat him with a stick, and bound him tight with cords. His eyes, his mouth, and his nose were bleeding.

At this moment the goose came back to drink his blood. The jeweler, furious, beat the goose to death. The monk said: "Is this goose quite dead?" The jeweler replied to him: "Why do you ask me whether the goose is dead or alive?" Then the monk turned towards the goose, and when he saw that she was dead, he wept and displayed no satisfaction. Then he uttered these stanzas:

I endured all the tortures
In the hope of sparing the life of this goose.

And now I remain alive still,
While the goose has died before me.

In the hope of saving your life,
I endured these horrible sufferings.

Why did you precede me in death?
No more do I deserve reward.

The jeweler asked the monk: "What affection have you for this goose, that you are so greatly afflicted [by her death]?" The monk replied to him: "I am sad because I have been unable to fulfil my vow. I formed the resolution to give my life for that of the goose. Now that this goose is dead, I am unable to fulfil my vow." The jeweler asked; "Why did you utter this vow?" The monk replied: "The Buddha, when he was still a Future Buddha, permitted his hands and his feet to be mutilated, and did not spare himself when the salvation of living beings was involved. I wished to imitate him." Then he uttered these stanzas:

In times past, the Future Buddha
Sacrificed himself to redeem the life of a dove;
I formed a similar resolution,
I was sacrificing my life for a goose.

I formed a noble resolution,
I desired to save the life of this goose.
But since you have just killed the goose,
I cannot fulfil my vow.

The jeweler said: "I do not yet understand your words. Explain to me in detail your reason for so acting." Then the monk replied to him with these stanzas:

My robe red in color
Threw on the pearl a reflection of flesh color.

This goose mistook it for a piece of meat
And swallowed it.

I endured all the sufferings
To save this goose.

In the midst of the tortures and the pains,
I hoped to save her life.

The living beings of the whole world
Are regarded by the Buddha as his children;

Even those who are destitute of all merit
Are embraced by the Buddha with pity.

Gautama is my Master:
How could I let a living being suffer?

This living being is my brother:
How could I wound him?

When the jeweler had heard these stanzas, he opened the belly of the goose and recovered his pearl. Then he lamented in a loud voice, and said to the monk: "To save the life of the goose, you have not spared your own! And thus you have caused me to act contrary to the Law." Then he uttered these stanzas:

You are a Treasury of Merits,
Like a fire that is covered with ashes.

The result of my folly will be
That I shall be punished in many hundreds of births.

You are altogether worthy
To bear the standard of the Buddha.

Blinded by my ignorance,
I have not been able to exercise good judgment.

The fire of ignorance burns me.
Therefore pray remain a moment longer
To receive the expression of my repentance;

As one who has stumbled,
Lift me up again from the earth, cause me to stand erect!
Accept a slight reparation from me!

Then the jeweler joined his hands, addressed himself to the monk, and pronounced in a loud voice the following stanzas:

Glory to him whose conduct is pure!
Glory to him who has kept the Precepts faithfully!

Placed in a difficult position,
He has shown no sign of wavering.

When one is not placed in a position similarly painful,
There is nothing extraordinary in keeping the Precepts.

But when, in the midst of tortures like these,
One has the courage to keep the Precepts,
This is called performing a difficult act.

To sustain tortures to save a goose,
And not violate the Precepts,—
This is in truth difficult to do.

When the jeweler had expressed his repentance, he permitted the monk to return to his residence.

211. RŪPĀVATĪ

"Only that I might attain Supreme Enlightenment!"

Synopsis of Divyāvadāna 472, 473, 478.

In a previous state of existence the Future Buddha was reborn as a woman named Rūpāvatī. One day Rūpāvatī came upon a starving woman who was about to devour her new-born child, whereupon she cut off her own breasts and gave them to the woman for food. When her husband learned of her act, he performed the following Act of Truth: "If it be true that so wonderful and marvelous thing has never been seen before or heard of before, then may your breasts be restored." Straightway her breasts were restored.

Indra, fearing that by the merit of her sacrifice Rūpāvatī might thrust him from his seat, went in disguise to Rūpāvatī and asked her: "Is it true that you sacrificed your breasts for the sake of a child?" "It is true." "Did you not, either in the act, or after the act, regret so doing?" "No." "Who will believe you?" Rūpāvatī replied: "Then I will make an Act of Truth:

" 'If it be true that neither in the act nor after the act had I any feeling of remorse or regret; if it be true that I acted, not for the sake of dominion, not for the sake of heaven, not that I might become an Indra or a Universal Monarch, but solely and only that I might attain Supreme Enlightenment: thereby to subdue the unsubdued, to emancipate the unemancipated, to console the unconsoled, to enable them that have attained not Nirvāṇa to attain unto Nirvāṇa;—if all this be true, then may I cease to be a woman and become a man.'" Straightway she ceased to be a woman and became a man, Rūpāvata.

Reborn as the Brahman Chandra-prabha, the Future Buddha one day came upon a starving tigress about to devour her young. He thereupon resolved to give his own body and blood to the tigress for food. So calling upon the deities of various ranks to witness, he announced his intention of making the highest and most sublime of all sacrifices; namely, the sacrifice of his own body and blood. Then, making an Act of Truth in terms identical with the preceding, he drew his sword, cut his own throat, and flung his body to the tigress.

212. KING SHIBI AND THE BIRD

"Thou alone, O my Heart, art called to be the Saviour of All!"

From E. Huber, Açvaghosha's Sūtrālaṁkāra, No. 64.

Moreover: It is difficult to obtain the privilege of hearing the Law of the Buddha. In times past, when the Tathāgata was yet a Future Buddha, he spared not his life when it was a matter of finding the Law. Accordingly, one should listen to the Law with heart full of zeal.

I HAVE heard related the parable of the pigeon:

There was an heretical teacher who expounded his false doctrine to Indra [king of the gods]. This heretical teacher, destitute of true knowledge, pretended to possess omniscience, and denied the existence of a being possessed of Perfect and Supreme Enlightenment. When Indra heard these words, he experienced displeasure, and became very sad. Then Indra proceeded to explore the universe, to discover whether there was an ascetic who had arrived at omniscience, at the end of his desires,—even as it is said in the stanzas of the Sūtras of the *Questions of Indra:*

My spirit seeks, but cannot find contentment;
Day and night, doubts agitate me;
I cannot distinguish the true from the false.

From afar am I come
With anxious desire never-ceasing
To complete my inquiries:

I know not in what place
The great and true Saviour is now to be found.

Vishva-karman [Vulcan] said to Indra: "A denizen of heaven should not give himself over to sadness. In the world of men, in the kingdom of Kushi-nagara, dwells a king named Shibi. He devotes himself with zeal to macerations and to the quest of Supreme Enlightenment. Men of intelligence who have watched him, believe that this king will presently attain the condition of a Buddha. Let us approach him!" Indra replied: "Is it perfectly certain that he will not be shaken in his resolution?" Then he uttered these stanzas:

Although the little fishes
Be very numerous, few among them grow big;
And among the fruits of the mango-tree,
Those that attain maturity are rare.

So also is it with Future Buddhas:
Those who utter the vow to attain Enlightenment are numerous;
Those who attain it are few indeed.

Those who practice austerities
Without ever flinching,
May be looked upon as Future Buddhas;
Those who desire to become Buddhas
Should show a heart full of constancy.

Vishva-karman said: "Let us make a journey and find out for ourselves. If, in reality, he has formed an unshakable resolution, we will pay our respects to him."

Then Indra, with the intention of sounding the heart of the Future Buddha, changed himself into a hawk, and said to Vishva-karman: "Change yourself into a pigeon!" Immediately Vishva-karman changed himself into a pigeon with a body as blue as the sky and eyes like red pearls, and took his place near Indra. At this moment Indra, filled with pity, said to Vishva-karman: "Why do we seek to increase the troubles of the Future Buddha? We shall cause the king of the Shibis to endure sufferings; it is true that he will suffer. But when one is selecting a precious jewel, one examines it repeatedly in order to make sure that it is not artificial. The way to examine a jewel is to cut it, to break it, to expose it to the fire, and to strike it; then alone does one know whether it is not artificial."

Then the pigeon, pursued by the hawk, displayed great fear, and in the presence of a great crowd, came and sought refuge under the arm-pit of the king of the Shibis. The pigeon had the blue color of a lotus-leaf, and his brightness shone like a rain-bow in the midst of a dark cloud; he gleamed with pure lustre. Thereat all the people were filled with wonderment, and uttered these stanzas:

In truth, he ought to be full of mercy,
In order that all living beings may have entire confidence in him.

Thus [the birds], when the sun disappears,
Fly away towards their nest.

But at this moment the hawk says:
"O king, give me back my prey!"

The king heard the words of the hawk, and saw the fright of the pigeon. Straightway he pronounced these stanzas:

This pigeon, seized with fear,
Has come towards me with wings outspread.

Although his mouth cannot speak,
His eyes are filled with tears.

It becomes me, therefore,
To grant him aid and protection.

Then the great king, in order to reassure the pigeon, uttered these stanzas further:

Have no fear!
Never will I permit your death.

Even should it become my duty to save you at the risk of my life,
In no wise will I refuse you my assistance.

Not only will I give you aid and help,
But I will protect also all living beings.

For the good of all living beings
I lavish my efforts.

The inhabitants of my kingdom pay heavy taxes to me;
Of six parts of their goods, they pay one to me.

Upon me [in return] rests the obligation, towards all living beings
To show myself a benevolent patron.

It is just for me to protect them,
And on no account to permit any to injure them.

Then the hawk said again to the king: "Great king! Deign to release the pigeon, for he is my food!" The king replied to the hawk: "Long ago I conceived pity towards all living beings, and I owe them all the assistance and protection I can give them." The hawk asked the king: "Why did you conceive long ago [pity towards all living beings]?" The king replied to him by pronouncing these stanzas:

When I uttered the vow to attain Enlightenment,
I granted my protection
To all living beings:
All shall win my profound compassion.

The hawk replied with these stanzas:

If your words are true,
Give me back the pigeon quickly;

For if you make me die of hunger,
You show no more compassion.

When the king had heard that, he reflected thus: "I am in an extremely difficult position. What expedient ought I to employ?" Having thus thought, he replied to the hawk and said: "Then you have no other meat to sustain your life?" The hawk replied to the king: "I can sustain my life only with fresh flesh and with blood." Then the king said to himself: "What means ought I to employ?" Then he pronounced these stanzas:

Towards all creatures
I have always shown profound compassion.

Blood and fresh flesh
Cannot be obtained without committing murder.

Having thus reflected, he found that it would be very easy to give his own flesh to feed the hawk. And he pronounced these stanzas further:

I will cut a piece of my own flesh
And give it to the hawk.

Even if it becomes my duty to sacrifice myself,
It is incumbent on me to protect the life of this frightened being.

When the great king had pronounced these verses, he said to the hawk: "Will my flesh be proper food for you?" The hawk said: "Yes! let the king deign to cut out of his body a piece of flesh equal [in weight] to that of the pigeon! Let him give it to me, and I will eat it." When the great king had heard these words, he became joyful. He ordered a servant: "Bring quickly a pair of scales! I am going to cut a piece of my flesh to redeem this pigeon. It is a fortunate day for me to-day! And why is it a fortunate day?" He uttered these stanzas:

This flesh is the seat of old age and of maladies,
Of numerous perils and of disgusting substances.

It is fitting that for the good of the Law
I sacrifice this flesh, vile and corrupt.

In the meantime the king's servant had executed the order, and brought a pair of scales. When the king saw the pair of scales coming, he showed no feeling. Immediately he bared the white flesh of his thigh, smooth as a tāla-leaf. He called the servant and recited these stanzas to him:

Take a sharp knife, and cut the flesh of my thigh!
Do as I tell you, without any fear!

For without submitting oneself to severe austerities,
One obtains not Omniscience.

For Omniscience,—
Is there aught more sublime in the three worlds?

Never, without sufficient cause,
Does one obtain Enlightenment.
Hence I ought to act with unshakable firmness.

At this moment the servant's eyes were filled with tears. Joining the palms of his hands, he spoke thus: "Have mercy on me! I cannot do it! I have always received good things from the king. How could I, with a knife, cut a piece of flesh from the thigh of the king?" He uttered these stanzas:

The king is the saviour and protector of all.
If I cut the flesh of the king,
Certainly, I myself, with the knife,
Should be overwhelmed, and should fall to the earth.

Then the great king took the knife in his own hand to cut the flesh from his thigh. The ministers and the great dignitaries, lamenting and weeping, made remonstrances to him without being able to stop him. All the inhabitants of the city pressed close to him. But he heard them not, and cut the flesh from his thigh. Those who were near him, turned their eyes away and dared not look. The Brahmans turned their eyes away and dared not look. The women of the palace uttered cries and wept. The deities, the dragons, the demons, the heavenly minstrels, the spirits, the fairies, and the great serpents said to each other throughout space: "It is not probable that the like of this deed has ever been done before." The king had a body that was feeble and tender. Born and reared at the palace, he had never been able to endure any pain. Now his body was tortured with pains, and he suffered intensely. But he exhorted himself, and pronounced these stanzas:

O my Heart, preserve thy firmness
Against this slight pain!

Why art thou cast down?
Only see how the whole universe

Is entangled in hundreds and thousands of evils!
Living beings are deprived of refuge and assistance;

They have no shelter and protection;
They live in utter dependence.

THOU ALONE, O MY HEART,
ART CALLED TO BE THE SAVIOUR OF ALL!

Art thou not ashamed of thyself
To yield thus to pain?

Then Indra reflected thus: "Will the great king preserve his constancy in the midst of the greatest sufferings?" And desiring to put him to the test, he said: "You have just endured sufferings difficult to endure. Why do you not stop torturing yourself? You have suffered enough. Leave off, and release the pigeon!" The Future Buddha smiled feebly, and replied to him: "Never will sufferings make me break my word. Even if I am destined to suffer yet more, I will not flinch. These insignificant sufferings cannot be compared with the sufferings of hell. Therefore it is incumbent upon me that I lift up my thought, and that even in the midst of these sufferings I increase my compassion [for living beings]." When he had made this reflection, he pronounced these stanzas:

I suffer now from my bodily wound.
But let not my heart be cast down!

Let it know the extent to which the irresolute and the heedless
Endure sufferings in hell,—

Tortures which never cease,—
Eternal and unending.

Who would wish to endure them?
Because I am filled with compassion for living beings,

I must make haste
To attain Enlightenment quickly.

All those who suffer from these miseries,—
Them will I save, and for them will I procure Deliverance.

Then Indra made this further reflection: "What the great king has just done, is not yet sufficiently painful. Will he preserve his constancy if I cause him to increase his sufferings? I will put him to the test!" Having made this reflection, he preserved silence and left off speaking.

In the meantime the great king had taken the piece of flesh which he had cut, and had placed it on one pan of the scales; he placed the pigeon on the other pan. It so happened that the pigeon made the scales tip. Then the king cut the two *pi* and placed this flesh in the scales. But it was still lighter than the pigeon. At this the great king was much surprised, and failed to understand what was the cause. Immediately he arose to place himself in the scales.

At this moment the hawk asked him: "Why do you fidget? Are you beginning to have regrets?" The great king replied to him: "I regret nothing. I wish to place myself whole and entire in the scales to save this pigeon." When the great king was on the point of ascending the scales, his face remained calm. The servants and the assistants dared look no more; all the members of his entourage turned their eyes away.

At this moment the king said: "Look freely!" *He cut off all of his flesh.* There remained no more anything but his bones and his joints. He was like a statue, which, when exposed to the rain, becomes dismembered and difficult to recognize.

Then cried aloud the great king as follows:

"IF I SACRIFICE MY BODY, IT IS NOT TO OBTAIN TREASURES, NOR FOR PLEASURE, NOR FOR LOVE OF MY WIFE AND MY CHILDREN AND MY KINSFOLK. WHAT I COVET IS ENLIGHTENMENT, THAT THEREBY I MAY BE ABLE TO PROCURE SALVATION FOR ALL LIVING BEINGS!"

Then he pronounced these stanzas:

Deities and spirits, heavenly musicians and ogres,
Dragons and demons,—all classes of living beings,

Seeing me in this state,
Will be incited to imitate my constancy.

Because I covet Supreme Enlightenment,
I make my body suffer, and I wound it.

He that would win Enlightenment,
Must prove himself possessed of compassion unshakable.

If one does not possess constancy that is proof against everything,
One should renounce the thought of winning Enlightenment.

At the instant when the great king, sacrificing his body, ascended the scales, the great earth trembled six times, like a blade of grass or a leaf, agitated in all the directions. In the sky, the deities expressed their wonderment at this extraordinary spectacle, and cried out: "Bravo! bravo! Thou dost deserve to be called zealous and of resolution unshakable."

And the great king uttered these stanzas:

To save the life of this living being,
I have cut my flesh to pieces.

I have acted from a heart that is sincere and full of compassion,
With a firm and unshakable resolution.

The whole company of the deities
Is filled with wonderment thereat.

At this moment the hawk expressed his wonderment at the sight of this extraordinary act: "His resolution is firm and sincere; he will soon become a Buddha; all living beings will put their confidence in him." Then Indra showed himself to the king under his true form, and told Vishva-karman to resume his true form also. And he added: "Let us pay him our respects! For this Future Buddha is imbued with resolution firm and unshakable, like Mount Sumeru, which lies in mid-ocean without ever being shaken. Such is the heart of this Future Buddha." Then he added these stanzas:

Let us pay our respects to this valiant and resolute man!
Let us lift up our voices and spread his praises abroad!
Let all that are harassed with cares seek shelter with him!
Let them unite closely with him whose conduct is unshakable!

He has planted in the ground of Compassion
The tree of Supreme Enlightenment.
His shoots begin to sprout,
And prudent men will seek a shelter under him.

Vishva-karman then addressed himself to Indra and said: "The great king has shown his compassion for all living beings. His body should be restored as it was before. May all living beings be able to seek after Enlightenment without faltering [as the king has done]!" Then Indra asked the king: "Had you no regret over sacrificing yourself for a pigeon?" The king replied to him with these stanzas:

This body is destined to perish;
It is like a piece of wood, or a rock:
It shall be thrown to the birds and to the beasts of prey;
It shall be burned, or it shall rot in the earth.

If, then, by means of this worthless body,
I can obtain great advantage,
I have only to rejoice over it;
It would not befit me to sorrow over it.

Where, then, is the prudent man,
Who would give this body, exposed to all dangers,
In exchange for the Law, stable and firm,
Without rejoicing?

Indra said to the king: "Such words are difficult to believe. Never has an act equal to it been seen. Who could give credence to it?" The great king replied: "I know myself. Were there in the world a great sage capable of fathoming my heart, he would see that it is pure and without duplicity." Indra replied: "You have spoken the truth." At this moment the great king made this declaration: "If I have no regret [for having done what I have just done], may my body become once more as it was before!" And the king surveyed his mutilated body and uttered these stanzas:

When I mutilated my body,
I was free from sorrow and joy,
From anger and grief;
I experienced no sadness.

If this be true,
May my body be restored as it was before,
And may I soon attain Enlightenment,
That I may bring salvation to all living beings!

When the great king had pronounced these stanzas, his mutilated body was transformed, and became as it was before. Here follow the stanzas:

The mountains, and the great earth as well,
Were all shaken;
The trees and the ocean
Began to stir, and lost their calm,
Like a timorous man
Who loses his confidence in battle.

The deities sang with joy,
And from the sky fell a rain of fragrant flowers.
Bells and drums were heard,
Mingling their sounds together.

The deities expressed their joy,
And all sang together.

All living beings were affected;
The ocean itself lifted up its voice;
From heaven fell fragrant dust,
Covering all the roads.

The sky was full of flowers
Which fell, some slowly, others quickly.

The celestial nymphs, assembled in heaven,
Covered the earth with flowers.

Garments of all colors,
Adorned with gold and precious stones,
Fell in a rain from heaven,
And caskets too, filled with heavenly robes,
Resounding as they clashed together.

In everybody's dwelling
Appeared spontaneously urns filled with precious stones,
Giving out, without a touch, sounds
Like the music of the heavenly musicians.

No cloud covered the heavens;
The four directions shone resplendent.

A gentle wind exhaled perfumes;
The streams flowed clear and noiseless.

The demons, ardently desirous to obtain the Law,
Once more redoubled zeal:
"Soon he will attain Enlightenment,"—
Thus they sang in praise of him.

All the heavenly musicians
Sang and made their music heard;
Their notes harmonious were sometimes soft, sometimes low.
And thus they sang the praises of the king:

"Soon he will obtain the condition of a Buddha;
"He will cross the ocean of his vow;
"Right quickly will he reach the place auspicious:
"When he shall attain the object of his desire,
"He will remember us, to win Salvation for us."

Then Indra and Vishva-karman paid their respects to the Future Buddha, and returned in their heavenly mansions.

C. ON THE SACRIFICE OF THE EYES

"Here is your eye! take it!"

213. KING SIVI AND THE BLIND BEGGAR

"Should any man name my eyes, I will pluck them out and give them to him!"

Synopsis of Jātaka 499: iv. 401-412.

King Sivi, who is already noted for his generosity, one day makes a vow that should any one beg of him, not something outside of him, but part of his very self, whether heart, flesh, blood, or eyes, he will give it to him.

"Should any man name the flesh of my heart, I will smite my breast with a spear, and like as if I were pulling up out of the clear water a lily, stalk and all, so will I draw forth my heart, dripping drops of blood, and give it to him. Should he name the flesh of my body, like as if I were graving with a graving tool, so I will remove the flesh of my body and give it to him. Should he name my blood, I will give him my blood, either dropping it into his mouth, or filling therewith a bowl held underneath. Should he say: 'My household work is at a standstill; do the work of a slave in my house!' I will lay aside my royal garments, stand outside, and proclaiming myself a slave, do the work of a slave. Should any man name my eyes, like as if I were removing the meat of a date-palm, so I will pluck out my eyes and give them to him."

> Whatever human gift there be that yet I have not given,
> Though one should ask my very eyes, I'll give them unafraid.

Sakka, king of the gods, hears his vow, disguises himself as a blind beggar, and asks him for one of his eyes. Sivi forthwith gives him both.

> "Dearer to me than this eye is the Eye of Omniscience!"

Afterwards, becoming depressed, he longs for death. Sakka tells him to make an Act of Truth with reference to his gift, assuring him that if he will do so, his eyes will be restored. Sivi thereupon makes the following Act of Truth: "Whatsoever sort or kind of beggar comes to me, is dear to my heart. If this be true, let one of my eyes be restored." Immediately one of his eyes is restored. To restore the other eye, he recites the following: "A Brahman came to me and asked me for one of my eyes; unto him gave I two. Great joy and delight filled me. If this be true, let my other eye be restored." Immediately his other eye is restored.

214. SUBHĀ OF JĪVAKA'S MANGO GROVE

"Here is your eye! take it!"

A. Prose version.

Therī-gāthā Commentary No. 71.

In the Division of Thirty Stanzas of the Book of the Stanzas of the Nuns, the stanzas beginning with the words *To Jīvaka's charming Mango Grove* are the stanzas of the nun Subhā of Jīvaka's Mango Grove.

She also, having made her Earnest Wish under previous Buddhas, developed Capacity for Sainthood and accumulated Merit in this state of existence and in that, and in due course having stimulated the Roots of Merit, having perfected the Conditions of Deliverance, with Knowledge fully ripe, was reborn in the dispensation of this present Buddha at Rājagaha in the household of a wealthy Brahman.

Subhā, or Beauty, was her name. Endowed with beauty, they say, were the members of her body. Therefore, appropriately enough, she was given the name Subhā, or Beauty.

When the Teacher entered Rājagaha, she received the gift of faith and became a lay disciple. Later on, terrified by the Round of Existences, seeing in the Pleasures of Sense danger, perceiving in Renunciation of the Pleasures of Sense security, she retired from the world and became a nun under Mahā Pajāpatī Gotamī, and performing the business of Insight, in but a few days became established in the Fruit of the Third Path.

Now one day a certain resident of Rājagaha, an unprincipled fellow, young, in the prime of youth, saw her going to Jīvaka's Mango Grove for her noonday siesta. Seeing her, he fell in love with her, and barring the way, invited her to enjoy the pleasures of sense. She preached the Doctrine to him, in divers ways making known the folly of the pleasures of sense, and her own determination to renounce the same. But even after hearing her discourse on the Doctrine, he would not leave her, but continued to importune her.

The nun, seeing that he paid no attention to what she said, and observing that he was fascinated with her eye, said: "Here is your eye! take it!" So saying, she plucked out one of her own eyes and handed it to him. Thereat that man was affrighted and terrified; for that nun his passion abated. Begging her to pardon him, he went his way. The nun went to the Teacher. The moment she looked upon him, her eye was restored to its former state. Thereat, as she stood there, her whole body was suffused with Joy in the Buddha.

The Teacher, knowing the course of her thoughts, preached the Doctrine to her; and that she might attain the Highest Path, assigned to her a Subject of Meditation. Suppressing Joy, she immediately developed Insight and attained Sainthood together with the Analytical Powers. And having attained Sainthood, she dwelt in the Bliss of the Fruit thereof, in the Bliss of Nibbāna. And surveying her own Attainment, by way of Solemn Utterance, she recited the following stanzas, previously uttered by her in conversation with that unprincipled fellow:

B. Poetical version.

Therī-gāthā 366-399.

366. To Jīvaka's charming Mango Grove went the nun Subhā.
An unprincipled fellow barred the way. To him spoke Subhā:

Subhā:

367. "What wrong have I done thee that thou standest barring me the way?
For, brother, it is not proper for a man to touch a religious.

368. "Following the revered religion of my Teacher,
Following the training proclaimed by the Happy One,
I am in the Way of Salvation, I am free from lust.
Why dost thou stand barring me the way?

369. "Stained are thy thoughts; I am free from stain.
Passionate art thou; I am free from passion, free from lust.
My heart is wholly free!
Why dost thou stand barring me the way?"

Libertine:

370. "Thou art young; thou art not bad-looking.
What shalt thou gain by the religious life?
Put off the yellow robe!
Come! let us take our pleasure in the flowering wood.

371. "Altogether sweet breathe the trees,
Swelling with the pollen of flowers.
Early spring's the time for pleasure!
Come! let us take our pleasure in the flowering wood.

372. "Flowering to their very tips, the trees
Roar away, swayed by the winds.
What pleasure shalt thou gain
If by thyself alone thou shalt plunge into the wood?

373. "The great wood is a solitude, a place of horrors,
Haunted by troops of beasts of prey,
Heaving with the dust of rutting elephants.
Wilt thou go thither without a companion?

374. "A very golden image, dost thou go about;
A very celestial nymph, in the garden Cittaratha;
With soft, beautiful garments of Benāres cloth
Art thou resplendent, O peerless one!

375. "With joy would I submit to thy will
If thou wilt reside in the heart of the forest,
For no living being is dearer to me than art thou,
O thou with the languid eyes of a sylph.

376. "If thou wilt do as I ask, thou shalt be happy.
Come, adopt the house-life.
Thou shalt dwell in mansions and places secure;
Women shall wait upon thee.

377. "Put on soft garments of Benāres cloth,
Deck thyself with all manner of garlands.
Of gold and gems and pearls
Will I make for thee ornaments many and various.

378. "Thy couch is new, spread with cotton mattresses
And fleecy woollen blankets, resplendent
With coverlets washed clean of dirt,
Of great price, adorned with sandalwood,
Of fragrant perfume. Mount thereon!

379. "And, like a lotus flower uplifted from the water,
Possessed by a demon, [enjoyed by none other,]
So thou, abiding chaste, thy own members unenjoyed,
Shalt go to old age."

Subhā:

380. "What meaning for thee has this body,
Full of corruption, augmenting the burning-ground,
Whose very nature is dissolution,
That seeing it thou dost gaze distraught?"

Libertine:

381. "Like the eyes of a deer are thine eyes,
Like the eyes of a sylph in the heart of the mountains;
Through gazing at thine eyes
The more doth my passion increase.

382. "O thou that dost resemble the crown of a lotus!
O thou spotless one! O thou whose face is like gold!
Through gazing at thine eyes
The more doth my passion increase.

383. "However far away thou be, I shall remember thee,
O thou of the long eyelashes! O thou of unblemished mien!
For no eyes are dearer to me than are thine eyes,
O thou with the languid eyes of a sylph!"

Subhā:

384. "Thou dost seek to walk where no path is,
Thou dost seek a toy moon,
Thou dost seek to leap over Meru,
When thou dost ask in marriage one that hath heard the Buddha.

385. "For neither in the world of men nor in the Worlds of Gods
Liveth any man for whom I lust, let be now who might be;
I do not even know what lust is like,
But by the Path lust with its roots hath been destroyed.

386. "For me lust is like a poison-bowl, once highly prized,
Consigned to the fire-pit for good and all;
I do not even understand what lust is like,
But by the Path lust with its roots hath been destroyed.

387. "If there be a woman that hath not well considered,
If there be a woman whose teacher is under instruction,
Such a woman do thou tempt.
In tempting her that knoweth, thou dost but vex thyself.

388. "For I am ever mindful, both in honor and in dishonor,
Both in pleasure and in pain;
I know that all existing things are foul;
Therefore cleaveth my heart to naught soever.

389. "I that stand here am a disciple of the Happy One;
In the Eightfold Vehicle of the Path do I make my way;
Drawn out are the arrows of the Depravities;
I delight to dwell in solitude.

390. "For what I see is a gaudily painted doll,
Newly made, fitted with little sticks and rods,
Fastened together with cords and little pins,
Dancing away to her heart's content.

391. "Remove the cords and pegs;
Unloosen, dismember, scatter the parts;
Reduce the members to fragments.
What! wilt thou set thy heart thereon?

392. "Precisely so do these wretched bodies of ours appear to me;
Without their constituent parts they exist not;
Without the constituent parts they exist not.
What! wilt thou set thy heart thereon?

393. "Not as I have looked upon a little picture
Plastered on a wall with yellow orpiment,
Not so hast thou looked upon this body;
Unprofitable is merely human judgment.

394. "Thou dost run after a phantom, as it were,
Wrought by a magician before thy very face,
Or after a tree of gold that appeareth in a dream,
O thou blind man!
Or after an image of silver, as it were,
A hollow piece of nothing!
Wrought by a magician in the crowd.

395. "Like a ball lodged in the hollow of a tree,
A mere bubble, floating in mucus, tears and all,
Is the eye.
Therein breed maggots of all sorts and kinds,—
As many kinds as there are kinds of eyes,—
In solid masses."

396. Straightway that maiden so fair to see,
With never a bond, never a care,
Tore out her eye and gave it to that man:
"Here is thine eye! take it!"

397. Straightway his passion abated;
Then and there he begged her to pardon him:
"I wish thee well, O maiden chaste;
Never again shall happen such a thing as this!

398. "Thou hast shattered me,—and such a man am I!
I have clasped, as it were, a blazing fire!
I have grasped, as it were, a poisonous serpent!
But I wish thee well! do thou pardon me!"

399. Then, free, that nun went to the Buddha,
To the All-glorious One;
She looked upon him, and her eye,
The product of surpassing merit,
Was restored to its former state.

215. THE PRINCE-ASCETIC

"Behold this, such as it is! take it, if you like!"

Kathāsaritsāgara vi. 28. 18-25.

To illustrate: In times past there lived a prince free from attachment for the things of earth. Youthful though he was, well-liking though he was, he adopted the life of a wandering ascetic.

One day this mendicant entered the house of a certain merchant. The young wife of the merchant, her eyes as long as the leaves of a lotus, saw him.

Her heart captivated by the beauty of his eyes, she addressed him: "How came such a man as you to take upon yourself this austere vow?

"Happy that woman who is gazed upon by these eyes of yours!" Thus addressed by that woman, that mendicant tore out one eye,

And having placed it in his hand, said: "Mother, behold this, such as it is! Take this loathsome gore and flesh, if you like!

"And the second is exactly like the first. Tell me, what is there delightful about these two eyes?" Thus addressed by him, seeing that, that merchant's wife became depressed

And said: "Alas! alas! An evil deed have I wrought, wretched woman that I am, in that I have caused you to tear out your eyes!"

Hearing this, the mendicant said: "Woman, be not distressed, for you have done me a service . . . by causing me to uproot my eyes, you have increased my self-mortification."

Thus spoke that self-controlled mendicant to that merchant's wife bent low before him; indifferent to his own body, well-liking though it was, he went to perfection.

216. PRINCE KUNĀLA

"Plucked out, the eye of flesh; but gained, the Eye of Knowledge!"

Divyāvadāna 406.

Kunāla, son of King Açoka, is famed throughout India for the beauty of his eyes. His stepmother falls in love with him, makes advances to him, and is repulsed. In revenge she forges an order in the name of the king, commanding that his eyes be put out. The order is carried out. Kunāla exclaims: "Plucked out, the eye of flesh; but gained, the Eye of Knowledge!"

Subsequently the king discovers the crime, fixes the guilt on his queen-consort, and in the presence of Kunāla, threatens her with the direst punishments. Kunāla begs his father not to harm the queen, extols the virtues of kindness, compassion, and forebearance, declares that in spite of the cruel suffering he has endured, pain has not stained him nor anger heated him, and concludes with the following Act of Truth: "If it be true that I have ever been kindly disposed to my mother, if it be true that I myself tore out my eyes, then may my eyes be restored!" Straightway his eyes are restored, yet more beautiful even than before.

217. ST. BRIGID OF KILDARE

Dearer the Eye of the Soul than the eye of the body
"Lo, here for thee is thy beautiful eye!"

The Sacrifice of an Eye appears for the first time in the Legends of St. Brigid in the fifteenth century.

A. Medieval Latin versions.

Acta Sanctorum, 4. Feb. 1, 119 *a*, 121 *b*.

The principal Medieval Latin versions are as follows:

St. Brigid, God-fearing virgin, seeing that the time of her betrothal was at hand, asked the Lord to send some deformity upon her, and that at any rate in this manner she might escape the importunity of her suitors. Then one of her eyes burst and dissolved in her head.

Not long afterwards came a certain nobleman to Dubthach to ask for his daughter in marriage, and this pleased her father and brothers. But Brigid refused him. And when they sternly insisted that she should marry the man, she asked the Lord to inflict some deformity on her body, so that men would cease to seek after her. Then one of her eyes burst and dissolved in her head. She, however, chose rather to lose the eye of the body than the Eye of the Soul, and loved beauty of soul more than beauty of body. But when her father saw this, he permitted her to take the veil; and the moment she took the veil, her eye was restored and she was made whole.

B. Middle Irish version.

From W. Stokes, Three Middle-Irish Homilies 64-65.

In the *Lebar Brecc,* a Middle Irish MS. of the fifteenth century, the following episode appears for the first time:

Shortly after that came a certain nobleman unto Dubthach to ask for his daughter. Dubthach and his sons were willing, but Brigid refused. Said a brother of her brethren named Beccán unto her: "Idle is the fair eye that is in thy head not to be on a pillow near a husband." "The Son of the Virgin knoweth," says Brigid; "it is not lively for us if it brings harm upon us." Then Brigid put her finger under her eye, and drew it out of her head so that it was on her cheek; and she said: "Lo, here for thee is thy beautiful eye, O Beccán!" Then *his* eye burst forthwith. When Dubthach and her brethren beheld that, they promised that she should never be told to go unto a husband. Then she put her palm to her eye and it was quite whole at once. But Beccán's eye was not whole till his death.

218. ST. LUCY OF SYRACUSE

"Here hast thou what thou hast desired! leave me in peace!"

From Mrs. Jameson's Sacred and Legendary Art ii. 615-617.

In the older legends of St. Lucy we are told that while she was praying at the tomb of St. Agatha for the restoration of her mother's health, St. Agatha appeared to her in a vision and said to her: "Well art thou called Lucy, who art indeed a light and a mirror to the faithful! What dost thou ask of me which shall not be granted to thine own faith and sanctity? Behold! thy mother is from this hour healed!" St. Lucy thereupon resolved to adopt the religious life, and sold all of her goods and gave to the poor. When the youth to whom she was betrothed saw this, he was enraged, and went and denounced her to the governor Pascasius as being a Christian. Pascasius ordered her to be brought before him, and commanded her to sacrifice to his idols. When she refused, he ordered her to be taken to a brothel and treated as a harlot. But when the governor's men tried to drag her away, she became rooted to the spot, and neither men and oxen nor magicians and enchanters were able to move her from the spot. Then Pascasius ordered her to be burnt alive, but the fire would not touch her. Finally one of his servants pierced her throat with a dagger.

The medieval legend is as follows:

In the city wherein the blessed Lucy dwelt, there dwelt also a youth who, having once beheld her, became enamored of her beauty, and by messages and promises and gifts, he ceased not to woo her; but Lucy, being a Christian and fearing God, resisted all these attacks on her virtue. Now this youth, in his letters and his tender speeches, was accustomed to protest that it was the brightness of her eyes which inflamed him, and that it was for the sake of those beautiful eyes he pursued her, leaving *her* no rest, because those eyes left *him* no rest, by day or by night.

Lucy, considering these things, and calling to mind the words of Christ, "If thine eye offend thee, pluck it out, and cast it from thee," and fearing lest her eyes should be the cause of damnation to the young man, and perhaps also to herself, called for a knife and took out her beautiful eyes, and sent them to her lover in a dish, with these words: "Here hast thou what thou hast so much desired; and for the rest, I beseech thee, leave me now in peace." Whereat the young man, being utterly astonished and full of grief and remorse, not only ceased his pursuit, but became also a convert of Christ, and lived ever afterwards an example of virtue and chastity.

But God would not suffer that the blessed Lucy, having given this proof of her courage and piety, should remain blind: for one day, as she knelt in prayer, behold! her eyes were restored to her more beautiful than before. And if any one doubts of this great miracle, let him consult the writings of that learned and praiseworthy man Filippo Bergomense, and also of that famous Spaniard Don Juan Maldonato, where they will find it all set down as I have related. And this is the reason that St. Lucy is invoked against blindness and all diseases of the eyes, and that in her effigy she is represented bearing two eyes in a dish.

219. ST. LUCY OF ALEXANDRIA

And seizing her spindle, she bit, and gouged out her two eyes.

John Moschus, Spiritual Meadow, 615 A. D. Patrologia Graeca 87. 3. 2911-4.

When we were in Alexandria, the lover of Christ related to us a story to the following effect:—A certain nun,—said he,—used to sit in her own house, aloof from the world, solicitous for her own soul, constant in fastings and supplications and watchings, generous in almsgiving. But the Devil, ever at enmity with mankind, intolerant of such virtues, stirred up the dust against her. For he excited in a certain youth a satanic longing for her. Now the youth was wont to wait outside the house. When, therefore, the nun desired to go out, and to depart from her own house to the house of prayer in order to pray, the youth would not permit her, but would importune and annoy her, as is the wont of the amorous, so that finally the nun was forced by the importunity of the youth not to leave her own house. On a certain day, therefore, the nun sent her maid-servant to the youth, saying: "Come, my mistress wishes you!" So the youth departed to her, rejoicing to think that he had attained his own purpose. Now the nun was sitting at her loom. Accordingly, she said to the youth: "Be seated." And having seated him, she said to him: "Tell me honestly, good brother,—why is it that you thus annoy me, and do not permit me to leave my house?" The youth replied, saying: "To tell you the truth, mistress,—I am deeply in love with you, and whenever I see you, I am all afire." And she said to him: "But what that is beautiful did you see in me, that you have such an affection for me?" And the youth said: "Your eyes! for it is even they that have led me astray." Now when the nun heard that it was her eyes that had led the youth astray, she seized her spindle, and bit, and gouged out her two eyes. And when the youth saw this, that by reason of him the nun had gouged out her two eyes, he was pricked to the heart, and departing for Scythia, became, himself also, an excellent monk.

220. KING (RICHARD OF ENGLAND) AND NUN

"*Behold the eyes that thou desirest! take them, and leave me in peace!*"

Lost, the eyes of the flesh; but kept, the Eyes of the Spirit.

Jacques de Vitry, Exemplum 57.

I HAVE heard a story about a certain consecrated virgin, that by reason of her beauty, a certain powerful and wealthy prince, in whose land a monastery had been founded, fell deeply in love with her at first sight; and that, unable to win her, either by entreaties or gifts, he sent men to take her by force and remove her from the monastery. But she, trembling and sorrowful, inquired of the bystanders why he seized her rather than some other inmate of the monastery. They replied that it was because she had such beautiful eyes. "Yonder ruler beheld them; this is the reason why he desires to obtain thee." When she heard this, she rejoiced above measure. And immediately she plucked out her own eyes and said: "Behold the eyes that he desires! Take them to him, and tell him to leave me in peace, and not to rob me of my soul!" And thus she lost the eyes of the flesh, but kept the Eyes of the Spirit.

TABLE OF PARALLELS

213. KING SIVI AND THE BLIND BEGGAR	**217. ST. BRIGID OF KILDARE**
"Dearer to me than this eye is the Eye of Omniscience!" By Acts of Truth both of his eyes were restored.	Dearer the Eye of the Soul than the eye of the body. Then one of her eyes burst. The moment she took the veil, her eye was restored and she was made whole.
214. SUBHĀ OF JĪVAKA'S MANGO-GROVE	
"Here is your eye! take it!" The moment she looked upon the Buddha, her eye was restored.	"Lo, here for thee is thy beautiful eye!" Then his eye burst. She put her palm to her eye, and it was quite whole at once. But his eye was not whole till his death.
215. PRINCE-ASCETIC	**220. KING AND NUN**
"Behold this, such as it is! take this loathsome gore and flesh, if you like!" The prince-ascetic "went to perfection."	"Behold the eyes that thou desirest! take them, and leave me in peace!" Lost, the eyes of the flesh; but kept, the Eyes of the Spirit.
216. PRINCE KUNĀLA	**218. ST. LUCY OF SYRACUSE**
"Plucked out, the eye of flesh; but gained, the Eye of Knowledge!" By Acts of Truth both of his eyes were restored, more beautiful than before.	"Here hast thou what thou hast desired! leave me in peace!" As she knelt in prayer, her eyes were restored to her, more beautiful than before.

INDEX